THE COMPLETE BOOK FOR
TRACING YOUR
IRISH ANCESTORS

by Michael C. O'Laughlin

Dedication

Dedicated to all those of Irish descent who are, or are soon to be, "the keepers of the family archives." In doing so they will enrich generations to come with the knowledge of the ages.

And to the elders of my own respective clans in America:

My Grandfather, Charles M. O'Laughlin;

My Grandmother, Mary Elizabeth "Sullivan" Donahue.

Special thanks to:

Jim and Monica O'Loughlin and family (Ennis, Ireland);

Mr. & Mrs. Denny Spillane (Glenflesk, Ireland).

Additional hardbound copies of this book are available at $29.95 from the publisher:

Irish Genealogical Foundation

P.O. Box 7575

Kansas City, MO 64116

(Write for free catalog.)

ISBN 0-940134-02-0

Library of Congress Catalog Card No.: 81-80710

THE COMPLETE BOOK FOR TRACING YOUR IRISH ANCESTORS

AT HOME AND ABROAD

Introduction 5

Important Notes

Case History and Background

20 Item Checklist Outline

Part I

20 Steps 13

A) Family Records: (1) Oral Testimony (2) Handwritten Documents (3) The Oldest Generation (4) Tradition and Legend (5) The Spelling of Your Name (6) Coat of Arms/Crest.

B) Local Records: (7) Newspapers (8) Cemetary (9) Church (10) Historians (11) Libraries.

C) Advanced Research: (12) Published Works (13) Census Study (14) National Archives (15) Passenger Lists (16) Ancient Pedigrees and History.

D) Final Steps: (17) Outside Assistance (18) Documentation and Record Keeping (19) Publishing and Preserving (20) Summary and Conclusions.

Part II

Research In Ireland 55

A) Terms and Understanding: Civil Units, Maps, Important Dates, Ancient Pedigrees and Legend.

Part III

Records & Repositories In Ireland 75

A) Church Records: Catholic, Presbyterian, Methodist, Huguenot, Quaker, Church of Ireland, Baptist, Congregationalists 99

B) Major Repositories for furthering research: Office of the Registrar General; Public Records Office; The Registry of Deeds; The National Library and Archives; Genealogical Office; Public Records Office of Northern Ireland; The Ulster Historical Foundation; Registrar General of Northern Ireland; Trinity College; The Royal Irish Acadamy; State Paper Office; Palatine Records; Irish Newspapers as sources; The National Library of Ireland; Other Libraries.

C) Census & Surveys (illustrated): Government Commissions; Statistical Surveys; Tithe Applotment Books; Books of Survey & Distribution, etc.

D) Ireland Parish Registers

E) 1891 Birth Index of Ireland: Number of births recorded by surname listing area of residence.

Part IV
Records & Repositories Abroad 140
A) American: National Archives; Library of Congress; Bounty Land Records; Birth, Marriage, and Death Records; Census Schedules; Mortality Schedules; Records about District of Columbia Residents; Land Records; Naturalization Records; Passenger Lists; Passport Applications; Personnel Records; Claims for Pensions and Bounty Land; Seamen's Protection Certificate Applications; Service Records Army; Service Records Navy and Marine; Coast Guard Records.
B) Canada 169
C) Other Countries: England, Australia, Wales, etc..........176

Part V
More Reference Sources 179
A) By Surname
B) By County
C) Other

General Outline and Important Instructions

Simply put, this book was written to enable you to trace your Irish Ancestors with all the information needed, contained in *one* authoritative book.

To this end we have included:

1. The basic methods of genealogical research.
2. Case histories and illustrations.
3. Records and repositories in Ireland, America, Canada (and elsewhere).
4. Records in the National Archives.
5. Hundreds of sources for furthering research.

The procedures outlined above will prove fruitful, regardless of the country you begin your search from.

The 20 item step by step checklist is particularly included for the 'novice' who does not know how to begin his research or where to go for further information. These steps are only a procedural outline, specific records to consult are given in following chapters. Thousands of avenues are available if only you know how and where to find them. Even a more experienced genealogist needs a handy procedure and reference guide, if only to help organize his thoughts and double check alternatives.

Specific sources covered are extensive but a partial list follows:

1. Census description and availability (Ireland, America, Canada).
2. Passenger Lists.
3. Church Records and Parish Registers.
4. Terminology necessary to understand the records.
5. Maps of the older divisions of Ireland.
6. Surveys and Estate Papers.
7. Records & Repositories throughout the world.

Based upon our own extensive genealogical research in Ireland and America, these sources can take years to discover, much less research. Using this book as a reference and a guideline can save you from not only months of lost time in searching for the proper source, but from coming to a complete dead end as well.

Our methods and resources, as outlined, based on true experience will show you how to proceed with your investigation, as well as giving you a basic understanding of the problems involved (i.e., handwriting, history, etc.). The names of the *records and repositories throughout the world* alone should save you much time.

In our special reference section are listed hundreds of publications and sources, some of which are indexed by last name or specific geographical area. These works can enable you to find works already in existance and documented on your family. We also invite any new sources or additions, which you may well turn up in the course of your study. They will be included in future editions of *The Complete Book for Tracing Your Irish Ancestors.*

Your journey to find your ancestors will prove a rewarding one, as it has been for me and thousands of others. Your family's future can be inevitably enriched with a knowledge of whence you came and why. This book is meant to encourage a little bit of that "Luck of the Irish" on your venture.

Important Advice

Having traced my O'Loughlin and Donaghue ancestors back to Ireland (in Counties Clare and Kerry respectively), I am aware of the problems involved in such research. Being fortunate and persistant enough to travel to Ireland to complete my search, I found the Baptismal records, churches and towns of both illustrious branches of my family. Carrying the interest even further, we researched the legend and manuscripts available concerning the thousands of years preceding my original emigrant ancestors in Ireland.

Everyday however, new sources of interest appear and more information comes to light. In addition, my sullivan and Buckley heritage is still being researched in a seemingly endless expansion of tracing my Irish heritage. It becomes apparent that there is an endless source of knowledge to draw upon, and the excitement and enjoyment involved increases as well. You will find that your research will enrich not only your life, but your entire family's as well, for generations to come.

If you are just beginning your research I would offer a few helpful hints:

1. Put all information down in writing immediately!
2. Prepare a family tree chart right now (even if it isn't too large) for your own understanding, as well as for others who may be interested.
3. Talk to the oldest generation in your family (before it's too late, and the information is lost forever).
4. Prepare to spend some time going through, or waiting for,

papers and records.

5. Check out the varient spellings of your name (i.e., my name is today O'Laughlin, but my ancestors spelled it O'Loglin, O'Loughlin, Lochlain, etc.). This can be quite helpful in tracing earlier generations.

In order to be successful you will have to spend a lot of time for ongoing research, i e., plan a trip to another country, send away for a death certificate, go through census returns of 1850, etc. Even if you hire research to be done for you, a good deal of time may lapse, so be patient and wait for the rewards.

Should you plan a trip in Ireland for this purpose do just that-*plan it*.Get all the names and addresses of repositories and records together and schedule your days accordingly. If you are going to be doing research locally you could plan to stay the night at a 'bed and breakfast,' where you live right in an Irish household and get a view of the Irish heritage right where it exists-with the Irish people (at an extremely reasonable rate). I was fortunate enough to stay with a family of the same last name as mine (Jim and Monica O'Loughlin), and you most probably could find a household bearing your last name as well. The Irish Tourist Board has a list of 'bed and breakfast' establishments throughout Ireland which is readily available. I strongly recommend this to those of you who are seriously interested in your genealogy as well as those wishing to have an enjoyable vacation.

Also in line with an Ireland trip, keep your eye out for the local unofficial 'historian' of the area. I found most gracious assistance from such individuals in Co. Kerry, and Co. Clare, who were most knowledgeable on Irish history. I found them out by making repeated inquiries about the families and history of the area. Finally someone would tell me to, 'see the man down the road three houses to the left, up the hill,' (which was in keeping with the Irish form of directions). It would be here that some of my most fascinating discoveries would turn up. Just keep asking questions and you're likely to find an answer somewhere.

Church records are often the only source of information for a time period, so any research you can do in this area beforehand will be beneficial. We have included a list of parish registers at the end of this book to help you in this manner. If you can narrow down the area or county of origin, the search will proceed much faster, particularly considering that you could end up traveling from parish to parish asking to see their old records as I did. With written permission from the parish priest beforehand however, you could search the parish records in comfort in Dublin where most of them have been recorded on microfilm Searching the 'original' register is much more time consuming, although I did find some scribbled information in the Baptism register concerning Peter O'Loughlin's marriage in 1865, which may have remained lost if I hadn't been looking at the local handwritten copy. At any rate, you should fully research the available records at home before attempting research in Ireland itself.

We have included source material in books and repositories for all the major religious denominations of Ireland in this book, to make your search a bit easier.

One last note on research in Ireland; you may wish to visit the cemetaries in order to record tombstone epitaphs, which are decaying more and more every year. If so, make careful note of the names and dates. They may not last another season.

CASE STUDIES

Throughout this book you will notice examples of data found in a genealogical search as it *actually* happened. This is intended to show some real results and peculiarities involved in such a venture as tracing your Irish ancestors.

The families in question are the O'Donaghues of the Glen from Co. Kerry, Ireland, and the Lords of the Burren, the O'Loughlins from Co. Clare, Ireland. We traced both families, one completely from scratch from Kansas City, Missouri to their city of origin in Ireland. Once this was established, existing pedigrees in Ireland led us to the first O'Loughlin (and O'Donaghue) and to their ancestors as well, back over 1,000 years in time and history.

The O'Loughlin Search

Starting from scratch with only the knowledge that we had always called ourselves Irish, after much research we found the original O'Loughlin who came to America. From there I traveled to Ireland and concluded the search with the extensive help of newly made Irish friends.

For your own possible enlightenment the following represent major developments in our research:

1. The 1860 census which listed our original ancestor who travelled from Ireland and gave Ireland as country of origin.
2. A death certificate in America listing Co. Clare as county of origin.
3. The birth register of Kilfenora, Co. Clare, Ireland confirmed the birth and residence of our ancestors near this town (1839).
4. The marriage records of Kilfenora (1865) documented the trip back to Ireland (and marriage there) of the son of our original American O'Loughlin.
5. Pedigrees from old books on *The History of County Clare, Ireland*, by Frost, White and Fahy, tracing families back into the 10th century,

CASE STUDY

Major Developments of Search:

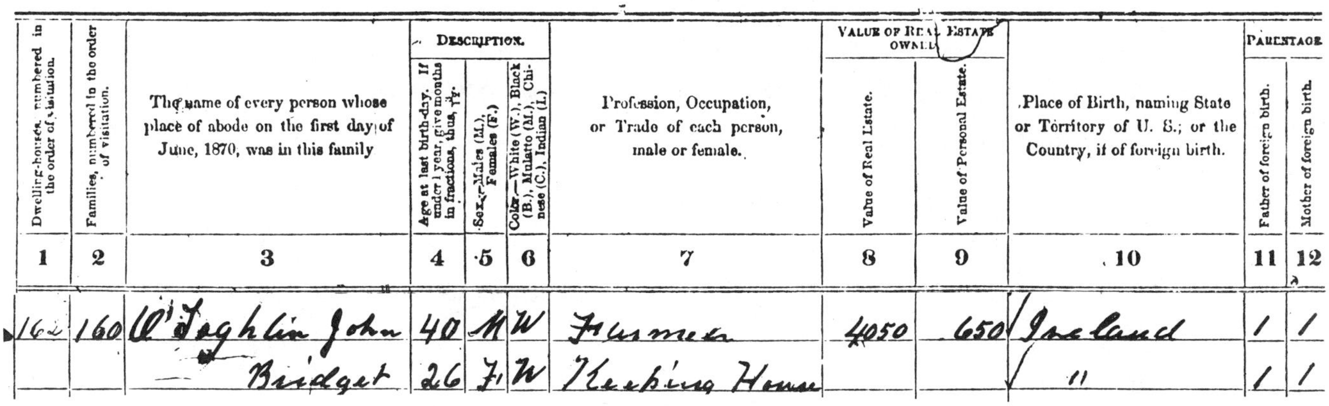

Dwelling-houses, numbered in the order of visitation.	Families, numbered in the order of visitation.	The name of every person whose place of abode on the first day of June, 1870, was in this family	Description: Age at last birth-day. If under 1 year, give months in fractions, thus, 3/12.	Description: Sex.—Males (M.), Females (F.)	Description: Color.—White (W.), Black (B.), Mulatto (M.), Chinese (C.), Indian (I.)	Profession, Occupation, or Trade of each person, male or female.	Value of Real Estate Owned: Value of Real Estate.	Value of Real Estate Owned: Value of Personal Estate.	Place of Birth, naming State or Territory of U. S.; or the Country, if of foreign birth.	Parentage: Father of foreign birth.	Parentage: Mother of foreign birth.
1	2	3	4	5	6	7	8	9	10	11	12
162	160	O'Loghlin John	40	M	W	Farmer	4050	650	Ireland	/	/
		Bridget	26	F	W	Keeping House			"	/	/

1870 Census Listing Ireland as Country of Origin

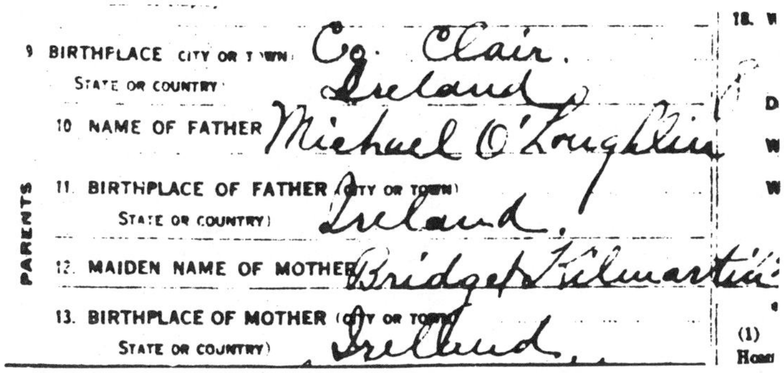

9 BIRTHPLACE CITY OR TOWN Co. Clair.
STATE OR COUNTRY Ireland
10 NAME OF FATHER Michael O'Loughlin
PARENTS
11. BIRTHPLACE OF FATHER (CITY OR TOWN)
STATE OR COUNTRY) Ireland.
12. MAIDEN NAME OF MOTHER Bridget Kilmartin
13. BIRTHPLACE OF MOTHER (CITY OR TOWN)
STATE OR COUNTRY) Ireland.

Death Certificate Showing "Co. Clair" as Birthplace

11/18/1839 Terence of Michael OLoughlin & Bid Kilmartin

Birth Register, Kilfenora Ireland

11/15/1865 Peter OLoughlin & Margarite Quin
Witness: Michael OLoughlin & Mary OLoughlin

Marriage Register of Kilfenora, Co. Clare

The Donahue Search

The Donahue search was a much easier one to trace to a specific area in Ireland due to the fact that by word of mouth, traditions had been handed down.

Known facts before search:

1. We were The O'Donahues of the Glen (whatever that meant)!
2. We knew of Cornelius Donahue, our original ancestor in American and his family.

Major breakthroughs:

1. Parish records of Glenflesk, Co. Kerry, confirming the above.
2. Passenger lists confirming names, dates, and place of origin.
3. Conversation and historical notes given to me by Mr. & Mrs. Denis Spillane of Glenflesk. (Which amounted to the collected archives of the area!)

It should be noted that most of this material was obtained by random search of the area in question and a good deal of time and luck were involved. But the results are well worth the efforts.

The Final Success!

I was able to walk the land of my ancestors in Kilfenora as well as in Glenflesk, Ireland. Furthermore I stood in the ruins of the churches in which they were married or baptized. This was not a guess, but fact.

Conversations with O'Loughlins born of the same ancestors as I was indeed a fateful event. There would I be, but for the trip made to America over 120 years ago.

Although all the O'Donahues of the Glen had died or left for other lands, their presence was nonetheless felt after reading the part they had played in the history of the area and talking with the present day residents.

Had I not asked a few questions at random (in Co. Clare and Co. Kerry) I could have left with next to nothing at all. As it turned out however I had succeeded beyond my own imagination.

I wish you the same success as I have had and hope that the case studies included in this book will assist you to that end.

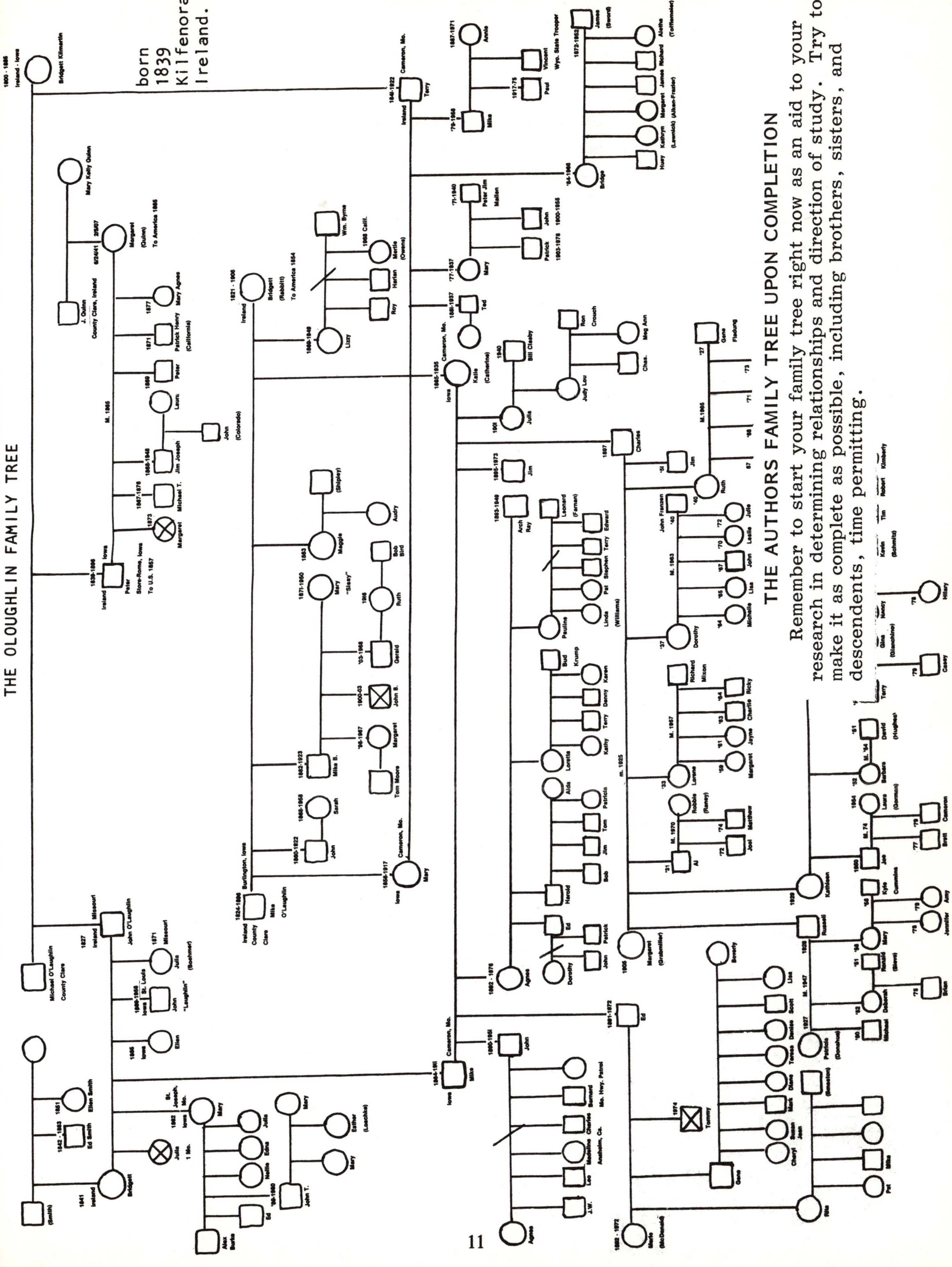

THE AUTHORS FAMILY TREE UPON COMPLETION

Remember to start your family tree right now as an aid to your research in determining relationships and direction of study. Try to make it as complete as possible, including brothers, sisters, and descendents, time permitting.

Having become so involved in Irish genealogy and history, I have decided to make a career out of helping others do so. The family histories and other materials we offer are all intended to open up your past, and enrich your family's future. To this end, let me know of any further help we may be, or any additional material we could include in this book for your benefit.

Much Success and Happiness,

Michael C. O'Laughlin

PART I

Only 20 Steps Away From...
Your "Irish Ancestors"

1. This section deals with the general resources and procedures necessary to conduct a complete search, regardless of the country involved. For more detailed information on particular records or countries see the following chapters: Ireland (Part II); American, Canada, Europe, Australia, etc. (Part III); specific source listing (Part IV).

20 ITEM GENEALOGICAL CHECKLIST

I. Family Records

1. Oral Testimony
2. Handwritten Documents
3. The Oldest Generation
4. Tradition and Legend
5. Spelling of Your Family Name
6. Coat of Arms or Crest

II. Local Records

7. Cemetery and Tombstone
8. Newspaper Articles and Obituaries
9. Baptism and Marriage Registers
10. Local and County Historians
11. Libraries

III. Advanced Research

12. Published Works
13. Census Study
14. National Archives and Government Records
15. Passenger Lists
16. Ancient Pedigrees and History

IV. Final Steps

17. Professional Assistance
18. Documentation and Record Keeping
19. Publish and Preserve Your Findings
20. Summary and Conclusion

RESEARCH AT HOME

1 • Oral Testimony

2 • Handwritten Documents

3 • The Oldest Generation

4 • Tradition & Legend

5 • Spelling of Your Name

6 • Coat of Arms or Crest

Beginning with the memories of the elders of the family along with existing documents such as letters, photoalbums, etc., the Family Records Section relies heavily on word of mouth data and personal interviews. Common sense and good sound reasoning can go a long way. Be sure to record all testimony and findings, even seemingly meaningless ones, for they can become key events in your search. These records are not only logically the best starting point, but represent valuable testimony which could be lost forever with the passing of the oldest living family members.

CASE HISTORY

Example: Step #1. Recording Oral Testimony

Oral Testimony Recorded in the Donaghue Search

1. We have always been called the "O'Donaghues of the Glen."

2. The first family member in America was "Cornelius."

3. Cornelius' wife's (Mary Kelliher) parents drowned in the "Shannon River," on the way home from church.

4. The elders of the family remember that they were related to Maur-ni-Dhuir.

5. Someone had researched the Donaghue family years ago, while in college.

6. Great Uncle Dan spoke of "Stealing an education from the British, under the hedgerows."

7. An oral pedigree had been handed down to my great aunt (unknown to the rest of the family) giving a five generation pedigree of Cornelius, the original Donaghue in America.

Results

1. The "Glen" led me to Glenflesk, Co. Kerry, Ireland.

2. Cornelius and family were located in the Parish records of Glenflesk.

3. The Shannon River gave a geographical landmark.

4. Maur-ni-Dhuir was a well remembered Donaghue in this area, being the grandmother of "The Liberator," Daniel O'Connell.

5. Old research was found done years ago on our family.

6. This type of education agrees with the tradition of the "Faha" school ("Faitche" meaning lawn), still remembered in the area. Students would gather in the open or in hovels as necessary, in order to obtain an education.

7. Still being researched, these names give us a valuable place to start when searching in Co. Kerry, Ireland.

Family Records

☑ Oral Testimony

Oral Testimony from the oldest living generations of your family often proves to be an intriguing (and necessary) starting point. Don't forget the more distant relatives out of town or unheard from in years. Another branch of the family may have valuable information unknown to your immediate family. Remember that "great Aunt Mary" may be the last living link to your heritage.

Be sure to commit all the names, dates and stories to writing-even the small details. A seemingly insignificant fact now, can become a major breakthrough later. Occupations, localities, nicknames and habits can be extremely important. Knowledge of, or marriage into another family is often vague, but the pieces can fall into place later.

A second interview (or a third) weeks or months later may prove more fruitful than the initial conversation with the elders of your clan. Old memories can come alive long after your first talk, and you yourself will have a better idea of what to look for.

☑ Handwritten Documentation

The family Bible is often the only written documentation which records successive generations in a family. Dates and names involving births, marriages, and deaths are commonly recorded in the family Bible. Documents of this type may still be in use or stored in the attic as an heirloom. All too often they have been lost in an estate sale or absent mindedly discarded, but if you are lucky enough to have one, it can make all the difference in the world to your search.

Letters, diaries and correspondence from earlier days can also shed much light on your ancestors and their surroundings. Correspondence between your ancestor and friends and neighbors at home or in "the old country" are invaluable. Old notes and memorabilia will offer the same exciting glimpse into your family's past. Names, titles, addresses, descriptions, and opinions expressed can fill missing links in your understanding of the family's history.

Old photographs (which are often captioned) can do the same thing, only more vividly. These photos can offer special clues found nowhere else. Note the following: What is in the background of the picture, and who are those other people standing with your ancestors? Family photos such as these can serve to bring many forgotten facts to life when shown to the elders of the family, and they begin to recall events such as the family or work picnic, or great Aunt Sally's wedding, etc.

If you've ever gone through a family photo album, you'll realize the value of captions to describe the event and the names of all the individuals in the shot. So, for the futures sake, be sure to caption and name every individual pictured in your current family photographs.

Special Notes on Handwriting & Abbreviations

When dealing with handwritten documents there are two items of special concern. First there is the *understanding of the old styles and forms of handwriting*; secondly, *proper interpretation of abbreviations* and other statements.

The first time you come across an example of older styles of handwriting, (i.e., Old English), not only will the spelling and use of some words be different from what you're use to, but the formation and style of handwriting may appear illegible at first glance. With a little study however, you should be able to make sense of it. A good book to consult on this subject is, *How to Read the Handwriting and Records of Early America*, by E. Kay Kirkham.

Abbreviations may be of a standardized nature, common to most writers of the day, or a specialized shorthand of the individual writer. An abbreviation is often denoted by the use of a superior notation (i.e., rect receipt). A few other examples are as follows:

1. Senr Senior
2. s^{d} said
3. Xofer Christopher
4. Test^{a} or Testa^{m}t Testament
5. ch^{h} church

A historical knowledge of the terms in use at the time and their meanings would, of course, make your interpretation of older handwritten documents much easier.

A further word to the wise would be to avoid abbreviations altogether (whenever possible) when recording your present day records, expecially informal ones. An abbreviation or incomplete notation may lead others (or even yourself at a later date) to an erroneous conclusion. Take for an example, recording the name of a city such as Springfield without making note of the state (or county) involved. There are several Springfields throughout America, and you can't just jump to the conclusion that this Springfield is the one you know best. Remember this when looking at older records as well.

A seemingly innocent notation such as S.A. can be taken to mean:

1. South America
2. South Africa
3. Southern Arizona
4. Santa Ana
5. Saint Augustine
6. San Antonio
7. San Angelo

Furthermor remember that just because you see it in writing, that doesn't make it true. (See checklist 18 for a full explanation.)

Some Widely Used Symbols and Their Meanings

1. Baptised or Christened	X
2. Born Illegitimate	(*)
3. Born	*
4. Died	+
5. Baptised or Christened	⬭
6. Baptised or Christened	∼
7. Bethrothed	O
8. Married	∞
9. Common-Law Marriage	OO
10. Divorced	O/O
11. Buried	□
12. No Further Issue	††
13. No Further Issue	(†)

Written Records

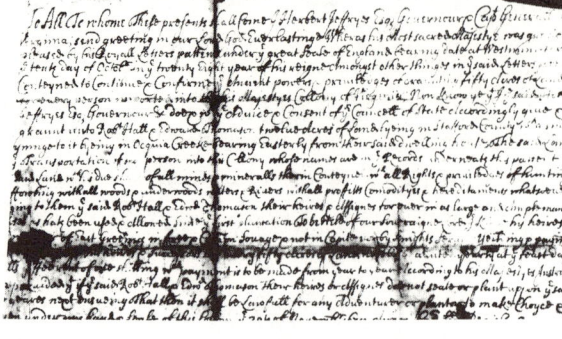

Example #3

Example #1

Example #2

Description of Illustrations:

#1 Family Bible showing births as they occurred.
#2 Captioned photograh showing long lost or hertofore unknown ancestors.
#3 Letters from the homeland telling of trip upcoming.

☑ Traditions and Legend

Unspoken or unrecognized family tradition are often living today in your own household, as well as the obvious well known habits peculiar to your own family. Particular holiday celebrations, names handed down from generation to generation, attitudes towards certain events or nationalities, can all lead toward an understanding of your family's past, date of immigration, etc. In my own family a bit of tradition was handed down by my mother's side:"that we were the O'Donaghues of the Glen.'

Having no idea what this really meant initially, it eventually led me to Glenflesk and Cumacullen Mountain in Co. Kerry, Ireland, to the house which the Donahues occupied in the 1800's and were my ancestors were born!

☑ The Oldest Generation Remembered

What were their names? They were often taken from their fathers or grandfathers, this can point you in the right direction when starting from scratch. Keep an eye out for similar names when searching old records for missing links. (I.E., my great grandfather was a 'Michael and his grandfather was a 'Michael .) Their occupations and peculiarities may prove to be a link as well.

"Of the Clanna Rory"

"The Lord of the Burren"

"Sons of County Cavan"

"The O'Donoghues of the Glen"

"A Stolen Education (under the hedgerows)"

"The Great Potatoe Famine"

"Drowned in the Shannon River"

Traditions handed down through generations often lead us to the location and time period of our early ancestors in Ireland.

CASE HISTORY

Example: Step #3. The Oldest Known Generation

Unknown family members must be found to continue your search

Great Great Grandfather: Still Unknown

Great Grandmother: Kate O'Loughlin

Great Grandfather: Michael O'Loughlin

Occupation: Farmer

Areas of Residence: Rome, Iowa

Relationship with Other Families: Somehow related to the Kilmartins and Rabbits.

Conclusion:

Search census for Rome, Iowa, for Michael O'Loughlin and Kate O'Loughlin. 1860 through 1890. If found, census may give parents name and country of origin, etc. Search adjoining counties if need be.

Keep an eye out for the Kilmartin and Rabbit families when doing local research.

Results:

1. Census gave country of origin as Ireland.
2. Great, great grandfather's mother was Bridget Kilmartin.
3. Great, great, great grandfather was also named "Michael."

CASE HISTORY

Example: Changes In Spelling

The original spelling of your name has most likely changed substantially since it first came into being, both in Ireland and on foreign shores.

To illustrate this point I will roughly trace the history of my own family name, O'Laughlin, in Ireland and America.

Name	Relation
Lochlain, 983 A.D.	Original Ancestor
O'LochLain	Early Descendents
O'Loglen, O'Loghlin, O'Loughlin	Later Descendents
O'Loughlin	My Great, Great, Great Grandfather
O'Laughlin	My Grandfather
O'Laughlin, 1980	Present Day Spelling in the U.S.A.
Laughlin	Corrupted spelling of another branch of the family dropping the O' altogether.

Keep this corruption of spelling in mind when searching even fairly recent records for your ancestors.

☑ The Spelling of Your Family Name

The spelling of your family name should be looked at very closely. Most often it has changed its form over the last hundred years. Prefixes such as the O' or the Mac preceding names were often dropped or added at will. Different individuals in the same family spelled their names differently (i.e., O'Loughlin, O'Laughlin, Loglen). The sound can be the important item to trace, not the spelling. Remember, as well, particularly for the more common names, that thousands of individuals may have born the same name as the ancestor you are looking for. This points out the need to look for other family members, as well as place of residence, etc., when doing your research.

☑ Family Crest or Coat of Arms

If genuine, a family crest, motto, or coat of arms can lead you directly to your ancestors place of origin and pedigree. A coat of arms alone however, is no proof of descent and in recent times many people have been misled into accepting false arms as their genuine heritage. A crest or coat of arms must be verified before being accepted. The same last name does not entitle you to a coat of arms. You may be completely unrelated to a family who bears the same last name as yours. Establishments such as the Genealogical Office in Dublin Castle, Ireland, would be a good place to confirm such matters.

CASE HISTORY

Coat of Arms

OLoughlin	O'Donoghues

Determined through direct male lineage, not your last name.

Note: Years ago my family received a "false" coat of arms by mail, which was really for MacLaughlin but sold as O'Laughlin to unsuspecting families.

7 • Cemetery & Tombstones

8 • Newspaper Articles & Obituaries

9 • Baptism & Marriage Registers

10 • Local & County Historians

11 • Libraries

Local records are a natural progression from data obtained in family records. Much time can be spent searching these sources, much of which can be unproductive. These local records may not only be available in the area of your present residence, but in areas where your ancestors lived as well. If you haven't already begun to make a few inquiries by mail, get ready to start, it may become a necessity.

Example: Step #7 Tombstone Records

The original O'Laughlin brothers from Ireland. In the left background, the unmarked gravestone of John O'Laughlin. Terry, his brother in the foreground.

Cameron, Missouri - Tombstones of two brothers who were original immigrants.

Note that the date given is actually 2 years off from other records found on the same individual.

☑ Tombstone and Cemetery Records

Inspecting tombstones in the family cemetery can give us names, dates and other hitherto unknown information. You may have to search several cemeteries if the exact one in unknown. Many cemeteries also have records of who paid for the tombstone, etc. This points towards other living family members or friends of the family.

☑ Newspapers

Articles and obituaries, particularly in the small towns of earlier days can appear telling of your great, great, grandfather's trip to town or trip back to the home country. Birth, death, and marriage notices are standard, along with biographies of local families. The social, economic and legal aspects of the community were most always covered.

Most newspapers began as weeklies and gradually became dailies. Although time consuming, a search can be very fruitful in this area.

Source Listing

History & Bibliography of American Newspapers, 1690-1820, Worcester, Mass. 1947. Clarence S. Bringham.

American Newspapers, 1821-1936, Winifred Godfrey. New York, 1937.

CASE HISTORY

Example: Step #8 Newspapers As Sources

An obituary column often gives us valuable information, as shown below:

Mt. Pleasant Daily News
Mt. Pleasant, Iowa
Tuesday, February 11, 1896
Page 4, Col. 4

Peter O'Loughlin Dead

Mr. Peter O'Loughlin, one of the staunch business men of Henry County, a man, who by natural ability and untiring energy arose from the condition of a comparatively poor man to wealth and influence, died at his home in Rome on Sunday evening about 10 o'clock. Mr. O'Loughlin has been an invalid for a great many years, and his demise was really a blessing to him.

Peter O'Loughlin was born in County Clare, Ireland, in 1839. While yet a young man he emigrated to America and settled in New Jersey in 1857. In 1858 he came west and settled in Henry County at Rome, then a stirring village. He received a business education in Burlington and afterward entered the flourishing business of O'Loughlin Bros. His heart feeling the emotion of love too strong to withstand, his mind naturally reverted to old Ireland the land of his birth and the home of his loved one. In 1865 he went home to Ireland and secured his bride. He was married to Miss Margaret Quinn. This good couple was blessed with six children. The eldest daughter, her monther's namesake, passed from life a few years ago and left a void in the family circle. The other children Michael, James, Peter Jr., Patrick, Marie, were present at the bedside of their father.

Mr. O'Loughlin, while in health, before the sad affliction befel him, was recognized as being one of the best financiers and business men in the county. He was noted for his integrity and honor. His word was as good as his bond. His friends were many and true. His good wife during the whole of his infirmity has been a noble and true support. Her life must have been sad, but how sweet to think she did her very best. Her reward will be great.

The funeral services took place at St. Alphonsus Catholic church this morning, Rev. Father Bassler conducting the services. His remains were laid to rest in the Catholic cemetary.

☑ Church Records

(Church records such a baptism, christening, marriage records, etc.). Often the only formal written records are those of the church to whom your forebearers belonged. Parish registers may be the only lead you have. Begin with the local parish records in the area of your concern. Birth, death, and marriage dates can be found in church records as well as witnesses to the events and other miscellaneous material.

The LDS Church out of Utah houses some of the most extensive genealogical records in existence, often going back hundred of years into foreign countries as well as America. You don't have to be of this particular denomination to obtain worthwhile information. Researchers are available for assistance. Address inquiries to: Chruch of Jesus Christ of Later Day Saints, Inc., Genealogical Society Library, 50 East North Temple Street, Salt Lake City, Utah 84150. (Also see our Irish Parish Registers listed at the end of this book.)

Source Listing

A Survey of American Church Records, Salt Lake City, 1959-60.

☑ Local or County Historians

A local historian may be able to shed light on your ancestors where no one else can. Check for local or county historical societies.

Also on a local level, an individual may appoint himself 'historian' of an area. Often just such an individual will have collected archives of his own over the years that no one else will possess or even be aware of! Ask about the elders of the area and make a few in person visits. You may turn up something (I have found this to be particularly true in Ireland.)

Source Listing

American Association for State and Local History, Directory: Historical Societies and Agencies in the U.S. and Canada, 1975-76. Nashville, 1976.

CASE HISTORY

Example: Step #9. Baptism & Marriage Registers

The Baptismal Register normally gives the date and Parents and Sponsors of the Newborn Child.

6/28/1838 - Sponsors: Michael O'Loughlin & Biddy Kilmartin. (Biddy=Bridget)

11/18/1839 - Terence (born of) Michael O'Loughlin & Bid Kilmartin.
Sponsors: Pat Hogan & Mary O'Loughlin

This listing confirmed the location and birth of one of the O'Loughlins we were searching for.

Also found incorrectly listed in the back of the Baptism Register were 2 or 3 pages of Marriages--Just what I'd been looking for:

11/15/1865 - Peter O'Loughlin & Margariet Quin
Witness: Michael O'Loughlin & Mary O'Loughlin

This listing confirmed Peter's trip back to Ireland, and marriage there, as reported in his obituary in America.

CASE HISTORY

Example: Step #10. Information from a "Local Historian"

Information obtained on a local level in Ireland.

Co. Clare - "The Burren" area - (The O'Loughlin Search)

1. The O'Loughlins were known as "Lords of the Burren"
2. Originally from the Ballyvaughan area in Co. Clare
3. One theory had been expressed that we were anciently descended from the Danes in some manner.
4. The names of several elders of the clan were obtained.
5. An ancient Gaelic pedigree of the first OLoughlin, (Lochlainn-983 A.D.) was found in a work published in Gaelic.

Co. Kerry - "The O'Donaghues of the Glen" Search

1. The Birth and Marriage register listing my ancestors.
2. The archives of the Glenflesk area, collected writings, etc.
3. The passenger list containing the names of the entire family who emigrated to America.

All this information was obtained simply by talking to a previously unknown resident of the area in question.

Glenflesk,
Killarney.
3rd. March 1981

Dear Mike,
I hope you and yours are in the best of health and happiness as we are ourselves (T.G.)

You are lucky in your research in that Con Daniel kept a family tree which is now very useful. So far I have found no confirmation of the fact that Jeremiah was born outside of Glenflesk If he Pat & Con are not in the parish Register of Births they might have been born before 1821 when the Register was started. I hope that Cornelius have recorded the families of his forefathers wives and families. Have you any record of why Mary Kellihers parents were across the Shannon? What connection had they with Clare, west of the Shannon?

During the 17th and 18th century the Catholic pesants were not allowed to have fire arms so the only arms allowed were long knives which they used for protection and attack on English settlers on their lands which the English Government had confiscated. The Donoghues were particularly noted for their long knives

☑ Library Research

You can check with the local public libraries as well as college and university libraries. Hundreds of unrecognized sources remain in little known published books in libraries. Keep an eye out for family or county histories in which your ancestors could appear. School yearbooks, city directories, and telephone directories are sometimes available for later day research.

There may also already be a book published on your family name or leading families of the area, which might include your forefathers. Check the indexes of all possible sources first for reference to your last name. The New York Public Library, The Newberry Library of Chicago, Illinois, and the Huntington Library of San Marino, California, all have fairly large collections of Irish published materials in America as well.

You may also request a search of the vast holdings in the Library of Congress (U.S.A.) for any book done on the name in question.

Source Listing

The Library of the National Society, Daughters of the American Revolution, 1776 D. Street, N.W., Washington, D.C. 20006

Old manuscripts and poems sometimes make excellent sources when tracing back your ancestors in Ireland.

As recorded by John O'Donovan from an old Irish Manuscript:

Standard of O'Loughlin

In O'Loughlin's camp was visible a fair satin sheet, to be at the head of each battle, to defend in the field, A fruit bearing oak, defended by a chieftain justly, And an anchor blue, with fold of a golden cable.

In the Irish Topographical Poem of Giolla-na-Naomh O'Huidhrin, written circa 1420, in which we are given the topography of pre-Norman Ireland, O'Loughlin is mentioned as Lord of Burren:

O'Lochlainn, hero over battalions,
Is over the soft drop-scattering Burren,
Over Tealach Chuirc by right
Of the cattle and wealth-abounding port.

Advanced research can come about only after you have laid the proper groundwork shown in the preceding sections. Without this groundwork, research of this type may prove totally useless and at best needlessly frustrating and time consuming. Detailed sources on material in the National Archives of the United States are contained in Part III of this book which covers repositories outside Ireland.

☑ Books and Publications

There are of course, thousands of books published dealing with genealogy. Some major catagories are as follows:

1. 'How to books' on genealogical research.
2. Family and County Histories.
3. General History Books on immigration, lifestyle, etc.
4. Estate papers, manuscripts, original documents, etc.
5. Indexed volumes highlighting government records and other compilations of available works.
6. Geographical census records and surveys.

We have included several hundred such references in this book for your use and inspection. Many of the more useful works we have tried to include in the text of this work, but there are many excellent works on more specific areas of research. While some works may not contain much new or useful material for you, a careful selection is sure to lead you in the right direction.

Out of Print Books

Classified telephone directories usually list booksellers who specialize in out of print publications. The New York Times Book Review and general literary periodicals like 'The Atlantic Monthly' often carry advertisements of out of print dealers and book search services. The collections of most large libraries contain several reference sources listing booksellers. Among these are the *American Book Trade Directory*, and the *A.B. Bookman's Yearbook*, which provides a list of U.S. and Canadian dealers arranged by subject specialty.

Special publishing companies often reprint books which have gone out of circulation as well. Many scarce materials are copied on microfilm and require special reading devices, usually on hand at most libraries.

A book such as *Irish Families*, by Edward MacLysaght is an excellent beginning source for locating your family's roots in Ireland, containing the origins of several hundred Irish families and their coat of arms.

Part II contains extensive sources available in and on Ireland as it pertains to genealogy. Part III of this book contains some of the books and publications in the American Archives as well as other countries. Part IV contains numerous sources some indexed by county name and specific surname, as well as general reference.

In the magazine "The Genealogical Helper," c/o Everton Publisher, Inc., P.O. Box 368, Logan, Utah, you can search for pedigrees, family trees, and find other individuals researching the same name as you.

Other Publications and Organizations

"National Genealogical Society Quarterly," published by the National Genealogical Society, 1921 Sunderland Place N.W., Washington, D.C. 20036.

Source Listing

Genealogical Research Methods and Sources, published by The American Society of Genealogists.

Searching for Your Ancestors, by Gilbert H. Doane.

The Researcher's Guide to American Genealogy, by Val D. Greenwood.

Genealogy as Pastime and Profession, by Donald Lines Jacobus.

Know Your Ancestors, by Ethel W. Williams.

Tracing Your Ancestry, by F. Wilburn Helmbold, 2 volumes includes a workbook.

American & British Genealogy & Heraldry, by P. William Filby.

Genealogical Books in Print, by Netti Schreiner-Yantis.

CASE STUDY

Example: Step #14. National Archives, Etc.

U.S. Published Guides to Government Records:

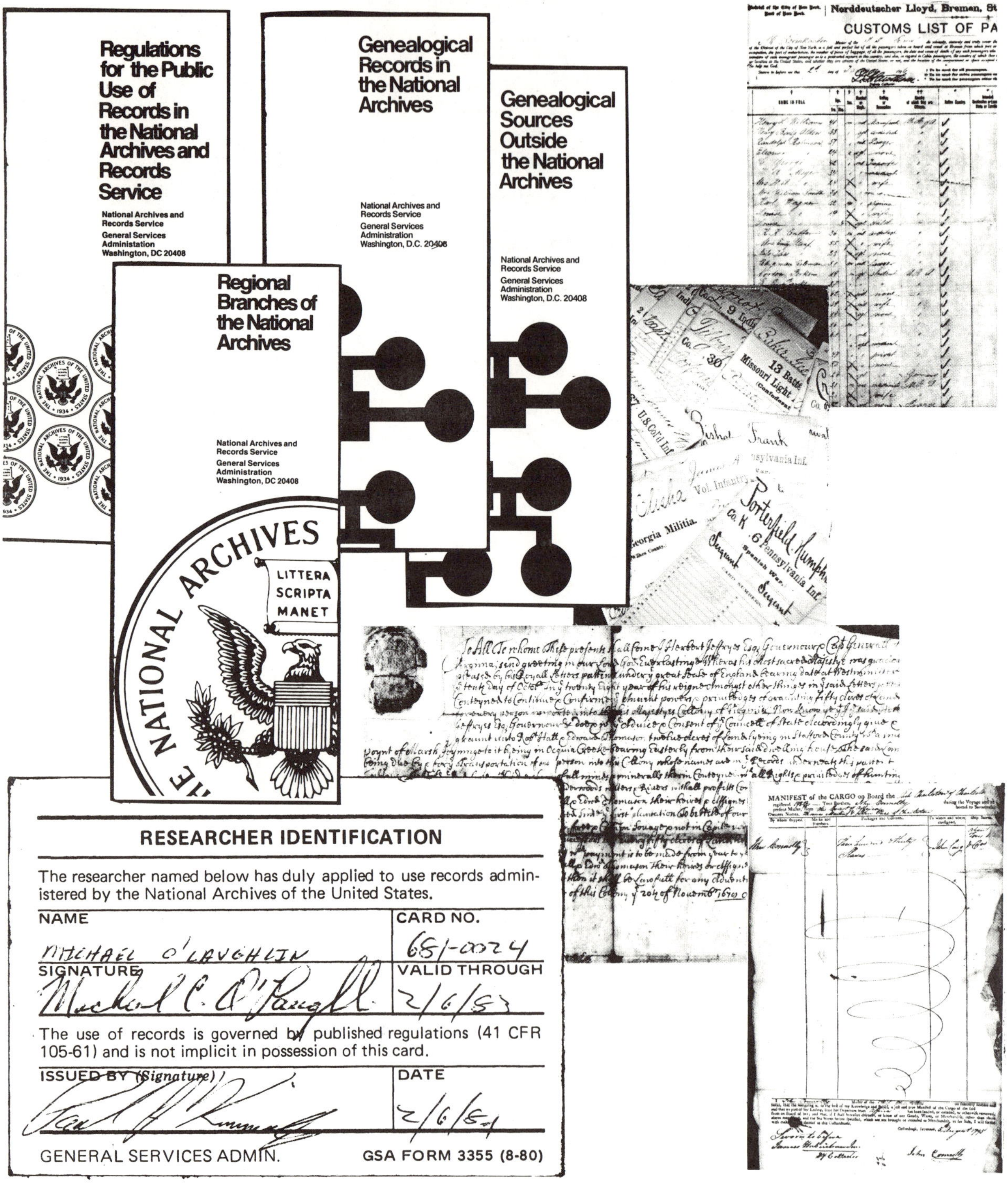

☑ Census & Survey Records

Perhaps the best documented census of ancient times were those of the Roman Empire, even being mentioned in the Bible. Since that time, the census has become a standard tool of government recordkeeping in countries throughout the world.

The federal census records in the United States are probably your best bet for furthering research. Regardless of the country involved, you should determine the states and counties (or specific locality) in which you'd like to search for names and then begin the tedious task of going county by county, census by census in order to trace family members living together, occupations, age, country of origin, etc. You can often trace your family back to the original country and county of origin simply by tracing back the earliest census on which your ancestor appears. In America there is sometimes available a soundex system of reference in which you can search for a name by sound, as well as spelling, which is often different or mis-recorded when compared to your present last name spelling.

(See special section of U.S., Canadian, and Irish National Archives, Part II & III for detail.)

Several surveys of land ownership and occupation exists in countries such as Ireland, going back several hundred years. These surveys were often used to inventory the land for occupying military forces, and record the transfer of land from the natives to the oppressors of the region.

☑ National Archives and Government Records

The National Archives will normally contain more material than you could possibly search in a given period of time. Containing such records as: census returns, military service records, criminal records, naturalizations, passenger lists, published works, etc. (See section later in this book, Part III, detailing the American records in the National Archives.)

On a local level, the county seat or state capitol (or their equivalents) will most often have birth, death, and marriage records (available from 'The Bureau of Vital Statistics' on a state level in the United States). Legal documents concerning land ownership, wills, probate, etc., are also good sources, but often take some time to locate and procure.

(See later sections for individual records by country.)

☑ Emigration and Passenger Lists

(In the U.S.A. see Reference Guide, ISSN 0163-1357, No. 6, Library of Congress, General Reading Rooms Division. Immigrant Arrivals.)

For one who is tracing the arrival of an ancestor, the published sources may prove disappointing. Too often, it seems, they do not contain the specific names and details that are sought. For this information one must usually turn to records and documents such as those held in the National Archives.

Study of the published sources may be valuable, however, if the general knowledge gained provides clues for further search, or ties together fragments gleaned earlier. For example, awareness of immigration patterns and the dispersal of ethnic groups throughout the country may serve to focus one's search on a particular time frame and geographic region. Similarly, a knowledge of changing ship design and construction through the years may illuminate some scrap of information that family legend has reported about an ancestor's travel.

The greatest emigration from Ireland occured in the 1800's, though many left much earlier for foreign shores. The main reason being due to poverty and affliction, as evidenced during the period of the well known "Great Potatoe Famine." During these times of great migration you will find individuals of the same first and last names who departed from Ireland in the same time period. It will be important to look for the names of accompanying passengers and family members as well as any single individual involved.

As evidenced by sources mentioned later in this book, there are many available passenger lists, (i.e., contained in the National Archives and various publications and libraries). Critical data of course, will be:

1. Name of the passenger.
2. Port of Entry (or departure).
3. The date.
4. The Name of the Ship.

Sometimes you will find the occupation, birth date, and area of residence of your ancestor as well, in the original passenger lists. There are several compilations of indexed passenger lists available for your inspection. Of course, not all passenger lists remain intact after the turbulent years of the past, but a surprising amount remain with us today.

A few other important points:

1. The Irish often traveled to England in order to catch a larger ship for passage abroad. Hence, the departure may

be from England (as well as a period of residence and occupation in England).

2. At times, occupiers of Ireland paid the passage of emigrants to the new world just to be rid of them.

4. The voyage took approximately 2 months to North America.

5. Bans were made on the immigration of skilled labor, so you will notice the abundance of laborers and farmers (as unskilled labor) which is not always correct.

The passenger list will most likely enable you to determine from whence your ancestors came and when they departed the "old country" for their new home. Once this has been determined, you can begin researching your Irish ancestor in Ireland.

(See Passenger Lists in the National Archives, Part III in this book.)

CASE STUDY

Example: Step #16. Ancient Pedigrees

Milesius	(504 B.C.) (Father of the Celtic Race in Ireland)
Oilioll Olium	(234 A.D.)
Donnchadh	(1063 A.D.) (The First Donaghue)
Conor	(Founder of the ODonoghues of the Glen)
Cornelius Donaghue	(1856 to U.S.A.)
Donaghue Family	(1980) (of Kansas City, Missouri, U.S.A.)

Taken to extremes, one could trace his family back into the legends of Irish heritage.

☑ Ancient Pedigrees, History and Legend

For those researchers who wish to pursue their family history beyond the normal limits of time, the study of ancient history and legend can be fascinating. At this point, it should be remembered that we begin dealing with theory and unproven conclusions more often than not.

The fact that the general use of surnames did not begin until around the 10th century (and for many, much later makes research even more perplexing.)

Proven facts and original documents soon become non-existant. Most of your time can easily be spent discovering general traits and movements of the population as a whole. Taken to the extreme, one could trace back to the first written records and then into the pre-history of the country in question.

The movement of the peoples of the world (Greeks, Romans, Spanish, etc.) can soon be seen to be a significant factor.When a country is conquered or invaded peacefully by another people, often these newcomers intermingle with the natives and become accepted as such. Actually they represent a new 'heritage,' with distinct ideas, customs, and beliefs.

Existing legends have been so often intertwined with fantasy and story telling that the facts are hopelessly clouded. With a sufficient amount of historical knowledge however, you can begin to uncover some basic 'truths.'

Conclusions must often be drawn from place names and traditions which travel unexplainably from area to area. At any rate, you will soon be dealing with generalities rather than specifics. While this may not add directly to your pedigree, it will definitely add to the knowledge of your heritage.

PART IV

Final steps. OKay, so you've done all you can possibly do. Making sure you've done it properly, and leaving this legacy to generations alive today, as well as to generations yet unborn is just as important.

Board for certification of Genealogists

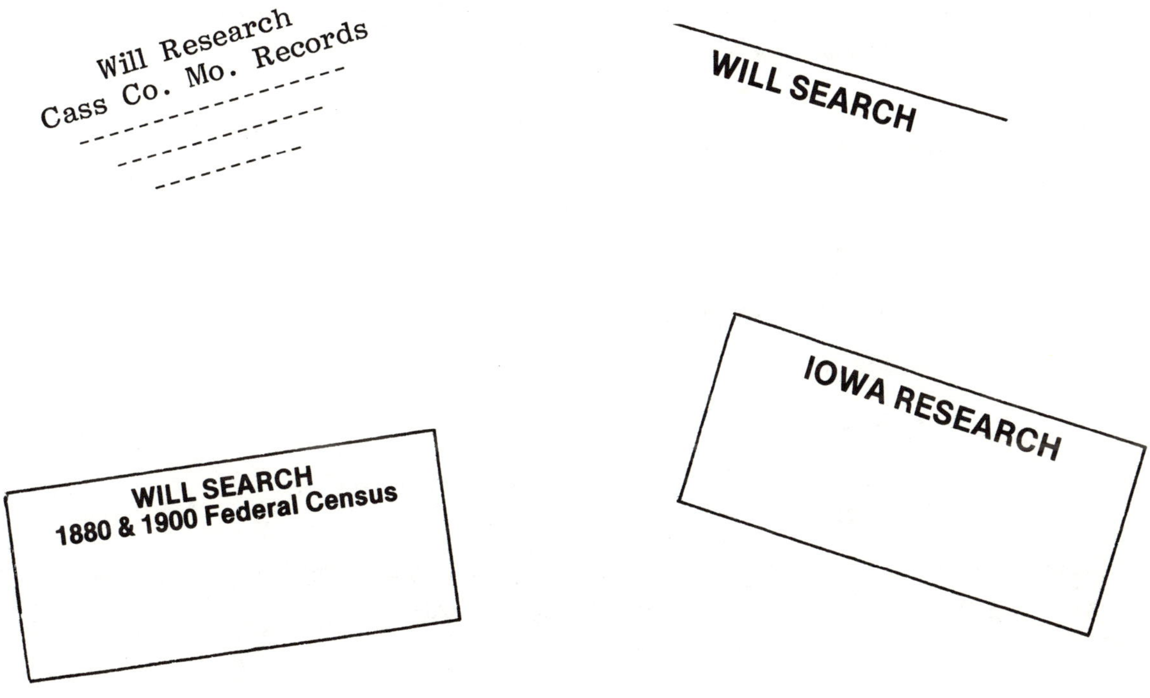

Be sure to ask for documentation of all facts presented to you as such.

☑ Outside and Professional Assistance

You may wish to enlist the help of a professional researcher or genealogist. Most libraries or areas of the country would have, or know of, someone available to search for you (i.e., search for records of Peter O'Loughlin in 1860 in New Jersey). You may wish to hire someone for a specific search such as a death notice in the local paper, or a will from 1863. You could hire a full fledged genealogical search to be done, but your cost will, of course, increase.

Be sure to check the credentials of any researcher and require documentation of all facts presented to you as such. For a list of qualified personnel write: Board for Certification of Genealogists, 1307 New Hampshire Avenue, N.W., Washington, D.C. 20036. Phone: (703) 560-3971.

Special Notes on Letters and Correspondence

In the course of your investigation you will undoubtedly need to correspond by mail. Whether your letters are addressed to professional genealogists, county historical societies, or family members, you will want to get the proper response, so it's best to follow a few common sense guidelines. (Which are too often overlooked):

Simply put, they are as follows:

- Ask for one thing at a time.
- Be brief and clear.
- Enclose a self addressed stamped envelope.
- Offer to share your results.
- Make a copy of the letter for your file.
- Enclose a brief family tree if necessary to identify your search.

Remember that your efforts may knowingly or unknowingly hinge upon the reply to your letter, so do it well and reap the rewards

☑ Documentation and Record Keeping

Whether your work is intended solely for your own satisfaction, or for other family members and interested parties, now and in the future, proper documentation and clear thinking is a must.

Someone may wish to begin a search where you left off, or confirm your findings. This could prove nearly impossible without some sort of documentation. Otherwise, all you have is your own 'oral testimony' which could well be lost in the passing of a few years.

You will probably not be aware of the significance of all your findings, nor understand all their implications if you are unable to sit back at your leisure and see some previously hidden conclusion. You can indeed find a whole new avenue of research when viewing your findings as a whole, well organized search. This points up the necessity of written records of all your efforts.

Keep a record of where *not* to look! As well as recording your successful finds, make a note of where not to look. This can help avoid needless duplications, or maybe raise the question of 'why you didn't find anything.' (I.E., no records of residence in 1880 in Missouri could be due to a move to another area or state.)

Some important facts to document (as an example):

1. The year of the census searched under what spelling of the name? It could be recorded under a varient spelling.
2. What newspaper, date, and issue, did you find the obituary article in (for future reference)?
3. Which book gave you a pedigree for your family name? (Different books can give altogether different information and you may have to go back and sort out the truth of the matter.)
4. Exactly what land survey listed your ancestors? (Perhaps you've uncovered another family of the same name and need to confirm your original conclusions.)
5. Another researcher wants to find access to the sources you considered most valuable. (Can you be of special help, i.e., date, title, author, repository?)
6. Your great grandchild wants to do the same research you did. Can you save him some time and trouble?

It becomes apparent that you can save yourself and others needless waste of time by documenting your sources. This will prove useful not only in your immediate lifetime, but to future generations a well.

When citing a particular written source be sure to include the following:

1. The location where you found the documents.
2. The name of the author.
3. Title, edition, and date of publication.
4. The Publisher.
5. The page numbers to which you refer.

Centuries of Errors

We have discussed some of the problems involved with older records accuracy and interpretation earlier in this book. The accuracy of records is a vital point in your research, and you must be able to understand the historic and personal distortions. which can affect the validity of your family's history. Errors made centuries ago can be looked upon as fact today.

Official Mistakes

Not only have census takers, historians, and clerks misrecorded names and dates in the past, but your own ancestors have furnished us with errors that have been faithfully copied down as well. The spelling of a last name for example, has been spelled differently by brothers and sisters in the same household. Census takers have spelled names according to their own 'beliefs' as to how it should be spelled. Dates of birth and death have often been recorded from oral testimony during periods of famine, in strange and often hostile environments, so it is little wonder that some errors occur.

Political reasons, as well as historical ones can affect documented, printed, so called 'fact.' In the same vein, it is not unheard of for an individual to alter the 'facts' of history in order to present a more favorable picture of his own life and philosophy. Remember that these errors have been copied down again and again until today they remain as unquestioned facts.

It becomes apparent that a working knowledge of history, politics and psychology of the individual is helpful in determining the accuracy of your information.

☑ Copy or Publish to Preserve Your Findings

You will most likely want to preserve your findings for your own benefit as well as others. You could decide to Xerox copy your notes and summary, have a microfilm copy made (sometimes at no expense to you through a historical or genealogical society), or go all out and print up a few copies of your genealogical findings in a family history format. You may even wish to include a brief section on living family members.

The finished product would make a nice gift for family members or it could be sold in order to recover some of your cost. There are several levels of quality and expense to choose from should you decide on publishing your work. Consult with several printers of different sizes and capabilities to get a proper picture of your alternatives.

Once you have completed your work you can have copies sent to the Library of Congress in America, where they will be indexed and held on file for future inquiries from any interested parties (in conjuction with the Library of Congress and Copyright application). There is a very modest fee for this service and well worth the few dollars of expense. Our own "Irish Genealogical Foundation" will also keep a copy of any Irish works you may have as well.

As we well know from printing many such publications, the cost can rise quite swiftly. There is no better way however of preserving your findings for generations to come.

Some of the most likely material to include in your family or personal history:

1. Dates concerning births, marriages, deaths.
2. Social and economic conditions.
3. Particular episodes of crises or achievement.
4. Friends and outside activities, hobbies.
5. History of your work or job.
6. Names of all children and descendents.
7. Religious Background.
8. Special days, holidays, or celebrations.
9. All the present day or past traditions.
10. The aspirations and dreams of family members.
11. Commentary and advice to future generations.

CASE STUDY

Example: Step #19. Publish & Preserve Your Findings

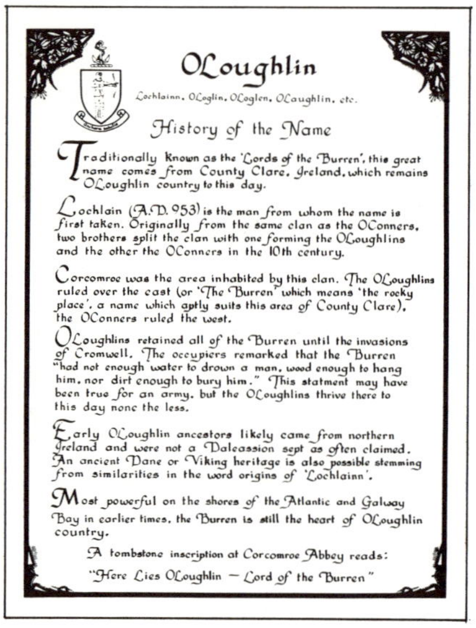

OLoughlin

Lochlainn, OLoglin, OLoglen, OLaughlin, etc.

History of the Name

Traditionally known as the 'Lords of the Burren', this great name comes from County Clare, Ireland, which remains OLoughlin country to this day.

Lochlain (A.D. 953) is the man from whom the name is first taken. Originally from the same clan as the OConners, two brothers split the clan with one forming the OLoughlins and the other the OConners in the 10th century.

Corcomroe was the area inhabited by this clan. The OLoughlins ruled over the east (or 'The Burren' which means 'the rocky place', a name which aptly suits this area of County Clare), the OConners ruled the west.

OLoughlins retained all of the Burren until the invasions of Cromwell. The occupiers remarked that the Burren "had not enough water to drown a man, wood enough to hang him, nor dirt enough to bury him." This statment may have been true for an army, but the OLoughlins thrive there to this day none the less.

Early OLoughlin ancestors likely came from northern Ireland and were not a Daleassion sept as often claimed. An ancient Dane or Viking heritage is also possible stemming from similarities in the word origins of 'Lochlainn'.

Most powerful on the shores of the Atlantic and Galway Bay in earlier times, the Burren is still the heart of OLoughlin country.

A tombstone inscription at Corcomroe Abbey reads:

"Here Lies OLoughlin — Lord of the Burren"

☑ **Summary and Conclusions** Once you have put all the facts and intriguing developments together, you will be able to view the 'big picture' of your genealogy. What traits have carried through the last 100 or 200 years down to the present? Have any of your likes and dislikes been shaped through the experience of your ancestors? Were they the strong silent type of people, or outspoken and boisterious more than likely? What role did 'personal freedom' or 'respect for the establishment' play? The possibilities are endless.

Often a certain type of occupation will repeat itself in a family through the generations. If not, why did they change? What was the effect of the changing world or new country of residence? Education and a love for learning, or the pioneer spirit can also manifest itself through the centuries.

Viewing the hardships in the history of the past can help us gain a better perspective on the challanges of the present and future.

Another part of your summary and conclusion would be to include estimates of the reliability of your sources (i.e., hearsay, little known books and publications). Just as important would be a comment on the direction of future research and sources still untapped. Where sould one go to further your research? You may be the only person who could answer this question for curious readers. You may even decide to continue the research yourself in later years. So, do everyone a favor and document your sources as well as the direction future research could take.

You can now take a great deal of satisfaction in preserving the genealogical history of your family and its effect on your family's future!

Example: Step #20. Summary & Conclusion

(continued)

were a proud family known for the ability to work hard, and valued honesty above all, as evidenced by these facts.

While information gathered from the 16th century and earlier is not hard fact, it is quite likely based on truth. These legends have proved more accurate than believed in the past, in view of recent discoveries. (See book #28 on following page for confirming data.)

Anyone wishing to do further research would do well to search the parish records in the Ballyvaughan area of Co. Clare for records of Michael O'Loughlin and Bridget Kilmartin.

In addition the following records should be sought:

1. 1865 Marriage Record in the Public Records Office in Dublin for Peter O'Loughlin and Margarite Quinn.

2. Parish registers in Corofin, Co. Clare, looking for the O'Loughlin and Quinn family.

3. Research the "Tullagha" area near Co. Clare which I believe may have been our ancestors land as well.

4. Further conversation with the individuals mentioned earlier in Kilfenora and Glenflesk.

PART II

RESEARCH IN IRELAND!!!

Chapter 1

• *Terms & Understanding*

Chapter 2

• *Religious Sources, Parish Registers* • *Ancient Pedigrees & History* • Records & Repositories
• *Census & Surveys* • 1891 Birth Index of Ireland

1. The material within this section will largely be self-explanatory (with sufficient review). It is necessary to understand the geographic divisions of Ireland to procure the proper material in continuing your search. One could theoretically continue tracing his ancestors back to the invasions of Ireland by the Celts in 504 B.C. and beyond, if he had the time and inclination.

ADMINISTRATIVE DIVISIONS OF IRELAND

Title	*Status (1883)*
Province	4 Civil Provinces (5 in earlier times)
County	32 Civil Counties
Barony	325 Civil Baronies
(Diocese)	(28 Church Diocese)
Parish	2447 Parishes
Townland	64,000 Civil Townlands

It is important for the researcher to understand these administrative divisions to further his study in Ireland. (See maps of the above on the following pages.)

UNDERSTANDING IRISH RECORDS & TERMINOLOGY

To walk into (or write) the Genealogical Office in Dublin with no idea of your heritage (or research) on your part, would most likely be a waste of time. If however, you do your homework and refer to the specific records as outlined in this book under Irish sources, half the battle is over. At least you have a place from which to start.

By understanding the geographical divisions of Ireland you will not only be able to research on your own, but you can talk intelligently to others who will be able to help.

You will, hopefully, at some point, find a reference to a locality or county in which your ancestors resided. From here you need to pinpoint this particular area. Two excellent sources to consult will be

1. Philips Handy Atlas of the Counties of Ireland, by P.W. Joyce, 1881. This publication is well indexed and outlines the counties as well as specific baronies and towns as well.

2. Topographical Dictionary of Ireland, by Lewis, published in two volumes, London, 1837.

Other sources to consult when looking for geographic locations in Ireland:

1. *A Topographical Index of the Parishes and Townlands of Ireland in Sir William Petty's MSS. Barony Maps, (1655-1659).* Dublin, 1932. Y.M. Goblet, Ed.

2. *The General Alphabetical Index of the Townlands and Towns, Parishes and Baronies of Ireland,* Ed. A. Thom. Dublin 1861, 1904, 1913. Published with the "Census of Ireland."

3. *Topographical Index; 1926.* For Northern Ireland, published with "Government of Northern Ireland, Census of Population of Northern Ireland."

4. *The Parliamentary Gazetteer of Ireland,* 1841, 1844, 1846. Gives a complete description of surroundings, castles, history and statistics.

The large "Ordinance Survey Maps" of Ireland are extremely detailed and readily available from the Government Publication Sales Office, GPO Arcade, Dublin, Ireland. These maps can be extraordinarily useful and interesting in tracing and understanding the localities of Ireland during earlier days.

The following pages should be self-explanatory and are available for study at your leisure. Use them well, for they can mean the difference between failure and success in the final stages of your search.

Before delving directly into Irish records and repositories, we will cover a brief explaination of terms, geographical divisions, and Irish background in order to understand some of the material you'll be searching for. To this end we have outlined the following:

1. Maps and descriptions of geographical divisions, ancient and modern.
2. A sample of Irish place names and terminology with modern translations.
3. Ancient Pedigrees and the Celts.
4. Initial sources to consult before continuing your search.
5. A surname map of Ireland, showing the counties of residence for Irish families.

Be prepared before continuing your search! Don't expect to go directly to the records of Ireland and have immediate results without the proper research beforehand. Looking for a Murphy, Sullivan or Donaghue can be like looking for a needle in a haystack.

Of prime importance to your search (if available) will be:

1. The name of your ancestor.
2. The name of other family members.
3. Area of residence.
4. Approximate date of departure from Ireland.

The Province

Ancient Kingdoms of Ireland. The four provinces were: (1) Ulster in the north; (2) Leinster in the east; (3) Connaught in the west; and (4) Munster in the south. The old province of Meath became incorporated into Leinster. The kingdoms of Oriel and Aileach merged with Ulster in the 17th century.

The County

The largest local administrative division of more modern times. The first 12 counties came into existence in the year 1210, and the last county (Wicklow) was formed in 1605.

The Barony

Another ancient division of Ireland based upon the great Irish families territorial holdings. A total of 325 baronies exist. They were used as a unit in the 19th Century Land Valuations. Normally composed of several parishes.

The Parish

Existing as both civil and ecclesiastical districts. The parish was the smallest administrative unit of the Catholic Church. This religious parish was a subdivision of the diocese (which were 28 in number in 1883). The civil parish was used for census and taxation purposes. Civil and religious parishes were often of different names entirely.

The Townland

The smallest civil district of Ireland. The words, "towne," "hamlet," and "vil" were also used to describe this 17th century geographic division. A rural subdivision of the civil parish.

Poor Law Unions

Usually comprised several townlands and came into begin as a result of the Poor Law Relief Act of 1838. Formed for taxation purposes to support the poor and destitute of the area. The "Poor House" itself was normally situated in a local market town of the area.

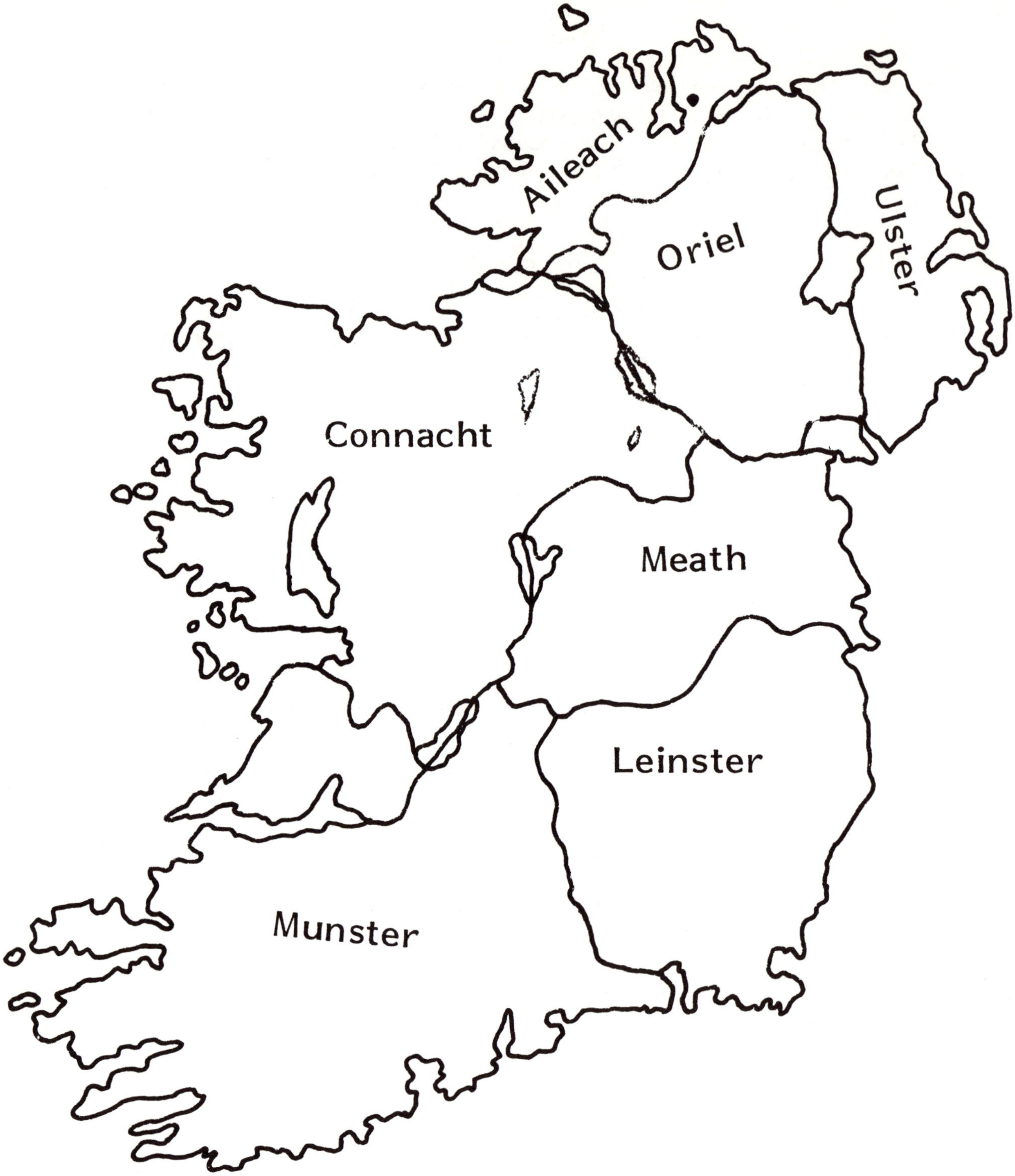

1. The Province – Ancient Kingdoms of Ireland. The four provinces were (1) Ulster in the north; (2) Leinster in the east; (3) Connaught in the west; and, (4) Munster in the south. The old province of Meath became incorporated into Leinster. The kingdoms of Oriel and Aileach merged with Ulster in the 17th century.

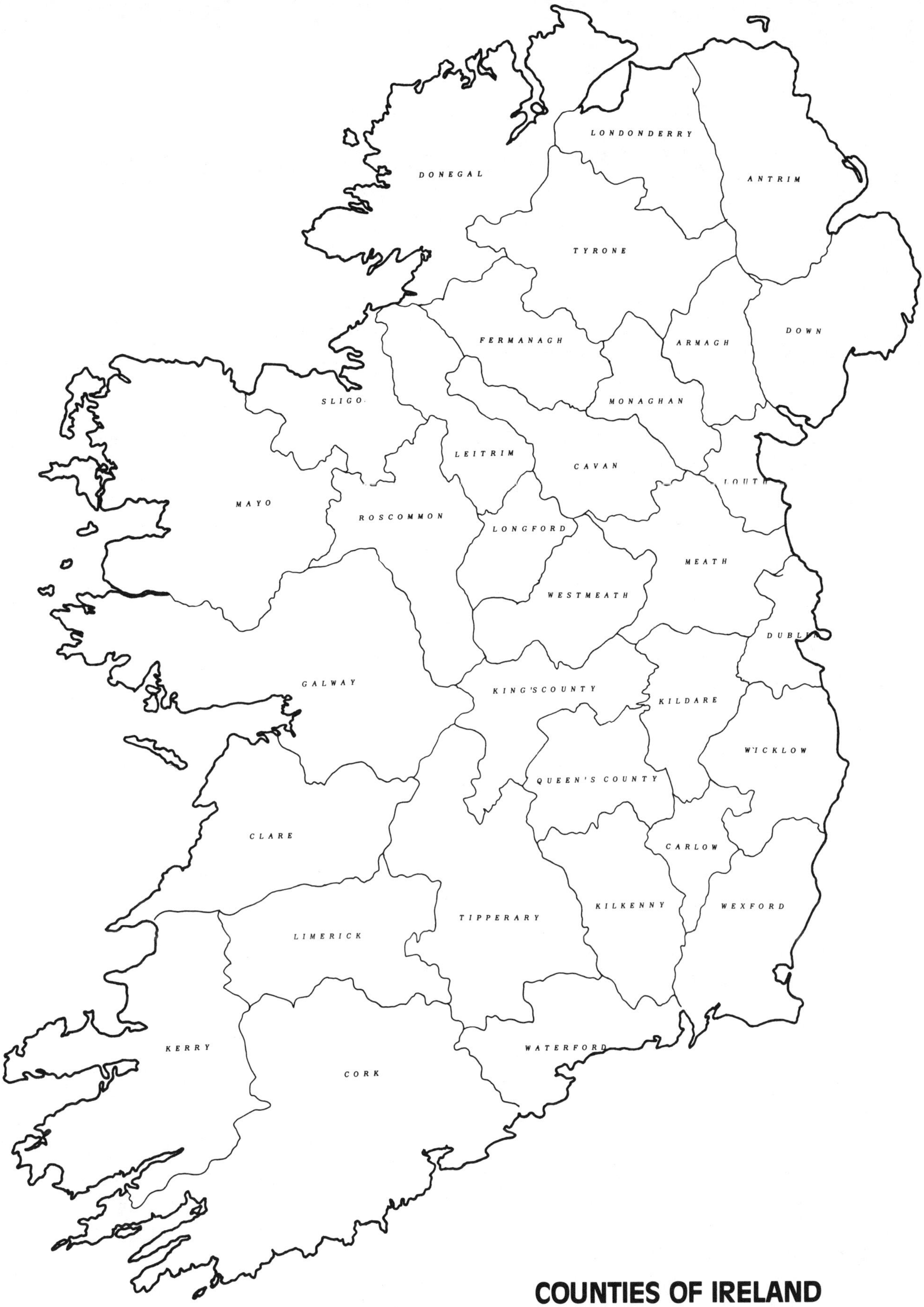

COUNTIES OF IRELAND

1. The County – The Largest local administrative divisions of more modern times. The first 12 counties came into existence in the year 1210, and the last county (Wicklow) was formed in 1605.

1883 LISTING OF COUNTIES AND THEIR BARONIES

County

Contains the following Baronies

Antrim

Lower Dunluce, Upper Dunluce, Cary, Kilconway, Lower Glenarm, Upper Glenarm, Lower Toome, Upper Toome, Lower Antrim, Upper Antrim, Carrickfergus, Lower Belfast, Upper Belfast, Lower Massareene, Upper Massareene.

Armagh

Oneilland West, Oneilland East, Tiranny, Armagh, Lower Fews, Upper Fews, Lower Orior, Upper Orior.

Carlow

Carlow, Rathvilly, Idrone West, Idrone East, Forth, St. Mullin's Upper, St. Mullin's lower.

Cavan

Tullyhaw, Tullyhunco, Lower Loughtee, Upper Loughtee, Tullygarvey, Clankee, Clanmahon, Castlerahan.

Clare

Burren, Corcomroe, Inchiquin, Ibrickan Islands, Upper Bunratty, Lower Bunratty, Upper Tulla, Lower Tulla, Moyarta, Clonderalaw.

Cork

Duhallow, Orrery and Kilmore, Fermoy, Condons and Clangibbon, West Muskerry, East Muskerry, Barretts, Barrymore, Kinnatalloon, Imokilly, Bear, Bantry, Kinalmeaky, Cork, Kerrycurrihy, Kinalea, West Carbery – West Division, West Carbery – East Division, East Carbery – West Division, East Carbery – East Division, Kinsale, Courceys, Ibane and Barryroe.

Donegal

Kilmacrenan, East Inishowen, West Inishowen, Boylagh, Raphoe, Banagh, Tirbugh,

Down

Lower Castlereagh, Upper Castlereagh, Dufferin, Lower Ards, Upper Ards, Lower Iveagh – Lower Part, Lower Iveagh – Upper Part, Kinelarty, Upper Lecale, Lower Lecale, Lordship of Newry, Mourne, Upper Iveagh – Lower Part, Upper Iveagh – Upper Part.

Dublin

Balrothery West, Balrothery East, Nethercross, Castleknock, Coolock, Newcastle, Uppercross, Dublin, Rathdown.

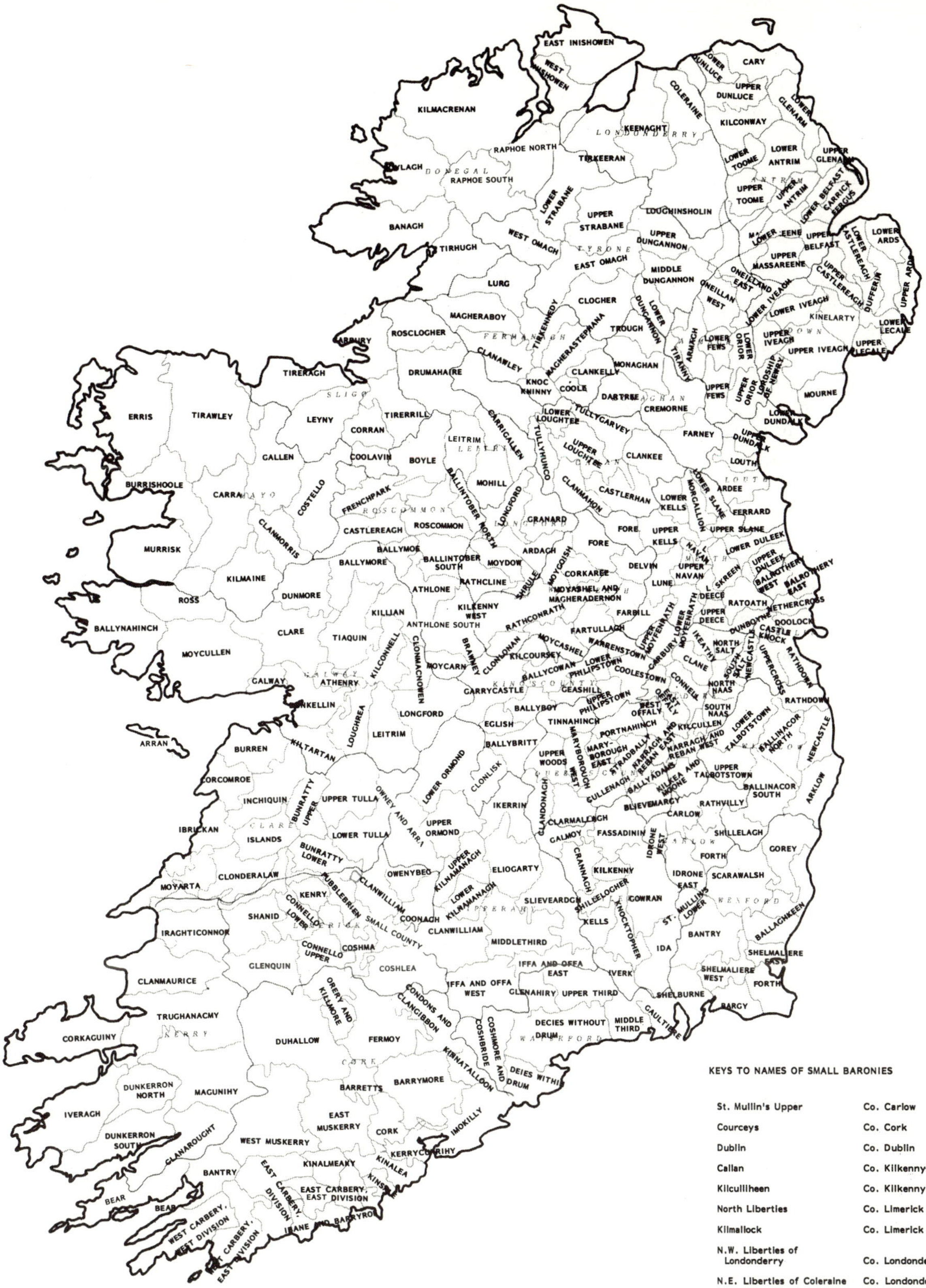

KEYS TO NAMES OF SMALL BARONIES

St. Mullin's Upper	Co. Carlow
Courceys	Co. Cork
Dublin	Co. Dublin
Callan	Co. Kilkenny
Kilculliheen	Co. Kilkenny
North Liberties	Co. Limerick
Kilmallock	Co. Limerick
N.W. Liberties of Londonderry	Co. Londonderry
N.E. Liberties of Coleraine	Co. Londonderry
Drogheda	Co. Louth

1. The Barony - Another ancient division of Ireland based upon the great Irish families territorial holdings. A total of 325 baronies exist. They were used as an unit in the 19th Century Land Valuations. Normally composed of several parishes

Fermanagh

Lurg, Magheraboy, Tirkennedy, Clanawley, Magherastephana, Knockninny, Coole, Clankelly.

Galway

Ballynahinch, Ross, Dunmore, Ballymore, Moycullen, Galway, Clare, Tiaquin, Killian, Aran, Dunkellin, Athenry, Kilconnell, Clonmacnowen, Loughrea, Longford, Kiltartan, Leitrim.

Kerry

Iraghticonnor, Clanmaurice, Corkaguiny, Trughanacmy, Iveragh, Dunkerron North, Dunkerron South, Magunihy, Glanarought.

Kildare

Carbury, Clane, Ikeathy and Oughterany, North Salt, South Salt, West Offaly, East Offaly, Connell, North Naas, South Naas, Kilcullen, Narragh and Reban West, Narragh and Reban East, Kilkea and Moone.

Kilkenny

Galmoy, Fassadinin, Crannagh, Gowran, Callan, Shillelogher, Kells, Knocktopher, Iverk, Ida.

King's County (now Offaly)

Kilcoursey, Garrycastle, Ballycowan, Geashill, Lower Philipstown, Upper Philipstown, Warrenstown, Coolestown, Eglish, Ballyboy, Ballybritt, Clonlisk.

Leitrim

Rosclogher, Drumahaire, Leitrim, Carrigallen, Mohil.

Limerick

Kenry, Pubblebrien, Limerick, North Liberties, Clanwilliam, Owenybeg, Coonagh, Shanid, Glenquin, Lower Connello, Upper Connello, Small County, Coshma, Killmallock, Coshlea.

Londonderry

Liberties of Londonderry, Tirkeeran, Keenaght, Coleraine, Northeast Liberties of Coleraine, Loughinsholin.

Longford

Longford, Granard, Moydow, Ardagh, Rathcline, Shrule.

Louth

Upper Dundalk, Lower Dundalk, Louth, Ardee, Ferrard, Drogheda.

Mayo

Erris, Tirawley, Gallen, Burrisholle, Murrisk, Carra, Clanmorris, Costello, Kilmaine.

Meath

Fore, Lower Kells, Upper Kells, Morgallion, Lower Slane, Upper Slane, Lune, Lower Navan, Upper Navan, Skreen, Drogheda, Lower Duleek, Upper Duleek, Upper Moyfenrath, Lower Moyfenrath, Lower Deece, Upper Deece, Ratoath, Dunboyne.

Monaghan

Trough, Monaghan, Dartree, Cremorne, Farney.

Queen's County (now Leix)

Tinnahinch, Portnahinch, Upper Woods, Maryborough West, Maryborough East, Stradbally, Clandonagh, Clarmallagh, Cullenagh, Ballyadams, Slievemargy.

Roscommon

Boyle, Frenchpark, Castlereagh, Ballymoe, Roscommon, Ballintober North, Ballintober South, Athlone, Moycarn.

Sligo

Canbury, Tireragh, Leyny, Corran, Tirerrill, Coolavin.

Tipperary

Owney and Arra, Lower Ormond, Upper Ormond, Ikerrin, Upper Kilnamanagh, Lower Kilnamanagh, Eliogarty, Slieveardagh, Clanwilliam, Middlethird, Iffa and Offa West, Iffa and Offa East.

Tyrone

Lower Strabane, Upper Strabane, West Omagh, East Omagh, Upper Dungannon, Middle Dungannon, Lower Dungannon, Clogher.

Waterford

Glenahiry, Upper Third, Middle Third, Gaultiere, Coshmore and Coshbride, Decies without Drum, Diecies within Drum.

West Meath

Moygoish, Fore, Corkaree, Delvin, Kilkenny West, Rathconrath, Moyashel and Magheradernon, Farbill, Brawney, Clonlonan, Moycashel, Fartullagh.

Wexford

Gorey, Scarawalsh, Bantry, Ballaghkeen, Shelburne, Shelmaliere West, Shelmaliere East, Bargy, Forth.

Wicklow

Lower Talbotstown, Upper Talbotstown, Rathdown, Ballinacor North, Ballinacor South, Newcastle, Arklow, Shillelagh.

THE PROVINCES OF IRELAND AND THE COUNTIES WHICH THEY CONTAIN.

Province:	*Counties within:*
Connaught	Galway, Leitrim, Mayo, Sligo, Roscommon.
Leinster	Carlow, Dublin, Kildare, Kilkenny, Leix, West Meath, Wexford, Wicklow. Longford, Louth, Meath, Offaly,
Munster	Clare, Cork, Kerry, Limerick, Tipperary, Waterford.
Ulster	Antrim, Armagh, Cavan, Donegal, Down, Fermanagh, Londonderry, Monaghan, Tyrone, (Cavan, Donegal, and Monaghan joined the republic in 1920).

COUNTIES OF IRELAND AND THEIR DIOCESAN JURISDICTIONS

County
Dioceses

Antrim

Connor, Derry, Down, Dromore.

Armagh

Armagh, Dromore.

Carlow

Leighlin.

Cavan

Ardagh, Meath, Kilmore.

Clare

Killaloe, Kilfenora, Limerick.

Cork

Cork, Ross, Cloyne, Ardfert.

Derry

Connor, Down, Dromore, Newry, Mourne.

Donegal

Clogher, Derry, Raphoe.

Down

Connor, Down, Dromore.

Dublin

Dublin

Fermanagh

Clogher, Kilmore

Galway

Clonfert, Elphin, Killaloe, Tuam

Kerry

Ardfert

Kildare

Dublin, Kildare

Kilkenny

Leighlin, Ossory

Laois (Queens)

Dublin, Kildare, Leighlin, Ossory

Leitrim

Ardagh, Kilmore

Limerick

Cashel, Emly, Killaloe, Limerick

Longford

Armagh, Meath

Louth

Armagh, Clogher, Drogheda.

Mayo

Killala, Achonry,Tuam

Meath

Armagh, Kildare, Kilmore, Meath

Monaghan

Clogher

Offaly (Kings)

Clonfert, Kildare, Killaloe, Meath, Ossory

Roscommon

Ardagh, Clonfert, Elphin, Tuam

Sligo

Ardagh, Elphin, Killala

Tipperary

Cashel, Killaloe, Waterford Lismore

Tyrone

Armagh, Clogher, Derry

Waterford

Waterford, Lismore

Westmeath

Ardagh, Meath

Wexford

Dublin, Ferns

Wicklow

Dublin, Ferns, Leighlin

DISTRICTS OF NORTHERN IRELAND

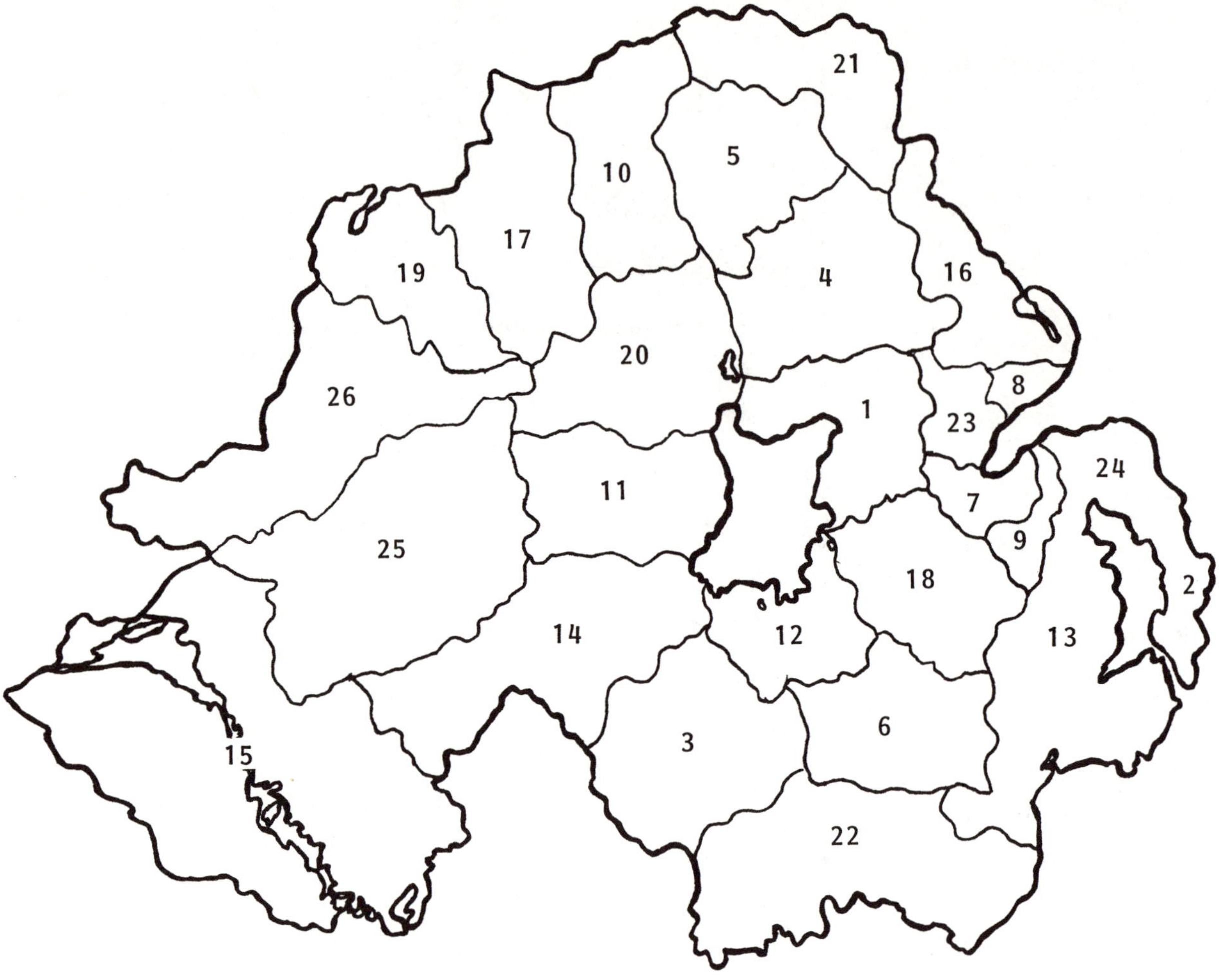

Antrim....................1
Ards.....................2
Armagh...................3
Ballymena................4
Ballymoney...............5
Banbridge................6
Belfast..................7
Carrickfergus............8
Castlereagh..............9
Coleraine...............10
Cookstown...............11
Craigavon...............12
Down....................13
Dungannon...............14
Fermanagh...............15
Larne...................16
Limavady................17
Lisburn.................18
Londonderry.............19
Magherafelt.............20
Moyle...................21
Newry and Mourne........22
Newtownabbey............23
North Down..............24
Omagh...................25
Strabane................26

THE MOST POPULOUS SURNAMES OF IRELAND (1890)

Murphy
Kelly
Sullivan
Walsh
Smith
O'Brien
Byrne
Ryan
Connor
Donaghue
O'Neill
Reilly
Doyle
McCarthy
Gallagher
Doherty
Kennedy
Lynch
Murray
Quinn
Stewart
Casey
Foley
Fitzpatrick
Leary
McDonnell
McMahon
Donnelly
Regan
Burns
Flanagan
Mullan
Barry

Kane
Moore
McLoughlin
Carroll
Connolly
Daly
Connell
Wilson
Dunne
Brennan
Burke
Collins
Campbell
Clark
Johnson
Hughes
Farrell
Fitzgerald
Brown
Martin
Robinson
Cunningham
Griffin
Kenny
Sheehan
Ward
Sheland
Lyons
Reid
Graham
Higgins
Sullen
Keane

King
Maguire
Nolan
Flynn
Thompson
Callaghan
O'Donnell
Dubby
Mahony
Boyle
Healy
Shea
White
Sweeny
Hayes
Kavanagh
Power
McGrath
Moran
Brady
Maher
McKenna
Bell
Scott
Hogan
Keefe
Magee
McNamara
McDonald
McDermott
Laloney
Rourke
Burkley
Dwyer

SURNAME MAP OF IRELAND

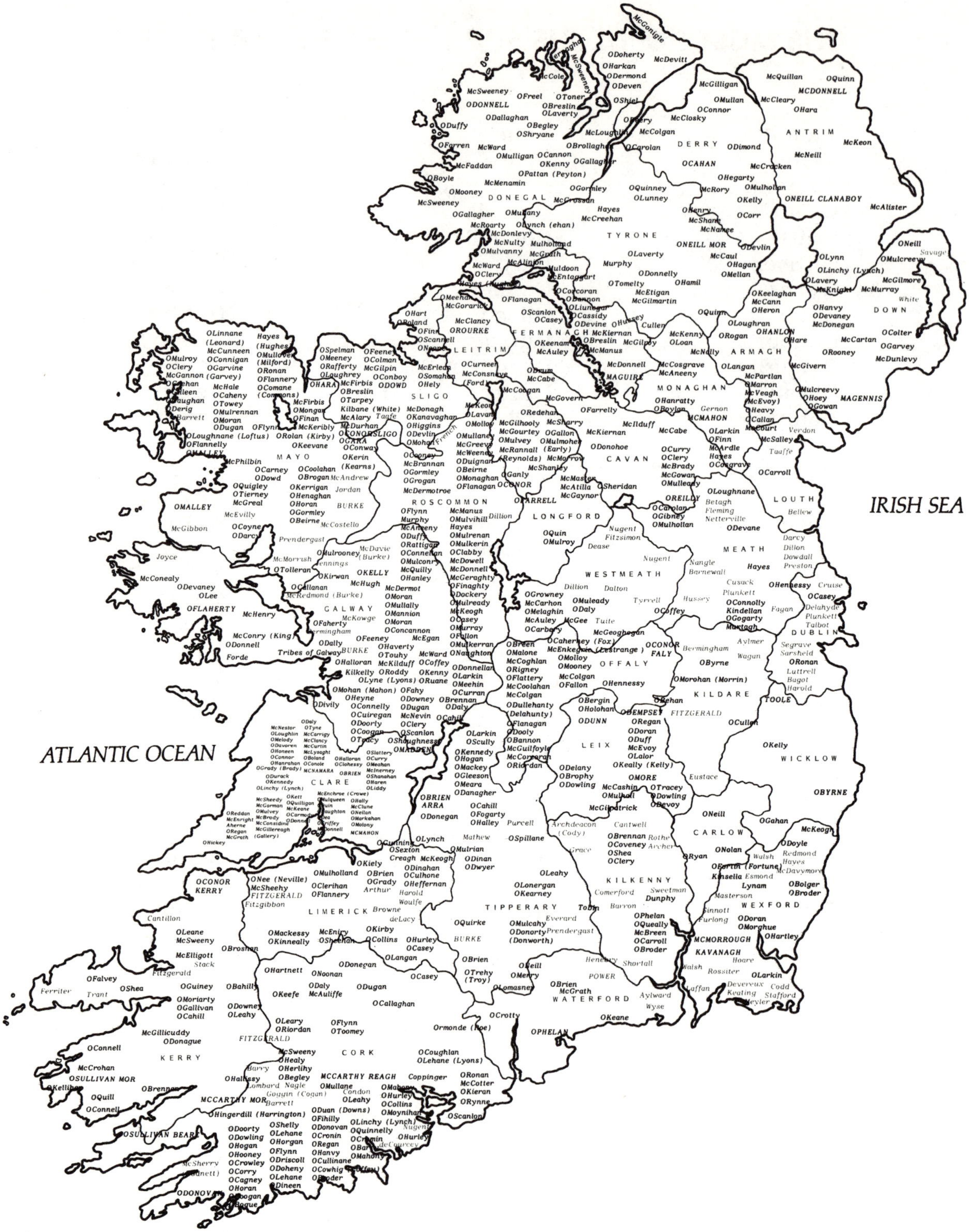

Gaelic Septs

Septs of Norman Ancestry

The 14 "Tribes of Galway" = Athys, Blakes, Bodkins, Brownes, D'Arcys, Deanes, ffonts, ffrenchs, Joyces, Kirwans, Lynches, Martins, Morrises, Skerretts.

ANCIENT HISTORY AND EARLY PEDIGREES

The first recorded people in Ireland were the Parthalonians from Greece (1484 B.C.). Other records include: The Nemedians (1154 B.C.), the Fomorian (978 B.C.), the Firbolgs (783 B.C.), the Dedannam (686 B.C.), and the Celts or Milesians (504 B.C.). The Celts were the first to fully rule Ireland.

The Celts were the descendents of Milesius from Spain. Many great Irish families trace their pedigree back to this man. The Celts kept careful records and pedigrees to insure their continued rule. In line with this, it was decreed that only Milesians could rule in Ireland. Hence we have pedigrees carefully preserved from the early days of Ireland. With the Celts came the notion of the "Clan" system of local government, allowing great individual freedom as well as the strict law and family customs of the "Clann."

Last Names Come into Being

Ireland was amoung the first countries to use surnames, which came into use in the 10th century near the reign of the great king of all Ireland, Brian Boru. Up until this time men lived without the use of surnames. Individuals now began to assume the names of ancestor or heroes of the past and used these names as family names. Hence, if your famous grandfather's name was "lochLainn" you might assume his name as your own last name. Further, if your name was Michael, you would then become Michael O'LochLainn. (The O' with the ancient Gaelic accent mark stood for "grandson of" or "male descendent of." Michael O'LochLainn would then mean that you were Michael, grandson of LochLainn. Similarly, if you were named Michael MacLochLainn (the Mac stood for "son of") you would be known as Michael, son of LochLainn.

The ancient Gaelic accent mark and symbol O, are carried on unknowlingly by present day living descendents in many families as an O with an apostrophe such as my name bears, O'Laughlin.

It should be noted that the name could have been taken from any individual known as "LochLainn," and entirely distinct individuals could have formed different O'LochLainn families. (This applies particularly to the most popular Irish names such as Murphy, where completely unrelated families now bear the same name.)

Furthermore, as time passed, names changed in their spelling. As language slowly changes, so does the spelling of that language. Social change, wars, foreign intervention and the attitude of the population all play a part.

Several times in Irish history foreign pressure was exerted to force the Irish to drop the O and the Mac from their names. These distinctive prefixes are seen as a mark of Irish heritage and pride, something the occupiers of the country wished to do away with. Hence it was forbidden at times to use the O' or Mac, preceeding so many Irish names. It was a common occurance to drop the O' while talking with the foreigners, only to add it again when back with friends and family. Indeed the O' has been dropped or added at will in modern times and most recently it is on the increase.

One of my distant relatives droppe the O' altogether stating that, "it didn't mean anything anyway."

When in foreign countries the Irish names often became spelled as the natives of the land believed it should be spelled or as similar names were spelled in their own language! This, of course, can lead to great confusion when tracing your heritage. Thus we have a name like Lochlainn in the year 983 A.D., becoming O'Laughlin in 1980. Similar transformations have occurred in most family names as well.

Older Irish Spelling	*Current Usage*
O'Suilleabhain	O'Sullivan
Murchada	Murphy
O'Cellaigh	Kelly
Raghallach	O'Reilly
Donnchadha	O'Donaghue (Donohoe, etc.)
Flaithbheartaigh	O'Flaherty
MagAonghuis	McGuinness

Further sources on ancient history and early pedigrees:

<u>Sources for the History of Irish Civilization</u>. Guide to books/periodicals, etc. by county. 1970.

Approx. Date	*Event*
10th Century	Use of Surnames declared manadatory.
1600's	A breakdown of Gaelic order and tradition begins to occur and pedigrees disappear, records are sparse.
1649	Cromwellian invasion.
1641-1647	Books of Survey and Distribution.
1651	30,000 Irish soldiers given leave to France & Spain.
	Thousands of Irish transported as "slaves" to the West Indies.
1691	Eleven thousand Irish sail to France to form the Irish Brigades.
1650	Strafford Survey
1654	The Civil Survey
1659	Census
1660-1670	Hearth Money Rolls
1740	Householders List
1766	Religious Census
1800	"Act of Union 1800" Emigration increase due to poverty, etc.
Early 1800's	Tithe Applotment Books
1845-1848	The Potatoe Famine: Causing great misery and migration.
1848-1864	Griffiths Valuation

SOME IRISH WORDS AND TRANSLATIONS

The meaning of the name of a particular town, area, or person may prove of interest to you during your research. Following are a few Irish words and translations.

1. Cill meaning ''Church''
2. Rath or dun meaning ''fort''
3. Druim meaning ''ridge''
4. Cnoc meaning ''hill''
5. Tulach meaning ''mound''
6. Gleann meaning ''glen'' (i.e. Glenflesk)
7. Baile meaning ''place, land farm''
8. Gal meaning ''stranger, foreigner'' (i.e. Galway)
9. Inis (Inch) meaning ''island, field near water''
10. Lough meaning ''lake'' (i.e. Loughlein = Lower Lake)
11. Muck meaning ''pig'' or ''boar''
12. Cavan meaning a ''hollow plain''
13. Goart or Furt meaning ''a field or garden''

Personal and Family Names

1. Gilchrist – servant of Christ
2. Kilbride – servant of St. Bridget
3. Mc – as a prefix. Meaning ''son of'' (i.e. McHugh = son of Hugh)
4. O – as a prefix. Meaning ''Grandson'' or ''male descendent'' of. (I.E., O'Conner = descendent of Conner)
5. Breheny – judge
6. Roe – red
7. Duff – black
8. Casey – valient
9. Eilis – Elizabeth
10. Sean – John
11. Oisin – Oscar
12. Liam – William
13. Mairead – Margaret
14. Eoghan – Owen
15. Seamus – James
16. Donnchadh – Denis
17. Art – Arthur
18. Criostoir – Christopher
19. Siobhan – Joan
20. Cait – Kate
21. Blathnaid – Florence
22. Aodh – Hugh
23. Tadhg – Timothy
25. Aine – Anne
26. Conal – Daniel
27. Caoimhin – Kevin
28. Aisling – Ester
29. Una – Agnes
30. Peadar – Peter
31. Gormfhlaith – Barbara
32. Diarmaid – Dermot
33. Grainne – Grace
34. Cathal – Charles
35. Eammonn – Edmund
36. Eoin – John
37. Lorcan – Laurance
38. Padraig – Patrick
39. Brian – Bryan

RECORDS & REPOSITORIES IN IRELAND

NOW, FINDING YOUR ANCESTORS IN IRELAND

Most of the items in the first section of this book could apply to any country. In this second section we will concentrate on researching in Ireland itself, to gain further information on your ancestry. For local and family records, the same principals apply as in the first section of this book.

- Public Records Office
- Office of the Registrar General
- The Registry of Deeds
- Genealogical Office
- Trinity College
- The Royal Irish Acadamy
- The National Library of Ireland
- Other Libraries
- Public Records Office of Northern Ireland, Belfast
- Registrar General of Northern Ireland
- State Paper Office
- Palatine Records
- Irish Newspapers as Sources

GENEALOGICAL OFFICE

Dublin Castle

For more advanced research. Contains pedigrees, coat of arms, will abstracts. Also houses the "Heraldic Museum." Open daily 9:30 A.M. to 5:00 P.M. Professional genealogical assistance may also be obtained here. Material on hand covers a wide range of subjects. Hundreds of volumes of manuscripts.

PUBLIC RECORDS OFFICE

Four Courts, Dublin, Ireland

The Tithe Applotment books are of particular interest. They are the first valuation office records and contain landowners names in the first half of the 19th century. Also: wills, abstracts, indexes, administrations and marriage bonds and the 1901 census.

Material contained herein covers all of Ireland and is of great benefit to the researcher. Searches will be made for a fee for specific documents.

The "Report of the Deputy Keeper of the Public Records in Ireland," was published from 1869-1921, and describes the collections of records on hand at that time. Copies of these reports are on hand at the major repositories in Ireland, and are of great assistance in locating records.

Thousands of family records are included in their manuscript collections, as well as records of the former Established Church of Ireland, Court Records and State papers.

Manuscripts relating to the following families are located in the Public Records Office, Dublin.

Ahmuty
Alcock
Alexander
Allen
Alley
Annesley
Archer
Ardery
Armstrong
Arthur
Atkins
Atkinson
Attwood
Auchmuty
Audley
Bacon
Baker
Balfour
Ball
Banastre
Barbor
Barker
Barlow
Barnard
Barnes
Barnewell
Bateman
Bateson
Beatty
Beck
Bell
Bellew
Bellingham
Beresford
Bermingham
Berry
Bianconi
Bibby
Bingham
Birch
Blackwood
Blake
Blakeney
Blood
Bolger
Bolton
Bond
Bourke
Bowen
Boxwell
Brabazon
Bradshaw
Brady
Brice
Bridgeman
Brisson
Bristow
Broderick
Broughton
Brown
Bruce
Budd
Bullock
Bunbury
Burke
Burnside
Burt
Busteed
Butler
Calbec
Caldwell
Cameron
Campbell
Cantwell
Carew
Carolan
Carpenter
Carroll
Carvill
Chinery
Chinnery
Christie
Clare
Clarke
Clinton
Cole
Colles
Colville
Comerford
Conly
Connell
Connolly
Conrahy
Cooke
Cooper
Coote
Coppinger
Corry
Cowley
Coyler
Cox
Crofton
Croker
Crone
Crookshanks
Crosby
Balzell
Dardis
Daunt
Davis
Dawson
De Burgho
Delaney
Delap
Dempsey
Denis
Dennehy
Denny
Despard
DeVigne
DeZouche
Dickson
Dillon
Disney
Dixon
Dobbin
Dobbyn
Dodwell
Dombille
Dowdall
Dowlin
Drought
Drury
Dunkett
Dunne
Durham
Dwyer
Eccles
Eckersley
Edgar
Edgeworth
Edwards
Elliot
Ellis
Elmes
England
Everard
Eyre
Fennell
Ferguson
Finch
Findlater
Finlay
Finn
Finston
Finucane
Finucane
Fitton
Fitzgerald
Fitzmaurice
Fitzpatrick
Fivey
Fleming
Foott
Forbes
Ford
Foss
Fox
Frayne
French
Fullam
Gernon
Gethin
Gibb
Gilbert
Glenny
Godley
Gordon
Gormley
Goslin
Grace
Granger
Gray
Green
Greene
Greer
Gregory
Grehan
Greville
Grubb
Guinness
Hamill
Hamilton
Handcock
Hardin
Harrison

Hatton
Hayes
Hedges
Hely-Hutchinson
Hendrick
Henry
Herbert
Hewson
Hickson
Higgenbotham
Hill
Hobart
Hogan
Holland
Howlin
Hubbart
Humphey
Hunt
Hussey
Irwin
Jacob
Jennens
Jennings
Johnson
Jones
Kearney
Kelly
Kemmis
Kennedy
Keogh
Kerr
King
King-Harmon
Knaresborough
Knight
Lacy
Lane
Langan
Langton
Larive
Latham
Latimer
Law
Lawless
Lecky
Lefroy
Lewis
Linton
Lisle
Lorton
Love
Lovekin
Lowther
Lucas
Ludlow
Lynch
Lysaght
MacGrath
MacKenzie
Madden
Maffit
Magill
Makesy
Malone
Markham
Martin
Massey
Mathews
McAuley
McClure
McDaniell
McDonell
McDonnell
McGarry
McGurty
McIntire
McKenna
McNamara
Meade
Meell
Meredith
Meredyth
Miltown
Minchin
Moland
Molineux
Montfort
Montgomery
Mooney
Moore
Moorehouse
Morgan
Morris
Morrison
Morrough
Murray
Naghten
Nash
Needham
Newport
Norris
North
Nowlan
Nugent
Nulty
Obins
O'Brien
O'Callaghan
O'Connor
O'Farrell
O'Flanagan
O'Grady
O'Huiginn
Oliver
O'Neill
Ormsby
Osborne
O'Shee
Paine
Palliser
Pearse
Pennefather
Perry
Phaire
Phayre
Plunkett
Poe
Pollock
Poulter
Prendergast
Purdon
Purefoy
Quin
Ram
Rambaut
Raymond
Read
Reddan
Readesdale
Reynell
Rice
Richardson
Riddal
Ringwood
Roberts
Robinson
Roche
Rosse
Roth
Towen
Royse
Rutherford
Ruxton
Ryan
Sandes
Sandford
Sarsfield
Saunders
Savage
Scool
Scott
Scull
Segrave
Seward
Sexton
Seymour
Shanley
Shearman
Shee
Shuckburgh
Silke
Simpson
Singleton
Skerrett
Slade
Smith
Smyth
Snell
Southwell
Sparks
Spence
Spencer
Spring
Stannard
Staples
Stawell
Steele
Steuart
Stewart
Stritch
Styles
Taylor
Thompson
Tiernan
Townsend
Travers
Trotter
Tuckey
Twigg
Tyrrell
Ulster
Upton
Usher
Vaughan
Verdon
Vernon
Vesey
Waddy
Wade
Walcott
Wall
Wallace
Waller
Walsh
Walton
Warburton
Ward
Warren
Watson
Webb
Welply
Wesley
West
Westby
White
Widenham
Wilder
Wilkinson
Willis
Wilson
Winder
Wolfe
Woodcock
Woodroffe
Wright
Yeo
Young

OFFICE OF THE REGISTRAR GENERAL
The Custom House, Dublin 1, Ireland

General Civil Registration of births, marriages, and deaths from 1864 on. Protestant weddings are recorded from April 1, 1845 on. Open 9:30 A.M. til 5:00 P.M. Monday through Friday.

THE REGISTRY OF DEEDS
Henrietta Street, Dublin 1, Ireland

Records dating from 1709 on. Property transactions, leases, mortages, and settlements. Research here may be tedious and many transactions were never recorded but much valuable genealogical information remains. Surname and place name indexes are available. Some data is microfilmed. Open 10:00 A.M. to 4:00 P.M., daily. An excellent publication to consult: *Registry of Deeds, Dublin, Abstracts of Wills, 1708-1745; 1745-1785*,containing over 1400 abstracts. Edited by P. Beryl Eustace, Dublin, Indexed.

When emigrating to America your ancestor may well have sold his land or made arrangements to adjust his lease. The Registry of Deeds is an excellent place to find just such information. One may be able not only to identify his ancestors, but their specific place of residence a well as surrounding circumstances.

Some types of documents on hand:

1. *Deeds of Sale*: Transfered ownership of property.

2. *Deeds in Trust*: Recorded property held in trust for specific individuals. Inheritance rights and specific mention of sons, daughters, etc., are of specific interest.

3. *Release*: Records of individuals giving up legal ownership or rights to lands, etc.

4. *Leases*: Often mentioning ancestors and descendents.

5. *Assignments*: Drawn in the form of a lease, the grantor gave his rights to a lease to another individual (sometimes due to emigration).

6. *Marriage Settlements, etc*: Containing much information of the couple involved. Pre-nuptual agreements concerning property, etc.

TRINITY COLLEGE

Dublin

The oldest such establishment in Ireland, houses the "Book of Kells," a famous ancient manuscript. The registers of the college from 1593 to 1860 are on record and contain details of over 30,000 former students.

Sources to Consult:

Catalog of the Manuscripts in the Library of Trinity College. Dublin 1900.
by T.K. Abbott & E.J. Gwynn.

THE ROYAL IRISH ACADAMY

19 Dawson Street, Dublin, Ireland

Manuscripts of particular interest to the Gaelic scholar. A large collection has been maintained.

THE NATIONAL LIBRARY OF IRELAND

Kildare Street, Dublin 2, Ireland

Directories, family histories, journals, newspapers, manuscript collections. A very good indexing system. Of special interest is, "Freeman's Journal Index: The Freeman Journal," a Dublin newspaper 1763-1780; 1783-1786. Open daily 10:00 A.M. to 10:00 P.M.

The historical and periodical journals here are particularly valuable to the genealogist. Everything from tombstone epitaphs to family pedigrees may be found in these compilations. Some of which were recorded before the burning of many records in 1922.

Among the many works of historical nature in the National Library are national, regional, and local histories. These publications often contain marriage bonds, wills, tax records, muster rolls, and cemetery records plus other rare genealogical information.

Items of particular interest available:

1. †Books of Survey and Distribution (1636-1703).
2. †Tithe Applotment Books (1824-1840).
3. Indexes to the Registry of Deeds

4. Freeman's Journal Index (a Dublin newspaper 1763-1780, 1783-1786). Much personal information is indexed.

5. Parish Registers

6. Forfeitures of 1641 and 1688 (manuscripts).

7. †Griffith's Valuation of Ireland (1844-1866).

†See detailed explanation and illustrations of these records under Census & Survey Records.

OTHER LIBRARIES

Other notable libraries of genealogical interest would, of course, include the official county libraries of the particular county in question. In addition to these we have the following repositories available (to name a few):

Armagh Public Library, (Manuscripts, histories, pedigrees).

The Linen Hall Library, Belfast.

The Presbyterian Historical Society Library, Belfast.

The Library of University College, Cork. Located in the city of Cork. (Containing many records national in scope).

Central Catholic Library, Dublin.

Church of Ireland Representative Church Body Library, 52 St. Stephens Green, Dublin, Ireland.

St. Colman's College Library, Fermoy. (Ulster genealogies).

Magee University College Library, Londonderry. (Many early newspapers.)

The Franciscan Friary Library, Athlone, Co. Westmeath.

St. Patrick's College Library, Catlow, Co. Carlow.

The Carnagie Library, Downpatrick, Co. Down.

Galway University College Library, Galway, Co. Galway.

St. Kiernans College Library, Kilkenny, Co. Kilkenny.

St. Mels College Library, Longford, Co. Longford.

Saint Patrick's College Library, Maymooth, Co. Kildare.

St. Marcartaus College Library, Monaghan, Co. Monaghan.

STATE PAPER OFFICE

Birmingham Tower, Dublin Castle, Dublin, Ireland.

Criminal and convict records of all sorts. Records may be consulted if they are 50 years old and have been declared public.

Public Records Office of Northern Ireland

66 Balmoral Avenue, Belfast, Ireland, BT96NY. Telephone: 661621

Tithe Applotment books, etc., for the six counties of Northern Ireland. "The Reports of the Deputy Keeper of the Records," are excellent sources for locating specific research material. These are available in the principal genealogical libraries of the U.S., Ireland, and Britain. Open 9:30 A.M. to 5:00 P.M.

PUBLIC RECORDS OFFICE OF NORTHERN IRELAND, BELFAST

Public Search Room.
Genealogical Searching.
Valuation Records
School Projects.
Local History Searching.
Business Records.
Maps and Plans c.1600-c.1830; Counties Antrim, Armagh, Down, Fermanagh, Londonderry and Tyrone.
Maps and Plans c.1600-c.1860; Belfast
Maps and Plans c1538-1830; General Maps: Ireland and Province of Ulster.
Landed Estate Records: Counties Antrim, Armagh, Down, Fermanagh, Londonderry and Tyrone.

Emigration Records in the Public Records Office of Northern Ireland, Belfast:

Emigration from Ulster to North Carolina, etc. from Papers of the late W.C. Houston. Philadelphia, USA, 1736-1737.

The Drumgooland Vestry Book, 1789-1828, published in 1892. Notes of Ulster emigration to America, 1789-1828.

Passenger lists sailing from Newry, Co. Down and Warrenspoint, Co. Down, 1791-1792.

Lists of persons naturalized in New York, 1802-1814.

The National Archives Library has copies of the Ordinance Survey Documents. Contains emigrantes 1833-1835 listed by parish.

REGISTRAR GENERAL OF NORTHERN IRELAND

Fermanagh House, Ormeau Avenue, Belfast, Ireland

Births, marriages and dates from 1921 on. Census returns 1931 and 1951.

THE ULSTER HISTORICAL FOUNDATION

Attached to the Public Records Office of Northern Ireland, Law Courts Building, Belfast, Ireland.

This is the genealogical section of the Public Records Office. You may hire research done, or perform your own study in person for Northern Ireland.

PALATINE RECORDS

Mainly from the County Limerick area (and somewhat in upper Co. Kerry) these settlers were fleeing religious persecution in the Palatine province of the Rhine (Early 1700's). Please consult,

The Palatine Families of Ireland. Author: Hank Jones, U.S.A.

IRISH NEWSPAPERS AS SOURCES

We are familiar with the newspapers of today and the type of information they offer. As well as a source of general social and economic conditions, they can cover specifics on a variety of subjects. Birth, death, and marriage records are just a sampling. Mention of individuals leaving the city or sailing to the new world have often been included as well.

Histories of the well established Irish families of the area may appear from time to time, tracing the genealogy of the names in question.

Some newspapers and repositories:

Additional Source Material

Linen Hall Library

Belfast Co-operative Advocate, Nos. 1-2. Belfast, 1830.

Belfast Evening Post, Nos. 300-315. June 12th to July 31st. 1786, missing No. 303. (See Belfast Mercury.)

Belfast Evening Post, "Letters by a Farmer," First published in 1787.

Belfast Magazine and Literary Journal. Belfast, 1825.

Belfast Mercury or Freeman's Chronicle. Began June, 1783. June 12, 1786, the name changed to the Belfast Evening Post.

Belfast Mercury, (2nd Publication), 1851-58.

Belfast Newsletter, (begins with Vol. 2, No. 152, dated Feb. 16). 1738-1915.

Belfast Penny Journal, Vols. 1-2. May, 1845 to July, 1846.

Belfast Penny Punch, May, 1847 to July, 1848.

Belfast Temperance Herald, June, 1846.

The Bible Christian, 1830-35. Second series, Vols. 1-2. 1836-37. Presbyterian.

Bolg an Tsolair; or, Gaelic Magazine, Belfast, No. 1, 1795.

The Christian Freeman. Vols. 1-3. Belfast, 1832-35. Presbyterian.

The Covenanter. Vols. 1-3. 1830-32. Presbyterian.

The Gleaner; or, Farmer's and Tradesman's Weekly Miscellany. No. 10. Belfast, 1821.

The Guardian and Constitutional Advocate. Belfast, 1829.

The Irishman: a weekly newspaper. 1819-22.

Irish Presbyterian. Vols. 1-6. 1853-58. Presbyterian.

Literary Museum; or Weekly Magazine. Vol. 1, Nos. 2-5. 1793.

The Magic Lanthorn. Vol. 1, Nos. 6-7. Vol. 2. 1815-16.

The Microscope; (Minute Observer). Vols. 2, 1800.

The Mirror: a Weekly Miscellany. Belfast, 1823.

New Belfast Magazine. 1833-34.

Northern Herald. Sept. 28th and Oct. 12th, 1833.

Northern Magazine. March, 1852 to Feb., 1853.

Northern Star. Belfast 1792-97. Supporting United Irishmen.

Northern Whig. Be fast, 1824-1915.

Orthodox Presbyterian: a monthly magazine. Vols. 1-8. 1829-37. New Series, Vols. 1-3. 1838-40.

Presbyterian Magazine. Belfast, 1835.

The Quizzing Glass. Sept. 1834, to Aug. 1835.

The Rushlight. (Weekly) Vol. 1, Nos. 1-41. 1824-25.

Temperance Advocate. Belfast, May, 1833.

Ulster Magazine. Jan. 1830. Vol. 1, No. 1.

The Ulster Miscellany. Belfast, 1873.

Ulster Register: a political and literary magazine. 1816-18. Vols. 1-4. Belfast.

Ulster Repository. Vol. 1, n.d. 1785.

Ulster Times. 1841-42. Belfast.

Irish Monthly Mercury. No. 1, 1649. (Reprint of No. 1 1649, is in the British Museum (Cat E 592, 5).

The Freeholder. 1716.

The Cork Newsletter. c. 1716-25.

The Medley. 1738.

The Serio-Jocular Medley. 1738.

Corke Journal. (George Swiney's), 1754.

The Cork Evening Post. 1754-96. The National Library of Ireland has Nov. 1757 to Oct. 1758. Trinity College Library has 1786-99.

The Corke Chronicle, or Universal Register. 1764.

The Hibernian Journal. Trinity College Library has 1760-71 (?).

The Corke Chronicle, or Free Intelligencer. 1764-68.

The Corke Chronicle, or True Intelligence. Trinity College Library has 1772, Jan. 2nd (Vol. IX, No. 1).

Hibernian Chronicle. 1769-1802. The baptisms, marriages and deaths are indexed. The Public Records Office of Northern Ireland has a copy of the index (1936 Report, P. 5; 1938-45 Report). Trinity College Library has some issues for 1779-87, and 1790-99.

The Cork General Advertiser. The National Library has Dec. 15, 1777 (Vol. II, No. 74).

The Volunteer Journal, or Weekly Advertiser. Trinity College Library has issues for 1782-84; and Jan. 2, 1786 (Vol. IV, No. 70).

The Cork Gazette and General Advertiser, 1789-1797. The National Library has issues for 1793, Vols. IV and V, and 1796, Vol. VIII. Trinity College Library has April 11, 1792 (No. 185).

The New Cork Evening Post. Trinity College Library has issue of Aug. 17, 1797 (No. 67, Vol. VII).

The Cork Herald or Munster Advertiser. The National Library has some issues from Nov. 3, 1798 to Dec. 5, 1798. Trinity College Library has Vol. 1, April, 1798 (No. 23) and Aug. 1798 (No. 58).

The Cork Advertiser and Commercial Register. The National Library has issues for 1799 (Jan. 29th, 31st; Feb. 2nd to July 18th). Trinity College Library has July 1799 (No. 75).

The Dublin Journal (Faulkner's). 1727/28-1800.

The Dublin Gazette. 1706-1800.

The Dublin Weekly Journal, (Carson), 1725-37.

Pue's Occurrences, 1717-1772/73.

Dublin News Letter, (Robert Reilly). 1737-43.

Sleater's Public Gazetter. 1758/59-1771/74.

The Public Register, or Freeman's Journal, 1763/64-1800.

Saunders' Dublin News Letter. 1767-1800.

Gentleman's Magazine, 1731-1868.

The Kilkenny Journal, began 1791.

Kilkenny Moderator.

Finn's Leinster Journal. 1766 (?)

The Munster Journal. Oldest journal in Munster.

Limerick Journal.

Limerick Chronicle.

Limerick Evening Post.

Clare Sentinel.

The Star.

Limerick Herald. ca 1821.

The Limerick Star and Evening Post, began 1834.

The Limerick Reporter, began 1839.

The Munster Telegraph, began 1832.

The Limerick Guardian, in 1833.

The Limerick Standard, in 1840/41.

The Limerick and Clare Examiner, in 1845.

The Munster News, began in 1852.

Limerick Southern Chronicle, began in 1863.

The Londonderry Sentinel. Published from 1829 to present.

The Londonderry Standard. Published from 1836 to present.

The Londonderry Chronicle. Feb. 18 to Oct. 7, 1829.

The Londerry Guardian. Sept. 30, 1857 to Sept. 28, 1871.

The Londonderry Journal. Feb. 14, 1825 to Mar. 19, 1880.
(Changed to Derry Journal, March 19, 1880).

Chute's Western Herald, 1812-35.

Kerry Evening Post, 1813-1917.

Tralee Mercury, 1829-39.

Kerry Examiner, 1840-56.

Tralee Chronicle, 1861-63.

Weekly Chronicle, 1873.

Kerry Sentinel, 1878-1917.

Kerry Independent, 1880-84.

Kerry Weekly Reporter, 1883-1925.

Kerry News, 1894-1917.

Munster Life, 1897.

Killarney Echo, 1899-1925.

The Post, 1774.

Journal, 1782.

Chronicle, 1783.

Mercury, 1793.

Herald, 1793.

Dispatch, 1807.

Kerry Evening Post, 1774-1917.

Clare Journal, 1778.

Ennis Chronicle, 1794.

Newspaper Press Directory: (United Kingdom and British Isles Annual) London 1846.

National Commercial Directory of Ireland. (Newspapers listed by town) I. Slater. London, 1846.

A brief historical survey of Ireland:

6000 B.C. Hunting and gathering peoples from Europe.

3500 B.C. Stone Age Farmers (who built great monuments).

308 B.C.

Celts conquered Ireland. Gaelic culture thrives. Dozens of kings rule throughout the country. Poets, Druids, Lawyers and oral tradition continue to develope. The Roman Legions stop short of Ireland, going no further than Britain.

450 A.D.

St. Patrick and the age of Christianity, which blends well with the society. Written records begin to supplant purely oral tradition.

800 A.D. Vikings raid and plunder. (Towns develope.)

1014 A.D. Brian Boru defeats Vikings. (The first High-King.)

1171 A.D. Normans control most of Ireland. Conflict.

1600 A.D. After years of Warfare, England dominates Ireland.

1649 A.D. Cromwell crushes Irish resistance.

1690 A.D. Gaelic culture and Catholic religion bitterly repressed

1800 A.D. Ireland formally joined with Britain. Continue revolt.

1922 A.D. Irish free state formed. Gaelic culture revived. Civil War.

1925 A.D. Northern Ireland forms a seperate state.

1949 A.D.

Republic of Ireland formed as a nation, but Ireland remains divided between the Republic and Northern Ireland.

It soon becomes evident to the researcher that Ireland has had a turbulent past. Destroyed records, and records of land confiscations and invasions will play a predominant role in your research. Not only have the Irish fought against foreign intervention, but they have often quarreled among themselves as well.

The following exerpt was taken from *The O'Donoghue Book* and illustrates some of the hostilities involved of years past in Ireland.

Hostilities

The following accounts show some of the hostilities involving the Donohues and their oppressors.

The following are excerpts from a copy of notes made by Lord Kenmare on the leasing of the town land, Ducorrig to Colonel Daniel ODonoghue:

GEOFFREY THE ODONOGHUE was the owner of Killaha in 1656 and it contained 20,000 acres. He was listed as a popish landowner in the "Down Survey". He was ordered "To hell or to Connaught", but he stayed among the mountains of Glenflesk and the Cromwellians, even though they destroyed his castle in 1653, they failed to apprehend him and no settler dared to occupy any part of his territory. The Cromwellian settlement did not touch Glenflesk.

The population of Killaha parish is given in the census of the year 1659 as 26 persons... It is very probable that the surveyors were unable to contact the people owing to the wild and inaccessible nature of the territory. We can be certain that the ODonoghue clan were not in the least co-operative with their oppressors...

On its expiration in 1752, I had a great mind to have changed my tenant who is an idle proud branch of the ODonoghues of Glenflesk and had never paid his rent to satisfaction... As to improvements he is not the man to make any, though many are mentioned in his leases.

CENSUS AND SURVEYS OF IRELAND

- *Government Commissions*
- *Statistical Surveys of the Royal Dublin Society*
- Ordinance Survey Maps
- The Census
- Census & Surveys (Detailed)

Time Period	Surveys and Census in Ireland
1635-1637	Strafford Survey
1654	The Down Survey
1659	The Census of 1659
1641-1670	The Books of Survey and Distribution
1660-1670	The Hearth Money Rolls
1740	1740 Householders List
1766	Religious Census of 1766
Early 1800's	Tithe Applotment Books
1848-1864	Griffiths Valuation
1841	1841 Census
1851	1851 Census

(See detail of above in the following pages of this book.)

GOVERNMENT COMMISSIONS

(1800-1850.) A minimum of 114 commissions and 61 committees were formed to investigate affairs in Ireland. The types of items included are as follows:

1. Civil and criminal offences. Trials. Maps of public works. Correspondence with engineers and officials. Reports on improvement projects. Mortality investigations.

2. *The General Index to the Accounts and Papers, Reports of Commissions, etc., 1801-1852*, is a good index to work by.

3. *The Devon Commission*– Reports, as does the above, giving insight into the daily life and problems of the rural Irishman (1847).

STATISTICAL SURVEYS OF THE ROYAL DUBLIN SOCIETY

These are primary sources for the early 1800's for this type of material. Covers the socio-economic background of Ireland before the Great Famine.

Prepared by the Royal Dublin Society these surveys can offer rare insight into the social and economic circumstances of the early 1800's. The main interests of these surveys were agriculture and the lay of the land. Geological descriptions and settlements are sometimes included.

Statistical Surveys of the Royal Dublin Society

Area	Author	Year
Antrim	Dubourdieu	1812
Cavan	- - - -	1802
Cork	Townsend	1810
Down	Dubourdieu	1802
Galway	Dutton	1824
Kilkenny	Tighe	1802
Leitrim	Coote	1802
Mayo	McParlan	1802
Queens Co.	Coote	1801
Sligo	McParian	1802
Wexford	Fraser	1807
Armagh	- - - -	1804
Clare	Dutton	1808
Donegal	McParlan	1802
Dublin	Archer	1801
Kildare	Rawson	1807
Kings Co.	Coote	1801
Derry	- - - -	1802
Monaghan	- - - -	1801
Roscommon	Weld	1832
Tyrone	McEvoy	1802
Wicklow	Fraser	1801

ORDINANCE SURVEY MAPS

Complete 1852 A detailed map and survey of Ireland containing an extreme volume and detail of work. Available from the Government Publications Sales Office, G.P.O. Arcade, Dublin, Ireland.

THE CENSUS

Complete census returns for Ireland do not truly exist until the year 1901. The ravages of time and fires, etc., have taken their toll. The first truly full census was taken in 1813. Census returns were also recorded in 1821, 1831-34, 1841, and every ten years thereafter. While full returns do not exist for the earlier years, many segments have survived and they can prove extremely useful.

The census format included the name, age, occupation, place of birth, and religious affiliations of every member of the household. The parish and county of residence were recorded as well.

Partial listing of Surveys and Census in Ireland:

Time Period	*Surveys and Census in Ireland*
1635-1637	Stafford Survey
1654	The Down Survey
1659	The Census of 1659
1641-1670	The Books of Survey and Distribution
1660-1670	The Hearth Money Rolls
1740	1740 Householders List
1766	Religious Census of 1766
Early 1800's	Tithe Applotment Books
1848-1864	Griffiths Valuation
1841	1841 Census
1851	1851 Census

(See detail of above in the following pages of this book.)

Strafford Survey - (1635-1637) Shows land ownership before English planation and is therefore a valuable genealogical reference.

The Civil Survey - (1654) After the confederacy wars, the Cromwellians confiscated the lands of Ireland and in part to help facilitate the confiscation of land made a civil survey in 1654. Much geographical information is covered as well as landowners and land value. I.E: Only fragments have survived for Munster, Leinster and Ulster.

Proprietor	Denominacion of lands	Acres	Profitable Lands	Unprofitable Lands	Total Value

The Down Survey - (1654-1656) Subsequent to the Civil Survey. Counties were mapped showing the baronies and parishes of the region in question. Castles, churches and the main geographic features are included as well as settlements. Concerned with confiscated lands.

Numbers in the Plot	Proprietors	Denominacion of lands	No. of Acres	Profitable Lands	Unprofitable Lands

The Census of 1659 - Concerned with confiscation land settlement. I.E:

Parishes	Townlands	Number of People	Tituladoes	English & Scotts, Irish

The Books of Survey and Distribution - Available in the Public Records Office, Dublin; The Royal Irish Acadamy Dublin, and the National Library which is in microfilm form. Contains abstracts circa 1636-1641 and 1701-1703. Contains details of the confiscated land distribution.

Proprietor (1641)	Denominacion of Lands	Acres	Profitable Lands	Unprofitable Lands	Proprietor (1670)

Also of interest in this concern are the Lodge Transcripts of the records of the rolls in the Public Records Office.

Hearth Money Rolls - Lists assessed house holders 1660-1670. For the following counties: Antrim 1669; Armagh 1664; Cavan 1664; Derry 1663; Donegal 1665; Dublin 1663; Fermanagh 1665; Louty 1664; Monaghan 1663-5; Sligo 1662; Tipperary 1665-7; Tyrone: Wicklow.

1740 Householders List

Griffiths Valuation - (Resulting from Poor Law Act of 1838) 1848-1864. Sir Richard Griffiths Primary Valuation of tenements.

Map Reference	Parishes, Townlands and Occupiers	Immediate Lessors	Description of Tenement	Content of Land	Net Annual Value Land Buildings	Total

Religious Census 1766 - (Available at Public Records Office, Dublin) Concentrated on heads of households. The originals were destroyed in 1922, but thanks to genealogist, Tension Groves who recorded thousands of names, we have a large remnant available today.

Tithe Composition Applotment Books - (1823-1837) Records tithe due to the Established Church of Ireland. For all religious denominations. Furnished name of tenent, townland, valuation, acreage and tithe due. Available at the Public Records Office, Dublin.

Poll Tax Rolls - Records of taxes levied to support the military in the last half of the 17th century.

The following excerpt was taken from *The O'Donoghue Book*, and shows the type of information you may uncover concerning your ancestors territory in Ireland, as well as surviving castles and ruins.

Castles - Ruins

The center of the ODonoghue clan was in the country immediately adjoining the three Killarney Lakes to the eastward. The main centers were at the famed 'Ross Castle', and here the ODonoghues held court at Gleanna Chapaill (The Horses Glen) in which lies the dark gloomy tarn called ODonoghues Ink Pot. ODonaghues horse may be seen here, doomed forever to stand poised in the depths.

Further north, along the little river which feeds Lough Leane (the lower lake), lay perhaps the most extensive holdings of the 'ODonoghues of the Glen'. This valley is a retreat (seldom visited by those who flock to Killarney) and of indescribable beauty and charm. Here, even after the avaricious rapacity of the oppressor had driven almost every family in Ireland from its land, and had stripped from ODonaghue most of its vast holdings around Lough Leane, the clan clung to its ground.

ROSS CASTLE

Ross Castle was the last place in Munster, and hence, the last place in all of Ireland to be taken by Cromwell. The garrison was gallantly defended until the fulfillment of an old prophecy, "that Ross Castle should not be taken until a ship would swim upon the lake". The garrison lost heart when they saw ships coming across Lough Leane and shortly afterwards, the castle fell, in 1652, after a cannon-ball was fired into the wall.

CHURCH RECORDS

- *Roman Catholic*
- *Church of Ireland (Episcopal)*
- Methodist
- Huguenot
- Presbyterian

RELIGIOUS SOURCES

Church Records

Due to the lack of government records for earlier time periods, church records are a main source of material for the researcher. Parish registers are usually in the care of the local clergy and contain birth and marriage records.

The main church related records available are for:

1. The Roman Catholic Church
2. The Church of Ireland
3. Methodist Church
4. Huguenot Church
5. Presbyterian Church
6. Quaker Church

ROMAN CATHOLIC CHURCH

Some registers date back to about 1750 but most rural registers begin closer to 1820. Most of the registers have been put on microfilm by the National Library of Ireland. The "Irish Catholic Directory" contains a listing of all the clergy and parishes. A list of parishes follows at the end of this chapter. Registers remain in the possession of the local parish priest. With written permission they may be viewed in Dublin repositories.

Archivium Hibernicum. (By the Catholic Record Society of Ireland) Dublin 1912.

Catholic Directory & Almanac, 1837.

THE CHURCH OF IRELAND (EPISCOPAL)

Parish registers for The Church of Ireland do not exist before the first half of the seventeenth century (1619 being the earliest available anywhere). A full listing of the church parish registers has been printed in the 28th "Report of the Deputy Keeper of the Public Records in Ireland," 1896. The "Irish Church Directory" lists the names and addresses of clergy. For further information see: "The Library of the Church Representative Body," Braemor Park, Dublin, or the Public Records Office.

It should be mentioned that individuals from the other denominations often crossed over to the Church of Ireland, including Roman Catholic. This was also often for a limited amount of time, due to duress and outside pressure.

(See end of this chapter for parish register listing.)

Armagh Diocesan Registry Office, Moniment Room (for the Church of Ireland).

METHODIST

The Wesleyan Methodist Society began around 1747 in Ireland. Most members were also members of the Established Church. Many were also of the Presbyterian persuasion. This double membership was allowed until the 1800's for the Established Church and the 19th century for the Presbyterians.

The National Library in Dublin, and the Linen Hall Library, Belfast, are good repositories for continuing your search in this direction, as are the following:

HUGUENOT RECORDS

The Huguenots were exiled French Protestant refugees, fleeing severe religious persecution which began in 1525. Most appeared in Ireland for a time, only to disappear shortly thereafter. There is a good chance that records on these individuals may be in Britain or Europe as well as Ireland.

The massacre of St. Bartholomew's Eve in 1572, in France, also created a great migration of Huguenots to England and Ireland. In the first half of the seventeenth century they began a new wave of settlement until the Roman Catholic rebellion broke out and they were forced to flee to safety in other countries.

With the coming of Cromwell and his army in 1649-1652, we find Huguenots enlisted from England as both officers and regular soldiers. Many of these soldiers were rewarded with Irish land confiscated from the Roman Catholics. The later half of the seventeenth century saw thousands of Huguenots continuing to leave their homeland due to increasing persecution.

The Pension List of 1702 shows most settled in Dublin, Belfast, Waterford, and Youghal. Huguenots are also to be found in Kilkenny, Lisburn, and Waterford (in linen establishments), in Dublin (as Weavers), and in Cork, Dundalk, and Lurgan (as manufacturers of cloth and cambric). Many came from Switzerland

and Holland as well.

Settlements recorded in the seventeenth century also include: Lisburn (coming from Holland), City of Cork (Christ Church), Portarlington Colony (records are available), and Carlow (coming from England).

The Huguenot's relationship with the Established Church of Ireland was a friendly one, and they often used the facilities of the Established Church for proceedings. Established Church parish registers often contain Huguenot records, particularly when no Huguenot parish had been established.

The Huguenot Society of London has published the parish records (1680-1830) of the four Dublin churches, (vol. 7 and 14), being: The French Conformed Churches of St. Patrick and St. Mary; The French Non-Donformist Churches of Lucy Land and Peter Street, Dublin. Volume 19 also contains the registers of Portarlington, in Co. Laois. The genealogical office in Dublin Castle has these records on file.

The following books may be used as source material:

Protestant Exiles from France in the Reign of Louis XIV. (Huguenot refugees and descendants in Ireland and Great Britain). London 1871-1874. D.C. Agnew.

Huguenot Settlement Records. (From the Ulster Journal of Archaeology. Vols. 1-4. 1853-56.)

Irish Pedigrees. Dublin, 1892. Vol. II. John O'Hart.

PRESBYTERIAN RECORDS

The first Presbyterian settlement from Scotland came to Ulster in the beginning of the 17th century. Because of persecution and bitter feelings of resentment from the native Irish and English, they remained quite seperate from the rest of the community. Here they remained a part of Scotland on the land of Ireland, keeping the religion and heritage of their homeland.

The Presbytery of Munster, on the other hand, was formed from English congregations in Leinster and Munster who were English Puritans and Independents. (Please note that Presbyterian individuals are also found in the Established Church Registers.)

A good source for further research: "The Presbyterian Historical Society," Church House, Fisherwick Place, Belfast, Ireland. Available are: 1766 religious census, 1775 census, 1740 householders records, birth, and marriage records, many of which are prior to 1820.

Source:

Fasti of the Irish Presbyterian Church. Belfast, 1935. McConnell.

History of the Irish Presbyterians. Belfast, 1902. Lattimer, W.T.

QUAKER

Excellent records exist from the 1650's onward. Included in these records are births, marriages, deaths, wills, letters, meetings, etc. Contact:

1. Friends Meeting House, Eustace Street, Dublin, Ireland.
2. Friends Meeting House, Lisburn, Co. Antrim, Ireland.
3. Public Records Office, Belfast, Ireland. Report of the deputy keeper 1951 to 1953.

Publications for further assistance:

Guide to Irish Quaker Records, by Olive Goodbody.

Quakers in Ireland, 1654-1900. London, 1927. Isabel Grubb.

Immigration of the Irish Quakers into Pennsylvania, 1682-1750. Albert Cook Meyers. 1902.

BAPTIST AND CONGREGATIONALIST RECORDS

The Baptist and Congregational (Independent religions in Ireland share a common background. They became politicall powerful during the Cromwellian Wars and took charge over confiscated lands. Many are found in the army around 1650.

They prospered for awhile but began to emigrate due to persecution after the Restoration (1660). "The Census of 1659," the books of "Survey and Distribution," and "The Hearth Money Rolls" can help in tracing these ancestors. Keep in mind that some of the lands of Ireland were distributed to the soldiers of Cromwells army, many of whom were of these denominations. Changes in land ownership during this period therefore, provide an important clue in your research.

"Thom's Irish Almanac and Official Directory for the Year 1847" provides us with a list of ministers and their locality in 1846. They are as follows:

Baptist

T. Berry, Abbeyleix, Queen's
(?), Aughavey, Tyrone
(?), Ballymoney, Antrim
R. Wilson, Belfast, Antrim
S. Jackman, Boyle, Roscommon
G. Moore, Carrickfergus, Antrim
C. Sharman, Clonmel, Tipperary
W.S. Eccles, Coleraine, Londonderry
(?), Cookstown, Tyrone
G.N. Watson, Cork, Cork
(?), Dublin, Dublin
(?), Easky, Sligo
(?), Grange, Antrim
(?), Knockconny, Tyrone
R. Bentley, Limerick, Limerick
(?), Monaghan, Monaghan
(?). Mullycar, Tyrone
I. M'Carthy, Rahue, Westmeath
R.H. Carson, Tubbermore (1st), Derry
C. Hardcastle, Waterford, Waterford
W. Thomas, Athlone, Westmeath
W. Hamilton, Ballina, Mayo
(?), Ballygawley, Tyrone
(?), Blackforth, Tyrone
(?), Brogshane, Antrim
(?), Carrandasy, Tyrone
M. Mullarky, Cloghjordan, Tipperary
D. Mulhern, Conlig, Down
(?), Coolaney, Sligo
(?), Crilly, Tyrone
J. Bates, Dunagannon, Tyronc
I. M'Carthy, Ferbane, King's
C. Sharman, Kilcolly Hills, Tipperary
(?), Letterkenny, Donegal
W. Thomas, Moate, Westmeath
(?), Mullaghmore, Tyrone
D. Cook, Omagh, Tyrone
(?), Siskanore, Tyrone
R.H. Carson, Tubbermore (2nd), Derry
M. Mullarky, Parsonstown, King's

Congregational

J. White, Armagh
W. Dowgan, Ballybay
J. Hodgens, Belfast
J. Murray and T. Jordan, Castlebar
H.G. Heathcote, Coleraine
H.G. Brien, Donegal
J. Mallagh, Kilkeel
J. Jennings, Londonderry
H.M. Torrens, Maryborough
S. Shaw, Moy
(?), Newry
J. Carroll, Richhill
N. Sheppard, Sligo
S. Browne, Tralee
E. Dillon, Wexford
J. Bewglass, W. Cooper, W.H. Cooper, W. Foley, J. Godkin, J. Hands, W. Urwick, A. King, Dublin
W. Fordyce, Aughnacloy
A. Bell, Ballycraigey
J. M'Assey, Carrickfergus
H. Martin, Clonmel
T. Shelley and J. Cranbrook, Cork
J. Hanson, Donoughmore
J. De K. Williams, Limerick
C.B. Gibson, Mallow
S.M. Coombs, Mountmellick
J. Gibbons, Newport
P. Finan, Newtownlimavady
G. Sampey, Roscommon
J. Bain, Straid
R. Murphy, Waterford
J.B. Grey, Youghal
(?), Dungarvan

The following exerpts may serve to give you an idea of conditions during the Great Famine in 19th century Ireland. (Example taken from *The O'Loughlin Book*).

The Great Famine

The famine rocked the society in County Clare to its very foundation. Hunger, disease and filth spread rapidly.

After a continuing increase in population during previous years, from 1841-1851, the population fell 25% from 286,000 to 212,000. Population continued to drop to 131,000 in 1881. Many landlords were forced into bankruptcy as well. Many land titles changed hands during this period.

(Quotes from 1847)

"Many of the habitations are no better than a fox earth, and the inmates, in their appearance, clothing and mode of living, hardly human".

"... we found the mother and three children stricken in fever at one side of the cabin; the father with a child who had been dead three days at the other. These horrors are too frequent...On entering the fever hospital a few days since, I found eight dead, the mortality of one night".

In a letter dated the 4th January, 1847 from Capt. Mann, a poor law inspector assigned to the county, we get a look at conditions in the Ennistymon union:

"On Monday I proceeded to Corofin. The place is eight miles distant from Ennis, the population in the town about 900, but situated in a mountain district representing 21,000 in committee, and greater misery or poverty I have not seen anywhere".

1. The parish registers of the churches in Ireland are a main source for genealogical research.
2. Most commonly they record births (baptisms), deaths (burials), and marriages, often including the wifes maiden name and witnesses to the event.
3. The dates these registers begin varies from parish to parish as indicated herein.

CO. ANTRIM

Ahoghill	1853
Antrim	1874
Armoy	1848
Ballintoy	
Ballyclare	1869
Ballymacarret	1841
Ballymoney & Derrykeighan	1853
Belfast (various city parishes)	
St. Malachy	1858
St. Peter	1866
St. Patrick	1875
St. Mary	1867
St. Joseph	1872
Braid (Ballymena)	1825
Carnlough	1869
Carrickfergus	1828
Culfeightrin (Ballycastle)	1825
Cushendall	1838
Cushendun	1862
Derryaghy	1855
Duneane (Toomebridge)	1834
Dunloy (Cloughmills)	1840
Glenavy & Killead	1849
Glenarm	1825
Greencastle	1854
Kirkinriola (Ballymena)	1848
Larne	1821
Loughuile	1845
Portglenone	1864
Portrush	1844
Ramoan (Ballycastle)	1838
Randalstown	1825
Rasharkin	1848
Tickmacrevan (Glenarm)	1825

CO. ARMAGH

Aghagallon & Ballinderry (Lurgan)	1828
Armagh	1796
Ballymacnab (Armagh)	1844
Ballymore & Mullaghbrac (Tandragee)	1843
Creggan (Crossmaglen)	1796
Derrynoose (Keady)	1835
Drumcree (Portadown)	1844
Forkhill	1845
Killeavy (Bessbrook)	1835
Kilmore (Rich Hill)	1845
Loughgall	1835
Loughgilly	1849
Seagoe	1836
Shankill (Lurgan)	1822
Tynan	1822

CO. CARLOW

Bagenalstown	1820
Ballon	1785
Borris	1782
Carlow	1774
Clonegall	1833
Clonmore	1819
Hacketstown	1820
Leighlinbridge	1783
Myshall	1822
St. Mullins	1796
Tinryland	1813
Tullow	1763

CO. CAVAN

Annagelliffe & Urney (Cavan)	1812
Annagh (Belturbet)	1855
Ballintemple	1862
Castlerahan (Ballyjamesduff)	1752
Castletera	1862
Crosserlough	1843
Denn	1856
Drumgoon	1829
Drumlane	1836
Drumlumman North	1859
Glangevlin (Swanlinbar)	1835
Kilbride & Mountnugent	1832
Killann (Bailieboro')	1835
Killinkere (Virginia)	1766
Killeshandra	1835
Kilmore	1859
Kilsherdany (Coothill)	1803
Kinawley (Swanlinbar)	1835
Kingscourt	1838
Knockbride	1835
Laragh	1860
Lavey	1866
Lurgan (Virginia)	1755
Templeport	1836

CO. CLARE

Ballina	1832
Ballyvaughan	1854
Broadford	1844
Carron	1853
O'Callaghan's Mills	1835
Carrigaholt	1853
Clareabbey	1853
Clondegad	1846
Clonrush	1846
Corofin	1819
Cratloe	1802
Crusheen	1860
Doonass & Trugh	1851
Doora & Kilraghtis	1821
Dysart	1845
Ennis	1841
Ennistymon	1870
Freakle Lr.	1860
Inagh	1850
Inch & Kilmaley	1828
Kilballyowen	1878
Kildysart	1829
Kilfarboy	1831
Kilfenora	1836
Kilfidane	1868
Kilkee	1869
Kilkeedy	1833
Killaloe	1825
Killanena	1842
Killard	1855
Killimer	1859
Kilmacduane	1854
Kilmihil	1849
Kilmurry-Ibrickane	1839
Kilmurry-M Mahon	1840
Kilnoe & Tuamgraney	1832
Kilrush	1827
Liscannor	1843
Lisdoonvarna	1854
Newmarket	1828
New Quay	1847
Ogonnelloe	1832
Parteen	1847
Quin	1816
Scariff & Moynoe	1852
Sixmilebridge	1828
Tulla	1819

CO. CORK

Aghabulloge	1856
Aghada	1815
Aghinagh	1848
Annakissy	1806
Ardfield & Rathbarry	1801
Aughadown	1822
Ballincollig	1820
Ballinhassig	1821
Ballyclogh	1807
Ballyhea	1809
Ballymacoda & Lady's Bridge	1835
Ballyvourney	1825
Bandon	1794
Bantry	1819
Blackrock	1810
Blarney	1791
Boherbue	1833
Bonane	1846
Barryroe	1804
Buttevant	1814
Caheragh	1818
Carrigaline	1826
Carrigtwohill	1817
Castlemagner	1832
Castlelyons	1791
Castletownroche	1811
Charlesville	1774
Clondrohid	1807
Clonmeen	1847
Clonthead & Ballingeary	1836
Cloyne	1791
Cobb	1812
Conna	1834
Cork	
St. Finbar	1756
St. Patrick	1831
St. Peter & Paul	1766
St. Mary	1748
Courceys	1819
Castletownbere	1819
Castlehaven	1842
Clonakilty & Darrara	1809
Donaghmore	1803
Doneraile	1815
Douglas	1812
Drimoleague	1817
Dromtariffe	1832
Dunmanway	1818
Enniskeane & Desertserges	1813
Eyeries	1843
Fermoy	1828
Freemount	1827
Glanmire	1806
Glanworth & Ballindangan	1836
Glounthane	1829
Goleen	1827
Grenagh	1840
Imogeela	1835
Inniscarra	1814
Innishannon	1825
Iveleary	1816
Kanturk	1822
Kilbehenny	1800
Kilbritain	1811
Kildorrery	1824
Killeigh	1829
Kilmichael	1819
Kilnamartyra	1803
Kilmurry	1786
Kilworth	1829
Kilmeen & Castleventry	1821

Parish	Year
Kinsale	1808
Liscarrol	1812
Lisgoold	1807
Macroom	1803
Mallow	1757
Midleton	1819
Millstreet	1853
Mitchelstown	1792
Monkstown	1795
Mourne Abbey	1829
Muintervara	1820
Murragh	1834
Newmarket	1821
Ovens	1816
Passage	1795
Rath & Islands	1818
Rathcormac	1792
Rathmore	1837
Roscarberry & Lissevard	1814
Schull	1827
Shandrum	1829
Skibbereen	1827
Timoleague & Cloghagh	1842
Tracton Abbey	1802
Watergrasshill	1836
Youghal	1803

CO. DERRY

Parish	Year
Ballinderry	1826
Ballynascreen	1825
Ballyscullion (Bellaghy)	1844
Banagher	1848
Coleraine	1843
Cumber Upr. (Claudy)	1863
Desertmartin	1848
Drumehose (Limavady)	1855
Dungiven	1847
Errigal	1846
Faughanvale	1860
Glendermot (Waterside, Derry)	1864
Kilrea	1846
Magilligan	1855
Maghera	1841
Magherafelt	1834
Moneymore	1832
Templemore (Derry City)	1823
Termoneeny	1837

CO. DONEGAL

Parish	Year
All Saints, Raymorky & Taughboyne (St. Johnston)	1843
Annagry	1868
Ardara	1869
Aughnish & Aghaninshin (Ramelton)	1873
Castlemacaward & Templecrone (Dungloe)	1876
Clonvaddog (Fanad)	1847
Clondahorky	1877
Conwal & Leck (Letterkenny)	1853
Drumhome	1866
Glencolumkille	1880
Gweedore	1868
Iniskeel (Glenties)	1866
Inver	1861
Kilcar	1848
Killybegs & Killaghtee	1845
Killygarvan & Tullyfern	1868
Killymard	1874
Kilbarron (Ballyshannon)	1854
Kilmacrenan	1862
Kilteevogue	1855
Mevagh (Carrigart)	1871
Raphoe	1876
Stranorlar	1860
Termon & Gartan	1862
Tullabegley E., Raymunterdoney & Tory	1868
Burt, Inch & Fahan	1859
Clonca (Malin)	1856
Clonleigh (Lifford)	1773
Clonmany	1852
Culdaff	1838
Desertegny & Lower Fahan (Buncrana)	1864
Donagh (Carndonagh)	1847
Donaghmore	1857
Iskaheen & Moville Upper	1858
Moville Lower	1847

CO. DOWN

Parish	Year
Aghaderg (Loughbrickland)	1816
Annaclone	1834
Ardkeen	1828
Ballygalget (Portaferry)	1828
Ballynahinch	1827
Banbridge	1843
Ballyphilip	1843
Bangor	1855
Bright (Ardglass)	1856
Clonallon (Warrenpoint)	1826
Clonduff (Hilltown)	1850
Donaghmore	1835
Dromara	1844
Dromore	1823
Drumaroad (Castlewellan)	1853
Drumbo	
Drumgath (Rathfriland)	1841
Drumgooland Upr.	1827
Drumgooland Lr.	1832
Downpatrick	1851
Dunsford	1848
Kilbroney (Rostrevor)	1808
Kilclief & Strangford	1866
Kilcoo (Rathfriland)	1832
Kilkeel	1839
Loughinisland	1806
Maghera & Bryansford (Newcastle)	1845
Magheralin	1815
Moira	1815
Mourne	1842
Newcastle	1845
Newry	1818
Newtownards, Comber & Donaghadee	1864
Saintfield (Downpatrick)	1865
Saul & Ballee	1844
Tullylish	1833
Tyrella & Dundrum	1854

CO. DUBLIN

Parish	Year
Balbriggan	1816
Baldoyle	1784
Balrothery	1816
Blanchardstown	1774
Booterstown	1796
Clondalkin	1778
Donabate	1760

Dublin City

Parish	Year
St. Agatha (North William Street)	1852
St. Andrew (Westland Row)	1741
St. Audeon (High Street)	1778
St. Catherine (Meath Street)	1740
St. James (James Street)	1752
St. Lawrence O'Toole (Seville Place)	1853
St. Mary (Pro-Cathedral, Marlborough Street)	1734
St. Michael & John (Lower Exchange Street)	1742
St. Michan (Halston Street)	1725
St. Nicholas of Myra (Francis Street)	1742
St. Paul (Arran Quay)	1731
Dun Laoire	1773
Finglas	1788
Garristown	1857
Howth	1784
Lucan	1818
Lusk	1757
Palmerstown	1798
Rathfarnham	1818
Rolestown	1857
Saggart	1857
Sandyford	1857
Skerries	1751
Swords	1763

CO. FERMANAGH

Parish	Year
Aghavea	1862
Aughalurcher (Lisnaskea)	1835
Carn (Belleek)	1851
Cleenish	1835
Culmaine	1836
Devenish	1853
Enniskillen	1838
Galloon	1853
Inishmacsaint	1848
Irvinestown	1846
Roslea	1862
Tempo	1845

CO. GALWAY

Parish	Year
Abbeyknockmoy	1834
Addergoole & Liskeevey	1858
Annaghdown	1834
Aran Islands	1872
Athenry	1858
Ahascragh	1840
Ardrahan	1839
Abbeygormican & Killoran	1859
Aughrim & Kilconnell	1828
Ballymacward & Clonkeenkerrill	1841
Ballinakill	1839
Bullaun, Grange & Killaan	1827
Beagh	1855
Ballinakill	1869
Boyounagh	1838
Creagh & Kilclooney (Ballinasloe)	1820
Clonfert, Donanaghta & Meelick	1829
Clontuskert	1827
Claregalway	1849
Castlegar	1827
Duniry & Kilnelahan	1849
Donaghpatrick & Kilcoona	1844
Dunmore	1833
Fahy & Kilquain	1836
Fohenagh & Kilgerrill	1827

Galway-St. Nicholas	1690
Kilconickny, Kilconieran & Lickerrig	1831
Kilcooley & Leitrim	1815
Killalaghten & Kilrickhill	1853
Killimorbologue & Tiranascragh	1831
Killimordaly & Kiltullagh	1830
Kilmalinoge & Lickmolassy (Portumna)	1830
Kilnadeema & Kilteskill (Loughera)	1836
Kiltomer & Oghill	1834
Killian & Killeroran (Ballygar)	1804
Kilcummin (Oughterard)	1809
Killannin	1875
Kilcameen & Ballynacourty	1855
Kinvarra	1831
Kilbeacanty	1854
Kilchreest	1855
Kilcolgan, Dromacoo & Killeenavara	1854
Kilcornan	1854
Killora & Killogilleen	1847
Kilmacduagh & Kiltartan	1848
Kilthomas	1854
Kilkerrin & Clonberne	1855
Killascobe	1807
Killeen (Carraroe)	1853
Killerein	1851
Kilmoylan & Cummer	1813
Loughrea	1827
Lettermore	1848
Lackagh	1842
Moycullen	1786
Moylough & Mountbellew	1848
Moyrus	1853
Oranmore	1833
Omey & Ballindoon	1838
Rahoon	1819
Roundstone	1872
Salthill	1840
Spiddal	1861
Tynagh	1809
Tuam	1790
Woodford	1821

CO. KERRY

Abbeydorney	1835
Annascaul	1829
Ardfert	1819
Ballybunion	1831
Ballyferriter	1807
Ballyheigue	1840
Ballylongford	1823
Ballymacelligott	1868
Boherbue	1833
Bonane & Glengarriff	1846
Brosna	1868
Cahirciveen	1846
Cahirdaniel	1831
Castlegregory	1828
Castleisland	1823
Castlemaine	1804
Causeway	1782
Dingle	1825
Dromod	1850
Duagh	1819
Firies	1830
Fossa	1857
Glenbeigh	1834
Glenflesk	1821
Kenmare	1819
Kilcummin	1821
Kilgarvan	1818
Killarney	1792
Killeentierna	1801
Killorglin	1886
Knocknagoshel	1850
Listowel	1802
Lixnaw	1810
Milltown	1825
Moyvane	1855
Prior	1832
Rathmore	1827
Sneem	1845
Spa	1866
Tarbert	1859
Tralee	1772
Tuogh	1844
Tuosist	1844
Valentia	1825

CO. KILDARE

Allen	1820
Athy	1779
Ballymore Eustace	1779
Balyna (Johnstown)	1818
Caragh (Downings)	1849
Carbury	1821
Castledermot	1789
Celbridge	1857
Clane	1785
Clonbullogue	1819
Kilcock	1771
Kilcullen	1777
Kildare	1815
Kill	1840
Maynooth	1814
Monasterevin	1819
Naas	1813
Narraghmore	1827
Newbridge	1786
Suncroft	1805

CO. KILKENNY

Aghaviller	1847
Ballyhale	1823
Ballyregget	1856
Callan	1821
Castlecomer	1812
Clara	1835
Clough	1858
Conahy	1832
Danesfort	1819
Dunnemaggan	1821
Durrow	1789
Freshford	1773
Galmory	1861
Glenmore	1831
Gowran	1809
Graignenamanagh	1818
Inistiogue	1810
Johnstown	1814
Johnstown	1814
Kilmacow	1858
Lisdowney	1817
Mooncoin	1779
Muckalee	1801
Mullinavat	1843
Paulstown	1828
Rosbercon	1817
St. Canice's (Kilkenny)	1768
St. John's (Kilkenny)	1809
St. Mary's (Kilkenny)	1754
St. Patrick's (Kilkenny)	1800
Slieverue	1766
Templeorum	1803
Thomastown	1782
Tullaherin	1782
Tulleroan	1843
Urlingford	1805
Windgap	1822

CO. LAOIS

Abbeyleix	1824
Aghaboe	1795
Arles	1821
Ballinakill	1794
Ballyadams	1820
Ballyfin	1824
Borris-in-Ossory	1840
Camross (Mountrath)	1816
Castletown	1772
Clonaslee	1849
Durrow	1789
Mountmellick	1814
Mountrath	1823
Portarlington	1820
Portaoise	1826
Raheen	1819
Rathdowney	1763
Rosenallis	1765
Stradbally	1820

CO. LEITRIM

Annaduff	1849
Aughavas	1825
Ballinamore	1869
Ballymeehan (Rossinver)	1851
Carrigallen	1829
Clooneclare (Manorhamilton)	1853
Drumlease (Dromahaire)	1859
Drumreilly	1867
Fenagh	1825
Glenade	1867
Gortletheragh	1830
Inishmagrath (Drumkeeran)	1854
Killargue	1852
Killasnet	1852
Killenummery & Killerny	1828
Kiltoghert	1826
Kiltubbrid	1841
Kinlough	1835
Mohill-Manachain	1836

CO. LIMERICK

Abbeyfeale	1856
Adare	1832
Ardagh	1845
Askeaton	1829
Athea	1830
Ballingarry	1825
Ballybricken	1800
Ballygran & Colman's well	1841
Ballylanders	1847
Banogue	1861
Bruff	1808
Bulgaden & Ballinvana	1812
Caherconlish	1841
Cappagh	1841
Cappamore	1845
Castleconnell	1850
Charleville	1774
Coolcappa	1833
Croagh	1836
Donaghmore	1830
Doon	1824
Dromin	1817
Drumcollogher	1830
Effin	1843
Emly	1810
Fedamore	1806
Feenagh	1854
Freemount	1835
Galbally	1810
Glenroe	1853
Glin	1851
Hospital	1810
Kilbenny	1824
Kildimo	1846
Kilfinane	1832
Kileedy	1840
Kilmallock	1837
Kilteely	1815
Knockaderry	1838
Knockaney	1808

Knocklong	1809
Loughill	1855
Mahoonagh	1812
Manistir	1845
Monagea	1777
Mungret	1844
Murroe & Boher	1814
Newcastle West	1815
Cola & Solohead	1809
Pallesgreen	1811
Parteen	1847
Patrick's well	1801
Rathkeale	1811
Rockhill	1842
St. John's (Limerick)	1788
St. Mary's (Limerick)	1745
St. Michael's (Limerick)	1776
St. Munchin's (Limerick)	1764
St. Patrick's (Limerick)	1812
Shanagolden	1824
Stonehall	1825
Templeglantine	1864
Tournafulla	1867

CO. LONGFORD

Abbeylara	1854
Ardagh & Moydow	1793
Carrickedmond	1825
Cashel	1850
Clonbroney	1849
Clonguish	1829
Columcille (Dring)	1845
Drumlish	1834
Kilcommuck	1859
Granard	1779
Kilglass & Rathreagh	1855
Kilashee	1826
Killoe (Drumlish)	1826
Mostrim	1838
Rathcline (Lanesboro')	1850
Scrabby & Columcille East (Cloonagh)	1833
Shrule (Ballymahon)	1820

CO. LOUTH

Ardee	1763
Carlingford	1811
Clogherhead	1744
Collon	1789
Darver	1787
Dundalk	1790
Dunleer	1772
Faughart	1851
Kilkerley	1752
Kilsaran	1809
Lordship & Ballymascanlan	1838
Louth	1833
Mellifont	1821
Monasterboice	1814
St. Mary's (Drogheda)	1835
St. Peter's (Drogheda)	1744
Tallanstown	1817
Termonfeckin	1823
Togher	1791

CO. MAYO

Attymass	1875
Addergoole	1840
Ardagh	1870
Aughaval (Westport)	1823
Achill	1867
Aghamore	1864
Aglish, Ballyheane & Breaghwy (Castlebar)	1824
Aghagower (Westport)	1828
Bohola	1857
Backs (Rathduff)	1848
Ballycastle	1864
Ballysokeary	1843
Belmullet	1841
Balla & Manulla	1837
Ballinrobe	1843
Ballyovey	1869
Bekan (Claremorris)	1832
Burriscarra & Ballintubber (Claremorris)	1839
Burrisholle (Newport)	1870
Ballyhaunis	1851
Crossmolina	1831
Clare Island	1851
Cong & Neale	1870
Crossboyne & Tagheen	1862
Clonbur	1853
Islandeady (Castlebar)	1839
Kilconduff & Meelick (Swinford)	1850
Kilgarvan (Ballina)	1844
Killasser (Swinford)	1847
Kilbeagh (Charlestown)	1845
Killedan	1834
Kilmovee	1854
Kilshalvey	1842
Kilfian	1826
Killala	1852
Kilmoremoy (Ballina)	1823
Kiltane (Bangor-Erris)	1860
Keelogues	1847
Kilcolman (Claremorris)	1835
Kilcommon & Robeen	1857
Kilgeever (Louisburg)	1850
Kilmaine	1854
Kilmeena	1858
Knock	1868
Kilbride	1853
Lackan	1852
Mayo & Roslee	1841
Templemore	1872
Toomore (Foxford)	1833
Turlough (Castlebar)	1847

CO. MEATH

Ardcath	1795
Athboy	1794
Ballinabrackey	1826
Ballivor & Kildalkey	1837
Beauparc (Yellow Furze)	1815
Blacklion	1815
Bohermeen (Navan)	1805
Carnaross	1806
Castletown (Navan)	1805
Clonmellon	1759
Curraha (Ashbourne)	1823
Drumconrath	1811
Duleek	1852
Dunboyne	1787
Dunderry	1837
Dunshaughlin	1789
Johnstown	1839
Kells	1791
Kilbride	1802
Kilmainham & Moybologue	1869
Kilcloon (Dunboyne)	1836
Kilbeg (Kells)	1817
Kilmessan & Dunsany	1742
Kilskyre (Ballinlough)	1784
Lobinstown (Navan)	1823
Longwood	1829
Moynalty	1811
Navan	1782
Nobber	1754
Oldcastle	1789
Oristown (Kells)	1757
Rathkenny	1784
Ratoath & Ashbourne	1781
Rosnaree & Donore	1840
Skyrne	1841
Slane	1851
Stamullen	1831
Summerhill	1812
Trim	1829

CO. MONAGHAN

Aghabog	1856
Aughmullen	1841
Clontibret	1861
Clones	1848
Donagh (Grasslough)	1836
Donaghmoyne	1852
Drumully (Scotshouse)	1845
Drumsnat & Kilmore	1836
Ematris (Rockcorry)	1848
Errigal Trough (Emyvale)	1835
Killevan (Newbliss)	1850
Monaghan	1835
Maghaire Rois	1836
Magheracloone (Carrickmacross)	1836
Muckno (Castleblaney)	1835
Tullycorbet (Ballybay)	1862
Tydavnet	1835

CO. OFFALY

Birr	1838
Clara	1821
Clonmacnoise	1826
Daingean	1795
Dunkerrin	1820
Edenderry	1820
Eglish	1809
Gallen & Reynagh (Banagher)	1811
Kilcormac	1821
Killeigh (Geashill)	1844
Killina (Rahan)	1810
Kinnetty	1833
Lemanaghan (Ferbane)	1821
Lusmagh	1850
Rhode	1829
Seirkieran	1830
Shinrone	1842
Tisaran & Fuithre (Ferbane)	1819
Tullamore	1809

CO. ROSCOMMON

Ardcarne	1843
Athleague & Fuerty	1808
Aughrim & Kilmore	1816
Ballintober, Ballymoe	1831

Boyle & Kilbryan	1793
Castlemore & Kilcolman	1851
Cloontuskert, Kilgeffin	1865
Dysert & Tissara	1850
Elphin & Creeve	1808
Glinsk & Kilbegnet	1836
Kilbride	1835
Kilcorkey & Frenchpark	1845
Kilglass & Rooskey	1865
Kilkeevan (Castlerea)	1804
Killukin	1811
Kilnamanagh & Estersnow	1853
Kiltoom	1835
Kiltrustan, Lissonuffy & Cloonfinlough (Strokestown)	1830
Loughglynn	1817
Ogulla & Baslick	1865
Oran	1845
Roscommon & Kilteevan	1820
St. John's (Knockcroghery)	1841
Tibohine	1833

CO. SLIGO

Aghanagh (Ballinafad)	1803
Ahamlish (Cliffoney)	1796
Ballisodare & Kilvarnet	1842
Cloonacool	1859
Curry	1867
Drumcliffe	1841
Drumrat	1843
Easky	1864
Emlefad & Kilmorgan	1824
Geevagh	1851
Kilfree & Killaraght	1844
Killoran	1846
Kilmacteigue	1845
Kilshalvey, Kilturra & Cloonoghill	1842
Riverstown	1803
Skreen & Dromard	1848
Sligo Coolera, Cairy, Rosses Point & St. Mary's	1858
Templeboy	1815
Tumore	1833

CO. TIPPERARY

Annacarty	1821
Ardfinnan	1809
Ballinahinch	1839
Ballingarry	1814
Ballylooby	1809
Ballyneale	1839
Ballyporeen	1817
Bansha & Kilmoyler	1820
Boherlahan & Dualla	1830
Borrisokane	1821
Borrisoleigh	1814
Burgess & Youghal	1828
Cahir	1809
Carrick-on-Suir	1784
Cashel	1793
Castletowarrha	1820
Clerihan	1852
Clogheen	1778
Cloghprior & Monsea	1835
Clonmel	1790
Clonoulty	1804
Cloughjordan	1833
Cappawhite	1815
Drangan	1811
Drom & Inch	1827
Dunkerrin	1820
Emly	1810
Fethard & Killusty	1806
Golden	1833
Gortnahoe	1805
Holycross	1835
Kilbarron	1827
Kilcommon	1813
Killenaule	1743
Kilsheelan	1836
Knockavilla	1834
Lattin & Cullen	1846
Loughmore	1798
Moycarky	1793
Mullinahone	1820
Nenagh	1792
Newcastle	1846
New Inn	1820
Newport	1795
Oola & Solohead	1809
Powerstown	1808
Roscrea	1810
Silvermines	1840
Templemore	1807
Templetuohy	1809
Thurles	1795
Toomevara	1831
Tipperary	1793
Upperchurch	1829

CO. TYRONE

Aghaloo	1846
Ardboe	1827
Ardstraw (Cappagh)	1846
Artrea	1832
Ballinderry (Cookstown)	1826
Ballyclog	1822
Beragh	1832
Bodoney	1850
Camus (Strabane)	1773
Cappagh	1846
Clogher	1856
Clonfeacle (Moy)	1814
Clonoe (Coalisland)	1810
Desertcreat	1827
Donaghcavey (Fintona)	1857
Donaghedy	1855
Donaghenry (Coalisland)	1822
Donaghmore	1837
Dromore	1855
Drumglass (Dungannon)	1821
Drumragh (Omagh)	1846
Eglish (Dungannon)	1862
Errigal Keeran (Ballygawley)	1847
Kildress	1835
Kileeshil (Tullyallen)	1845
Kilskerry (Trillick)	1840
Leckpatrick (Strabane)	1863
Lissan (Cookstown)	1832
Longfield	1846
Pomeroy	1837
Termonamongan	1863
Termonmaguirk (Carrickmore)	1834
Urney	

CO. WATERFORD

Abbeyside	1828
Aglish	1837
Ardmore	1823
Ballyduff	1805
Cappoquin	1810
Carrickbeg	1842
Clashmore	1811
Dungarvan	1787
Dunhill	1829
Kilgobnet	1848
Kill	1831
Killea	1780
Kilrossanty	1822
Kilsheelan	1840
Knockanore	1833
Lismore	1820
Modelligo	1846
Newcastle	1846
Portlaw	1809
Ring	1813
St. John's (Waterford)	1759
St. Patrick's (Saterford)	1731
St. Peter & Paul's	1737
Tallow	1797
Touraneena	1851
Tramore	1798
Trinity Within (Waterford)	1729
Trinity Without (Waterford)	1752

CO. WESTMEATH

Ballinacargy	1837
Ballymore	1824
Castlepollard	1763
Castletown	1829
Churchtown	1816
Clara	1821
Clonmellion	1785
Collinstown	1807
Delvin	1785
Drumraney	1834
Kilbeggan	1818
Kilbride	1832
Kilkenny West	1829
Killucan	1821
Kinnegad	1827
Lemanaghan & Ballynahowen	1821
Miltown	1781
Moate & Colry	1823
Moyvore	1831
Mullingar	1737
Multyfarnham	1824
Rathaspick & Russagh	1822
Rochfortbridge	1823
St. Mary's (Athlone)	1813
Streete	1820
Taghmon	1781
Tubber	1821
Tullamore	1801
Turbotstown	1819

CO. WEXFORD

Adamstown	1807
Ballindaggin	1841
Ballygarrett	1828
Ballyoughter	1810
Bennow	1832
Blackwater	1815
Bree	1837
Bunclody	1834
Castlebridge	1832
Clongen	1847
Cloughbawn	1816
Craanford	1853
Crossebeg	1856
Cushinstown	1759
Davidstown	1805
Enniscorthy	1794
Ferns	1819
Glynn	1817
Gorey	1847
Kilanieran	1852
Kilaveny	1800
Kilmore	1752
Kilrush	1842
Lady's-Island	1773
Litter	1789
Marshallstown	1854
Mayglass	1843
Monageer	1838
New Ross	1789

Oulart	1837
Oylegate	1804
Piercestown	1839
Ramsgrange	1835
Rathengan	1803
Suttons	1824
Taghmon	1801
Tagoat	1853
Tintern	1827
Templetown	1792
Wexford	1671

CO. WICKLOW

Arklow	1809
Ashford	1864
Avoca	1791
Baltiglass	1807
Blessington	1852
Bray:	
Bray Town	1800
Dunlavin	1815
Enniskerry	1825
Glendalough	1807
Kilbride & Barnderrig	1835
Kilquade	1826
Rathdrum	1795
Rathvilly	1797
Valleymount	1810
Tinahealy	1835
Wicklow	1747

PRESBYTERIAN REGISTERS

*In Presbyterian Historical Society's Archives, Belfast.

CO. ANTRIM

*Antrim	1674
Armoy	1842
Ballycarny	1832
Ballycastle	1829
Ballyeaston (Ballyclare)	1821
Ballylinney (Ballyclare)	1837
Ballymena	1825
Ballymoney	1827
Ballynure	1819
Ballywillan (Portrush)	1816
Ballymacarrett (Belfast)	1837
Ballysillan	1839
Belfast	
Fisherwick Place	1810
*Rosemary St.	1722
Broadmills (Lisburn)	1824
Broughshane	1830
Buckal	1841
*Carnmoney	1708
Carrickfergus	1823
Castlereagh	1807
*Cliftonville	1825
Cloughwater	1852
Connor (Ballymeana)	1819
Crumlin	1839
Dullybackey	1812
*Dongore (Templepatrick)	1806
*Drumbo (Lisburn)	1764
*Dundonald (Belfast)	1829
Dundron (Belfast	1829
Finvoy (Ballymoney)	1843
Gilnahurk (Belfast)	1797
Glenarn	1850
Glenwherry (Ballymena)	1845
Grange (Toomebridge)	1824
Kilraught (Ballymorey)	1836
Larne	1824
Loughmourne	1848
*Lylehill (Templepatrick)	1832
Masside	1843
Portrush	1843
Raloo (Larne)	1840
Randalstown	1837
Rasharkin	1834
Templepatrick	1831
Tobberleigh	1831

CO. ARMAGH

Ahorey (Loughgall)	1838
*Armagh	1707
Bessbrook	1854
Cladymore	1848
Clare (Tandragee)	1838
Cremore	1831
Donacloney (Lurgan)	1798
Gilford	1843
Keady	1819
Kingsmills (Whitecross)	1842
Knappagh	1842
Lislooney	1836
Loughgall	1842
Lurgan	1746
Markethill	1821
*Mountnorris	1804
Newmills (Portadown)	1838
Newtownhamilton	1823
Portadown	1822
Poyntzpass	1850
Richhill	1856
Tandragee	1835
Tullyallen	1795
Vinecash (Portadown)	1838

CO. CORK

Bandon	1842
Cork	1832
Cobh (Queenstown)	1847

CO DERRY

*Ballykelly	1699
Banagher (Derry)	1834
Boveedy (Kilrea)	1841
Castledawson	1835
*Coleraine	1842
Crossgar (Coleraine)	1839
*Cumber (Claudy)	1827
Derrymore (Limavady)	1825
Derry	1815
Draperstown	1837
Drumachose (Limavady)	1838
Dunboe (Boleraine)	1843
Dungiven	1835
*Faughanval (Eglinton)	1819
Garvagh	1795
Gortnassy (Derry)	1839
*Killaigh (Coleraine)	1805
Kilrea	1825
Lecompher (Moneymore)	1825
Limavady	1832
Maghera	1843
*Magherafelt	1703
Magilligan	1814
Moneymore	1827
Portstewart	1829

CO. CONEGAL

Ballindrait	1819
Ballyshannon	1836
Buncrana	1836
Burt	1834
Carnone (Raphoe)	1834
*Carrigart	1844
Convoy	1822
Donegal	1825
Donoughmore (Castlefin)	1844
Knowhead (Muff)	1826
Letterkenny	1841
Monreagh (Derry)	1845
Moville	1834
Newtowncunningham	1830
Ramelton	1808
Raphoe	1829
St. Johnston	1838
Trentagh (Kilmacrennan)	1836

CO. DOWN

Anaghlone (Banbridge)	1839
Anahilt (Hillsborough)	1780
Annalong	1840
Ardaragh (Newry)	1804
Balltdown (Banbridge)	1809
Ballygilbert	1841
Ballygraney (Bangor)	1838
Ballynahinch	1841
Ballyroney (Banbridge)	1831
Ballywalter	1824
*Banbridge	1756
Bangor	1833

Carrowdore (Greyabbey)	1843
Clarkesbridge (Newry)	1833
Clonduff (Banbridge)	1842
Clough (Downpatrick)	1836
Cloughey	1844
Comber	1847
Conligh (Newtownards)	1845
Donaghadee	1822
Downpatrick	1827
Dromara	1823
Dromore	1834
Drumbanagher (Derry)	1832
Drumgooland	1833
Drumlee (Banbridge)	1826
Edengrove (Ballynahinch)	1829
Glastry	1728
Groomsport	1841
Hillsborough	1832
Kilkeel	1842
Killinchy	1835
*Killyleagh	1693
Kilmore (Crossgar)	1833
*Kirkcubbin	1785
Leitrim (Banbridge)	1837
Lissera (Crossgar)	1809
Loughagherry (Hillsborough)	1801
Loughbrickland	1842
Magherally (Banbridge)	1837
Millisle	1773
Mourne (Kilkeel)	1840
Newry	1829
Newtownards	1833
*Portaferry	1699
Raffrey (Crossgar)	1843
Rathfriland	1804
Rostrevor	1851
Saintfield	1831
*Scarva	1807
Seaforde	1826
Strangford	1846
Tullylish (Gilford)	1813
Warrenpoint	1832
CO DUBLIN	
Abbey (Abbey St.)	1777
Ormond Quay	1787
Clontarf	1836
CO. FERMANAGH	
Enniskillen	1837
Lisbellaw	1849
Pettigo	1844
CO. GALWAY	
Galway	1831
CO. KERRY	
Tralee	1840
CO. LAOIS (QUEENS)	
*Mountmellick	1849
CO. LEITRIM	
Carrigallen	1844
CO. LIMERICK	
Limerick	1829
CO. LONGFORD	
Tully (Edgeworthstown)	1844
CO. LOUTH	
Corvally (Dundalk)	1840
Dundalk	1819
CO. MAYO	
Dromore (Balina)	1849
CO. MONAGHAN	
Ballyalbany	1802
Ballybay	1833
Ballyhobridge (Clones)	1846
Broomfield (Castleblaney)	1841
*Cahans (Ballybay)	1752
Castleblaney	1832
Clones	1856
Clontibret	1825
Corlea	1835
Derryvalley (Ballybay)	1816
Drumkeen (Newbliss)	1856
*Frankford (Castleblaney)	1820
*Glennan (Glasslough)	1805
Middletown (Glasslough)	1829
Monaghan	1824
Newbliss	1856
Scotstown	1856
Stonebridge (Newbliss)	1821
CO. TYRONE	
Albany (Stewartstown)	1838
Ardstraw	1837
Aughtaire (Fivemiletown)	1836
Aughnacloy	1843
Ballygawley	1843
Ballygorey (Cookstown)	1834
Ballynahatty (Omagh)	1843
Ballyreagh (Ballygawley)	1843
Brigh (Stewartstown)	1836
Carland (Castlecaulfield)	1759
Castlederg	1823
Cleggan (Cookstown)	1848
Clenanees (Castlecaulfield)	1840
Clogher	1819
Coagh	1839
Cookstown	1836
Donaghheady (Strabane)	1838
Drumguin	1845
Dungannon	1790
Edenderry (Omagh)	1845
Eglish (Dungannon)	1839
Fintona	1836
Gillygooly (Omagh)	1848
Gortin	1843
Leckpatrick (Strabane)	1838
Minterburn (Caledon)	1829
Moy	1851
Newmills (Dungannon)	1850
Omagh	1821
Orritor (Cookstown)	1831
Pomeroy	1841
Sandholey (Cookstown)	1844
Strabane	1828
Urney (Sion Mills)	1837
CO. WATERFORD	
Waterford	1770
CO. WEXFORD	
Wexford	1844
CO. WICKLOW	
Bray	1836

CHURCH OF IRELAND

CO. ANTRIM

Aghalee	1782
Ahoghill (Ballymena)	1811
Antrim	1700
Ballinderry	1805
Ballintoy (Ballycastle)	1712
Ballyclug	1841
Ballymacarrett	1827
Ballymena	1815
Ballymoney	1807
Ballynure	1812
Ballysillan	1856
Belfast	
Christ Church	1868
Mariner's	1745
St. Anne (Shankill)	1819
St. George	1853
St. John	1853
St. Mark (see Ballysillan)	
St. Mary	1867
St. Matthew	1846
Trinity	1844
Upper Falls	1855
Carnamoney	1789
Carrickfergus	1740
Craigs (Belfast)	1839
Derryaghey (Lisburn)	1696
Derrykeighan	1802
Drummaul (Randalstown)	1823
Dunluce (Bushmills)	1809
Dunseverick (Bushmills)	1832
Finvoy (Ballymoney)	1811
Glenarm	1788
Glenary	1707
Glynn (Larne)	1838
Inver (Larne)	1806
Lambeg	1810
Layde (Cushendall)	1826
Lisburn (Blaris)	1639
Magheragall (Lisburn)	1772
Muckamore (Antrim)	1847
Skerry	1805
Stoneyford	1845
Templecorran	1848
Templepatrick	1827
Whitehouse (Belfast)	1840

CO. ARMAGH

Aghavilly (Armagh)	1844
Annaghmore (Loughgall)	1856
Ardmore	1822
Armagh	1750
Ballymore (Tandragee)	1783
Ballymoyer (Whitecross)	1820
Camlough (Newry)	1832
Creggan (Crossmaglen)	1808
Derrynoose (Armagh)	1710
Drumbanagher (Newry)	1838
Drumcree (Portadown)	1780
Eglish (Moy)	1803
Grange (Armagh)	1780
Keady	1780
Kilcluney (Markethill)	1832
Killylea	1845
Loughgall	1706
Loughgilly (Markethill)	1804
Milltown (Magheramoy)	1840
Mullavilly (Tandragee)	1821
Newtownhamilton	1823
Sankill	1681
Tartaraghan (Loughgall)	1824
Tynan	1686

CO. CARLOW

Aghade (Carlow)	1740
Aghold	1700
Barragh (Enniscorthy)	1831
Carlow	1744
Dunleckney	1791
Fenagh (Carlow)	1809
Hacketstown	
Killeshir (Carlow)	1824
Kiltennell (New Ross)	1837
Myshall	1814
Painestown (Carlow)	1833
Rathvilly	1826
Rullow	1696
Urglin (Carlow)	1710

CO. CAVAN

Annagelliffe (Cavan)	1804
Annagh (Belturbet)	1801
Ashfield (Cootehill)	1821
Bailieborough	1744
Ballymachugh	1816
Billis (Virginia)	1840
Castleterra (Ballyhaise)	1800
Cavan	1842
Cloverhill	1861
Drumgoon (Cootehill)	1802
Drung	1785
Kildallon (Ballyconnell)	1856
Kildrumferton (Kilnelack)	1801
Killeshandra	1735
Killsherdaney (Cootehill)	1810
Killoughter (Redhills)	1827
Kilmore (Cavan)	1702
Knockbride (Bailieborough)	1825
Lurgan (Virginia)	1831
Quivy (Belturbet)	1854
Swanlinbar	1798
Tomregan (Ballyconnell)	1797

CO. CLARE

Ennis	1805
Killaloe	1679
Kilnasoolagh (Newmarket)	1731
Kilrush	1773
Ogonnilloe (Scariff)	1807

CO. CORK

Abbeymahon (Timoleague)	1827
Abbeystrewry (Skibbereen)	1778
Aghabullog (Coachford)	1808
Aghada (Cloyne)	1815
Ardfield (Clonakilty)	1835
Ballyclough (Mallow)	1795
Ballydehob (Skull)	1826
Ballyhay (Charleville)	1728
Ballyhooly (Mallow)	1788
Ballymartyl (Ballinhassig)	1785
Ballymodan (Bandon)	1695
Ballymoney (Ballineen)	1805
Berehaven	1787
Blackrock (St. Michael)	1828
Brigown (Mitchelstown)	1775
Buttevant	1757
Carrigaline	1723
Carrigamleary (Mallow)	1779
Carrig Park	1779
Carrigtwohill	1779
Castlemagner	1810
Castletownroche	1728
Churchtown (Mallow)	1806

Clenore (Mallow)	1813
Clonfert (Newmarket)	1771
Clonmeen (Mallow)	1764
Cloyne	1708
Cork	
Christ Church	1643
St. Luke	1837
St. Nicholas	1721
St. Anne	1772
St. Finbarr	1752
Corbeg	1836
Desertserges (Bandon)	1837
Doneraile	1730
Douglas (Cork)	1792
Drishane	1792
Dromdaleague	1812
Dromtariff (Millstreet)	1825
Fanlobbus (Dunmanway)	1855
Farrihy (Kildorrery)	1765
Fermoy	1801
Garrane (Middleton)	1856
Glanworth	1805
Inniscarra (Cork)	1820
Innishannon	1693
Kanturk	1818
Kilbolane (Kanturk)	1779
Kilbrogan (Bandon)	1752
Kilcummer (Fermoy)	1856
Killanully (Carrigaline)	1831
Killowen (Bandon)	1833
Kilmeen (Clonakilty)	1806
Kilworth	1766
Knocavilly (Bandon)	1837
Liscarrol	1805
Lisgould (Middleton)	1847
Lislee (Bandon)	1809
Litter (Fermoy)	1811
Macroom	1727
Magourney (Coachford)	1757
Mallow	1776
Marmulland (Passage West)	1801
Middleton	1810
Monanimy (Mallow)	1812
Monkstown	1842
Mourne Abbey (Mallow)	1807
Murragh (Bandon)	1754
Nathlash (Kildorrery)	1844
Nohoval (Kinsale)	1785
Queenstown (Cobh)	1761
Rahan (Mallow)	1773
Rathcooney (Glanmire)	1749
Rincurran (Kinsale)	1793
Rushbrook	1806
Templemartin (Bandon)	1806
Timoleague	1823
Tullylease	1850
Wallstown (Doneraile)	1829
Youghal	1665

CO. DERRY

Ballinderry (Moneymore)	1802
Ballyeglish (Moneymore)	1868
Ballynascreen	1808
Banagher (Derry)	1839
Castledawson	1744
Clooney	1867
Coleraine	1769
Cumber (Clady)	1804
Desartlyn (Moneymore)	1797
Desartmartin	1797
Drumachose (Limavady)	1728
Dungiven	1778
Glendermot	1810
Kilcronaghan (Tubbermore)	1749
Killowen (Coleraine)	1824
Kilrea	1801
Learmount (Kerry)	1832
Londonderry	1642
Maghera	1785
Magherafelt	1718
Tamlaght (Portglenone)	1858
Tamlaghard (Magilligan)	1747
Tamlaghfinlagan	1796
Termoneeny (Castledawson)	1821
Woods Chapel	1800

CO. DONEGAL

Ardara	1829
Burt	1802
Clondevadock (Ramelton)	1794
Donegal	1803
Drumholm (Ballintra)	1691
Fahan (Buncrana)	1761
Finner	1815
Glencolumbkille	1827
Inniskeel (Ardara)	1826
Inver	1805
Kilbarrow (Ballyshannon)	1785
Kilcar (Killybegs)	1819
Killaghtee (Glenties)	1810
Killybegs	1789
Kilteevogue (Stranorlar)	1818
Moville	1814
Muff	1803
Raphoe	1831
Stranorlar	1821
Taughboyne (Derry)	1819
Templecarn	1825
Tullyaughnish (Ramelton)	1798

CO. DOWN

Aghaderg (Loughbrickland)	1814
Annalong (Castlewellan)	1842
Ardkeen	1746
Ballee (Downpatrick)	1792
Ballyculter (Strangford)	1777
Ballyhalbert (Kircubbin)	1852
Ballyphilip (Portaferry)	1745
Ballywalter (Newtowards)	1844
Bangor	1803
Clonduff (Hilltown)	1782
Comber	1683
Donaghadee	1778
Donaghcloney	1834
Downpatrick	1750
Drumballyroney (Rathfriland)	1831
Drumbeg (Lisburn)	1823
Drumbo (Lisburn)	1791
Drumgooland	1779
Dundonald (Belfast)	1811
Gilford	1869
Hillsborough	1777
Holywood	1806
Inch (Downpatrick)	1767
Innishargy	1783
Kilbroney (Rostrevor)	1814
Kilcoo	1786
Killaney	1858
Killinchy	1819
Kilmood (Killinchy)	1822
Kilmore	1820
Knockbreda (Belfast)	1784
Knocknamuckley (Gilford)	1838
Loughlin Island (Clough)	1760
Magheralin	1692
Moira	1845
Moyntags (Lurgan)	1822
Newcastle	1823
Newry	1822
Saintfield	1724
Seagoe	1672
Seapatrick (Banbridge)	1802
Tullylish (Banbridge)	1820
Tyrella (Clough)	1839
Warrenpoint	1825

CO. DUBLIN

Balbriggan	1838
Blackrock	1855
Castleknock	1709
Chapelizod	1812
Clondalkin	1728
Clonsilla	1830
Donabate	1811
Donnybrook	1712
Holmpatrick	1779
Howth	1804
Irishtown (Sandymount)	1812
Killesk	1829
Kilmainham	1857
Kilsallaghan	1818
Kilternan	1917
Kingstown (Dun Laoghaire)	1843
Lusk	1809
Malahide	1822
Monkstown	1680
Newcastle	1773
Santry	1753
Swords	1705
Taney (Dundrum)	1835
Whitechurch (Terenure)	1825

CO. FERMANAGH

Aghadrumsee (Clones)	1821
Aghalurcher (Lisnaskea)	1788
Aghaveagh (Lisnaskea)	1815
Belleek	1822
Bohoe (Enniskillen)	1840
Clabby (Fivemiletown)	1862
Coolaghty (Kesh)	1835
Derryvullan (Enniskillen)	1803

Devenish (Ballyshannon)	1800
Drumkeeran (Kesh)	1801
Galloon	1798
Innishmacsaint	1813
Killesher (Enniskillen)	1798
Kinawley	1761
Lisnaskea	1804
Mullaghafad (Scotstown)	1836
Magheracross	1800
Magheraculmoney (Kesh)	1767
Maguiresbridge	1840
Tempo	1836
Trory (Enniskillen)	1779

CO. GALWAY

Ahascragh	1775
Ardrahan	1804
Aughrim	1814
Ballinacourty (Oranmore)	1838
Ballinakill (Clifden)	1852
Ballinakill (Portumna)	1766
Creagh (Ballinasloe)	1823
Galway St. Nicholas	1782
Inniscaltra (Mountshannon)	1851
Kilcolgan	1847
Kilcummin (Oughterard)	1812
Killannin (Headford)	1844
Loughrea	1747
Moylough (Mountbellew)	1821
Moyrus (Roundstone)	1841
Omey (Clifden)	1831
Tuam	1808

CO. KERRY

Aghadoe (Killarney)	1842
Ballymacelligot	1817
Ballynacourty (Kilflynn)	1803
Ballyseedy (Tralee)	1830
Castleisland	1835
Dingle	1707
Dromod (Prior)	1827
Kenmare	1799
Kilcolman (Killorglin)	1802
Kilgarvan	1811
Kilnaughton (Tarbert)	1793
Liselton	1840
Listowel	1790
Tralee	1771
Valentia	1826

CO. KILDARE

Athy	1669
Ballymore-Eustace	1838
Ballysax	1830
Carbery	1814
Celbridge	1777
Clane	1802
Clonsast (Celbridge)	1805
Harristown (Athy)	1666
Kilcullen	1778
Kildare St. Bridget	1801
Kill	1814
Lackagh (Monastereven)	1830
Naas	1679
Straffan (Naas)	1838
Timolin (Baltinglass)	1812

CO. KILKENNY

Blackrath (Kilkenny)	1810
Castlecomer	1799
Clonmore	1817
Fertagh (Johnstown)	1797
Fiddown (Pilltown)	1686
Gallskill (Pilltown)	1753
Graig	1827
Grangesylvae (Gowran)	1850
Innistiogue	1797
Kilbeacon (Pilltown)	1813
Kilcollum	1817
Kilkenny St. Canice	1789
Kilkenny St. Mary	1729
Kilmacow	1792
Kilmanagh (Callan)	1784
Kilmoganny (Knocktopher)	1782
Macully (Pilltown)	1817

CO. LEITRIM

Drumlease (Dromahaire)	1828
Kiltoghert (Carrick-on-Shannon)	1810
Manorhamilton	1816
Outragh (Ballinamore)	1833

CO. LEIX (QUEEN'S)

Abbeyleix	1781
Ballyfin	1821
Castletown	1802
Clonenagh (Mountrath)	1749
Coolbanagher	1802
Durrow	1731
Killeban	1802
Lea (Portarlington)	1801
Maryborough (Portlaoise)	1793
Mountmellick	1840
Offerland (Borris-in-Ossory)	1807
Oregan (Rosenallis)	1801
Portarlington	1694
Rathdowney	1756
Rathsaran (Rathdowney)	1810
Stradbally	1772
Timahoe	1845

CO. LIMERICK

Abington	1811
Adare	1804
Ardcanny (Pallaskenry)	1802
Ballingarry	1785
Bruff	1850
Cahernarry (Nr. Limerick)	1857
Cappamore	1858
Doon	1804
Fedamore	1840
Kildimo	1809
Kilfergus (Foynes)	1812
Kilfinane	1804
Kilflyn (Ardpatrick)	1813
Kilkeedy (Mungret)	1799
Kilmoylan	1812
Limerick St. John	1697
Limerick St. Mary	1726
Limerick St. Michael	1801
Limerick St. Munchin	1700
Rathkeale	1746
Rathronan (Ardagh)	1818
Shanagolden	1803
Tullybrackey (Bruff)	1820

CO. LONGFORD

Ardagh	1811
Clonbroney	1821
Clogesh	1820
Forgney (Ballymahon)	1803
Granard	1820
Kilcommick (Ballymahon)	1795
Killashee (Lanesboro)	1771
Mostrim (Edgeworthstown)	1801
Moydow	1794
Street	1801
Shrule	1821
Templemichael (Longford)	1795

CO. LOUTH

Ardee	1735
Charlestown	1822
Collon	1790
Drogheda St. Peter	1654
Drogheda St. Mary	1811
Dundalk	1729
Jonesborough	1812
Mellifont	1812
Tullyallen	1812

CO. MAYO

Achill	1854
Aghagower (Westport)	1825
Ballincholla (The Neale)	1831
Ballysakeery (Ballina)	1802
Cong	1811
Crossmolina	1768
Dugort	1838
Killala	1757
Kilmainemore (Ballinrobe)	1744
Kilmoremoy (Ballinahaglish)	1801
Knappagh (Westport)	1855
Turlough (Castlebar)	1821
Westport	1801

CO. MONAGHAN

Ballybay	1813
Carrickmacross	1796
Castleblaney	1810
Clones	1682
Currin (Rockcorry)	1810
Donagh (Glasslough)	1796
Emyvale (Trough)	1809
Killarney (Carrickmacross)	1825
Killeevan (Clones)	1811
Kilmore	1796
Magheracloone	1806
Monaghan	1802
Newbliss	1841
Tedavnet (Scotstown)	1822
Tyholland (Monaghan)	1806

CO. MEATH

Athboy 1736
Ballymaglasson (Dunshaughlin) 1800
Clonard 1792
Drumconrath 1785
Dunshaughlin 1800
Kells 1773
Killochonagan (Trim) 1853
Kilmore (Kilcock) 1800
Knockmark (Dunshaughlin) 1825
Nobber 1828
Oldcastle 1814
Rathbeggan (Dunboyne) 1821
Rathcore (Enfield) 1810
Syddan (Navan) 1720
Trim 1836

CO. OFFALY (KING'S)

Ballyboy (Frankford) 1796
Birr 1772
Castlejordan (Edenderry) 1823
Cloneyhork (Portarlington) 1824
Clonmacnoise 1824
Durrow 1816
Ettagh (Roscrea) 1825
Ferbane 1819
Gallen (Cloghan) 1842
Geashill 1713
Kilbride (Tullamore) 1811
Killeigh (Tullamore) 1808
Kinnitty 1800
Monasteroris (Edenderry) 1698
Shinrone 1741
Templeharry (Shinroe) 1800

CO. ROSCOMMON

Ardcarna (Boyle) 1820
Boyle 1793
Bumlin (Strokestown) 1811
Croghan (Boyle) 1862
Estersrow (Boyle 1800
Kilbryan (Boyle) 1852
Kilglass (Rooskey) 1823
Kiltoom (Athlone) 1797
Kiltullagh (Castlerea) 1822

CO. SLIGO

Ballysumaghan (Collooney) 1828
Drumcliff 1805
Easkey 1822
Emlafad (Ballymote) 1831
Kilmactranny (Boyle) 1816
Knocknarea (Sligo) 1842
Lissadell 1836
Sligo
St. John 1802

CO. TIPPERARY

Aghnameadle (Moneygall) 1834
Ballingarry (Cashel) 1816
Ballintemple 1805
Borrisnafarney (Roscrea) 1827
Cahir 1801
Carrick-on-Suir 1803
Cashel 1668
Clonmel 1766
Clonoulty (Cashel) 1817
Cloughjordan 1827
Cullen (Tipperary) 1770
Dunkerrin 1800
Fethard 1804
Holycross 1784
Inislonagh (Clonmel) 1801
Mealiffe (Thurles) 1791
Modreeny 1827
Newport 1782
Shanrahan (Clogheen) 1793
Templemichael (Carrick-on-Suir) 1791
Terry Glass (Borrisokane) 1809
Tipperary 1779
Toem (Cashel) 1802
Tullamelan (Clonmel) 1823

CO. TYRONE

Arboe (Cookstown) 1773
Ardtrea (Cookstown) 1811
Badoney (Gortin) 1818
Ballyclog (Stewartstown) 1818
Brackaville 1836
Caledon 1791
Camus 1803
Cappagh 1758
Carnteel (Aughnacloy) 1805
Clonfeacle (Dungannon) 1763
Derg (Castlederg) 1807
Derrylorgan (Cookstown) 1796
Desertcreat (Cookstown) 1812
Donagheady (Strabane) 1754
Donaghenry (Dungannon) 1734
Donaghmore (Castlefin) 1748
Drumglass (Dungannon) 1664
Drumrath (Omagh) 1800
Edenderry (Omagh) 1841
Errigal (Garvagh) 1812
Findonagh (Donacavey) 1777
Fivemiletown 1804
Kildress (Cookstown) 1749
Killyman (Dungannon) 1741
Kilskerry (Enniskillen) 1772
Lissan (Cookstown) 1753
Sixmilecross 1836
Termonmongan (Castlederg) 1812
Tullyniskin (Dungannon) 1794
Urney (Strabane) 1813

CO. WATERFORD

Cappoquin 1844
Dungarvan 1741
Innislonagh 1800
Killea (Dunmore) 1816
Kilmeadon 1683
Killrosantry 1838
Kilwatermoy 1860
Kill (Passage) 1730
Lismore 1693
Macully 1817
Portlaw 1741
Tallow 1772
Templemichael 1801
Waterford
St. Olave's 1658
St. Patrick's 1723

CO. WESTMEATH

Abbeyshrule 1821
Athlone
St. Mary 1746
Delvin 1817
Kilbixy (Ballinacargy) 1843
Killucan 1700
Mayne (Castlepollard) 1808
Willbrooke (Athlone) 1756

CO. WEXFORD

Ardamine (Gorey) 1807
Ballycanew 1733
Ballycarney (Ferns) 1835
Carnew 1749
Clonegal 1792
Clonmore 1828
Enniscorthy 1798
Ferns 1775
Gorey 1801
Inch (New Ross) 1726
Killanne 1771
Killegney (Enniscorthy) 1800
Killeney 1788
Killinick (Wexford) 1804
Killurin 1816
Kilmallog (Wexford) 1813
Kilnehue (Gorey) 1817
Kilpipe (Arklow) 1828
Kiltennell (Gorey) 1806
Leskinfere (Gorey) 1806
Mulrankin 1768
Newtownbarry (Bunclody) 1779
Owneduff (Taghmon) 1752
Rathaspick 1844
Rossdroit (Enniscorthy) 1802
Tacumshane (Rosslare) 1832
Templescobin (Enniscorthy) 1802
Tomhaggard (Rosslare) 1809
Toombe (Ferns) 1770
Wexford 1674

CO WICKLOW

Ballinaclash (Rathdrum) 1839
Ballintemple (Arklow) 1823
Ballunure (Dunlavin) 1807
Blessington 1695
Bray 1666
Castlemacadam (Ovoca) 1720
Crosspatrick (Tinahely) 1830
Delgany 1666
Dunlavin 1697
Glenealy 1825
Kilcommon (Hacketstown) 1814
Killiskey (Ashford) 1818
Mullinacuff (Tinahely) 1838
Newcastle 1698
Ovoca 1720
Powerscourt 1677
Preban (Tinahely) 1827
Rathdrum 1706
Shillelagh 1833
Stratford (Baltinglass) 1812
Wicklow 1655

1891 BIRTH INDEX (EXTRACT)

The following pages list the surnames of Ireland as recorded by the number of births in the year 1890. *(Per Report of the Registrar General,* published in 1894).

A minimum of five births must have been recorded to appear in this listing. An asterisk indicates that there were different spellings of the name as listed. The number in parenthesis immediately following the surname indicates those names spelled exactly as listed.

The total number of births recorded is listed in the second column. The counties listed in the last column represent the primary area of residence for the name in question,(though not necessarily exclusive to these counties).

NAME	BIRTHS	PREDOMINANT COUNTIES
*Abbott (10)	11	
Abernethy	6	
*Abraham (8)	9	Armagh
*Acheson (17)	27	Antrim, ARmagh, Down.
Adair	29	Antrim, Down, Londonderry
Adams	77	Antrim, Londonderry
Adamson	9	Armagh, Down
Agnew	39	Antrim, Armagh, Down
*Ahern (92)		
Aherne (15)		
Ahearn (9)	122	Cork, Limerick
*Aiken (15)	19	Antrim
Alcock	5	
Alcorn	6	Donegal, Londonderry
Alderdice	6	Antrim, Armagh
Alexander	53	Antrim, Down
*Allen (158)	163	Antrim, Armagh, Dublin
Allingham	5	Leitrim
Allison	5	Antrim
Ambrose	12	Cork, Limerick
Anderson	175	Antrim, Dublin, Down,
		Londonderry
Andrews	42	Antrim, Down
Anglin	5	Cork
Angus	10	Down, Antrim
Annett	8	Down, Antrim
Archbold	8	Dublin, Kildare
Archer	15	Armagh, Antrim, Dublin
Archiblad	8	Londonderry
Armour	10	Antrim
Armstrong	140	Antrim, Fermanagh, Cavan,
		Tyrone
Arnold	22	Antrim, Dublin
Arnott	5	Cork
Arthur	9	
Arthurs	11	Antrim, Tyrone
*Ashe (18)	22	Kerry, Antrim
*Aspel (8)	11	Wexford
Atkins	6	Cork
Atkinson	37	Antrim, Armagh, Down
Auld	6	Antrim, Monaghan
*Austin (19)	20	Antrim, Dublin
Aylward	14	Waterford, Kilkenny
Bacon	7	
*Bagnall (6)	9	King's
*Balley (34)		Antrim, Wesford
Bailie (29)		Antrim, Down
Bayley (7)	80	Tipperary, Dublin
Baird	39	Antrim, Down
Baker	30	Dublin, Antrim
Baldwin	10	Waterford
*Balfe (7)	9	
Balfour	5	Antrim
Ball	16	Antrim, Meath, Dublin
*Ballantine (8)	19	Antrim
Ballentine (8)		
Balmer	8	Down
Bamford	9	Antrim
Banks	8	
Bannister	5	
*Bannon (21)	23	Tipperary
*Barber (15)	18	Antrim
Barclay	6	Antrim, Galway
Barker	7	
*Barkley (6)	9	Antrim
Barlow	7	
*Barnes (22)	26	Antrim
Barnett	15	
Barr	60	Antrim, Londonderry, Down
*Barrett (141)	146	Dublin, Cork, Kerry,
		Limerick, Galway, Mayo
Barrington	7	
*Barron (41)	43	Antrim, Donegal, Wexford,
		Waterford
Barry	217	Cork, Limerick, Waterford
*Bartley (8)	10	
Barton	20	Fermanagh, Dublin
*Bassett (6)	9	
Bateman	19	Cork, Dublin
Bates	22	Dublin
Battersby	5	Dublin
Battle	6	Sligo
Baxter	31	Antrim
Beamish	5	Cork
*Beattie (61)	101	Antrim, Down
Beatty (36)		Dublin, Armagh, Tyrone
Beck	7	Antrim, Down
Beckett	6	Antrim
*Beggan (5)	7	Monaghan
Beggs	30	Antrim, Dublin
*Begley (36)	39	Kerry, Donegal
*Behan (37)	46	Dublin, Kildare
Beirne	64	Roscommon, Leitrim
Bell	197	Antrim, Down, Tyrone,
		Armagh, Dublin
Bellew	8	Louth
Belton	12	Longford, Louth
*Bennett (79)	81	Cork, Dublin, Antrim,
		Armagh, Down
*Benson (15)	16	
Beresford	6	
*Bergin (40)	45	Tipperary, Queen's, Dublin
Berkery	6	Tipperary, Limerick
Bermingham (23)	40	Dublin, King's, Cork
Birmingham (17)		
Bernard	6	
Berry	30	Antrim, King's, Mayo
Best	21	Armagh, Tyrone
Bickerstaff	5	Down, Antrim
Biggins	6	Mayo
Bill	5	Antrim
Bingham	30	Down, Antrim
Birch	9	
*Bird (21)	22	Dublin, Cork
*Birney (6)	7	
Bishop	9	Dublin
Black	116	Antrim, Armagh, Tyrone, Down
*Balckburn (6)	8	Antrim
Blackstock	5	Antrim, Armagh
Blackwood	7	Antrim
*Blain (6)		Down, Antrim
Blair	78	Antrim, Londonderry, Tyrone
Blake	58	Cork, Galway, Clare,
		Antrim, Dublin
*Blaney (7)	9	Antrim
*Bleakley (7)	11	Antrim
Bloomer	6	Antrim, Tyrone
*Boal (12)	17	Antrim, Down
*Bogan (7)	12	Wexford
Bogue	9	Fermanagh
*Bohan (27)	30	Leitrim, Galway
Bohane	5	Cork
Boland	57	Clare, Kildare, Roscommon
*Boles (7)	12	
Bowles (5)		
*Bolger (64)	70	Wexford, Kildare, Wicklow
Bollard	7	Dublin
Bolton	22	
*Bonar (22)	38	Donegal
Bond	18	Dublin
Bones	7	
*Booth (14)	17	Antrim, Dublin
Bothwell	7	
*Boucher (5)	7	
Bourke	140	Tipperary, Limerick, Mayo,
		Kerry, Cork
Bowden	8	
Bowe	14	Kilkenny
Bowen	14	Cork
Bowers	5	

NAME	BIRTHS	PREDOMINANT COUNTIES
Bowes	10	Dublin
Bowler	14	Kerry
Bowman	11	Antrim, Down
*Boyce (39)	40	Donegal, Down, Londonderry
*Boyd (154)	155	Antrim, Down, Londonderry
Boylan	49	Dublin, Monaghan, Cavan, Meath
Boyle	273	Donegal, Antrim, Mayo, Tyrone Armagh, Louth
Boyne	7	Dublin
Brabazon	5	
*Bracken (24)	26	Dublin, King's
*Bradley (132)	135	Londonderry, Antrim, Tyrone, Donegal, Dublin, Cork
Bradshaw	25	Antrim, Tipperary, Dublin
Brady	261	Cavan, Dublin, Antrim, Meath, Longford
Brandon	8	
*Brannan (8)	18	Donegal
Brannon (7)		
Brannigan (20)	38	Armagh, Monaghan
Branagan (7)		Dublin
Bransfield	5	Cork
Bray	14	Cavan, Dublin
*Brazil (10)	19	Dublin, Waterford
*Breadon (7)	13	Fermanagh, Tyrone
*Breen (110)	112	Wexford, Dublin, Kerry
*Breheny (7)	16	Roscommon, Sligo
*Brennan (336)	358	Kilkenny, Dublin, Sligo, Mayo, Carlow, Roscommon
*Brereton (8)	15	Dublin, King's
*Breslin (42)	43	Donegal
Brett	20	Sligo, Dublin
Brew	9	Clare
*Brick (9)	10	Kerry
Brickley	5	Cork
*Bridget (5)	7	
Brien	246	Cork, Dublin, Tipperary, Wexford, Waterford
*Briggs (16)	17	Antrim, Down
Bright	7	Dublin
Briody	13	Longford, Cavan
Britt	12	Tipperary, Waterford
*Britton (9)	13	
Brock	6	
Broder	11	Kerry, Limerick
*Broderick (37)	39	Galway, Cork, Kerry, Dublin
*Brody (6)	7	Clare
Broe	8	Kildare, Dublin
Brogan	33	Mayo, Donegal
*Brolly (7)	8	Londonderry, Tyrone
*Brooks (20)	25	Cork, Dublin
Brophy	50	Dublin, Kilkenny, Queen's, Tipperary
*Brosnan (47)	66	Kerry
Brown	327	Antrim, Londonderry, Down, Dublin
Browne	146	Cork, Mayo, Wexford, Dublin
Brownlee	19	Antrim, Armagh
Bruce	7	
Bruen	10	Roscommon
Bruton	9	Dublin
*Bryan (38)	47	Dublin, Kilkenny, Wexford, Cork, Down
Bryans	16	Antrim, Down
Bryson	9	Londonderry
*Buchanan (20)	24	Tyrone
*Buckley (176)	184	Cork, Kerry, Dublin, Kilkenny, Tipperary
Buggy	12	Kilkenny, Queen's
Buick	7	Antrim
Bullman	5	Cork
Bunting	17	Antrim, Armagh
*Burchill (6)	7	Cork
Burgess	19	Dublin
*Burke (353)	357	Galway, Cork, Dublin, Mayo, Tipperary, Waterford

NAME	BIRTHS	PREDOMINANT COUNTIES
*Burnett (7)	8	
*Burns (215)	219	Antrim, Down, Armagh, Clare, Cork, Kerry, Tipperary
Burnside	8	Londonderry, Antrim
Burrell	5	Amagh
*Burrows (15)	19	Down
Burton	10	Dublin, Antrim
Bustard	7	Donegal
*Butler (168)	172	Dublin, Kilkenny, Tipperary, Waterford
Butterfield	7	Dublin, Kildare
Byers	7	Cavan
*Byrne (715)	734	Dublin, Wicklow, Wexford, Louth, Kildare, Kilkenny, Cork, Waterford, Donegal, Galway, Mayo, Roscommon
Byron	10	Dublin, Antrim
*Caddell (5)	6	
Cadden	5	
*Cadogan (6)	8	Cork
*Cafferky (19)	25	Mayo, Roscommon
Cafferty	6	Cavan
*Caffrey (32)	35	Dublin, Meath, Cavan
*Cahalane (13)	27	Cork, Kerry
Cahill	147	Cork, Kerry, Dublin, Kilkenny Tipperary
*Cain (23)	31	Mayo
*Cairns (43)	44	Antrim, Down, Armagh
Calderwood	12	Antrim
*Caldwell (40)	42	Antrim, Londonderry, Tyrone
*Callaghan (243)	250	Cork, Kerry, Dublin
Callan	33	Louth, Monaghan
*Callanan (18)	41	Galway, Cork
Callinan (13)		Clare
Calvert	15	Antrim, Armagh, Down
*Calvey (7)	9	Sligo
Cambridge	5	Cork, Antrim
Cameron	30	Antrim, Londonderry
Campbell	349	Antrim, Down, Armagh, Tyrone Londonderry, Donegal
Campion	13	Kilkenny, Queen's
*Canavan (22)	26	
*Canniff (5)	6	Cork
Canning	25	Londonderry
Cannon	49	Donegal, Leitrim, Mayo
Canny	8	Clare, Mayo
Cantwell	15	Tipperary, Dublin
Canty	23	Cork, Limerick
*Carberry (15)	26	Antrim
Cardiff	5	
Cardwell	9	Antrim
Carew	12	Tipperary
Carey	118	Cork, Dublin, Tipperary, Mayo, Kerry
Carleton	15	Antrim
*Carley (6)	8	Wexford
*Carlin (17)	20	Tyrone, Londonderry
*Carlisle (22)	24	Antrim, Down
Carmichael	19	Antrim
Carmody	33	Clare, Kerry, Limerick
*Carney (48)	49	Mayo
*Carolan (39)	47	Mayo, Cavan
Carpenter	10	Dublin
*Carr (85)	90	Donegal, Galway, Dublin
*Carrick (7)	12	
Carrigan	9	Fermanagh
*Carroll (374)	386	Dublin, Kilkenny, Cork, Tipperary, Limerick, Leinster, Munster, Connaught
*Carruthers (7)	11	
Carry	5	Louth
Carson	77	Antrim, Down, Tyrone
Carter	38	Dublin, Galway
Carthy	25	Wicklow, Waterford, Cork
Cartmill	5	Armagh
*Carton (27)	32	Dublin, Wexford, Londonderry

NAME	BIRTHS	PREDOMINANT COUNTIES
Carty	68	Roscommon, Wexford, Galway, Longford
*Carvill (8)	14	Armagh, Down
*Casey (252)	254	Cork, Kerry, Dublin, Limerick
Cash	12	Tipperary, Wexford
*Cashin (11)	21	
Cashman	16	Cork
Caskey	6	Antrim
*Cassells (16)	17	Armagh
Casserly	16	Roscommon
*Cassidy (140)	141	Donegal, Dublin, Antrim, Fermanagh
Cassin	5	
Cathcart	16	Antrim
Catherwood	9	Antrim
*Caughey (12)	13	Down, Antrim
*Caulfield (55)	59	Mayo, Antrim, Monaghan
Cawley	17	Mayo, Sligo
Chambers	69	Antrim, Mayo, Down, Armagh
Chandler	7	Dublin
Chapman	19	Dublin, Down, Antrim
*Charles (7)	8	
Charleton (7)	14	Tyrone, Antrim
Charlton (7)		
*Charters (8)	10	
Cherry	10	Down
Christian	12	
Christopher	6	Waterford, Leitrim
Christy (17)	33	Antrim
Christie (16)		
Church	7	
Claffey	7	
Clancy (95)	100	Clare, Leitrim, Galway, Tipperary
Clare	9	Dublin
*Clarke (327)	345	Antrim, Dublin, Mayo, Caven, Louth, Ulster
Clarkson	5	
Clay	5	
Clayton	12	
*Clear (11)	12	Queen's, Wexford
*Cleary (122)	127	Dublin, Tipperary, Clare, Limerick, Waterford
Clegg	12	Down, Antrim
*Cleland (9)	14	Down, Antrim
Clements	25	Antrim
Clenaghan	5	
*Clendinning (8)	10	Antrim
*Clerkin (11)	15	
*Clifford (82)	83	Kerry
Clinton	18	Dublin, Louth
*Cloherty (12)	13	Galway
*Clohessy (10)	12	Clare, Limerick
*Cloonan (7)	8	Galway
Close	16	Antrim
Clune	10	Clare
Clyde	7	Antrim, Londonderry
Clyne	11	Leitrim, Longford
*Coakley (31)	36	Cork
Colelough (4)		Leinster
*Coates (14)	15	Antrim
*Coburn (9)	10	Down, Armagh, Louth
*Cochrane (38)	42	Antrim, Londonderry, Down, Tyrone
Codd	10	Wexford
*Code (8)	10	
*Cody (23)	35	Kilkenny, Tipperary, Galway, Cork
Coady (12)		
*Coen (21)	27	Galway, Roscommon
Coey	6	Antrim, Down
*Coffey (90)	98	Kerry, Tipperary, Dublin, Cork, Roscommon
Cogan	14	Cork, Kildare
Colbert	11	Cork, Waterford
*Cole (36)	37	Dublin, Londonderry, Armagh, Down, King's

NAME	BIRTHS	PREDOMINANT COUNTIES
*Coleman (128)	138	Cork, Roscommon, Dublin, Waterford
*Colgan (31)	32	Dublin, King's, Antrim
*Colhous (20)	22	Londonderry, Tyrone
Coll	28	Donegal
Colleran	7	Mayo, Galway
Collier	7	Wexford
Colligan	5	
*Collins (350)	352	Cork, Limerick, Dublin, Galway Antrim, Kerry, Clare
Colvin	6	
Comber	5	Mayo
*Comerford (28)	30	Kilkenny, Dublin
*Commins (17)	20	Mayo, Waterford
*Commons (13)	14	Kilkenny, Galway, Mayo
Compton	5	Antrim
Conaghan	7	Donegal, Londonderry
*Conaty (12)	14	Cavan
*Conboy (11)	12	Roscommon, Sligo
*Concannon (17)	18	Galway, Mayo, Roscommon
*Condon (63)	64	Cork, Tipperary, Kerry
*Condron (19)	23	Carlow, Dublin, Kildare, King's
Condy	5	Tyrone, Fermanagh
*Conefry (6)	7	Leitrim
*Conlon (66)	107	Roscommon, Mayo, Sligo, Leinster, Ulster
Conlan (36)		
Conn	9	Down, Armagh
*Connaughton (9)	10	Galway, Roscommon
*Conneely (81)	92	Galway
*Connell (236)	242	Cork, Kerry, Limerick, Tipperary, Galway
*Connellan (6)	8	
Conney	5	
*Connolly (303)	381	Cork, Monaghan, Galway, Antrim, Dublin
Connelly (43)		Galway
*Connor (423)	432	Kerry, Dublin, Mayo, Cork, Roscommon, Galway, Antrim, Londonderry
*Connors (141)	142	Cork, Wexford, Tipperary
Conroy	78	Galway, Queen's, Dublin
*Conry (36)	52	Mayo, Roscommon
Considine	21	Clare, Limerick
*Convery (10)	11	Londonderry
Convey	5	Mayo, Down
Conway	169	Mayo, Tyrone, Dublin, Munster
Coogan	23	Dublin, Kilkenny, Monaghan
*Cooke (74)	89	Antrim, Dublin, Cork, Limerick, Galway, Sligo
*Cooley (8)	9	Antrim, Galway
Cooney	76	Mayo, Dublin
Cooper	36	Antrim, Dublin
Coote	6	Dublin
Copeland	17	Armagh, Antrim
Copley	5	Cork
*Corbett (54)	64	Cork, Tipperary, Galway
*Corcoran (127)	132	Mayo, Cork, Tipperary, Dublin, Kerry
Cordner	5	Armagh
Corish	5	
*Corkery (12)	15	Cork, Limerick, Kerry
Corkin	5	Down
*Corless (5)	6	Galway
Corley	6	
Cormack	18	Kilkenny, Tipperary
*Cormican (8)	10	Galway
Corr	55	Dublin, Tyrone
Corrigan	74	Dublin, Mayo, Fermanagh, Monaghan, Louth
*Corry (42)	44	Antrim, Clare
*Cosgrave (33)	34	Dublin, Wexford
Cosgrove	40	Mayo, Galway, Ulster
*Costello (80)	147	Mayo, Dublin, Galway
Costelloe (58)		Limerick, Galway, Clare
Costigan	8	Dublin, Kilkenny, Queen's
Cotter	64	Cork
*Cotton (8)	9	

NAME	BIRTHS	PREDOMINANT COUNTIES
*Coughlan (65)	125	Cork
Coghlan (49)		Cork, Dublin
*Coulter (44)	45	Antrim, Down, Fermanagh
Counihan	8	Kerry
*Cournane (8)	9	Kerry
Courtney (55)	59	Kerry, Antrim, Dublin
Cousins	18	
*Cowan (31)	33	Antrim, Down, Armagh
*Cowley (14)	15	Mayo
Cox	75	Roscommon, Dublin
Coy	5	
Coyle	90	Donegal, Cavan, Londonderry, Dublin, Tyrone, Longford
Coyne	54	Galway, Mayo
Craig	120	Antrim, Londonderry, Tyrone
*Crampsy (5)	9	Donegal
Crampton	7	
Crane	8	
Cranny	6	
Cranston	9	Armagh, Antrim
*Craven (9)	10	
Crawford	96	Antrim, Down, Londonderry, Tyrone
Crawley	19	Louth, Roscommon
Creagh	17	
*Crean (24)	27	Kerry, Cork, Wexford
Creaney	5	Armagh, Down
Creaton	8	
*Creed (7)	9	Cork
*Creedon (14)	15	Cork
*Cregan (20)	33	Limerick, Meath
Creegan (13)		Leitrim, Sligo
Cregg	13	Roscommon
*Crehan (15)	17	Galway
*Creigton (20)	23	Antrim, Dublin
*Cremin (20)	25	Cork, Kerry
*Crilly (18)	23	Antrim, Londonderry, Louth
*Croghan (6)	9	
Croke	12	Tipperary, Waterford
Cromie (20)	21	Armagh, Down
Crone	9	Cork, Antrim
*Cronin (168)	176	Cork, Kerry, Limerick
Crooks	15	Antrim, Londonderry
*Crosbie (15)	28	Dublin
Cross	19	Dublin, Cork, Armagh
*Crossan (15)	17	Londonderry
Crothers	17	Antrim, Down
Crotty	26	Clare, Waterford, Cork
*Crowe (62)	68	Antrim, Tipperary, Clare
*Crowley (149)	161	Cork
Crozier	22	Armagh
*Cruise (7)	8	Dublin
Cryan	15	Roscommon
Crymble	6	Antrim
*Cuddihy (5)	6	Kilkenny
Cuddy	8	
*Cuffe (12)	14	Mayo, Wexford
Culbert	8	Antrim
Culhane	16	Limerick
Cull	10	
*Cullen (196)	203	Dublin, Wexford
*Culleton (10)	12	Wexford
Culligan	5	Clare
*Cullinane (26)	40	Cork, Waterford
Cullinan (19)		Clare
Culloty	6	Kerry
*Cully	22	Armagh, Antrim
*Cumiskey (7)	11	Cavan, Longford, Westmeath
*Cummings (10)	20	Antrim
Cumming	77	Dublin, Cork, Tipperary
*Cunnane (16)	18	Mayo, Roscommon
*Cunniffe (11)	16	Galway, Mayo, Roscommon
*Cunningham (202)	215	Down, Antrim, Dublin, Galway, Roscommon, Cork
Cupples	7	Antrim, Armagh
*Curley (28)	36	Roscommon, Galway, Dublin
*Curran (161)	169	Donegal, Dublin, Waterford, Galway
Currane	19	Kerry
Currid	6	Sligo, Wexford
Currigan	9	Roscommon, Mayo
*Curry (60	75	Antrim
Currie (15)		
*Curtin (68)	69	Cork Limerick, Clare, Kerry
Curtis	23	Dublin
Cusack	46	Limerick, Cavan, Clare
*Cussen (6)	9	Cork, Limerick
Cuthbert	7	Dublin, Londonderry
Dagg	7	
Dahill	5	Tipperary
Dallas	6	Antrim
Dalton	75	Dublin, Waterford, Limerick, Kilkenny, Westmeath
*Daly (360)	381	Cork, Dublin, Kerry, Galway, King's
Dalzell	12	Down
Danaher	8	Limerick, Dublin
*Daniel (16)	17	Dublin, Tipperary, Waterford
*Darby (10)	11	
*Darcy (77)	86	Dublin, Tipperary
Dardis	6	
*Dargan (11)	13	Dublin
Darling	5	
Darmody	12	Tipperary
*Darragh (17)	18	Antrim
*Davern (5)	8	Tipperary
*Davey (18)	31	Sligo, Antrim
Davy (12)		
Davidson	58	Antrim, Down
*Davin (11)	12	Tipperary, Galway
*Davis (95)	104	Dublin, Antrim
*Davison (44)	45	Antrim
Davitt	8	
Dawson	55	Antrim
Day	13	
Dea	10	
Deacon	5	
Deady	8	Kerry
*Deane (35)	45	Mayo, Cork, Donegal
*Deasy (32)	35	Cork, Mayo
Dee	16	Waterford, Cork, Tipperary
*Deegan (26)	28	Dublin, King's, Queen's
Deehan	6	Londonderry
*Deely (7)	8	Galway
*Deeney (8)	15	Donegal, Londonderry
Deeny (7)		
Deering	6	Monaghan
Deery	14	Tyrone, Monaghan
*Deevy (7)	9	Kilkenny
Delahunt	6	Kildare
Delahunty	10	
*Delaney (93)	158	Dublin, Queen's, Tipperary, Kilkenny
Delany (65)		
*Dempsey (108)	117	Dublin, Antrim, Cork, Wexford, King's
*Dempster (12)	13	Antrim, Down
*Dennehy (30)	36	Cork, Kerry
*Dennis (7)	10	Dublin, Cork
Dennison	6	Armagh
Derby	6	Antrim
Dermody	9	
Dermott	6	Leitrim
Desmond	34	Cork
Devane	16	Kerry
*Devany (15)	44	Mayo, Galway, Leitrim
Devaney (11)		
Devenny (8)		
*Dever (8)	15	Mayo
Devers (6)		
Devereux	16	Wexford
Devery	5	King's, Dublin

NAME	BIRTHS	PREDOMINANT COUNTIES
*Devine (70)	81	Tyrone, Dublin, Roscommon
*Devitt (16)	17	Clare, Dublin
*Devlin (102)	112	Antrim, Tyrone, Dublin, Armagh, Londonderry
*Diamond (13)	16	Londonderry, Antrim
*Dick (12)	13	Antrim, Down
*Dickey (11)	13	Antrim
Digan	5	King's
Diggin (6)	8	Kerry
*Dignan (10)	11	Westmeath
Dillane	19	Limerick, Galway, Kerry
*Dillon (116)	117	Dublin, Limerick, Antrim, Galway
Dinan	14	Cork
*Dinneen (22)	42	Cork
Dineen (18)		
Dinsmore	6	Londonderry
*Dirrane (13)	14	Galway
*Diskin (10)	14	Galway
Diver	29	Donegal
*Dixon (51)	100	Dublin, Mayo
Dickson (49)		Down, Antrim
*Dobbin (17)	21	Antrim
Dobbs	6	
Dobson	14	
*Dockery (7)	9	Roscommon
Dockrell	5	Dublin
Dodds (18)	31	Down, Armagh
Dodd (12)		
*Doherty (414)	457	Donegal, Londonderry, Mayo
Dogherty (27)		Donegal
Dolan	142	Fermanagh, Roscommon, Cavan, Galway, Leitrim, Dublin
Dollard	5	
*Donaghy (40)	49	Antrim, Londonderry, Tyrone
Donald	6	Antrim
Donaldson	33	Antrim, Armagh
*Donegan (28)	31	
*Donnan (10)	11	Down
Donnell	18	Londonderry, Tyrone, Tipperary
*Donnellan (19)	76	Clare, Mayo
Donelan (16)		Galway
Donlan (13)		Galway
Donlon (14)		Longford
*Donnelly (228)	240	Antrim, Tyrone, Armagh, Dublin
*Donoghue (84)	97	Kerry, Cork
*Donohoe (137)	162	Dublin, Longford, Cavan, Galway
Donovan	211	Cork
Doody	27	Limerick, Cork, Waterford
*Doogan (32)	53	Donegal
Dougan (13)		Antrim, Armagh
Doohan	11	Donegal, Clare
*Doolan (35)	66	Dublin, Louth, Cork, Tipperary
Doolin (13)		
*Dooley (49)	60	Dublin, King's
Doonan	15	Leitrim, Roscommon
Dooney	5	Roscommon
Doran	97	Dublin, Wexford, Down, Armagh
Dore	12	Limerick
Dorgan	13	Cork
Dorman	14	Down
*Dornan (10)	11	Antrim, Down
Dorney	7	Cork, Tipperary
*Dorrian (5)	7	
*Douglas (47)	54	Antrim, Londonderry
*Dowd (64)	84	Roscommon, Dublin, Kerry, Galway
*Dowdall (17)	20	Dublin, Louth
Dowling	109	Dublin, Kilkenny, Queen's, Leinster
*Downes (35)	47	Clare, Limerick, Dublin
*Downey (90)	91	Cork, Kerry, Antrim, Galway, Limerick
Downing	15	Kerry, Cork

NAME	BIRTHS	PREDOMINANT COUNTIES
Doyle	514	Dublin, Wexford, Wicklow Carlow, Kerry, Cork
Drain	5	Antrim
Drake	6	Down, Monaghan
Draper	5	
*Drennan (19)	20	Antrim, Tipperary
Drew	12	Louth
*Driscoll (120)	121	Cork
Drohan	10	Waterford, Cork
Drought	5	
*Drum (12)	13	Fermanagh
Drummond	6	Antrim
*Drummy (6)	9	Cork, Sligo
*Drury (10)	11	Roscommon
Duddy	13	Londonderry
Dudgeon	6	
*Dudley (5)	6	
*Duff (41)	45	Antrim, Dublin, Louth
Duffin	17	Antrim, Waterford
*Duffy (282)	305	Mayo, Monaghan, Donegal, Dublin, Louth, Roscommon
*Dugan (18)	20	Antrim, Down, Londonderry
Duggan	89	Cork, Dublin, Tipperary, Waterford
Duhig	7	Cork, Kerry
*Duignan (21)	22	Leitrim, Roscommon
Duke	12	Armagh, Roscommon
Dullaghan	7	Louth
Dullard	6	Kilkenny, Queen's
Dullea	5	Cork
*Dunbar (17)	26	Wexford, Antrim, Down, Tyrone
*Duncan (35)	41	Antrim, Tyrone
Dundon	12	Clare, Limerick, Dublin
Dunlea	11	Cork
*Dunlcavy (27)	40	Mayo, Sligo
Dunlop	35	Antrim
*Dunne (313)	365	Dublin, Queen's, Kildare, King's, Kilkenny, Cork, Tipperary, Ulster, Cavan
Dunn (51)		Ulster, Antrim, Down, Londonderry, Tyrone
Dunphy	34	Waterford, Dublin
Dunwoody	11	Antrim
*Durkan (48)	62	Mayo, Sligo
*Durnin (6)	10	Louth
*Dwane (11)	22	Tipperary, Cork, Kerry
Duane (6)		Galway
*Dwyer (152)	155	Tipperary, Cork, Dublin, Limerick, Kerry, Kilkenny
Dyas	5	Dublin
*Dyer (14)	16	Roscommon, Sligo
*Eagar (4)	7	
Eager (3)		
*Eakins (6)	14	
Eakin (5)		
*Earl (5)	16	
Earle (5)		
*Early (37)	42	Leitrim
Eaton	8	Londonderry
Eccles	15	Tyrone, Antrim
Edgar	17	Antrim, Down
*Edmonds (5)	10	
Edwards	36	Dublin, Wexford, Antrim
*Egan (165)	171	Galway, Dublin, King's, Mayo, Roscommon, Munster
*Elder (14)	16	Antrim, Londonderry
*Elliott (71)	76	Fermanagh, Antrim, Donegal, Dublin
Ellis	38	Dublin, Antrim
Ellison	13	Antrim, Down
*Elwood (10)	11	Mayo
Emerson	18	Down, Antrim
England	5	
English	53	Tipperary, Antrim, Dublin

NAME	BIRTHS	PREDOMINANT COUNTIES
Ennis	44	Dublin, Kildare
Enright	49	Limerick, Kerry, Cork, Clare
Erskine	12	Antrim
*Ervine (14)	19	Antrim, Down
*Erwin (18)	19	Antrim
Esler	8	Antrim
Eustace	9	Dublin
Evans	55	Dublin, Londonderry, Antrim
*Evers (5)	9	Longford, Dublin
Ewart	14	Antrim
*Ewing (21)	24	Londonderry, Tyrone, Antrim
*Fagan (47)	48	Leinster, Dublin
Faherty	26	Galway
*Fahy (72)	119	Galway, Tipperary, Mayo
Fahey (47)		
Fair	6	
*Fallon (68)	70	Roscommon, Galway
*Falloon (9)	12	Armagh
Falvey	17	Cork, Clare, Kerry
*Fanning (22)	45	Wexford, Tipperary, Waterford
Fannin (13)		
Farley	7	
Farmer	6	
Farnan	10	
Farr	5	Antrim
*Farragher (7)	9	Mayo, Galway
*Farrar (6)	7	Wicklow
*Farrell (302)	311	Dublin, Longford, Louth, Meath, Westmeath, Roscommon
Farrelly	69	Cavan, Meath, Dublin
*Farren (12)	13	Donegal, Londonderry
Farrington	5	
Farry	5	
Faughnan	8	Leitrim
*Faulkner (18)	35	Antrim
Fay	27	Dublin
Fearon	21	Armagh, Down, Louth
*Fee (22)	23	Antrim, Cavan, Fermanagh
*Feehan (14)	17	Louth
*Feely (28)	41	Donegal, Roscommon
*Feeney (46)	73	Sligo, Mayo, Galway
Feeny (26)		Galway, Roscommon
Feerick	13	Mayo, Galway
Fegan	26	Armagh, Dublin, Louth
*Fehily (6)	11	
*Fenlon (18)	28	Carlow, Dublin, Wexford
*Fennell (28)	29	Clare, Dublin
*Fennelly (14)	15	Kilkenny
Fennessy	8	Waterford
Fenton	19	Kerry, Antrim
Fergus	8	Mayo
*Ferguson (130)	133	Antrim, Down, Londonderry
*Ferris (32)	33	Antrim
*Ferry (26)	27	Donegal
Fetherston	6	Dublin, Roscommon
*Field (18)	29	Dublin, Cork
*Finan (9)	18	Roscommon, Sligo
*Finegan (52)	115	Monaghan, Galway, Louth
Finnegan (39)		Armagh, Cavan
*Finlay (69)	76	Antrim, Down
*Finn (110)	111	Cork, Mayo, Dublin, Roscommon
Finneran	9	Galway
*Finnerty (14)	28	Galway
Finerty (10)		
*Finney (7)	8	
Finucane	10	
Fisher	29	Antrim, Wicklow
*Fitzgerald (327)	330	Munster, Cork, Limerick, Kerry, Dublin
*Fitzgibbon (31)	34	Limerick
Fitzmaurice	21	Kerry
Fitzpatrick	249	Dublin, Queen's Cork, Tipperary, Cavan, Antrim, Down, Mayo, Galway

NAME	BIRTHS	PREDOMINANT COUNTIES
*Fitzsimons (70)	80	Dublin, Down, Cavan
Flack	8	
*Flahavan (6)	12	Cork, Waterford
Flaherty	88	Galway, Kerry
*Flanagan (173)	219	Roscommon, Dublin, Mayo, Clare, Galway, Fermanagh, Cavan, Monaghan
*Flannery (59)	64	Mayo, Tipperary, Galway, Clare
Flattery	6	King's
*Flattley (6)	11	Mayo
Flavell	5	
*Fleming (157)	170	Antrim, Dublin, Galway, Londonderry, Cork, Mayo
Fletcher	22	Antrim, Dublin
Flood	64	Dublin
*Flynn (304)	319	Cork, Dublin, Waterford, Roscommon, Leitrim, Cavan
*Fogarty (57)	61	Tipperary, Dublin
*Folan (26)	28	Galway, Mayo
*Foley (249)	250	Kerry, Cork, Waterford, Dublin
Folliard	5	Mayo, Roscommon
*Foran (18)	26	Dublin, Limerick, Waterford
*Forbes (20)	22	Antrim, Tyrone
*Forde (114)	154	Galway, Cork, Mayo, Dublin
Ford (39)		
Foreman	5	
*Forkin (7)	11	Mayo
*Forrest (8)	9	Cork
*Forsythe (29)	33	Antrim, Down
Fortune	22	Wexford
*Foster (51)	57	Antrim, Dublin
Fowler	17	
*Fox (124)	125	Dublin, Longford, Tyrone, Leitrim.
Foy	38	Mayo, Cavan, Dublin
Fraher	5	Waterford, Limerick
*Frain (16)	20	Mayo, Roscommon
*Francy (8)	10	Antrim
Francis	13	
Franklin	12	Limerick, Tipperary
*Frawley (19)	20	Clare, Limerick
*Frazer (27)	41	Dublin, Antrim, Down
Fraser (14)		
*Freeburn (7)	9	Antrim
Freeman	20	
*French (23)	24	Antrim
*Friel (40)	43	Donegal, Tyrone, Londonderry
*Frizell (6)		
Frost	7	
Fry	9	Dublin
*Fulham (5)	8	Dublin, King's
Fuller	6	Cork
Fullerton	25	Antrim, Down
Fulton	32	Antrim
Furlong	36	Wexford
Fury (10)	17	Galway
Furey (7)		
Gabbey	5	Down, Antrim
*Gaffey (9)	10	Roscommon, Galway
Gaffney	68	Cavan, Dublin, Roscommon
Gahan	11	Wexford
Galbraith	15	Antrim
*Gallagher (471)	488	Donegal, Mayo, Tyrone, Sligo, Londonderry, Dublin, Ulster
*Gallen (10)	13	Donegal, Tyrone
*Galligan (25)	26	Cavan
*Gallivan (31)	32	Kerry
Galloway	9	Antrim
*Galvin (60)	62	Cork, Clare, Kerry, Roscommon
*Galway (12)	13	Antrim
*Gamble (38)	40	Antrim, Down, Londonderry
*Ganley (7)	11	
*Gannon (71)	73	Mayo, Dublin, Leitrim

NAME	BIRTHS	PREDOMINANT COUNTIES
Gara	20	Donegal, Roscommon, Mayo, Down
*Gardiner (25)	26	Antrim, Dublin
Gardner	23	Antrim
Gargan	7	
*Garland (13)	24	Dublin, Monaghan
Garrett	24	Down, Antrim, Dublin
Garry	14	
*Garvey (60)	64	Kerry, Mayo, Galway, Louth
Garvin	5	
Gaskin	5	Dublin
Gaston	13	Antrim
*Gately (10)	11	Roscommon
*Gaughan (25)	26	Mayo, Sligo
Gaughran	5	Meath, Louth
Gaul (6)	11	Wexford, Waterford, Kilkenny
Gaule (5)		Kildare
Gault	16	Antrim
*Gavaghan (13)	23	Mayo, Sligo
*Gavin (44)	66	Mary, Glaway
Gavan (19)		
Gaw	6	Down, Antrim
Gawley	6	Sligo
*Gaynard (5)	6	Mayo
*Gaynor (21)	22	Dublin, Westmeath, Cavan
*Geaney (8)	15	Cork
Geany (7)		
*Geary (24)	26	Cork
Geddis	13	Antrim, Down
Geeland	6	
*Geoghegan (33)	38	Dublin, Galway
George	12	
*Geraghty (54)	72	Galway, Mayo, Dublin
Getty	8	Antrim, Londonderry
*Gibb (5)	8	
*Gibbons (76)	78	Mayo, Galway
*Giblin (29)	30	Roscommon, Mayo
Gibney	26	Cavan, Dublin
Gibson	96	Down, Antrim
*Giffen (8)	10	Antrim
Gilbert	16	Dublin, Antrim
*Gilchrist (12)	18	
*Gildea (13)	18	Donegal, Mayo
Giles	6	
*Gilgan (8)	13	Sligo
*Gilhooly (8)	9	Leitrim
Gill	62	Dulbin, Galway, Mayo, Longford
*Gillan (18)	40	Antrim, Sligo
Gillen (16)		Antrim, Donegal, Tyrone
*Gilleece (6)	14	
*Gillespie (84)	86	Antrim, Donegal, Armagh, Tyrone
Gillick	9	Cavan
Gilligan	32	Dublin
Gilliland	11	Antrim
Gilmartin	24	Sligo, Leitrim
*Gilmore (54)	79	Antrim
Gilmour (18)		
Gilpin	9	Armagh, Cavan
Gilroy	16	Leitrim, Mayo
*Gilsenan (6)	12	
Ginn	6	
*Ginty (16)	19	Mayo
*Girvin (8)	15	Antrim
Girvan (6)		
Glancy	5	
Glasgow	7	Tyrone, Antrim, Armagh
Glass	17	Antrim, Londonderry
Glavin	7	Cork, Kerry
*Gleeson (81)	82	Tipperary, Limerick, Dublin, Kilkenny, Cork.
Glenn	12	Antrim, Londonderry
*Glennon (22)	28	
Glover	20	Antrim
*Glynn (66)	72	Galway, Mayo, Dublin, Clare
*Godfrey (17)	18	Mayo, Tipperary, Kerry
*Godkin (6)	7	Wexford

NAME	BIRTHS	PREDOMINANT COUNTIES
Gogarty	7	Meath, Louth
*Goggin (26)	34	Cork, Kerry
*Golden (22)	24	Mayo, Sligo, Kerry, Cork
*Good (16)	19	Cork
Goodbody	5	
Goodman	9	Armagh, Monaghan
*Goodwin (24)	26	Dublin, Monaghan
Goold	6	Cork
*Gordon (118)	122	Antrim, Down, Dublin, Antrim
*Gorham (11)	12	Galway
Gorman	140	Antrim, Dublin, Tipperary, Leinster, Munster
*Gormley (31)	44	Antrim, Tyrone
*Gough (17)	30	Dublin, Waterford
Goff (13)		
*Gould (10)	12	
*Goulding (15)	27	Dublin, Cork
Golding (9)		Galway
*Gourley (20)	23	Antrim
Gowen	5	Cork
Grace	36	Dublin, Kilkenny
Gracey	9	Down, Armagh
Grady	68	Mayo, Clare, Kerry, Roscommon
*Graham (195)	204	Antrim, Down, Dublin, Tyrone, Armagh, Monaghan
*Grainger (9)	11	
Grange	6	Dublin, Antrim
Grant	77	Antrim, Donegal
*Grattan (3)	5	
*Graves (5)	6	
*Gray (97)	117	Antrim, Down, Londonderry, Dublin
*Graydon (6)	7	
Gready	22	Tipperary
*Grealish (6)	7	Galway
*Greally (9)	15	Galway, Mayo
*Greany (19)	30	Kerry, Galway
Greehy	5	Waterford, Cork
*Green (105)	152	Dublin, Antrim, Galway,
Greene (47)		Tipperary, Clare
Greenan	8	Cavan
Greenaway	7	Down, Antrim
Greer	63	Antrim, Armagh, Down
Gregan	5	
Gregg	29	Antrim, Down
Gregory	14	
*Grehan (22)	23	Mayo, Galway, Sligo, Westmeath
*Grennan (18)	19	Mayo, Dublin
*Gribben (18)	28	Antrim, Armagh, Down
*Griffin (206)	216	Kerry, Clare, Cork, Limerick, Galway, Mayo, Dublin
*Griffith (16)	22	
Grimason	5	Armagh
Grimes	39	Tyrone, Mayo
Grimley	7	Armagh
*Groarke (7)	9	Mayo
*Grogan (39)	44	Dublin, Tipeprary, Mayo, Clare
Groves	8	Kerry, Antrim
*Gubbins (5)	7	Limerick
*Guerin (11)	12	Limerick
*Guihen (7)	10	Roscommon
Guilfoyle	11	Dublin
*Guinan (13)	21	Kins's
Guinane (7)		Tipperary
*Guiney (16)	17	Cork
Guiry	8	Limerick
Gunn	9	
Gunning	12	Antrim
Gurry	5	
*Guthrie (9)	11	Clare
Guy	11	Armagh, Londonderry

NAME	BIRTHS	PREDOMINANT COUNTIES
*Hackett (30)	34	Tyrone, Dublin, Kilkenny
*Haddock (10)	12	Armagh
*Haddon (8)	14	
Hadden (6)		
*Hagan (49)	63	Antrim, Tyrone, Armagh
*Hale (8)	13	Cork, Antrim
*Halfpenny (8)	12	Louth
Hall	120	Antrim, Dublin, Armagh
*Hallahan (4)	8	Cork
*Halliday (18)	19	Antrim
Halligan	27	Roscommon, Dublin, Louth, Armagh, Mayo
*Hailinan (9)	10	Clare
*Hallissy (6)	12	Cork, Kerry
*Halloran (65)	67	Clare, Galway, Cork
Hally	13	Tipperary
Halpin	33	Dublin, Clare
Halton	9	Meath
*Hamill (68)	77	Antrim, Armagh, Louth
*Hamilton (166)	167	Antrim, Down, Tyrone, Londonderry
Hammond	13	Donegal
Hampton	5	
Hand	28	Dublin
*Hanifin (6)	17	Kerry
Hanafin (5)		
*Hanlon (93)	95	Dulbin, Kerry, Louth, Wexford
*Hanly (60)	95	Roscommon, Glaway, Limerick Tipperary
Hanley (35)		Cork
*Hanna (81)	86	Antrim, Down, Armagh
*Hannigan (25)	30	Dublin, Waterford, Tyrone
*Hannon (44)	92	Galway, Roscommon, Limerick
Hannan (32)		Cork, Sligo
Hanrahan	54	Clare, Limerick
Hanratty	30	Louth, Armagh, Monaghan, Dublin
Hanvey	5	
Hara	5	Galway
*Haran (16)	37	Mayo
Haren (11)		Clare
Harbison	11	Antrim
Hardiman	7	Galway
Harding	17	Dublin, Tipperary
Hardy	19	Louth, Dublin, Tyrone
*Hare (11)	22	Antrim
Haire (10)		
*Harford (16)	17	Dublin
*Hargadon (8)	11	Sligo, Leitrim, Roscommon
*Hargan (5)	6	
*Harkin (53)	56	Donegal, Londonderry
Harkness	13	Antrim
Harley	7	
*Harmon (7)	12	Wicklow
Harnett	15	Limerick, Kerry
Harney	11	Tipperary, Galway
*Harold (9)	15	Cork
Harrold (6)		Limerick
*Harper (32)	51	Antrim
Harpur (18)		Wexford
*Harrell (4)	5	
Harrington	119	Cork, Kerry, Mayo
*Harris (58)	59	Dublin, Cork, Antrim
*Harrison (44)	48	Antrim, Dublin, Down
*Hart (64)	122	Antrim, Dublin, Cork
Harte (58)		Sligo, Leitrim, Roscommon
Hartigan	16	Limerick
Hartin (5)	10	Antrim, Longford
*Hartnett (24)	27	Limerick, Cork
Hartney	8	Limerick, Clare
Harty	17	Tipperary, Cork, Kerry
*Harvey (53)	54	Antrim, Dublin, Down, Donegal
Haslam	6	Dublin
Hassard	7	
Hassett	11	Clare, Tipperary
Hastings	22	Mayo, Clare

NAME	BIRTHS	PREDOMINANT COUNTIES
Hatton	7	
*Haugh (20)	27	Clare
Hough (7)		Tipperary, Limerick
Haughey	14	Armagh, Donegal
Haughton	9	
*Hawe (7)	10	
Hawes	5	
*Hawkes (6)	7	Cork
Hawkins	18	Antrim, Galway, Cork
*Hawthorne (15)	27	Antrim, Down, Armagh
*Hay	6	
*Hayden (43)	45	Dublin, Carlow, Tipperary
*Hayes (271)	275	Cork, Limerick, Tipperary, Dublin, Wexford, Antrim, Galway
*Hazlett (10)	19	Antrim, Londonderry
Haslett (9)		
*Healy (272)	291	Cork, Kerry, Dublin, Galway, Roscommon, Mayo
*Heaney (39)	56	Antrim, Armagh, Louth
Heanue	14	Galway, Donegal
Heaphy	8	Cork
*Hearne (6)	11	Waterford
Hearn (5)		
Hearty	8	Louth, Monaghan
*Heavey (6)	12	
Heavy (5)		
*Helan (6)	7	Waterford
Heenan	6	Tipperary
Heffernan	53	Tipperary
*Heffron (7)	20	Mayo
Hegan	5	Armagh
*Hegarty (96)	100	Cork, Donegal, Clare, Londonderry, Mayo
*Hehir (24)	28	Clare, Limericks
Hemphill	7	Londonderry, Tyrone
Henderson	72	Antrim, Tyrone
Hendrick	12	Dublin
*Henehan (14)	49	Mayo
Heneghan (11)		
*Henneberry (7)	13	Waterford, Tipperary
*Hennessy (95)	111	Cork, Limerick, Tipperary, Dublin
*Henry (124)	132	Antrim, Sligo, Tyrone
*Heraghty (12)	16	Mayo, Donegal
Herbert	25	Dublin, Limerick
Herdman	6	Antrim
*Herlihy (38)	42	Cork, Kerry
*Hernon (6)	8	Glaway
*Herron (23)	45	Antrim, Donegal Down
Heron (22)		
Heslin	8	Leitrim
*Hession (17)	21	Galway, Mayo
Hester	8	Mayo, Roscommon
*Hetherington (7)	8	Tyrone
*Hewitt (36)	40	Antrim, Armagh
*Hickey (132)	139	Cork, Tipperary, Dublin, Limerick, Clare
Hicks	10	
*Higgins (203)	205	Mayo, Galway, Dublin, Roscommon, Cork, Antrim
Higginson	8	Antrim
Hill	118	Antrim, Dublin, Down
*Hilland (6)	7	Antrim, Down
Hilliard	11	Dublin
*Hillis (10)	12	Antrim
Hilton	6	
*Hinchy (7)	14	
*Hinds (14)	20	Down, Roscommon
Hynds (6)		
*Hoare (18)	30	Kerry, Cork, Dublin
Hoban	22	Mayo, Killkenny
Hobbs	5	
Hobson	11	Antrim
*Hodges (6)	12	
Hodge (6)		

NAME	BIRTHS	PREDOMINANT COUNTIES
*Hodgins (11)	19	Tipperary
Hodgen (5)		Down
Hodnett	5	Cork, Tipperary
Hoey	33	Louth, Dublin
Hogan	193	Tipperary, Dublin, Limerick, Clare, Cork
*Hogg (17)	18	Antrim, Londonderry
Holden	20	Dublin, Waterford, Antrim
Holland	52	Cork, Galway, Dublin
*Holleran (6)	9	Glaway, Mayo
Holly	8	Londonderry, Cork
Hollywood	9	Louth
Holman	5	
*Holmes (81)	84	Antrim, Dublin
Holt	8	
Homan	5	
Hood	9	Antrim
Hope	6	
Hopkins	44	Mayo, Dublin
Hopper	8	Tyrone
Horan	63	Mayo, Kerry, Tipperary, Roscommon
Horgan	66	Cork, Kerry
*Horne (4)	6	
Horner	6	Antrim
Hornibrook	5	Cork
Horrigan	7	Cork
Hosford	10	Cork
Hosty	6	Mayo, Galway
*Houlihan (38)	71	Kerry, Limerick, Cork, Clare
Holohan (11)		Kilkenny
*Hourigan (17)	22	Limerick, Tipperary
*Hourihane (9)	16	Cork
*Houston (49)	76	Antrim, Londonderry, Armagh
Huston (19)		Down
Howard	61	Dublin, Cork, Clare, Limerick
Howe	16	
Howell	8	Cork
Howlett	5	Wexford, Dublin
Howley	14	Clare, Mayo, Sligo
*Howlin (5)	6	Wexford
Hoy	15	Antrim, Down
*Hoyne (5)	6	Kilkenny
Hudson	23	Dublin
Huggard	8	
*Hughes (328)	334	Armagh, Antrim, Dublin, Tyrone, Monaghan, Galway, Mayo
Hughey	6	Tyrone
Hull	10	Antrim, Armagh
*Hume (8)	10	Antrim
*Humphries (15)	32	Armagh, Dublin
Hunt	76	Mayo, Roscommon, Dublin, Waterford
Hunter	95	Antrim, Londonderry, Dcwn
*Hurley (129)	134	Cork, Waterford, Dublin, Galway
Hurson	5	Longford, Tyrone
Hurst	10	
*Hussey (21)	26	Kerry, Galway, Roscommon
*Hutchinson (44)	64	Londonderry, Antrim, Down,
Hutchison (15)		Dublin
Hutton	15	Antrim, Londonderry
*Hyde (11)	15	Cork, Antrim
Hyland	55	Mayo, Dublin, Queen's
Hyndman	14	Antrim, Londonderry
*Hynes (81)	83	Galway, Clare, Mayo, Dublin
*Igoe (6)	10	Longford, Mayo, Roscommon
*Ingram (12)	13	Antrim
Ireland	21	Antrim, Armagh
*Irvine (66)	68	Antrim, Fermanagh

NAME	BIRTHS	PREDOMINANT COUNTIES
Irwin	118	Armagh, Antrim, Tyrone, Londonderry
*Ivers (8)	11	Dublin, Louth
*Ivory (8)	9	Dublin
Jack	8	
*Jackson (100)	101	Antrim, Armagh, Dublin, Munster, Cork, Connaught, Mayo
*Jacob (9)	11	Dublin
(Jagoe (4)	6	Cork
James	12	
*Jamison (24)	52	Antrim, Down
Jameson (20)		Dublin
Jamieson (7)		Antrim, Down
*Jeffers (12)	16	
*Jenkins (25)	29	Antrim, Dublin
Jenkinson	7	Dublin
*Jennings (61)	63	Mayo, Galway, Cork, Armagh
Jess	7	Down
Johnson	58	Cork, Dublin, Antrim
*Johnston (320)	341	Antrim, Down, Armagh, Fermanagh, Dublin
Johnstone (21)		Cavan, Londonderry
Jolly	5	Dublin
Jones	152	Dublin, Cork, Antrim, Armagh
*Jordan (91)	98	Dublin, Mayo, Antrim, Galway
*Joy (14)	15	Waterford
Joyce	164	Galway, Mayo
Judge	30	Mayo, Dublin, Tyrone
*Kane (175)	190	Antrim, Londonderry, Dublin
*Kavanagh (230)	274	Dublin, Wexford, Wicklow
Keady	16	Galway
*Keane (185)	202	Galway, Clare, Kerry, Mayo
*Keany (18)	33	Leitrim, Galway, Donegal
*Kearney (137)	147	Dublin, Cork, Antrim
*Kearns (71)	87	Dublin, Mayo
Kearon	7	Wicklow
*Keating (121)	130	Cork, Kerry, Tipperary, Dublin
*Keaveny (15)	33	Galway, Sligo
Kee	6	
*Keeffe (93)	110	Cork, Waterford, Kerry, Kilkenny
*Keegan (93)	95	Dublin, Roscommon, Wicklow, Leitrim
Keena	7	
Keenan	103	Antrim, Monaghan, Dublin, Down
Keith	7	Antrim, Down
Kell	6	Antrim
*Kelleher (92)	148	Cork, Kerry
Kelliher (24)		
*Kellett (7)	8	Cavan, Dublin
Kells	10	
*Kelly (1,238)	1242	Dublin, Galway, Mayo, Roscommon, Cork
Kelso	7	Antrim
Kemp	6	
Kempton	5	Antrim
Kenna	21	Dublin, Tipperary
*Kenneally (10)	36	Cork, Waterford, Tipperary
Kennelly (9)		
*Kennedy (436)	446	Tipperary, Dublin, Antrim
*Kenny (211)	216	Dublin, Galway, Roscommon
Kenrick	5	
Kent	13	Cork
*Keogh (96)	163	Dublin
Kehoe (51)		Wexford
*Keohane (21)	25	Cork
*Keon (8)	18	Down, Donegal, Fermanagh
Keown (8)		
*Kerin (15)	17	Kerry, Clare

NAME	BIRTHS	PREDOMINANT COUNTIES
Kerley	8	Louth
*Kernaghan (11)	26	Armagh
Kernohan (8)		Antrim
Kerr	142	Antrim, Down, Tyrone, Ulster
Kerrane	7	Mayo, Galway
*Kerrigan (37)	41	Mayo, Donegal
Kerrisk	5	Kerry
Kerwick	5	Kilkenny
*Kevane (13)	19	Kerry
*Keys (22)	32	Fermanagh, Antrim
Keyes (10)		Tipperary, Wexford
Kidd	28	Antrim, Armagh, Dublin
Kidney	7	Cork
*Kielty (6)	9	Galway, Roscommon
*Kiely (36)	110	Cork, Limerick, Waterford
Keely (27)		Dublin, Wicklow, Galway
Kealy (18)		Kilkenny
Keily (10)		Cork, Limerick, Waterford
Keeley (9)		Dublin, Wicklow, Galway
*Kiernan (56)	70	Longford, Cavan, Dublin, Leitrim
Kilbane	8	Mayo
Kilbride	7	
Kilcoyne	15	Mayo, Sligo
Kilcullen	6	Sligo
Kilduff	5	
Kilgallon	8	Mayo
Kilgannon	8	Galway, Sligo
*Kilkelly (6)	7	Galway, Roscommon
Kilkenny	18	Leitrim, Mayo, Roscommon
Kileen	40	Clare, Mayo, King's
*Killelea (6)	10	Galway, Roscommon
Killen	14	Antrim
*Killian (13)	18	Roscommon, Westmeath
Killoran	7	Roscommon, Sligo
Kilmartin	22	Roscommon
Kilpatrick	24	Antrim
Kilroy	15	Mayo, Roscommon, Sligo
*Kinahan (7)	15	Dublin, Louth
*Kinane (9)	18	Tipperary
Kinnane (5)		
King	203	Galway, Dublin, Antrim, Mayo, Limerick
Kinghan	5	Down, Mayo
Kingston	40	Cork, Dublin
Kinnear	5	
*Kinsella (75)	81	Dublin, Wesford, Wicklow, Kildare
Kirby	33	Mayo, Kerry, Limerick
*Kirk (28)	38	Antrim, Louth
Kirkland	6	
Kirkpatrick	25	Antrim
Kirkwood	8	Antrim, Limerick
*Kirrane (6)	8	Mayo
*Kirwan (42)	59	Dublin, Wexford, Tipperary
Kissane	19	Kerry
*Kitterick (5)	6	Mayo
Knight	13	
Knowles	13	Dublin, Antrim
Knox	45	Antrim
Kyle	26	Antrim, Londonderry
Kyne	27	Galway, Mayo
*Lacey (21)	50	Wexford, Dublin, Galway
Lacy (19)		
Leacy (8)		
Laffan	8	Limerick, Tipperary, Wexford
Lafferty	17	Donegal, Londonderry, Tyrone
*Laffey (5)	7	Galway, Mayo
Lagan	8	Londonderry
*Lahey (4)	7	
Lahiff	8	Dublin, Clare
Laird	17	Antrim
*Lally (33)	34	Mayo, Galway
*Lamb (37)	50	Dublin
Lambe (13)		
Lambert	22	Wexford, Dublin
*Lamont (16)	18	Antrim
*Landers (18)	19	Waterford, Kerry
Landy	9	Tipperary, Galway
Lane	69	Cork, Limerick
Lang	15	Cavan
Langan	19	Mayo
Langton	6	
*Lanigan (18)	21	Kilkenny
*Lannon (7)	11	Kilkenny
Lappin	26	Armagh, Tyrone, Antrim
Larkin	85	Dublin, Armagh, Galway, Tipper
*Larmour (15)	17	Antrim, Down
Latimer	8	Dublin
*Lavelle (33)	38	Mayo, Galway
Laverty	26	Antrim
Lavery	51	Armagh, Antrim, Down
*Lavin (28)	42	Mayo, Roscommon
Lavan (14)		
*Law (18)	19	Antrim
*Lawder (3)	6	
Lauder (3)		
Lawless	42	Dublin, Galway
*Lawlor (59)	142	Dublin, Queen's, Wicklow Wexford
Lalor (42)		
Lawler (41)		
*Lawn (6)	7	Donegal, Tyrone
*Lawrence (12)	19	Dublin, Tipperary
Laurence (7)		
Lawson	15	Dublin, Armagh, Down
Lawton	10	Cork
*Leahy (99)	105	Cork, Kerry, Limerick, Tipperary
*Leane (9)	11	Kerry, Limerick
*Leary (185)	186	Cork, Kerry, Ewxford
*Leathem (8)	11	Armagh
*Leavy (22)	31	Longford, Westmeath
*Leckey (6)	10	
Leddy	15	Cavan
*Ledwith (5)	10	Dublin
*Lee (118)	120	Antrim, Dublin, Galway, Limerick
Leeson	6	Dublin
*Leech (28)	35	Dublin
Leeson	6	
*Legge (6)	8	
*Lehane (23)	30	Cork, Kerry
Leigh	8	
*Lemon (13)	15	Antrim
*Lennon (102)	103	Dublin, Armagh
Lennox	18	Antrim, Londonderry
Leo	5	Limerick
Leonard	99	Dublin, Sligo, Cork
Leslie	15	Londonderry
Lester	5	
L'Estrange	8	
*Levins (6)	7	
Lewis	51	Dublin, Antrim, Cork, Tipperary
*Leyden (10)	11	Sligo, Clare
*Liddane (6)	7	Clare
*Liddy (8)	9	Clare, Antrim
Liggett	6	Armagh, Antrim
Lightbody	6	Down
Lillis	5	
*Lilly (8)	14	Antrim, Down
Lilley (6)		
*Linane (10)	15	Limerick, Kerry, Calre
Linnane (5)		
*Lindsay (36)	38	Antrim
*Linehan (50)	104	Cork
Lenaghan (18)		Antrim
Lenihan (14)		Limerick
Linton	13	Antrim

NAME	BIRTHS	PREDOMINANT COUNTIES
*Lipsett (6)	7	
Liston	12	Limerick
*Little (43)	59	Antrim, Dublin, Fermanagh
*Livingston (19)	43	Armagh, Antrim, Down
Livingstone (14)		
Levingston (10)		
*Lloyd (19)	20	Tipperary
*Locke (5)	8	
Lockhart	21	Armagh, Antrim
Loftus	34	Mayo
Logan	55	Antrim
Logue	31	Londonderry, Donegal
*Lohan (12)	14	Galway
Lombard	6	Cork
*Lonergan (49)	56	Tipperary, Waterford, Kilkenny, Cork
Londrigan (5)		
Long	91	Cork, Dublin, Limerick, Kerry, Donegal
*Looby (11)	16	Tipperary
Luby (5)		
*Looney (22)	23	Cork, Clare
Lord	5	
*Lordan (12)	13	Cork
*Lorimer (7)	8	Antrim
*Lougheed (5)	7	
*Loughlin (39)	57	Leitrim, Dublin, Kilkenny
Laughlin (14)		Tyrone, Antrim
*Loughman (9)	10	
*Loughnane (10)	13	
Loughran (37)	41	Tyrone, Antrim, Armagh
*Loughrey (12)	13	
Love	22	Londonderry
Lovett	9	Kerry
*Lowe (18)	21	Dublin
Lowney	6	Cork
*Lowry (53)	71	Dublin, Antrim, Down
Loy	5	
Lucas	22	Tyrone, Cavan
*Lucey (29)	42	Cork, Kerry
Luke	9	Antrim
Lundy	12	
Lunn	9	Armagh
*Lunney (11)	24	Fermanagh
Lunny (9)		
*Lydon (49)	57	Galway, Mayo
Lyle	5	Antrim
Lynagh	6	
Lynam	22	Dublin, King's
*Lynas (10)	23	Antrim, Down
Lyness (9)		
Lynch	444	Cork, Cavan, Dublin, Kerry, Limerick, Clare, Meath, Londonderry
Lyne	17	Kerry
Lynn	24	Antrim
*Lynskey (9)	11	Galway, Mayo
Lyons	210	Mayo, Cork, Galway, Dublin, Kerry, Limerick, Leinster
*Lysaght (12)	13	Limerick
Mack	20	Limerick, Tipperary, Antrim
Macken (29)	38	Mayo, Louth, Dublin
Mackin (9)		Monaghan
*Mackey (33)	38	Dublin, Cork, Tipperary, Antrim
Mackie	8	Armagh
*Madden (106)	107	Galway, Cork, Dublin, Antrim
*Maddock (7)	10	Wexford
*Madigan (26)	27	Limerick, Clare
Madill	5	
*Magauran (9)	10	Cavan
Magee (138)	193	Antrim, Armagh, Down
McGee (55)		Donegal, Tyrone
*Magill (65)	84	Antrim, Armagh, Down
McGill (19)		Donegal, Tyrone
*Magner (12)	17	Cork, Limerick
*Magrane (12)	22	Dublin
McGrane (8)		
Maguire (248)	322	Fermanagh, Dublin, Cavan, Donegal
McGuire (74)		Roscommon, Mayo
Maher (176)	203	Tipperary, Dublin, Kilkenny
Meagher (27)		
*Mahon (85)	87	Dublin, Galway
*Mahony (243)	276	Cork, Kerry, Limerick
Mahood	8	Antrim, Down
Mailey	6	Antrim
*Mairs (8)	12	Antrim
Maitland	7	
Major	12	Antrim, Down
Malcolm	10	Antrim
*Malcomson (11)	14	Armagh
Malcolmson (3)		
*Malley (65)	85	Mayo, Galway
*Mallon (44)	48	Armagh, Antrim, Tyrone
Malone	100	Dublin, Wexford, Clare
Malseed	5	Donegal, Londonderry
*Mangan (50)	52	Dublin, Limerick, Kerry, Mayo
*Manley (15)	21	Cork, Wicklow
Mann	19	Antrim
Manning	54	Cork, Dublin
*Mannion (73)	91	Galway, Roscommon
Mannix	6	Cork, Kerry
Mansfield	13	Cork, Kerry
Markey	16	Dublin, Monaghan
Markham	5	Clare
*Marks (13)	19	Antrim
*Marley (12)	14	Donegal, Mayo
Marlow	7	Dublin, Tyrone
*Marron (23)	31	Monaghan
Marren (6)		Sligo
Marsh	5	
*Marshall (58)	59	Antrim, Londonderry, Down, Dublin
*Martin (325)	326	Antrim, Down, Dublin, Monaghan
Mason	32	Dublin
*Massey (10)	11	Down
Masterson	47	Dublin, Longford, Cavan
*Matchett (12)	14	Armagh, Antrim, Down
Mateer	9	Antrim
Mathers	9	Armagh
*Mathews (51)	78	Louth, Dublin, Antrim, Down
Mathews (26)		
Maughan	9	Mayo
Mawhinney (10)	18	Antrim
Mawhinny (8)		
Maxwell	68	Antrim, Down, Dublin
*May (25)	28	Sligo
*Mayberry (9)	12	Antrim
Maybury (3)		Kerry, Limerick
*Mayes (6)	7	Antrim, Armagh
*Mayne (13)	16	Antrim
*McAdams (21)	25	Monaghan
*McAfee (8)	11	Antrim
*McAleavey (5)	10	Down, Armagh
McAleer	17	Tyrone
*McAleese (10)	12	Antrim, Londonderry
*McAlinden (19)	24	Armagh
*McAllen (6)	13	Antrim
McCallan (5)		
*McAllister (40)	87	Antrim
McAlister (34)		
McAloney	5	Antrim, Down
McAndrew	16	Mayo
*McAneny (9)	32	Tyrone
McEneaney (8)		Louth
McEneany (5)		Monaghan
*McArdle (45)	55	Louth, Monaghan, Armagh

NAME	BIRTHS	PREDOMINANT COUNTIES
McAree	6	Antrim, Monaghan
McAtamney	6	Londonderry
McAteer	36	Armagh, Antrim, Donegal
*McAuley (49) McCauley (30)	107	Antrim, Donegal
*McAuliffe (39)	40	Cork
McBarron	5	Fermanagh, Donegal
McBratney	5	Antrim, Down
McBrearty	8	Tyrone, Donegal
McBride	118	Antrim, Donegal, Down
*McBrien (13)	16	Fermanagh, Cavan
*McBurney (11) McBirney (6)	19	Down, Antrim
McCabe	145	Cavan, Monaghan, Dublin
*McCafferty (24)	25	Donegal, Londonderry, Antrim
&McCaffrey (31)	61	Fermanagh, Tyrone
McCahon	6	Antrim
McCallion	24	Londonderry, Donegal
McCambridge	9	Antrim, Donegal
McCamley	5	
*McCandless (5)	7	
*McCann (175)	177	Antrim, Armagh, Dublin, Tyrone
*McCarroll (9)	13	Londonderry
McCarron	33	Donegal, Londonderry
McCarry	5	Donegal
*McCart (5)	6	Antrim
*McCartan (21)	35	Down, Armagh
McCarter	9	Antrim, Londonderry
*McCarthy (481)	498	Cork, Kerry, Limerick, Dublin, Antrim, Munster
*McCartney (44)	53	Antrim
*McCaughan (7)	10	Antrim
*McCaughey (23)	24	Antrim, Tyrone
*McCaul (12)	24	Armagh, Cavan
McCausland	16	Antrim
McCaw	9	Antrim
McClafferty	11	Donegal, Tyrone
*McClatchey (7)	8	Antrim, Armagh
*McClay (5)	7	Londonderry, Donegal
&McClean (54) McLean (43)	106	Antrim, Derry
*McCleery (14)	19	Antrim, Dondonderry
*McClelland (57)	66	Antrim, Down, Armagh, Londonderry, Monaghan
*McClenaghan (8) McLenaghan (5)	19	Antrim
McClintock	25	Antrim, Londonderry
*McClory (10)	11	Down
*McCloskey (47) McCluskey (24)	79	Londonderry Antrim, Dublin
McCloy	14	Antrim
McClughan	5	Antrim, Down
McClung	7	
McClure	35	Antrim, Down
McClurg	10	Antrim, Down
*McCole (9)	12	Donegal
McColgan	16	Donegal, Londonderry
*McCollum (10)	19	Antrim, Tyrone, Donegal
*McComb (23)	26	Antrim, Down, Londonderry
*McConaghy (14)	16	Antrim
McConkey	17	Antrim
*McConnell (98)	101	Antrim, Down, Tyrone
McConnon	9	Louth
*McConville (24)	29	Armagh, Antrim
McCoo	10	Armagh, Antrim
McCool	22	Donegal, Tyrone
McCord	15	Antrim
*McCormack (111)	118	Dublin, Mayo, Roscommon, Limerick
*McCormick (164)	165	Antrim, Dublin, Down
McCorry	16	Armagh, Down
*McCoubrey (5)	11	Down, Antrim
McCourt	44	Louth, Armagh, Antrim
McCoy	41	Antrim, Armagh, Monaghan

NAME	BIRTHS	PREDOMINANT COUNTIES
McCraken	33	Antrim, Down
*McCrea (28)	33	Antrim, Tyrone
*McCready (27)	39	Down, Antrim, Londonderry
McCreary	5	
McCreesh	6	Monaghan
McCrohan	5	Kerry
*McCrory (32)	34	Tyrone, Antrim
*McCrossan (13)	14	Tyrone
McCrudden	8	Antrim
McCrum	8	
*McCullough (69) McCullagh (40)	130	Antrim, Tyrone, Down
McCully	5	
McCune	8	Antrim, Armagh
*McCurdy (15)	19	Antrim, Londonderry
*McCurry (11)	12	Antrim
McCusker	19	Tyrone
*McCutcheon (25)	27	Tyrone, Antrim, Down,
*McDaid (35)	48	Donegal, Londonderry, Tyrone
*McDaniel (8)	9	
*McDermott (176)	189	Roscommon, Dublin, Donegal, Galway, Tyrone
*McDevitt (13)	15	Donegal, Londonderry, Tyrone
*McDonagh (100)	174	Galway, Roscommon, Mayo
*McDonald (173)	191	Dublin, Antrim, Cavan, Wexford, Carlow
*McDonnell (237)	247	Dublin, Mayo, Antrim, Galway, Cork
*McDowell (89)	91	Antrim, Down
McEldowney	6	Londonderry
*McElhinney (17)	26	Donegal, Tyrone, Londonderry
McElligott	24	Kerry
McElmeel	6	Monaghan
McElwee	7	Donegal, Londonderry
McEnroe	9	Cavan
McEntee	13	Monaghan, Cavan
*McErlain (11) McErlean (8)	21	Antrim, Derry
*McEvoy (85)	99	Dublin, Louth, Armagh, Queen's
*McFadden (72)	79	Donegal, Antrim, Londonderry
*McFall (20)	24	Antrim, Londonderry
McFarland	46	Tyrone, Armagh
*McFarlane (7)	12	
*McFeeters (6)	7	Londonderry
McFerran	7	Antrim
*McFetridge (8)	9	Antrim, Londonderry
McGahan	13	Louth
McGahey (12)	13	Antrim, Monaghan
*McGann (18)	21	
*McGarry (64)	79	Antrim, Dublin, Roscommon, Leit
*McGarvey (28)	30	Donegal, Londonderry
McGaughey	7	Antrim, Armagh
McGready	5	Donegal
McGeary	8	Tyrone
*McGeehan (7)	11	Donegal
McGeough	11	Monaghan, Louth
McGeown	19	Armagh
McGettigan	10	Donegal
McGillicuddy	6	Kerry
*McGilloway (8)	10	Londonderry, Donegal
McGimpsey	8	Down, Antrim
McGing	10	Mayo, Leitrim
*McGinley (45)	47	Donegal
*McGinn (17) Maginn (13)	31	Ulster
*McGinty (10)	12	Donegal
McGirr	12	Tyrone
*McGivern (17)	18	Armagh, Down, Antrim
McGivney	6	Cavan
McGlade	8	Antrim, Londonderry
*McGlinchey (17)	22	Tyrone, Donegal
*McGloin (14)	16	Donegal, Slibo
McGlone	12	Tyrone
*McGlynn (26)	39	
McGoey	5	
*McGoldrick (34)	41	Tyrone, Fermanagh, Sligo

NAME	BIRTHS	PREDOMINANT COUNTIES
*McGonigle (24)	38	Donegal, Londonderry
McGookin	7	Antrim, Armagh
*McGough (8)	11	Mayo
McGourty	5	Leitrim
*McGovern (92)	102	Fermanagh, Cavan, Leitrim
*McGowan (112)	152	Donegal, Leitrim, Sligo
Magowan (28)		
McGrady	6	Antrim, Down
*McGrath (233)	266	Tipperary, Cork, Waterford,
Magrath (31)		Waterford, Antrim, Tyrone
McGraw	5	
*McGreal (21)	22	Mayo, Leitrim
*McGreevy (16)	18	Down, Antrim
*McGregor (14)	16	Londonderry
McGrory	12	Donegal, Londonderry
McGuane	6	Clare
*McGuckin (8)	11	Londonderry
*McGuigan (36)	43	Antrim, Tyrone
McGuinn	5	Sligo
*McGuinness (47)	128	Dublin, Monaghan, Louth
*McGurk (32)	51	Tyrone, Antrim
McGuirk (17)		Dublin
McHale	51	Mayo
*McHenry (14)	27	Antrim, Londonderry,
McEniry (5)		Limerick
*McHugh (165)	176	Mayo, Donegal, Fermanagh,
		Galway, Leitrim
*McIlroy (40)	79	Antrim, Down, Fermanagh,
McElroy (39)		Londonderry
*McIlveen (15)	16	Antrim, Down
*McIlwaine (20)	29	Antrim, Down, Armagh
*McInerney (40)	64	Clare, Limerick
McIntosh	7	Antrim
*McIntyre (42)	58	Londonderry, Antrim, Sligo
*McIvor (19)	24	Tyrone, Londonderry
McKane	8	
*McKay (53)	64	Antrim
*McKeag (11)	16	
McKee	96	Antrim, Down, Armagh
*McKeever (30)	34	Londonderry, Antrim
*McKelvey (21)	24	
McKendry	19	Antrim
McKenna	201	Antrim, Monaghan, Tyrone,
		Kerry, Armagh, Dublin,
		Louth
*McKenzie (21)	22	Antrim, Dublin
*McKeogh (12)	13	Westmeath
*McKeown (119)	175	Antrim, Down, Armagh,
		Londonderry, Louth
McKeon (40)		Leitrim Louth
McKeone (12)		
*McKernan (12)	18	
McKevitt	9	Louth
*McKibbin (14)	20	Down, Antrim
McKiernan	9	
*McKillen (8)	9	Antrim
*McKinley (23)	35	Antrim, Donegal
*McKinney (37)	42	Antrim, Tyrone
McKinstry	11	Antrim, Down
*McKitterick (5)	9	
McKnight (38)	39	Antrim, Down
McLarnon (8)	13	Antrim
McClarnon (5)		
*McLaughlin (191)	391	Antrim, Donegal, Londonderry,
McLoughlin (170)		Tyrone, Dublin, Connaught
McLernon	8	
*McLoone (9)	8	Donegal
*McMahon (236)	241	Clare, Monaghan, Limerick,
		Dublin
McManamon	6	Mayo
*McManus (129)	138	Fermanagh
McMaster	38	Antrim, Down
McMeekin	7	Antrim
*McMenamin (34)	36	Donegal, Tyrone
McMichael	5	
*McMillen (12)	25	Antrim, Down
McMillan (11)		

NAME	BIRTHS	PREDOMINANT COUNTIES
*McMinn (12)	13	Antrim
*McMonagle (10)	12	Donegal
McMorrow	21	Leitrim
*McMullan (80)	108	Antrim, Down
*McMurray (16)	19	Antrim, Armagh
*McMurtry (6)	7	Antrim
*McNabb (8)	10	
McNair	5	Antrim
*McNally (72)	101	Antrim, Armagh, Monaghan,
McAnally (23)		Dublin
*McNamara (175)	192	Clare, Limerick, Mayo, Dublin,
		Cork
McNamee	40	Londonderry
*McNeice (8)	16	Antrim
McNiece (8)		
*McNeill (53)	58	Antrim, Londonderry
McNeilly	7	Antrim, Down
McNelis	8	Donegal
McNicholas	32	Mayo
*McNickle (10)	13	Tyrone
*McNiff (13)	14	Leitrim
McNinch	5	Antrim
*McNulty (59)	69	Donegal, Mayo
*McPaden (6)	8	Mayo
*McParland (24)	55	Armagh
McPartlan (12)		Leitrim
McPartlin (11)		
*McPhillips (13)	17	Cavan, Monaghan
McPolin	5	Armagh
*McQuaid (28)	55	Monaghan, Fermanagh
McQuade (25)		Antrim
*McQuillan (30	33	Antrim, Monaghan
*McQuinn (5)	7	Kerry
McQuiston	5	Antrim
McRedmond	5	King's
McReynolds	9	Antrim
McRoberts	9	Down, Antrim
McShane	34	Donegal, Louth
McSharry	29	Leitrim, Donegal, Sligo
McSherry	10	Armagh
McSorley	14	Tyrone, Fermanagh
*M'Stay (9)	10	Armagh
McStravick	6	Armagh, Antrim
*McSweeney (13)	29	Cork
*McTigue (12)	19	Mayo
McTague (4)		Cavan
McTeague (3)		Donegal
*McVeigh (47)	68	Antrim, Down
*McVicker (10)	13	Antrim, Londonderry
McWatters	6	Antrim
*McWeeney (6)	8	Leitrim
*McWhinney (6)	7	Down, Antrim
Mc Whirter	5	Antrim, Armagh
*McWilliams (40)	43	Antrim, Londonderry
*Meade (24)	25	Cork
*Meany (25)	34	Kilkenny, Clare
Meara (33)	54	Tipperary
Mara (21)		
*Mee (10)	15	Roscommon
Mea (5)		Mayo
*Meegan (11)	12	Monaghan
*Meehan (112)	121	Galway, Sligo, Donegal, Dublin,
		Clare
Meek	7	Antrim
*Meenan (9)	14	Donegal, Tyrone
Meharg	5	Antrim
Melia	11	Galway
*Mellon (11)	12	Tyrone
Melody	5	
Melville	6	Antrim, Down
Melvin	11	Mayo
Mercer	22	Antrim, Down
*Meredith (5)	7	
*Merrick (6)	7	
Merrigan	7	Dublin

NAME	BIRTHS	PREDOMINANT COUNTIES
*Metcalf (7)	9	Armagh
Meyler	9	Wexford
*Middleton (5)	6	
*Millar (87)	166	Antrim, Londonderry, Dublin
Miller (79)		
Millen	10	Antrim
*Milligan (22)	40	Antrim, Down Londonderry
Milliken (17)		
Mills	59	Antrim
*Minihane (12)	28	Cork
Minnis	6	Antrim
Minnock	5	King's
*Minogue (16)	17	Clare
Miskelly	5	Antrim
*Mitchell (120)	128	Antrim, Glaway, Dublin
Mitten	7	
*Mockler (7)	9	Tipperary
*Moffatt (17)	68	Antrim, Sligo, Tyrone
Moffat (11)		
Moffctt (12)		
Moffet (10)		
Moffitt (11)		
Moffit (7)		
*Mohan (11)	25	Monaghan
Moan (9)		
*Molloy (127)	153	Dublin, Glaway, Mayo, King's Donegal
*Moloney (119)	187	Limerick, Clare, Tipperary, Waterford
Molony (34)		
*Molyneaux (6)	10	
*Monaghan (96)	140	Galway, Mayo, Dublin, Fermanagh
Monahan (42)		
Mongan	6	
Monks	12	Dublin
Monnelly (9)	15	Mayo
Munnelly (6)		
*Montague (8)	9	Tyrone
*Montgomery (110)	111	Antrim, Down
*Moody (12)	13	Antrim, Down
*Moon (6)	8	
Mooney	136	Dublin, Antrim, King's
*Moore (395)	396	Antrim, Dublin, Londonderry, Cork, Kildare, Tyrone, Westmeath
*Moorehead (17)	25	Antrim
*Morahan (7)	10	Leitrim
Moran	265	Mayo, Dublin, Galway, Roscommon, Leitrim, Kerry
Moreland	11	Antrim, Down
Morey	7	
Morgan	132	Antrim, Armagh, Down, Dublin, Louth
Moriarty	83	Kerry
Morley	23	Mayo
*Moroney (35)	44	Clare, Limerick, Tipperary
*Morrin (6)	8	
*Morris (102)	115	Dublin, Mayo, Tyrone, Monaghan
*Morrison (93)	111	Antrim, Down, Dublin
Morrisroe	7	Roscommon
*Morrissey (62)	90	Waterford, Limerick, Cork
*Morrow (90)	91	Antrim, Donegal, Armagh, Down
*Morton (30)	32	Antrim
Moss	6	Tyrone
Motherway	5	Cork
Moylan	23	Clare, Cork, Tipperary
*Moynihan (50)	66	Kerry, Cork
Muir	5	
Mulcahy	76	Cork, Limerick, Waterford, Tipperary
Muldoon	26	Fermanagh, Galway
*Muldowney (5)	7	
Mulgrew	7	Tyrone
Mulnall	33	Dublin, Kilkenny, Carlow, Queen's

NAME	BIRTHS	PREDOMINANT COUNTIES
*Mulhern (8)	21	
Mulherin (7)		
*Mulholland (71)	73	Antrim, Down, Londonderry
Mulkeen	7	Mayo, Roscommon
*Mulkerrin (5)	10	Galway
*Mullally (8)	14	
*Mullan (92)	218	Tyrone, Londonderry, Galway, Antrim
Mullen (72)		
Mullin (53)		
Mullane	31	Cork, Limerick
*Mullany (27)	32	Roscommon, Mayo, Sligo
Mullarkey	21	Mayo, Galway, Sligo
Mulligan	105	Dublin, Mayo, Monaghan
Mullins	47	Cork, Clare
Mulqueen	6	Limerick, Clare
Mulrennan	5	
Mulroe	5	Mayo, Glaway
*Mulrooney (9)	12	
Mulroy	12	Mayo
Mulry	5	Galway
*Mulvany (4)	15	
Mulvanny (4)		
Mulvenna	5	Antrim
*Mulvey (21)	27	Leitrim
*Mulvihill (18)	21	Kerry, Limerick
*Murdock (18)	30	Antrim
Murdock (12)		
*Murnane (13)	14	Limerick, Cork
*Murphy (1385)	1386	Cork, Dublin, Wexford, Westmeath, Tyrone, Sligo
*Murray (405)	438	Dublin, Antrim, Cork, Down, Galway, Mayo
*Murrin (6)	8	
*Murtagh (58)	66	Dublin, Sligo
*Meyers (10)	11	Wexford, Antrim
*Myles (7)	12	
Miles (5)		
*Nagle (32)	39	Cork
Nally	20	Mayo, Roscommon
Napier	8	Antrim, Down
*Nash (20)	21	Kerry, Limerick
*Naughton (52)	71	Galway, Mayo, Roscommon, Clare
Navin	6	Mayo
*Naylor (5)	6	Dublin
*Neal (6)	10	
Neale (4)		
*Neary (34)	43	Mayo, Roscommon, Dublin, Louth
Nee	17	Galway
Needham	7	Mayo
*Neely (9)	12	
Neenan	7	Clare
Neeson	17	Antrim
*Neilan (12)	36	Galway, Roscommon, Sligo
Nilan (7)		
*Neill (215)	244	Antrim, Cork, Kerry, Carlow, Dublin, Wexford
Nelis	5	Londonderry, Mayo
Nelson	72	Antrim, Down, Londonderry, Tyrone
*Nesbitt (25)	30	Antrim, Armagh, Dublin
*Nestor (13)	15	Galway, Clare
*Neville (36)	39	Limerick, Cork
*Nevin (22)	23	
(Newell (31)	34	Down, Antrim
Newman	36	Cork, Meath, Dublin
*Neylon (10)	13	Clare
Niblock	6	Antrim
*Nicholl (25)	49	Antrim, Londonderry
*Nicholson (43)	44	Antrim, Sligo, Dublin
*Nixon (46)	47	Antrim, Cavan, Fermanagh
Noble	25	Antrim, Dublin
*Nolan (313)	321	Dublin, Wexford, Carlow, Wicklow, Kildare, Kerry, Tipperary, Mayo, Galway

NAME	BIRTHS	PREDOMINANT COUNTIES
*Noonan (69)	83	Cork, Clare, Limerick, Tipperary
*Noone (29)	48	Galway, Roscommon, Mayo
*Normile (5)	9	Limerick, Clare
*Norris (21)	22	
*North (8)	9	
Northridge	5	Cork
Norton	11	Dublin
Nugent	73	Armagh, Dublin, Cork, Tipperary, Tyrone
Nulty	16	Meath
Oakley	5	
*O'Beirne (9)	10	
O'Boyle	20	Mayo, Antrim
*O'Brien (488)	502	Dublin, Munster, Cavan, Galway
O'Byrne	8	Dublin
*O'Callaghan (63)	54	Cork
O'Carroll	5	
*O'Connell (128)	130	Cork, Limerick, Kerry, Dublin
*O'Connor (259)	266	Kerry, Cork, Limerick, Dublin, Calre, Galway
*O'Dea (34)	35	Clare, Limerick
*O'Doherty (7)	8	
*O'Donnell (292)	294	Donegal, Mayo, Galway
*O'Donoghue (28)	39	Kerry, Cork
O'Donovan	11	Cork, Limerick
O'Dowd	15	Sligo
O'Driscoll	13	Cork
O'Dwyer	25	Tipperary, Limerick, Clare
O'Farrell	19	
O'Flaherty	16	
O'Flynn	5	
*O'Gara (6)	7	Roscommon, Mayo
Ogle	6	
*O'Gorman (22)	24	Clare
*O'Grady (46)	47	Clare, Limerick, Dublin, Roscommon
*O'Hagan (32)	33	Armagh, Louth, Down
*O'Halloran (17)	25	Limerick
O'Hanlon	22	Dublin, Armagh
*O'Hara (104)	105	Dublin, Antrim, Sligo
*O'Hare (57)	59	Armagh, Louth, Down
*O'Hora (6)	8	Mayo
*O'Kane (27)	29	Londonderry, Antrim
*O'Keeffe (76)	83	Cork, Limerick, Dublin
O'Kelly	9	
O'Leary	64	Cork, Kerry, Limerick
*Oliver (15)	16	
*O'Loughlin (30)	40	Clare, Dublin
*O'Mahony (18)	25	Cork
*O'Malley (25)	30	Mayo
*O'Meara (20)	31	Dublin, Limerick, Tipperary
*O'Neill (359)	407	Dublin, Antrim, Cork, Tyrone,
*O'Rawe (7)	10	Antrim
O'Regan	16	Cork, Limerick
*O'Reilly (58)	62	Dublin
O'Riordan	11	Cork
*Ormond (6)	8	
Ormsby	10	
*O'Rourke (31)	49	
Orr	73	Antrim, Down, Londonderry, Tyrone
Osborne	23	
O'Shaughnessy	30	Limerick
O'Shea	46	Cork, Kerry, Limerick
O'Sullivan	136	Kerry, Cork, Limerick
Oswald	5	
*O'Toole (36)	39	Dublin, Wicklow, Limerick
*Owens (84)	89	Dublin, Roscommon, Cork

NAME	BIRTHS	PREDOMINANT COUNTIES
*Padden (5)	10	Mayo
Page	15	Antrim, Dublin
Paisley	12	Dublin, Antrim
Palmer	32	Antrim
*Park (15)	21	Antrim, Tyrone
Parker	40	Antrim, Cork
Parkhill	8	Londonderry
Parkinson	14	Dublin, Antrim, Down
*Parks (16)	23	Antrim, Armagh
Parle	5	Wexford
Parr	5	
Parsons	12	
*Patterson (137)	153	Down, Antrim, Armagh, Londonderry, Tyrone
*Patton (49)	60	Antrim, Down
Patten (10)		Mayo
*Paul (13)	14	Londonderry, Antrim
*Payne (25)	26	Dublin, Antrim
*Peacock (7)	9	
*Pearson (26)	31	Antrim, Dublin
*Peel (11)	12	Antrim
Pender	25	Wexford
Penny	5	Antrim, Dublin
Pentland	7	Down, Armagh
*Peoples (9)	10	Donegal
Pepper	10	Dublin, Antrim
*Perrott (5)	6	Cork
Perry	23	Dublin, Down
Peters	12	Tipperary
Petticrew (7)	12	Antrim
Pettigrew (5)		
Peyton	11	Mayo
*Phelan (91)	92	Waterford, Kilkenny, Queen's, Tipperary
Phibbs	6	Sligo
*Philbin (9)	10	Mayo, Galway
*Phillips (64)	77	Mayo, Antrim, Dublin
*Picken (5)	6	Antrim
*Pidgeon (5)	6	
*Pierce (22)	38	Dublin, Wexford
*Pigott (15)	20	Cork, Dublin
Pilkington	8	
Pinkerton	7	Antrim
Platt	8	Londonderry
*Plunkett (21)	28	Dublin
Poland	5	
Pollard	15	Dublin, Kilkenny
*Pollock (39)	41	Antrim, Tyrone
Poots	5	Down, Antrim
Pope	6	
Porter	73	Antrim, Down, Londonderry, Armagh
Potter	14	
Powell	23	
*Power (271)	272	Waterford, Cork, Dublin, Tipperary, Wexford, Kilkenny, Limerick
Pratt	10	
*Prendergast (46)	52	Mayo, Dublin, Waterford
Prentice	8	
*Prescott (5)	6	
Preston	17	
*Price (45)	47	Dublin, Antrim
Prior	15	Cavan
Pritchard	11	Antrim
Proctor	15	Antrim
Prunty	10	Longford
Punch	6	Cork, Limerick
*Purcell (76)	79	Kilkenny, Dublin, Leinster, Tipperary
*Purdy (15)	16	Antrim
*Purtill (6)	9	Limerick
Purvis	8	
Pyne	11	Cork, Clare

NAME	BIRTHS	PREDOMINANT COUNTIES
*Quail (10)	14	Antirm, Down
Quee	5	Antrim
Quigg	6	
*Quigley (82)	89	Londonderry, Dublin, Donegal, Galway, Louth, Sligo
Quill	10	Cork
Quilligan	7	Limerick, Cork
Quillinan	5	Tipperary
Quilty	9	Limerick, Waterford
*Quinlan (52)	54	Tipperary, Kerry
*Quinlivan (12)	13	Clare
*Quinn (349) Quin (58)	408	Dublin, Tyrone, Antrim, Roscommon, Galway, Cavan
*Quirke (27)	40	Tipperary, Kerry
*Rabbit (10)	13	
Ractigan	5	Mayo
Radford	7	
*Rafferty (54)	44	Antrim, Tyrone, Louth
*Rafter (17)	20	Dublin, Queen's Mayo
*Raftery (25)	26	Galway, Roscommon
Rahilly	11	Kerry, Cork
Rainey	39	Antrim, Down
Raleigh	11	Limerick, Tipperary
*Ralph (12)	14	
*Ramsay (16) Ramsey (12)	28	Antrim
Rankin	36	Londonderry, Donegal
*Ratigan (4) Rattigan (4)	8	Mayo, Roscommon
Ray	7	
Raymond	6	
Rea	49	Antrim, Down
*Reaney (5)	9	
*Reddan (7) Reddin (6)	15	
Reddington (7) Redington (7)	14	Mayo, Galway
*Reddy (25)	32	Dublin, Kilkenny
Redfern	5	
Redmond	79	Wexford, Dublin, Wicklow
Redpath	9	Antrim
Reel	5	
Reen	10	Cork, Kerry
Regan	219	Cork, Roscommon, Mayo
*Reid (181)	205	Antrim, Dublin, Down, Tyrone, Armagh
Reidy	49	Kerry, Clare
*Reilly (503) Reilly (58)	586	Cavan, Longford, Dublin, Meath, Mayo, Cork
Reihan	7	Cork, Kerry
*Reville (5)	6	Wexford
*Reynolds (112)	113	Leitrim, Dublin, Antrim. Louth
Rice	99	Antrim, Armagh, Louth, Dublin
Richards	9	
*Richardson (53)	54	Dublin, Antrim
Richmond	9	Antrim
*Rickard (6)	7	
*Riddell (8)	12	Antrim
Ridge	10	Galway
Rigney	9	King's
Ring	18	Cork
Ringland	7	Down, Antrim
*Riordan (134)	159	Cork, Kerry, Limerick
*Ritchie (23)	24	Antrim
Roarty	5	Donegal, Tyrone
Robb	21	Antrim
Roberts	40	
Robertson	18	
Robinson	217	Antrim, Down, Dublin, Armagh, Tyrone
Robson	5	Down

NAME	BIRTHS	PREDOMINANT COUNTIES
*Roche (141)	183	Cork, Wexford, Dublin, Limerick, Mayo
*Rochford (16)	18	Dublin
*Rock (17)	23	Dublin
*Rodden (9)	11	Donegal
*Roddy (15)	17	Mayo, Roscommon
Roe	21	
Rogan	24	Antrim, Down, Leitrim
*Rogers (100) Rodgers (68)	170	Antrim, Down, Dublin, Roscommon
Rohan	8	Kerry, Queen's
Rollins	7	Antrim, Down
*Ronayne (13) Ronan (12)	25	Cork
Rooney	119	Dublin, Leitrim, Down, Antrim, Mayo
Rose	10	
Ross	73	Antrim, Londonderry, Cork, Down
*Rossiter (12)	14	Wexford, Wicklow
Rothwell	10	Wexford, Dublin
*Roulston (8) Rolston (7)	25	Tyrone, Antrim
*Rountree (5)	9	Armagh
*Rourke (90)	136	Dublin, Leitrim, Roscommon, Wexford
*Rowan (15) Roughan (5)	27	
*Rowland (11)	12	Mayo, Galway
Rowe	21	Wexford
Rowley	11	Mayo
Roy	16	Antrim, Down
*Roycroft (5)	7	Cork
*Ruane (35)	37	Mayo, Galway
Rudden	9	Cavan
*Ruddle (5) Ruddell (4)	9	Limerick, Armagh
Ruddock	6	Down, Armagh
*Ruddy (22)	23	Mayo, Donegal, Armagh
Rush	22	Mayo
*Russell (99)	101	Antrim, Dublin, Down
Ruth	6	
*Rutherford (25)	26	Antrim, Londonderry, Down
*Rutledge (19)	23	Tyrone
Ruttle	6	
Ryan	715	Tipperary, Limerick, Dublin, Cork, Waterford, Kilkenny, Wexford, Clare, Galway
Ryder	9	Mayo
*Ryle (6)	9	Kerry
*Sadlier (6)	12	
*Salmon (21)	24	
*Sands (17)	18	Antrim, Armagh
Santry	7	Cork
*Sargent (7)	11	
*Sarsfield (10)	11	
*Saunders (22)	29	Dublin, Antrim
*Savage	61	Antrim, Down, Dublin, Cork
Sayers	8	
Scallan	10	Wexford
*Scally (24)	25	Roscommon, Westmeath, Dublin
*Scanlon (54) · Scanlan (42)	97	Kerry, Clare, Sligo, Limerick, Cork
*Scannell (40	42	Cork, Kerry
Scott	196	Antrim, Down, Londonderry, Dublin
Scullion	17	Antrim, Londonderry
Scully	65	Cork, Dublin, Carlow, King's
Seaton	6	
*Seeds (6)	7	Antrim, Down

NAME	BIRTHS	PREDOMINANT COUNTIES
*Seery (20)	22	Westmeath, Dublin
Semple	19	Antrim
Sewell	6	
Sexton	43	Munster, Cork, Clare, Limerick, Ulster, Cavan
Seymour	15	
*Shally (6)	7	Galway
*Shanahan (53)	65	Cork, Kerry, Tipperary, Liberick, Waterford
Shanks	21	Antrim, Down
*Shanley (14)	22	Leitrim
Shannon	72	Antrim, Clare, Roscommon
*Sharkey (57)	58	Roscommon, Donegal, Tyrone, Dublin, Louth
*Sharpe (10	17	Antrim
*Shaughnessy (40)	41	Galway
Shaw	80	Antrim, Down, Dublin
Shea	246	Kerry, Cork, Killkenny, Tipperary, Waterford
Shearer	5	
Sheedy	13	Clare
*Sheehan (171) Sheahan (43)	215	Cork, Kerry, Limerick, Munster
*Sheehy (54)	55	Kerry, Limerick, Cork
*Sheeran (18)	30	
*Shelly (16)	17	Dublin, Tipperary
*Shepard (12)	22	
*Sheidan (135)	145	Cavan, Dublin, Mayo
Sherlock	23	Dublin
Sherman	5	
Sherrard	7	Londonderry, Antrim
Sherry	25	Monaghan, Dublin, Meath
Sherwood	8	
*Shevlin (8)	11	
*Shields (36) Sheilds (19)	55	Antrim, Down
*Shiels (28) Sheils (28)	88	Dublin, Donegal, Londonderry
*Shilliday (5)	6	Antrim, Down
Shine	26	Cork
Shirley	7	
*Short (21) Shortt (8)	30	
*Shortall (10)	11	Dublin, Kilkenny
Shorten	7	Cork
*Silk (7)	8	Galway
Silver	5	Galway
*Simmons (6)	11	
*Simms (11)	24	Antrim
Simpson	75	Antrim
Sinclair	18	Armagh, Londonderry
Singleton	17	Cork, Down
*Sinnott (22) Synnott (12	37	Wexford Dublin
*Skeffington (6)	8	
*Skehan (7)	8	
Skelly	18	Dublin, Down
Skelton	8	
Skillen	6	Down, Antrim
*Slator (5)	10	Dublin
Slattery	69	Munster Tipperary, Kerry Cork, Clare, Limerick
*Slavin (11)	14	
Slevin	13	
*Sloan (44) Sloane (16)	61	Antrim
Small	30	Antrim, Armagh, Down
*Smiley (5) Smylie (5)	13	Antrim
*Smith (471) Smyth (277)	753	Antrim, Cavan, Dublin, Kerry
Smullen	8	Dublin
Snee	7	Mayo
Snoddy	7	Antrim
*Somers (29)	38	Wexford, Dublin
*Somerville (18)	24	

NAME	BIRTHS	PREDOMINANT COUNTIES
*Spain (7)	8	
Sparks	6	
*Speers (17)	38	Antrim
*Spelman (24)	30	Galway, Roscommon, Mayo
*Spence (57)	58	Antrim, Down
Spencer	19	Dublin, Cork
Spillane	44	Cork, Kerry
Spratt	14	Antrim
Spring	6	
Sproule	17	Tyrone
Stacey	5	
Stack	54	Kerry, Cork Limerick
Stafford	33	Wexford, Dublin
*Stanley (20)	21	Dublin
*Stanton (39) Staunton (28)	67	Mayo, Cork Mayo, Galway
Stapleton	28	Tipperary, Kilkenny
*Starrett (7)	10	Antrim, Londonderry
*Steele (37) Steel (17)	54	Antrim, Londonderry
Steen	6	
Steenson	19	Antrim, Armagh
Stenson	15	Sligo
*Stephens (32)	36	Mayo
*Stevenson (81) Stephenson (20)	106	Antrim, Armagh, Down
*Stewart (236)	255	Antrim, Down, Londonderry, Donegal, Tyrone
Stinson	12	
*Stirling (9) Sterling (7)	16	Antrim
Stitt	12	Antrim
St. John	10	Tipperary
*St. Leger (5)	7	
Stockman	7	
Stokes	28	
*Stone (7)	12	
*Storey (9)	13	Antrim
*Strahan (9)	11	
Strain	14	Down
Strange	6	Antrim
Stringer	9	
*Strong (12)	14	
Studdert	6	Clare, Kerry
Sturgeon	8	
*Sugrue (21)	23	Kerry, Cork
*Sullivan (838)	839	Cork, Kerry, Leinster, Dublin Ulster, Antrim, Connaught, Galway
Sunderland	7	Wexford
*Supple (5)	6	
*Surgeoner (5) Surgenor (4)	10	Antrim
Sutherland	6	
Sutton	27	Dublin, Wexford, Cork
*Swan (19)	23	Dublin, Antrim
Swanton	7	Cork, Dublin
*Sweeney (166) Sweeny (82)	254	Cork, Donegal, Mayo, Kerry
*Sweetman (6)	8	Cork, Dublin
Swift	12	Mayo
Switzer	7	
Swords	8	Dublin
*Taaffe (11)	15	
*Taggart (27)	42	Antrim
*Talbot (17)	18	
Tallon	15	Dublin
Talty	12	Clare
Tangney	8	Kerry, Cork
Tanner	7	
*Tansey (10)	13	
*Tarpey (10)	12	Mayo, Roscommon, Galway
*Tarrant (6)	7	Cork
*Tate (25)	36	Antrim, Down

NAME	BIRTHS	PREDOMINANT COUNTIES
Tait (10)	36	Londonderry
*Taylor (150)	151	Antrim, Down, Londonderry, Dublin
*Teague (5)	6	
*Teahan (10)	11	Kerry
Teeling	6	Dublin
Telford	14	Antrim
Temple	6	
Templeton	18	Antrim
Tennant	5	
Terry	9	Cork
Thomas	28	Antrim
*Thompson (304)	317	Antrim, Down, Armagh, Londonderry, Dublin, Fermanagh, Longford
Thornton	54	Galway, Dublin, Mayo
*Thorpe (5)	6	
Thunder	5	Dublin
*Tiernan (26)	27	Louth
*Tierney (74)	78	Dublin, Tipperary, Galway
Tighe	33	Mayo
Timlin	13	Mayo, Sligo
*Timmins (16)	25	Dublin, Kildare, Wicklow
*Timony (9)	14	
Tinsley	5	
Tisdall	6	Dublin
*Toal (19)	20	Armagh, Antrim
*Tobin (97)	98	Waterford, Cork, Tipperary, Limerick, Dublin, Kilkenny
Todd	38	Antrim, Down
Tolan	19	Mayo
Toland	9	Antrim
Toman	5	Down, Antrim
*Tomkins (7)	9	
Tomlinson	5	
*Toner (39)	42	Armagh, Londonderry, Antrim
Tooher	5	
Toolan	10	Roscommon
*Toole (98)	100	Dublin, Galway, Mayo, Wicklow, Kildare
*Topping (8)	10	Antrim, Armagh
*Tormey (9)	11	
*Torrens (8)	9	Antrim
*Totten (9)	17	Antrim
Totton (8)		Armagh
Tougher	5	Mayo
*Towey (28)	30	Roscommon, Mayo
*Townsend (9)	11	
Trant	6	Kerry
Travers	38	Donegal, Dublin, Leitrim
*Traynor (35)	77	Dublin
Treanor (28)		Antrim, Armagh, Monaghan,
Trainor (12)		Tyrone
*Treacy (37)	84	Tipperary, Galway
Tracey (31)		Dublin
Tracy (16)		Dublin
*Trimble (12)	13	
Trotter	12	
Troy	31	King's, Cork, Tipperary
Trueman	5	
Tucker	10	
Tuite	14	
Tully	45	Galway, Dublin, Cavan
*Tumelty (5)	10	
*Tuohy (22)	40	Clare, Galway
Turkington	12	Armagh
*Turley (7)	9	
Turnbull	5	
Turner	67	Dublin, Antrim, Cork
Turtle	9	Antrim, Armagh
Tutty	5	
Twamley	6	
*Tweedie (10)	15	
Twohig	15	Cork
*Twomey (63)	80	Cork, Kerry
Toomey (15)		Dublin, Limerick
Tynan	20	Queen's

NAME	BIRTHS	PREDOMINANT COUNTIES
Tyner	6	
*Tyrrell (27)	30	Dublin, Kildare, Wicklow
*Uprichard (9)	10	Armagh, Antrim
Upton	6	
*Usher (6)	8	
*Valentine (8)	9	Dublin
*Vallely (7)	9	Armagh
Vance	19	Antrim
Vaughan	35	Cork, Clare, Limerick, Antrim, Down
Veale	12	Waterford
Vickers	5	
Vincent	8	
Vogan	5	
Waddell	12	
Wade	30	Dublin
Waldron	43	Mayo, Roscommon, Dublin
Walker	123	Antrim, Dublin, Down, Derry
Wall	58	Dublin, Waterford, Cork, Kilkenny, Limerick, Tipperary
*Wallace (140)	144	Antrim, Galway, Cork, Limerick, Dublin, Down, Londonderry
Waller	6	
Walls	11	
*Walsh (877)	932	Cork, Mayo, Waterford,
Walshe (55)		Galway, Dublin, Wexford
*Walters (5)	7	
Walton	8	
*Ward (211)	213	Donegal, Dublin, Galway
Wardlow	5	Antrim, Armagh
Waring	7	
Warner	6	Cork
Warnock	15	Tyrone, Down
*Warren (31)	35	Kerry, Dublin, Cork
*Warwick (6)	7	Antrim
*Wasson (5)	8	
Waters	47	Sligo, Wexford, Monaghan
Watkins	7	
Watson	120	Antrim, Armagh, Down
Watt	33	Antrim
Watters	22	Tyrone, Antrim, Louth
Watterson	14	Antrim
Waugh	5	
Weatherup	6	Antrim
Webb	33	Dublin, Antrim
Webster	21	Antrim, Dublin
Weir	56	Antrim, Armagh
Welby	5	Galway
Weldon	14	
Wells	9	Armagh
*Welsh (27)	32	Antrim
West	26	
Weston	7	
Wharry	5	Antrim
Wharton	5	
Wheeler	14	Dublin
*Whelan (213)	214	Dublin, Wexford, Waterford, Tipperary, Carlow, Queen's
*Whelehan (5)	8	
Whelton	11	Cork, Kerry
White (269)	291	Antrim, Cork, Dublin,
Whyte (22)		Wexford
Whiteside	18	Antrim, Armagh
Whitney	5	Longford, Wexford
Whittle	6	
*Whitton (5)	8	
Whitty	19	Wexford
Wickham	6	Wexford

NAME	BIRTHS	PREDOMINANT COUNTIES
Wiggins	6	
Wightman	6	Down
Wilkinson	33	Antrim, Armagh
Williams	90	Dublin, Cork, Limerick, Antrim
*Williamson (56)	57	Antrim, Armagh, Londonderry Tyrone
Willis	33	Antrim, Down
Wills	9	
*Wilson (365)	366	Antrim, Armagh, Down, Tyrone, Dublin, Londonderry Fermanagh
*Winters (15)	18	
*Wise (5)	8	
Wyse (3)		
Wiseman	5	
Withers	5	
Wood	14	
Woodhouse	6	
Woods	137	Antrim, Armagh, Down, Monaghan, Tyrone, Dublin, Louth, Cork
Woodside	9	Antrim, Dublin
Workman	5	Antrim
*Woulfe (12)	22	Limerick
Wray	15	Donegal, Londonderry
Wren	12	
Wright	103	Antrim, Down, Dublin, Armagh
*Wylie (32)	51	Antrim
*Wynne (46)	47	Dublin, Sligo
*Yeates (14)	18	Antrim, Dublin
Yates (4)		Cork
*Young (131)	132	Antrim, Tyrone, Dublin, Cork Down, Londonderry

THE IRISH SETTLERS OF THE WORLD

A Word of Caution

Remember when tracing your ancestors through written documents not to jump to erroneous conclusions. A document may say that an individual came from Liverpool, but that does not necessarily mean that he was born or even lived there. It may just simply mean that the ship he came over on happened to leave from Liverpool, or that he traveled to Liverpool from his residence in order to catch the ship before it departed.

Furthermore, remember that sailing dates were uncertain, and hence a long wait could force the immigrant to take a job or temporary residence near the port of departure.

From the 17th century onwards an Irish immigrant could have been an indentured servant working to regain his former status, which had been destroyed by the conquerors of the land. Some were convicted of treason by the British and shipped to southern plantations in America. Others settled in the Amazon (1612-1623), the Barbados, Montserrat and St. Christophers as well.

Thousands of non-military Irish also settled in the West Indies after the fall of Limerick in 1651.

THE IRISH ABROAD

Thousands have left Ireland and settled in North America, Canada, Australia, Great Britain, Europe, etc. This small Emerald Isle has indeed helped shape the history of the worlds population.

PART III

SOURCES IN COUNTRIES OUTSIDE OF IRELAND

Chapter 1 • Detail of the American Archives

Chapter 2 • Canada
• England, Scotland, Wales
• Australia

The Irish have spread all across the world and left quite an impact on it. Having settled abroad due to famine, military service, religious persecution, etc., it can be very frustrating to trace ones origin back to the Emerald Isle. It is hoped that these sources will make it easier for you to trace your own ancestors. Part II, which preceeds this section gives details of all the major Irish records and repositories in Ireland itself.

If your ancestors were in America at these times there is a chance they fought in (or were affected by) these wars. Records can be checked accordingly.

Wars in which your Irish Ancestors could have fought.

1690 - King Williams War

1702 - Queen Ann's War

1744 - King George's War

1745 - French & Indian War

1775 - Revolutionary War

1812 - War of 1812

1846 - Mexican War

1861 - Civil War

1898 - Spanish American War

The Irish began to migrate to North America during the late 1600's, after the Cromwellian oppresion. By the time of the American Revolutionary War there were a fair amount of the Irish already in America and Canada (and about 35% of the Conntinental Army). The following list shows some of the Irish surnames involved:

Per Charles Lucy's Book Harp and Sword, the following surnames were found among the ranks of George Washington's Revolutionary Army.

695 Kellys	231 Mullens
484 Murphys	201 Walshes or Welshes
331 McCarthys	183 Carrolls
327 Connors or O'Connors	178 O'Neills
322 Ryans	184 Fitzgeralds
285 Reillys	142 Farrells
248 Doughertys	138 Flynns
243 Connollys	108 Gallaghers
266 Sullivans	168 McGuires
231 O'Briens	165 Magees
128 Lynchs	115 Hogans

The Soundex System of Recording Names by Sound (Not Spelling).

Note:

(A) Different spellings used within the same family.

(B) This phonetic system of searching the U.S. Census is available only for certain periods.

(C) Code No. for this name is 0424-which represents its phonetic sounds.

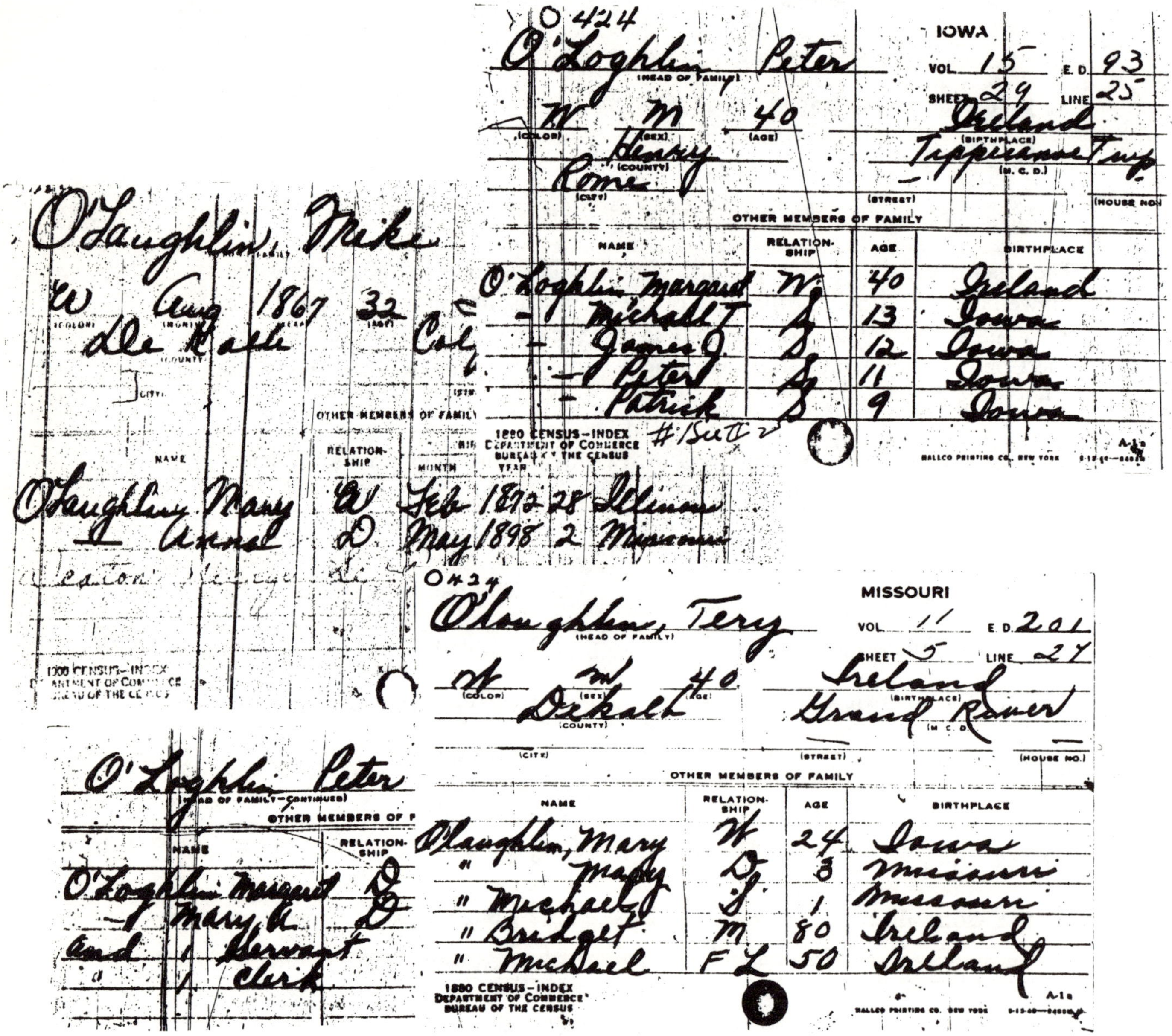

0424

O'Loghlin Peter (HEAD OF FAMILY)

IOWA VOL. 15 E.D. 93 SHEET 29 LINE 25

W (COLOR) M (SEX) 40 (AGE) Ireland (BIRTHPLACE)

Henry (COUNTY) Tippecanoe Twp (M.C.D.)

Rome (CITY) (STREET) (HOUSE NO.)

OTHER MEMBERS OF FAMILY

NAME	RELATION-SHIP	AGE	BIRTHPLACE
O'Loghlin Margaret	W	40	Ireland
" Michael T	S	13	Iowa
" James J	S	12	Iowa
" Peter	S	11	Iowa
" Patrick	S	9	Iowa

1880 CENSUS—INDEX DEPARTMENT OF COMMERCE BUREAU OF THE CENSUS

O'Laughlin Mike

W Aug 1867 32

De Kalb (COUNTY)

OTHER MEMBERS OF FAMILY

NAME	RELATION-SHIP	MONTH	YEAR		
O'Laughlin Mary	W	Feb	1872	28	Illinois
Annie	D	May	1898	2	Missouri

1900 CENSUS—INDEX DEPARTMENT OF COMMERCE BUREAU OF THE CENSUS

0424

O'Laughlin Tery (HEAD OF FAMILY)

MISSOURI VOL. 11 E.D. 201 SHEET 5 LINE 27

W (COLOR) M (SEX) 40 (AGE) Ireland (BIRTHPLACE)

Dekalb (COUNTY) Grand River (M.C.D.)

OTHER MEMBERS OF FAMILY

NAME	RELATION-SHIP	AGE	BIRTHPLACE
O'Laughlin Mary	W	24	Iowa
" Mary	D	3	Missouri
" Michael	S	1	Missouri
" Bridget	M	80	Ireland
" McNeil	FL	50	Ireland

1880 CENSUS—INDEX DEPARTMENT OF COMMERCE BUREAU OF THE CENSUS

O'Loghlin Peter (HEAD OF FAMILY—CONTINUED)

OTHER MEMBERS OF FAMILY

NAME	RELATION-SHIP
O'Loghlin Margaret	D
Mary A.	D
and 1 Servant	
1 Clerk	

• National Archives
• Census Records
• Naturalization, Passport and War Records
• Selected Publications
• Emigration Records

THE NATIONAL ARCHIVES

National Archives & Records Service, General Services Administration, Washington, D.C. 20408.

Well over 30 million Americans are of Irish heritage, and many missing links in Irish genealogy are to be found in the National Archives. Due to the extensive nature of material available in the American National Archives we will outline in this chapter the available sources and material therein. It should be noted that the General Reading Rooms Division distributes free upon request, four short bibliographies:

Guides ot Genealogical Research; A selected list of publications that explain how to trace your ancestors.

Surnames; A selected list of references on family names, including those of Irish origin.

Immigrant Arrivals; a short guide to published sources, which can aid in identifying ships and passenger lists; and

Heraldry, a selected list of references, listing publications on the origins, design and identification of coat of arms. Much material within these publications are contained in these chapters.

The rest of this chapter deals with the following areas of the national archives:

1. Census Records – nature and availability
2. Military Service Records
3. The General Reading Rooms Division
4. Naturalization, Passport and War Records
5. Land Records
6. Selected Lists of Books and Publications

Because of the millions of records in the National Archives, they are unable to make extensive searches for you. If however you can furnish enough specific information, a particular can be searched for. A search can also be made for publications dealing with your family name in the Archives in Washington, D.C., or the General Archives Division in Suitland, Md. Photocopies can be supplied as well.

The following information was taken from a publication entitled:

Genealogical Records in the National Archives, by the General Services Administration.

Birth, Marriage, and Death Records

The National Archives has records of births, marriages, and deaths at U.S. Army facilities, 1884-1912, with some records dated as late as 1928. It will search these records if provided with the following:

1. Birth Records: Name of child, names of his parents, place of birth, and month and year of birth.
2. Marriage Records: Names of contracting parties.
3. Death Records: Name, date, place, and rank of deceased.

The National Archives also has some records of births and marriages, through 1941, and reports of some deaths, through 1949, of American citizens abroad, registered at Foreign Service posts. Requests for information about registrations made less than 75 years ago should be addressed to the Department of State, Washington, D.C. 20520. Requests for information about earlier registrations should be addressed to the Civil Archives Division, National Archives (GSA), Washington, D.C. 20408.

For information about other original records of birth, marriage, and death an inquirer should address the bureau of vital statistics, the church, or other appropriate local depository in the appropriate State, county, or city. To obtain a birth certificate, he should address the bureau of vital statistics in the capital city of the state in which the birth occured, giving the date and the place of birth. If there is no record of birth on file, the bureau will explain the procedure for filing a delayed birth certificate. The Superintendent of Documents, U.S. Government Printing Office, Washington, D.C. 20402, can supply the leaflets,

Where to Write for Birth and Death Records, (35 cents);

Where to Write for Marriage Records, (35 cents); and

Where to Write for Divorce Records, (35 cents).

CENSUS SCHEDULES

Population Censuses

A census of the population has been taken every 10 years since 1790. The National Archives has the 1790-1870 schedules, a microfilm copy of the 1880 schedules, the surviving fragments of the 1890 schedules, and a microfilm copy of the 1900 schedules. Practicall all of the 1890 census schedules were destroyed by fire in 1921. The remaining entries are for small segments of the populations of Perry County, Ala., the District of Columbia, Columbus, Georgia, Mound

Township, Ill., Rockford, Minn., Jersey City, Eastchester and Brookhaven Township, N.Y., Cleveland and Gaston Counties, N.C., Cincinnati and Wayne Township, Ohio, Jefferson Township, S. Dak., and Ellis, Hood, Kaufman, Rusk, and Trinity Counties, Tex.

The 1790-1840 schedules give the name of the head of household only; other family members are tallied unnamed by age and sex. For the 1850 and 1860 censuses, seperate schedules list slaveowners and the age, sex, and color (but not the name) of each free person in a household. Additional information is included with each succeeding census.

The available schedules for the 1790 census were published by the Federal Government in the early 1900's and have since been privately reprinted. The published census schedules for 1790 are for Connecticut Maine, Maryland, Massachusetts, New Hampshire, New York, North Carolina Pennsylvania, Rhode Island, South Carolina, and Vermont. Schedules for each State are listed in a separate, indexed volume. The schedules for the remaining States – Delaware, Georgia, Kentucky, New Jersey, Tennessee, and Virginia – were burned during the War of 1812. As a substitute for the Virginia schedules, the Federal Government published names obtained from State censuses and tax lists, thereby listing about half of the known population of the State in 1790. Over the years additional lists of names have been published privately, and they provide more of the missing information for Virginia and other States whose 1790 schedules were destroyed. The Government has not published other census listings, but many privately published lists are available from libraries and other sources. Although the lists vary considerably in format and geographic scope, they frequently save researchers from fruitless searches and help locate a specific entry in the actual records.

Also helpful in locating specific census entries are the following unpublished indexes in the National Archives:

1. 1810 Census – A card index for Virginia only.
2. 1880 Census – A microfilm copy of a card index to entries for each household that included a child aged 10 or under. On the cards are the name, age, and birthplace of each member of such households, and there is a separate cross reference card for each child aged 10 or under whose surname is different from that of the head of the household in which he is listed. The cards are arranged by State and thereunder by the Soundex system; that is, alphabetically by the first letter of the surname, thereunder by the sound of the surname, and thereunder alphabetically by given name of the head of the household.

3. 1890 Census – A card index to the 6,160 names on the surviving 1890 schedules.

4. 1900 Census – A microfilm copy of a card index to all heads of families. Otherwise, content is similar to 1880 index.

Other Censuses

The National Archives has the 1890 special schedules of Union Veterans ans Widows of Veterans for Washington, D.C., about half of Kentucky, and for states in alphabetical order from Louisiana through Wyoming. Schedules for the other states no longer exists. The schedules give the name and post office address of each living veteran and of each veteran's widow (along with the name of her veteran husband) and information about the service of each veteran named.

Microfilm

The National Archives has microfilmed all of the available census schedules and the indexes to them, and positive microfilm copies are available at a moderate cost per roll. These microfilm rolls are arranged alphabetically by state and thereunder alphabetically by county. Each roll usually contains all of the schedules for one or several counties. The National Archives publication

Federal Population Censuses, 1790-1890, which contains a roll listing and indicates the price for each roll, will be mailed upon request.

Microfilm copies of census schedules, 1790-1900, are available in the regional archives branches listed at the end of this chapter and are available for use in the branches research rooms. Microfilm copies of census schedules, except those for 1900, which are under restriction, are also available on interinstitutional loan. Individual users may borrow the microfilm through libraries and research institutions located within a particular region and in accordance with the "National Interlibrary Loan Code, 1968." Inquiries concerning microfilm publications should be directed to the appropriate regional archives branch.

Mortality Schedules

Whenever possible, the National Archives is acquiring microfilm copies of the mortality schedules of the 1850-80 censuses from the various depositories where they are held. The schedules show the name, the month, and cause of death, and the state, territory, or country of birth of each person who died during the year that preceded the taking of each of the censuses.

The National Archives has some or all of the available mortality schedules on microfilm for the following states: Arizona, Colorado, District of Columbia, Delaware, Georgia, Illinois, Kansas, Kentucky, Louisiana, Massachusetts, Minnesota, Montana, Nebraska, New Jersey, North Carolina, North Dakota, South

Carolina, Tennessee, Texas, Utah, Vermont, Virginia, and Washington.

Mortality schedules for other states are available in state archives, libraries, historical societies, university libraries, and in a few instances the Library National Society, Daughters of the American Revolution, 1776 D Street N.W., Washington, D.C. 100006.

Records about District of Columbia Residents

Records relating to District of Columbia residents in the Washington National Records Center, Suitland, Md., include, in addition to naturalization records, copies of wills, 1801-88; records relating to the administration of estates, 1701-78; and guardianship papers, 1802-78. Although the records relating to the administration of estates are concerned mostly with financial transactions involving the property and debts of a decedent, they show his name and sometimes the names of members of his family. Copies of wills contain, besides the name of the decedent, the names of legatees and their relationship to him. Guardianship papers give the name of each ward of the court and at times his age and the names of his parents.

A search of these records requires the name of the person in question, the type of record involved, and the approximate date of the transaction.

Land Records

The land records (dated chiefly 1800-1950) in the General Archives Division include bounty land warrant files, donation land entry of individual settlers on land in the public land states. There are no land records for the thirteen original states and Maine, Vermont, West Virginia, Kentudky, Tennessee, Texas, and Hawaii. Records tor these states are maintained by state officials, usually in the State capital. The donation land entry files and homestead application files show, in addition to the name of the applicant, the location of the land and the date he acquired it, his residence or post office address, his age or date and place of birth, his marital status, and, if applicable, the given name of his wife or the size of his family. If an applicant for homestead land was of foreign birth, his application file contains evidence of his naturalization or of his intention to become a citizen. Supporting documents show the immigrant's country of birth and sometimes the date and port of arrival. Genealogical information in records relating to private land claims varies from the mention of the claimant's name and location of the land to such additional information as the claimant's place of residence when he made the claim and the names of his relatives, both living and dead.

The General Archives Division will search these land records for Alabama, Alaska, Arizona, Florida, Louisiana, Nevada, or Utah for the period 1800 to July 1, 1908, if the full name of the applicant and the name of the state or territory in which the land was located are given. A search of the records for all other public land states or territories, 1800-1950, requires in addition to the applicant's name, (1) the number of the land entry file or a description of the land by township, range, section, and fraction of section or (2) the name of the land office and either the date when the original application was filed or the date of the final certificate. An inquirer may be able to obtain the legal description of land by writing to the county recorder of deeds in the county seat of the county in which the land was located.

Naturalization Records

The General Archives Division has naturalization proceedings of the District of Columbia Courts, 1802-1926. These records show, for each person who petitioned for naturalization, his age or date of birth, his nationality, and whether citizenship was granted. The National Archives has photocopies and indexes of naturalization documents, 1787-1906, filed by courts in Maine, Massachusetts, New Hampshire, and Rhode Island. These records were copied and indexed by the Work Projects Administration in the late 1930's. The General Archives Division and the National Archives will search these records for information about naturalizations that occurred before September 27, 1906, if given the full name of the petitioner and the approximate date of naturalization. Persons who wish information about citizenship granted elsewhere before September 27, 1906, should send their inquiries to the clerk of the Federal, State, or other court that issued the naturalization certificate.

EMIGRATION RECORDS

Lists of early immigrants were often published in local history and genealogical journals or as small monographs. A bibliography first compiled by Harold Lancour gives the locations of many of these lists. The third edition, *A Bibliography of Ship Passenger Lists, 1538-1835;* Being a guide to published lists of early immigrants to North America, revised and enlarged by Richard J. Wolfe, was published in 1963 by the New York Public Library (137 p. Z7164.I3L2). Appendixes include "Published Lists of Ship Passengers and Immigrants after 1825" (p. 87-91) and "Passenger Arrival Records in the National Archives" (p. 93-99). The book is obtainable from the publisher, the New York Public Library for $10. The order number is ISBN 0-87104-023-9. There is no index to the family names that appear in the various lists, but publication of such a list, compiled by P. William Filby for Gale Research Co., is expected.

Items that appear in the Lancour bibliography are not included in the list that follows, except in instances where they have been reprinted in a more accessible form.

Other published works on hand:

The body of material published about individual ethnic groups is far too extensive to be listed here. By way of introduction a few general histories of American immigration (some of which contain lengthy bibliographies) are described within the free government publications mentioned earlier.

Bibliography of Other Published Irish Passenger Lists

Ulster, Emigration to Colonial America, 1718-1775. R.J. Dickson. London, Routledge & K. Paul (1966) xiv, 320 pp. map. (Ulster-Scot Historical Series, No. 1). E184.S4D47
Bibliography: pp. 208-311
Appendixes contain data on ships, emigrants, and ports.

Emigrants from Ireland, 1847-1852. Elish Ellis. State-aided emigration schemes from crown estates.

A Dictionary of Scottish Emigrants to the USA Baltimore. Donald Whyte. Magna Carta Book Co., 1972. 504 pp. E184.S3W49
Bibliography: p. 467-472. Index of places of origin: pp. 493-504.
Names of over 6,000 immigrants are alphabetically arranged.

Passengers to America: a consolidation of ship passenger lists from the New England Historical and Genealogical Register. Michael Tepper (editor). Baltimore, Genealogical Publishing Company, 1977. 544 pp. 1977. CS68.P37

San Francisco Ship Passenger Lists. Louis J. Rasmussen. Baltimore, Genealogical Pub. Co., 1978. xvi, 273 pp. CS68.R37
Originally published in Colma, California, 1965. "This volume is the first in a series of volumes which will reflect the names of passengers arriving by vessels in the Port of San Francisco during the period of 1850 to 1875." Arrivals from 1850 to 1864 are included in this volume. Surname index: pp. 174-264.

American-Irish Historical Society Journal, New York, volume 28. "Passenger Lists for American Ports printed in Ireland 1811."

American-Irish Historical Society Journal, New York, volume 29. "Passenger Lists for American Ports printed in Ireland 1815-1816."

Passenger Lists of Ships Coming to North America, 1607-1825; A Bibliography. A. Harold Lancour. (New York Public Library Bulletin, 41; No. 5, pp. 389-410.)

New England Historical and Genealogical Register:
"Two Early Passenger Lists, 1635-1637"
"List of Emigrants from England, 1773-1776"
"List of Emigrants to America from Liverpool, 1697-1707"
"Irish Passenger Lists; Ireland to the USA, 1803-1806" (Copy by Fothergill from British Museum Add. MSS. No. 35932.) Vols. 60, 61, 62, 66.

The Recorder. (Bulletin of the American-Irish Historical Society, Boston, vol.3.) "Early Irish Emigrants, 1803-1806."

The National Archives has incomplete series of customs passenger lists and immigration passenger lists of ships arriving from abroad at Atlantic and Gulf of Mexico ports. The following table shows the dates of passenger lists and related indexes in the National Archives:

Port	*Customs Passenger Lists*	*Immigration Passenger Lists*	*Indexes*
Baltimore	1820-1891	1891-1909	1820-1952
Boston	1820-74 and 1883-91	1891-1943	1848-91 and 1902-20
New Orleans	1820-1902	1903-1945	1853-1952
New York	1820-1897	1897-1942	1820-46 and 1897-1943
Philadelphia	1800-1882	1883-1945	1800-1948
Certain Minor Ports	1820-1873	1893-1945	1890-1924

Supplementing the indexes listed above in a general index to quarterly reports of arrivals at most ports except New York, 1820-74

A customs passenger list normally contains the following information for each passenger: his name, age, sex, and occupation; the country from which he came; and the country to which he was going; and, if he died in passage, the date and circumstances of his death. The immigration passenger lists that are more than 50 years old (those less than 50 years old are not available for reference purposes) vary in information content but usually show the place of birth and last place of residence in addition to the information found in the customs passenger lists. Some of the immigration passenger lists included the name and address of a relative in the country from which the passenger came.

The National Archives will search the customs passenger lists if in addition to the name of the passenger and the name of the port of entry an inquirer can supply the following information: the name of the vessel and the approximate date of its arrival or the name of the port of its arrival or the name of the port of embarkation and the exact date of arrival. It will also search the immigration passenger lists over 50 years old if an inquirer can give the full name and age of the passenger and names and ages of accompanying passengers, the name of the port of entry, the name of the vessel, and the exact date of arrival. The National Archives will also consult such indexes as it has to the names on the customs and immigration passenger lists provided an inquirer can give the full name and age of the passenger and names and ages of accompanying passengers, the name of the port of entry, the name of the vessel, and the exact date of arrival. The National Archives will also consult such indexes as it has to the names on the customs and immigration passenger lists provided an inquirer can supply the name of the port of entry and the supposed year of arrival. Requests for searches should be made on GSA Form 7111, Order and Billing for Copies of Passenger Lists.

Microfilm copies of passenger lists more than 50 years old are available for use in the National Archives.

The Morton Allan Directory of European Passenger Steamship Arrivals(New York, 1931) lists by year, steamship company, and exact date the names of vessels arriving at the ports of New York, 1890-1930, and Baltimore, Boston, and Philadelphia, 1904-26. This publication is available in some of the larger public and research libraries.

Passport Applications

The National Archives has passport applications and related papers, 1791-1905, of U.S. citizens who intended to travel abroad and will make limited searches for age and citizenship information in such of these records that are at least 75 years old. The name of the person who applied for a passort and the place and approximate date of application should be supplied. Requests for information from passport records less than 75 years old should be addressed to the Passport Office, Department of State, Washington, D.C. 20420.

Personnel Records

Most of the extant personnel records for civilian employees of the Federal Government whose service terminated before 1910 are in the National Archives. These records may contain information about the date and place of birth of an employee. The National Archives will search personnel records if given the full name and address of the employing agency, and the approximate dates of employment. The personnel records for most civilian employees whose service terminated after 1909 are in Civilian Personnel Records (GSA), 111 Winnebago Street, St. Louis, Mo. 63118.

Claims for Pensions and Bounty Land

Under numerous laws passed since the Revolutionary War period, money and land have been awarded to Army, Navy, and Marine veterans and their widows and other dependents. Each claim, whether for bounty land or pensions, whether submitted by the veteran, or whether approved, is filed under the name of veteran on whose service the applicant based his claim. The National Archives has bounty land warrant application files based on service in wartime between 1775 and 1855 and pension application files based on service between 1775 and 1916. Pensions based on military service for the confederate states of America were authorized by some southern states but not by the Federal Government until 1959. Inquiries about State pensions should be addressed to the State archives or equivalent agency at the capital of the veteran's state of residence after the war.

Since the form and contents of the papers submitted in support of claims have varied over the years, the information in the files is not uniform. A veteran's claim will probably show his place and date of birth, place of residence after service, and a summary of military service. A dependent's claim normally includes the dependent's age and residence, relationship to the veteran, and information about the Veteran's death. A widow's application usually includes her maiden name, the date of her marriage to the veteran, and the names of their children.

Inquiries about pension and bounty land claims should be submitted on GSA Form 6751, Order and Billing for Copies of Veterans Records. Printed on the form are instructions for its use and an explanation of how orders are processed. When a claim file is found, documents that normally contain information of a personal nature about the veteran and his family will be selected and photocopied. The photocopies will be sent to the inquirer with a bill for the cost of the reproductions. The selected documents furnished generally contain the basic information in the pension file, as the remaining documents rarely contain any additional genealogical data. If an inquirer wished to have photocopies of all the reproductible papers in the claim file, they can be furnished for a moderate cost per page.

The National Archives staff cannot undertake to read all the documents in the claim file or to answer questions about them. Some of the information requested on the form will be found in

Index of Revolutionary War Pension Applications, revised and published in 1966 by the National Genealogical Society; in

Report From the Secretary of War...in Relation to the Pension Establishment of the United States, published in three volumes in 1835 as Senate Document 514,23d Congress, 1st session; and in

List of Pensioners on the Roll January 1, 1883, published in five volumes in 1883 as Senate Executive Document 84, 47th Congress, 2d session. These publications are available in some of the larger public and research libraries.

A note on the Revolutionary War Pension and Bounty Land Records (from the Veterans Administration Archives in the National Archives). These records include a large number of Irish men and widows of Irish origin. Frequently they contain information about the country of origin as well as place of birth and several localities of residence while in America.

A veteran's widow would often send supporting evidence when submitting a claim (i.e. Family Bible, records of marriage and offspring, etc.). These items can prove very fruitful. Most pension records are from 1818 onwards. Also in the Archives are records from "The War of 1812."

Seamen's Protection-Certificate Applications

The National Archives has applications of seamen on American vessels for "protection certificates," or certificates of American citizenship, 1916-40. Such applications are usually supported by evidence of the date and place of birth and of the citizenship of the seaman. The National Archives will search the application files if give the following information: the full name of the seaman and the port from which the certificate was issued and, if available, the number or date of the certificates.

Service Records – Army

Records relating to service in the U.S. Regular Army of officers (1789-1916) and enlisted men (1789-1912) during both peacetime and wartime, as well as those of persons serving during wartime in volunteer units raised by states and mustered into Federal Service (1775-1903), are in the National Archives. Records of officers serving in the Regular Army vary in content so much that it is not feasible to describe here their form or content. Records of enlisted men serving in the Regular Army are contained in registers of enlistments which show for each recruit his name, age, place of birth, date and place of enlistment, regiment or company, and date and cause of discharge, or where applicable, date of death or date of desertion and sometimes of apprehension or return after desertion. There are also compiled military service records for soldiers of the Confederate Army. The compiled military service records of both volunteer officers and enlisted men serving in wartime and of Confederate soldiers normally show the soldier's rank, military organization, and term of service and occasionally his age, place of birth, date and place of enlistment, regiment or company, and date and cause of discharge, or where applicable, date of death or date of desertion and sometimes of apprehension or return after desertion. There are also compiled military service records for soldiers of the Confederate Army. The compiled military service records of both volunteer officers and enlisted men serving in wartime and of Confederate soldiers normally show the soldier's rank, military organization, and term of service and occasionally his age, place of enlistment, and place of birth. These records do not contain information about the soldier's family.

The National Archives will search the registers of enlistments or the compiled military service records in response to an inquiry on GSA Form 6751, Order and Billing for Copies of Veterans Records. For an effective search it is necessary that the form be as complete as possible. Whenever information is desired about military service in the Union Army in the Civil War, the name of the state from which the soldier served must be given. If a compiled military service record or an entry in an enlistment register is found, photocopies of the records will be supplied if the service was rendered more than 75 years ago (records of more recent service are subject to restrictions imposed by the Department of Defense). If the records in the National Archives relate to service within the past 75 years, a written statement of the service of the soldier will be sent free of charge.

Requests for information about Army officers separated after 1916 and Army enlisted personnel separated after 1912 should be made on Standard Form 180, Request Pertaining to Military Records, and sent to Military Personnel Records (GSA), 9700 Page Boulevard, St. Louis, MO 63132.

Service Records – Naval and Marine

The National Archives has records relating to American naval and marine service in the Revolutionary War (1775-83), in the U.S. Navy (for officers, 1798-1902, and enlisted men, 1798-1885), and in the U.S. Marine Corps (1798–1895). There are also records for some persons who served in the Confederate Navy and Marine Corps (1861-65).

Naval and marine service records of the Revolutionary War period are fragmentary, including only such information as a serviceman's name and rank, the name of the vessel on which he served, and the dates of his service or the dates when he was paid. Confederate naval and marine service records give the serviceman's name and rank and sometimes his station. If he was imprisoned, a record may give such information as the date of his capture, the place of his imprisonment, and the date of his parole. Only those requests for information about naval and marine service during the Revolutionary War and about service in the Confederate Navy and Marine Corps should be sent on GSA Form 6751, Order and Billing for Copies of Veterans Records. All other requests regarding naval and marine service records in the National Archives should be by letter, as the National Archives does not have compiled service records for naval and marine personnel.

The National Archives has records books of Revenue-Cutter Service officer personnel, 1791-1919, which are indexed by name of officer and give for each the state from which he was appointed, dates of birth and death (if he died while in the service), his successive promotions, and the names of vessels upon which he served. There are also record copies of officers commissions, 1791-1909; applications for cadet appointments and officers commissions, ca 1833-90; and "muster rolls and payrolls" (after 1871 muster rolls) of revenue cutters, 1832-1914. The muster rolls and payrolls show for each crewmember the name, rating, date and place of enlistment, place of birth, age, occupation, and personal description; the number of days served during the reported month; and the manner of separation, detachment, transferal, discharge, desertion, or death.

The officer personnel records, 1890-1929, in the General Archives Division, Washington National Records Center, include records of former Revenue-Cutter Service officers whose terms of service extended beyond 1915.

The inspectors of the Life-Saving Service were also military personnel, but the superintendents, keepers, and other employees at the Life-Saving stations were civilian employees. The inspectors and engineers of the Lighthouse Districts were officers detailed from the Navy and Army. All other employees of the Lighthouse Service were civilians. Personnel and card records, some dating back to 1864, for civilians formerly employed by the Revenue-Cutter Service, Life-Saving Service, and Lighthouse Service are on file at the National Personnel Records Center (Civilian Personnel Records). There are no separate lists by area or activity. Information can only be furnished on an individual name basis if sufficient identifying data is furnished.

Civilian employment records are subject to U.S. Civil Service Commission regulations governing the release of information from Federal employees' personnel records under the terms of the Freedom of Information Act of 1967 (5 USC/552). Information furnished is limited to names, position titles, grades, salaries, and duty stations. Inquiries, with as much identification as possible, should be submitted to Civilian Personnel Records (GSA), 111 Winnebago Street, St. Louis, MO 63118.

Library of Congress

GENERAL READING ROOMS DIVISION

Subject: Reference Services and Facilities of the Local History and Genealogy Room.

Location:

5th Floor of the Thomas Jefferson Bldg., adjacent to the Thomas Jefferson Reading Room.

Hours:

8:30 A.M. to 9:30 P.M., Monday thru Friday; 8:30 A.M. to 5:00 P.M., Saturday; 1:00 P.M. to 5:00 P.M., Sunday.

Resources:

Local history and genealogy publications. 5,000 volumes of reference books which are well indexed for the readers use and understanding. Indexes are often by family name. Mainly for research within the area of the United States.

Important Comments:

1. A small reference staff is available to assist readers who come to the library.

2. The staff cannot undertake general research in family history or heraldry because of the time involved.

3. Readers should familiarize themselves with genealogical research by reading at least one book on the subject before coming to the library. (In order to make proper use of your time and improve the chances of success.)

4. A complete transcript of the "Family Name Index" in the LH&G room as of 12/71 was published by the Magna Carta Book Company, 5502 Magnolia Avenue, Baltimore, Md. 21215. Entitled,

Genealogies in the Library of Congress, a Bibliography, containing over 20,000 genealogies.

5. *U.S. Local Histories in the Library of Congress, a Bibliography,* also by the Magna Carta Book Company, lists 90,000 works.

6. The library does not permit genealogy books to circulate on interlibrary loan.

7. The library does not have copies of genealogies for sale.

8. Inquiries for information on passenger lists, census, land, naturalization and military records should be made to the National Archives, Washington D.C., 20408.

9. Photocopies may be made of the libraries collection. Inquire at: Library of Congress, Photoduplication Service, Washington, D.C., 20540.

Surnames: A Selected List of References

Note: Publications on this list can be consulted in the Library of Congress; They are not, however, available on interlibrary loan. Some of them may be in the collections of a library to which you have access.

Irish Family Names, with origins, meanings, clans, arms, crests, and mottos. Patrick Kelly. Collected from the living Gaelic and from authoritative books, mss., and public documents. 2d ed. (n.p.) 1958. 136 pp. CS2415.K4

Some Ulster Surnames. Padraig MacGiolla Domhnaigh. (New ed.) with foreword by Edward MdLysaght. Baile Atha Cliath (Dublin) Clodhanna Teo. 64, (5) p. First published in 1923 under the title, Some Anglicised Surnames in Ireland.

A Guide to Irish Surnames. Edward MacLysaght. (2d ed., rev. and enl) Dublin, Helicon (1965, c 1965) 256 pp. CS2415.M23 "Bibliography of Irish family history." pp. 207-247.

Irish Families; their names, arms, and origins. Edward MacLysaght. Illustrated by Myra Maquire. (3d ed., rev.) New York, Crown Publishers (1972). Bibliography, pp. 316-336. 365 pp. illus. CS498.M3

More Irish Families. O'Gorman. Galway Ireland 1960. 320 pp. color coat of arms. Bibliography, pp. 285-290. CS498.M32

Supplement to Irish Families. Genealogical Book Co., Galtimore. 1964. 163 pp. "Additional notes on names dealt with in Irish Families and More Irish Families": pp. 157-163. CS498.M33

The Surnames of Ireland. Edward MacLysaght. Dublin. Irish University Press (1973) xxi. 337 pp. maps. "Bibliography of Irish family history": pp. 305-368. CS2411.M25

Sloinnte Gaedheal is Gall: Irish Names and Surnames, collected and edited with explanatory and historical notes by Patrick Woulfe. Dublin, M.H. Gill, 1923. xlvi. 696 pp. CS2411.W6

Some of the Military Records of America, before 1900; their use and value in genealogical and historical research. E. Kay Kirkham. (Washington? 1963) 35 pp. illus. CS49.K49

A Survey of American Census Schedules; an explanation and description of our Federal Census enumerations 1790 to 1950. E. Kay Kirkham. Salt Lake City, Seseret Book Co. (1959) 102 pp. illus. (The Columbia series in genealogy) CS49.K5

Directory of Genealogical Periodicals. J.A. Konrad. Munroe Falls, Ohio, Summit Publications. 1975. 61 pp. CS1.K66

A Bibliography of Ship Passenger Lists, 1538-1825; being a guide to published lists of early immigrants to North America. 3d ed., rev. and enl. by Richard J. Wolfe. Harold Lancour. With a list of passenger arrival records in the National Archives by Frank E. Bridgers. New Yoruk, New York Public Library, 1963. 137 pp. Z7164.I3L2

United States Directory of Post Offices, Washington, D.C.: Post Office Department (annual). Alphabetical arrangement of towns by state with county indicated. It is, of course, limited to towns with Post Offices.

Bullinger's Postal and Shippers Guide for the United States and Canada. Westwood, N.J.: Bullinger's Guides, Inc. (1897-?). Alphabetical listing of all towns (and cover towns without Post Offices as well).

Columbia-Lippincott Gazetteer of the World. Morningside Heights, N.Y.: Columbia University Press and J.B. Lippincott Co. (1905-1952). While not covering all localities, the information contained on the places included in this book is excellent.

Webster's Geographical Dictionary. Springfield, Massachusetts: G & C Merriam Company, 1957. Over 40,000 listings throughout the world.

Other Published Research Aids:

Some books that may be of assistance in the use of state and local records are listed below:

Church records contain information about births, baptisms, marriages, deaths, and burials and give the names of members of families. Church records may also help trace movements of individuals from one community to another.

Information about the record holdings of many of the leading denomination can be found in the October 1961 and other issues of *The American Archivist,* published quarterly by the Society of American Archivists.

The following books may also help locate church records:

Check List of Historical Records Survey Publications. Sargent B. Child and Dorothy P. Holmes. Rev. Ed. Washington, D.C., 1943. Lists published inventories of State, county, and municipal records; transcriptions of public records in the States; and guides to bital records.

An Annotated Bibliography of Censuses of Population Taken After the Year 1790 by States and Territories of the United States. Henry J. Dubester. Washington, D.C., 1948. Out of print.

Search and Research. Noel C. Stevenson. Rev. Ed. Salt Lake City, 1973.

Directory of State and Provincial Archivests. Society of American Archivists. Chicago, 1975.

Directory: Historical Societies and Agencies in the United States and Canada, 1975-76. American Association for State and Local History. Nashville, 1976.

How to Trace Your Family Tree; a complete and easy to understand guide for the beginner. American Genealogical Research Institute. (Arlington, Va., c 1973) 197 pp. Bibliography: pp. 194-197. CS16.A48

Genealogical Research. American Society of Genealogists. Washington, 1960 port. CS16.A5

Practical Research in Genealogy; a compilation of genealogical research data, compiled by Galdys Busby and Evelyn Fish. Arizona Temple District Genealogical Library, Messa Ariz. c 1955. 150 pp. maps. Includes bibliographical references. CS47.A75

Basic Course in Genealogy; instruction to help beginners in genealogical research. Thomas Nelson Community College, Hampton, Va. 1972. 109 pp. Includes bibliographical references. CS16.B34

Advanced Genealogical Research. Archibald F. Bennett. Salt Lake City, Bookcraft. 1959. 256 pp. illus. CS16.B38

A Guide for Genealogical Research. Archibald F. Bennett. Salt Lake City. Genealogical Society of the Church of Jesus Christ of Latter Day Saints, 1951. 339 pp. illus. facsims., ports. CS16.B4

Searching with Success; a genealogical text. Archibald F. Bennett. Salt Lake City, Deseret Book Co., 1962. 262 pp. illus. CS16.B42

Guide to Genealogical Records in The National Archives. Meredith B. Colket. Washington, National Archives, National Archives and Records Service, General Services Administration, 1964. 145 pp. (National Archives publication no. 65-8) CS15.C6

Seven Lesson Course in Irish Research and Sources. Betty L. McCay. (Indianapolis? c 1972) 36 leaves. map. CS483.M3

Irish and Scotch-Irish Ancestral Research; a guide to the genealogical records, methods and sources in Ireland. Margaret D. Falley. Evanston, Ill. 1962. 2 vol. Contents: v.1 Reporitories and records. v.2 Bibliography and family index. CS483.F32.

Wills and Where to Find Them. Jeremy S.W. Gibson. Baltimore, Genealogical Pub. Co. 1974. xxii, 210 pp. maps. CS1068.A2G5

In Search of Scottish Ancestry. Gerald K.S. Hamilton-Edwards. Baltimore, Genealogical Pub. Co. 1972. 252 pp. illus. facsims, geneal. tables, map. Bibliography: pp. 233-283.

A Survey of American Church Records. E. Kay Kirkham. 2 vols. Salt Lake City, 1959-60.

For each of the following, address inquiries to:

Chief, Archives Branch

Federal Archives and Records Center

Boston

380 Trapelo Road
Waltham, MA 02154
(Telephone 617-223-2657; hours 8 a.m.-4:30 p.m., Monday-Friday. Serves Connecticut, Maine, Massachusetts, New Hampshire, Rhode Island, and Vermont.)

New York

Building 22-MOT Bayonne
Bayonne, N.J. 07002
(Telephone 201-858-7245; hours 8:30 a.m.-5:00 p.m., Monday-Friday. Serves New Jersey, New York, Puerto Rico, and the Virgin Islands.)

Philadelphia

5000 Wissahickon Avenue
Philadelphia, PA 19144
(Telephone 215-951-5591; hours 7:30 a.m.-4:00 p.m., Monday-Friday. Serves Delaware and Pennsylvania; for the loan of microfilm also serves the District of Columbia, Maryland, Virginia, and West Virginia.)

Atlanta

1557 St. Joseph Avenue
East Point, GA 30344
(Telephone 404-763-7477; hours 8 a.m.-4:30 p.m., Monday-Friday. Serves Alabama, Georgia, Florida, Kentucky, Mississippi, North Carolina, South Carolina, and Tennessee.)

Chicago

7358 South Pulaski Road
Chicago, IL 60629
(Telephone 312-353-0161; hours 8 a.m.-4:30 p.m., Monday-Friday. Serves Illinois, Indiana, Michigan, Minnesota, Ohio, and Wisconsin.)

Kansas City

2306 East Bannister Road
Kansas City, MO 64131
(Telephone 816-926-7271; hours 8 a.m.-4:30 p.m., Monday-Friday. Serves Iowa, Kansas, Missouri, and Nebraska.)

Forth Worth

4900 Hemphill Street (building address)
P.O. Box 6216 (mailing address)
Forth Worth, TX 76115
(Telephone 817-334-5515; hours 8 a.m.-4:30 p.m., Monday-Friday. Serves Arkansas, Louisiana, New Mexico, Oklahoma, and Texas.)

Denver

Building 48, Denver Federal Center
Denver, CO 80225
(Telephone 303-234-5271; hours 7:30 a.m.-4 p.m., Monday-Friday. Serves Colorado, Montana, North Dakota, South Dakota, Utah, and Wyoming.)

San Francisco

1000 Commodore Drive
San Bruno, CA 94066
(Telephone 415-876-9009; hours 7:45 a.m.-7:15 p.m., Monday-Friday. Serves California except Southern California, Hawaii, Nevada except Clark County, and the Pacific Ocean area.)

Los Angeles

24000 Avila Road
Laguna Niguel, CA 92677
(Telephone 714-831-4242; hours 8 a.m.-4:30 p.m., Monday-Friday. Serves Arizona; the Southern California counties of Imperial, Inyo, Kern, Los Angeles, Orange, Riverside, San Bernardino, San Diego, San Luis Obispo, Santa Barbara, and Ventura; and Clark County, Nev.)

Seattle

6125 San Point Way N.E.
Seattle, WA 98115
(Telephone 206-442-4502; hours 8 a.m.-4:30 p.m., Monday-Friday. Serves Alaska, Idaho, Oregon, and Washington.)

Holdings of Microfilm Publications

NARS is depositing in regional archives branches copies of its microfilm publications. These publications, on 35– and 16-mm. microfilm, reproduce with introductions and annotations some of the most significant records in the National Archives Building. They contain basic documentation for the study of history, economics, public administrations, political science, law, ethnology, genealogy, and other subjects. Included are records of U.S. diplomatic missions, large bodies of material relating to the Revolutionary and Civil Wars, German records captured at the end of World War II, territorial papers, and census returns, including the 1900 census. *Prologue: The Journal of the National Archives* periodically lists the microfilm publications deposited in the regional archives branches.

Microfilm publications in the regional archives branches are available for use in the branches' research rooms and on interinstitutional loan. Individual users may borrow the microfilm through libraries and research institutions located within a particular region and in accordance with the "National Interlibrary Loan Code, 1968."

Microfilms of Passenger Lists

The National Archives, Washington, D.C. has microfilm of Irish Passenger lists, Ireland to ports in the USA, 1803-1806.

CENSUS FORMATS IN THE U.S.A.

1790

NAME OF HEAD OF FAMILY
Free white males of 16 years and upward including heads of families.
Free white males under 16 years.
Free white females including heads of families.
All other free persons.
Slaves

1790

This census has been published and fully indexed for simple and easy examination. Covers the original colonies.

1800

Names of heads of families.	Name of county, parish, township, town or city, where the family resides.
Free white males: Under 10 years of age Of 10 and under 16 Of 16 and under 26, including heads of families Of 26 and under 45, including heads of families Of 45 and upwards, including heads of families	
Free white females: Under 10 years of age Of 16 and under 26, including heads of families Of 26 and under 45, including heads of families Of 45 and upwards, including heads of families	
All other free persons, except Indians not taxed	
Slaves	

1800-1840

You must search county by county. Not indexed.

1820

1820
Name of county, parish, township, town or city, where the family resides.
Names of heads of families.
Free white males: Under 10 years of age; Of 10 and under 16; Between 16 and 18; Of 16 and under 26, including heads of families; Of 26 and under 45, including heads of families; Of 45 and upwards, including heads of families
Free white females: Under 10 years of age; Of 10 and under 16; Of 16 and under 26, including heads of families; Of 26 and under 45, including heads of families; Of 45 and upwards, including heads of families
Foreigners not naturalized
Number of persons engaged in: Agriculture; Commerce; Manufacture
Slaves: Males: Under 14 years; Of 14 and under 26; Of 26 and under 45; Of 45 and upwards. Females: Under 14 years; Of 14 and under 26; Of 26 and under 45; Of 45 and upwards
Free colored persons: Males: Under 14 years; Of 14 and under 26; Of 26 and under 45; Of 45 and upwards. Females: Under 14 years; Of 14 and under 26; Of 26 and under 45; Of 45 and upwards
All other persons, except Indians not taxed

1830

1830	
Name of county, city, ward, town, township, parish, precinct, hundred or district	
Name of heads of families	
Free white persons, including heads of families — Males:	Under 5 years of age; Of 5 and under 10; Of 10 and under 15; Of 15 and under 20; Of 20 and under 30; Of 30 and under 40; Of 40 and under 50; Of 50 and under 60; Of 60 and under 70; Of 70 and under 80; Of 80 and under 90; Of 90 and under 100; Of 100 and upwards
Free white persons, including heads of families — Females:	Under 5 years of age; Of 5 and under 10; Of 10 and under 15; Of 15 and under 20; Of 20 and under 30; Of 30 and under 40; Of 40 and under 50; Of 50 and under 60; Of 60 and under 70; Of 70 and under 80; Of 80 and under 90; Of 90 and under 100; Of 100 and upwards
Slaves — Males:	Under 10 years of age; Of 10 and under 25; Of 24 and under 36; Of 36 and under 55; Of 55 and under 100; Of 100 and upwards
Slaves — Females:	Under 10 years of age; Of 10 and under 24; Of 24 and under 36; Of 36 and under 55; Of 55 and under 100; Of 100 and upwards
Total	
White persons included in the foregoing	Who are deaf and dumb, under 14 years of age
	Who are deaf and dumb, of 14 and under 25
	Who are deaf and dumb, of 25 and upwards
	Who are blind
Aliens--foreigners not Naturalized	

1840

1840	
Name of county, city, ward, town, township parish, precinct, hundred, or district	
Name of heads of families	
Free white persons, including heads of families — Males:	Under 5 years of age; Of 5 and under 10; Of 15 and under 20; Of 20 and under 30; Of 30 and under 40; Of 40 and under 50; Of 50 and under 60; Of 60 and under 70; Of 70 and under 80; Of 80 and under 90; Of 90 and under 100; Of 100 and upwards
Free white persons, including heads of families — Females:	Under 5 years of age; Of 5 and under 10; Of 10 and under 15; Of 15 and under 20; Of 20 and under 30; Of 30 and under 40; Of 40 and under 50; Of 50 and under 60; Of 60 and under 70; Of 70 and under 80; Of 80 and under 90; Of 90 and under 100; Of 100 and upwards
Slaves — Males:	Under 10 years of age; Of 10 and under 24; Of 24 and under 36; Of 36 and under 55; Of 55 and under 100; Of 100 and upwards
Slaves — Females:	Under 10 years of age; Of 10 and under 24; Of 24 and under 36; Of 36 and under 55; Of 55 and under 100; Of 100 and upwards
Total	
Number of persons in each family engaged in-	
Pensioners for Revolutionary or military services, included in the foregoing	Name
	Age

1850

1850
Dwelling-houses numbered in the order of visitation
Families numbered in the order of visitation
The name of every person whose usual place of abode on the first day of June, 1850, was in this family.
Description: Age
Description: Sex
Description: Color--White, black or mulatto.
Profession, Occupation, or Trade of each male person over 15 years of age
Value of Real Estate owned
Place of Birth, naming the State, Territory, or Country.
Married within the year.
Attended school within the year.
Persons over 20 years of age who cannot read and write.
Whether deaf and dumb, blind, insane, idiotic, pauper, or convict.

1850-1870 These years enumerate every member of a household (not just heads of households). Not indexed.

1860

1860
Dwelling Houses--number in the order of visitation.
Families numbered in the order of visitation.
The name of every person whose usual place of abode on the first day of June, 1860, was in this family.
Description. Age
Description. Sex
Description. Color, White, Black, or Mulatto
Profession, Occupation, or Trade of each person, male and female, over 15 years of age.
Value of Estate Owned. Value of Real Estate
Value of Estate Owned. Value of Personal Estate
Place of Birth, Naming the State, Territory, or Country.
Married within the year.
Attended school within the year.
Persons over 20 years of age who cannot read and write.
Whether deaf and dumb, blind, insane idiotic, pauper, or convict.

1880 Relationship to head of household listed for every individual. Place of birth for each person's mother and father is listed. Partially indexed.

State	Date Records Begin Death	Birth	First Census	Available Census Mortality Records	Locations	Location of Land Records
Alabama	1908	1908	1830	1850/60/70/80	Dept of Archives & History, Montg.	Probate Judge of County
Arizona	1909	1909	1870	1870/80	NSDAR Library	County Recorder
Arkansas	1914	1914	1830	1850/60/70/80	Univ. of Arkansas	County Recorder
California	1905	1905	1850	1850/60/70/80	Calif. State Library	County Recorder
Colorado	1907	1907	1870	1870/80	NSDAR Library	County Recorder
Connecticut	1897	1897	1790	1850/60/70/80	Conn. State Library	Town Clerk
Delaware	1881	1881	1800	1850/60/70/80	Public Archives Comm. Hall of Records	County Recorder of Deeds
District of Columbia	1855	1871		1850/60/70/80	NSDAR Library	Recorder of Deeds
Florida	1899	1899	1830	1850/60/70/80	Dept of Agriculture	Clerk of County Circuit Court
Georgia	1919	1919	1820	1850/60/70/80	NSDAR Library	Clerk of County Superior Court
Idaho	1911	1911	1870	1870/80	Idaho State Library	County Recorder
Illinois	1916	1916	1820	1850/60/70/80	Ill. State Archives	County Recorder of Deeds
Indiana	1900	1907	1820	1850/60/70/80	Indiana State Library	County Recorder
Iowa	1880	1880	1840	1850/60/70/80	Iowa State Historical Society	County Recorder of Deeds
Kansas	1911	1911	1860	1860/70/80	Kansas State Historical Society	County Clerk
Kentucky	1911	1911	1860	1850/60/70/80	NSDAR Library	County Clerk
Louisiana	1914	1914	1810	1850/60/70/80	NSDAR Library	Recorder of Mortgages & Register of Conveyanc in the Parish
Maine	1892	1892	1790	1850/60/70/80	Office of Vital Statistics, Dept of Health & Welfare	Register of Deeds
Maryland	1898	1898	1790	1850/60/70/80	Maryland State Library	Circuit Court Clerk for the County
Massachusetts	1841	1841	1790	1850/60/70/80	State Archives	Registry of Deeds of County
Michigan	1867	1867	1820	1850/60/70/80	Mich. Historical Comm.	County Register of Deeds
Minnesota	1900	1900	1850	1850/60/70/80	Minn. State Library	County Register of Deeds
Misssissippi	1912	1912	1820	1850/60/70/80	Dept of Archives & History	Clerk of the Chance Court
Missouri	1910	1910	1830	1850/60/70/80	Mo. State Historical Society	Recorder of Deeds
Montana	1907	1907	1860	1870/80	Mon. State Historical Society	County Clerk & Recorder

Nebraska	1905	1905	1860	1860/70/80	Neb. State Historical Society	Register of Deeds
Nevada	1911	1911	1860	1860/70/80	State Historical Society	County Recorder
New Hampshire	1850	1850	1790	1850/60/70/80	State Library	Town Clerk
New Jersey	1848	1848	1830	1850/60/70/80	State Library Archives & History Bureau	County Register
New Mexico	1919	1919	1850	1850/60/70	State Historical Society	County Recorder
New York	1880	1880	1790	1850/60/70/80	State Library	County Clerk
No. Carolina	1913	1913	1790	1850/60/70/80	State Dept of Archives & History	Co. Register of Deeds
No. Dakota	1908	1908	1860	1860/70/80	State Historical Society	Co. Register of Deeds
Ohio	1909	1909	1820	1850/60/80	State Historical Society	County Recorder
Oklahoma	1908	1908				County Recorder of Deeds
Oregon	1903	1903	1850	1850/60/70/80	State Archives	County Clerk
Pennsylvania	1906	1906	1790	1850/60/70/80	State Library	County Recorder of Deeds
Rhode Island	1852	1852	1790	1850/60/70/80	State Library	Town & City Clerk
So. Carolina	1915	1915	1790	1850/60/70/80	Dept of Archives & History	Register of Mesne
So. Dakota	1905	1905	1860	1860/70/80	State Historical Society	Co. Register of Deeds
Tennessee	1914	1914	1820	1850/60/80	NSDAR Library	Co. Register of Deeds
Texas	1903	1903	1850	1850/60/70/80	Archives Div. State Library	County Clerk
Utah	1905	1905	1850	1850/60/70/80	Texas State Library	County Recorder
Vermont	1857	1857	1790	1850/60/70/80	State Library	Town & City Clerks
Virginia	1912	1912	1810	1850/60/70/80	State Library	Co. Circuit Judge
Washington	1907	1907	1860	1860/70/80	State Library	County Auditor
West Virginia	1912	1912	1810	1860/70/80	Dept of Archives & History	Clerk of the County Court
Wisconsin	1907	1907	1820	1850/60/70/80	State Historical Society	County Register of Deeds
Wyoming	1909	1909	1860	1870/80	State Law Library	County Clerk
Alaska	1913	1913	1880			Recorder of Judicial District
Hawaii	1896	1896				Registrar of Conveyances
Puerto Rico	1931	1931				
Virgin Islands	1919	1919				

It has been estimated that 20% of Canada's population is of Irish heritage. Indeed, ships passed through Canadian ports, i.e., St. Johns, Halifax, Quebec, on their journey from Ireland. In the first half of the 18th century strong commercial links existed between Co. Cork, Ireland and Canada. Some of our Irish ancestors resided in both Canada and America, so research is often necessary in both counties.

CANADA

Records of Canadian affairs vary from area to area, mainly as a result of the history of the formation of the country itself. The location as well as the type of information available in Canadian records will be determined by the particular province or land division in question.

The information contained in this chapter will acquaint you with the available records and dates covered. For further information consult the sources listed at the end of this section.

We will cover in the following pages some of the geographical and judicial divisions of Canada as they pertain to genealogical research. Each province will be dealt with seperately and will include census, vital records and probate jurisdiction. The next few paragraphs will give you vital information needed to organize and begin your search with a proper understanding of Canada's background and records.

Historical Notes on Land Division

Upper Canada (Ontario) and Lower Canada (Quebec) were merged as Canada West and Canada East in 1841. On July 1, 1867, New Brunswick and Nova Scotia joined the above to form the Dominion of Canada. Manitoba was added in 1870; British Columbia, 1871; Prince Edward Island, 1873; Saskatchewan, 1905; and Newfoundland (and Labrador) joined the Dominion in 1950.

Land Records

The Ottowa Public Archives contain original grants in Upper Canada (1791-1867) and Lower Canada (1764-1829). Country of birth, military service and family members are often included as well.

Most land records are in the hands of the local land registries, so you would need to know the land area in question to continue your search easily in this direction.

Church Records

As in Ireland, the church registers are a major source of information which normally remains in the hands of the local pastor. In some instances church records are on hand as far back as 1617, but in most cases they begin much later.

The province of Quebec required church records to be kept as vital information by law. Hence, Quebec has the oldest and most complete church registers for both Catholic and Protestant denominations.

Marriage bonds for Ontario (Upper Canada) 1803-1845, and Quebec (Lower Canada) 1779, 1919-1967, are on hand in the Public Archives of Ottowa, Ontario.

Divorce Records are kept in the proper court jurisdiction for each province. At times you find that divorce is allowed only by act of Parliament. For all practical purposes under these conditions, divorce records are nearly non-existant since divorce was seldom officially recognized or allowed.

Census Returns

While several census' were taken earlier, beginning in 1851, a census has been taken every 10 years, listing all persons in a household. Information includes name, sex, place of birth, religious affiliation, occupation, education, marriage status, and disabilities.

Military Service records can be obtained if you have specific knowledge of the regiment in question. The Public Archives contain some records on microfilm.

Peterboro Library, Ontario, contains some 2,000 Irish names of men who traveled from Co. Cork, Ireland (1823-1825) to Canada. Their ship names were: Star, Fortitude, Regulus, Resolution, Elizabeth, Brunswick, Hebe, and Stakesby.

A knowledge of the geographical divisions in Canada will prove to be a necessary starting point in your research. The following is an overview of the records for the particular provinces in question.

Alberta

Two main recordkeeping centers exist in: (1) Edmonton for northern areas, and (2) Lethleridge for the southern areas of Alberta. The province records for Alberta, dating from 1855, are in the hands of the Deputy Registrar General in Edmonton.

Vital records. Edmonton is the center. Most records are incomplete up until the beginning of the 20th century.

Early Census Returns. Did not join the Dominion until 1905.

Probate Records. District Courts.

British Columbia

The following counties are important references for jurisdiction:

1. Cariboo
2. Kootenay
3. Nanaimo
4. Prince Rupert
5. Vancouver
6. Victoria
7. West Minster
8. Yale

British Columbia is also divided into land districts, some of which have land registry offices.

Vital Records. 1872 on. The Director of Vital Statistics, Parliament Building, Victoria Canada.

Probate Records. County Courts (under $5,000).

Manitoba

The following judicial districts can give you access to legal records:

District	Center
Eastern Judicial District	Winnepeg
Central Judicial District	Portage la Prairie
Western Judicial District	Brandon
Dauphin Judicial District	Dauphin
Northern Judicial District	The Pas

Vital Statistics. (The late 1800's for complete records.) Department of Health, Vital Statistics Branch, Wennegeg, Canada.

Census. Family heads: 1832,1834,1835,1840, 1843, 1846, 1849. All persons: 1870.

Probate. Provincial Surrogate Clerk at Winnepeg.

New Brunswick

Probate and land records are kept by county and county seat. Vital Statistics. (Good records 1888 on.) Registrar General, Department of Health, Federiction.

Census. All persons: 1851, 1861, 1871.

Probate. County Probate Court of Area at time of death.

Newfoundland

The capitol of St. Johns is the record center.

Vital Statistics. (1892 on.) Register of Vital Statistics, Department of Health, St. Johns.

Census. Family heads: 1704; All persons: 1691-1693. (Also special census for Plaisance alone.)

Probate. Newfoundland Supreme Court at St. Johns.

Nova Scotia

The 18 county seats of this province house most legal and civil records.

Vital Statistics. (1864 on.) Registrar General, Department of Public Health, Halifax. (From 1876-1909, marriage records only.)

Census. Family heads: 1770, 1773, 1775, 1787, 1861. All persons: 1871 (per Acadia).

Probate. Probate Court of area of residence.

Ontario

The counties and district of Ontario house civil and legal records. Land records are an independent division within the counties.

Vital Statistics. (July 1st, 1869 on.) Deputy Registrar General, Bay and Wellesley Streets, Toronto.

Census. Family heads: 1842. All persons: 1851, 1861, 1871.

Probate. County Surrogate Court of Area of residence.

Prince Edward Island

The three main divisions are as follows:

Kings County (Seat at Georgetown)

Prince County (Seat at Summerside)

Queens County (Seat at Charlottetown)

Vital Statistics. (Good records 1883 on.) Director of Vital Statistics, Department of Health, Charlottetown.

Census. Family heads: 1841, 1861.

Probate. The Supreme Court of Charlottetown.

Quebec

The eight probate (Superior Court) divisions of this province are as follows:

District	Center
Quebec	Quebec City, Thetford Mines Rimouski, Beauc
Montreal	Montreal
Sherbrooke (St. Francois)	Sherbrooke
Trois-Rivieres	Trois-Riveres
Hull	Hull
Amos & Rouyn	Abitibi and Rouyn
Chicoutimi	Chicoutimi
St. Maurice	Shawinigan

In addition, 32 judicial district contain vital records prior to 1926. Land registration divisions are also worthy of note.

Vital statistics. (1621-1926) Superior Court of Area. Based upon church location. (1926 on.) Department of Health, Demography Branch, Quebec City.

Census. Family heads: 1825,1831, 1842. All persons: 1666, 1667, 1851, 1861, 1871.

Probate. District Superior Court of place of residence (or notary records).

Saskatchewan

Division of Vital Statistics, Health & Welfare Building, Regina. (1878+)

Probate. District Surrogate Court.

Acadia

An early French holding which new comprises most of what is now Nova Scotia.

Census. Family heads: 1703, 1707, 1739. All persons: 1671, 1686, 1693, 1698, 1701, 1714. (Also available, individual city census.)

Irish Families in Ancient Quebec Reocrds, by John O'Farrell, 1872.

Records of Genealogical Interest in the Public Archives of Canada, by James J. Atherton. (Area I, No. 43) Seminar paper from World Conference on REcords and Genealogical Seminar. Salt Lake City: The Genealogical Society of The Church of Jesus Christ of Latter-day Saints, 1969.

Tracing Ancestors Through the Province of Quebec and Acadia to France, by Roland J. Auger. (Area F, No. 6) Se inar paper from World Conference on Records and Genealogical Seminar. Salt Lake City: The Genealogical Society of The Church of Jesus Christ of Latter-day Saints, 1969.

Billinger's Postal and Shippers Guide for the United States and Canada. Westwood, N.J.: Bullinger's Buides, Inc. (annual). This is a good source for helping to locate places.

Gazetteer of Canada. Canadian Permanent Committee on Geographical Names. (For each individual province). Ottawa: Queen's Printer and Controller of Stationery (various dates). These have good maps, good historical data, and are excellent for locating places.

Directory-History Societies and Agencies in the United States and Canada. Nashville, Tenn: American Association of State and Local History. (Bi-annual.)

Pre-Revolutionary Settlements in Nova Scotia, by D. Bruce Fergusson. (Area I, No. 45). Seminar paper from World Conference on Records and Genealogical Seminar. Salt Lake City: The Genealogical Society of The Church of Jesus Christ of Latter-day Saints, 1969.

Sources for Genealogical Research in Ontario, by Sandra Guillaume. (Area I, No. 44). Seminar paper from World Conference on Records and Genealogical Seminar. Salt Lake City: The Genealogical Society of The Church of Jesus Christ of Latter-day Saints, 1969.

The Exodus of British Loyalist (Royalists) from the U.S. to Canada, England, the Caribbean, and Spanish Territories, by Robert F. Kirk and Audrey Kirk. (Area I, No. 46). Seminar paper from World Conference on Records and Genealogical Seminar. Salt Lake City: The Genealogical Society of The Church of Jesus Christ of Latter-day Saints, 1969.

Major Genealogical Sources for Canada, Quebec and Acadia. (Series B, No. 3, of Research Papers.) Salt Lake City: The Genealogical Society of The Church of Jesus Christ of Latter-day Saints, 1969.

Martindale-Hubbell Law Directory. Vol. V. Summit, N.J.: Martindale-Hubbell, Inc. (annual). This is an excellent guide to courts, laws and legal procedures.

McGraw-Hill Directory and Almanac of Canada. Toronto: McGraw-Hill Company of Canada, Ltd. (various dates). This book gives good information on court jurisdictions and land divisions in the provinces.

Church Records of Canada by Marget Meikleham and Glenn Lucus, T.R. Millman, Francois Beaudin, Erich Schults. (Area I, Nos. 48 and 49). Seminar papers from World Conference on Records and Genealogical Seminar. Salt Lake City: The Genealogical Society of The Church of Jesus Christ of Latter-day Saints, 1969.

Municipal Guide for the Province of Quebec City: Quebec Bureau of Statistics, 1966. This useful guide is available for fifty cents from the Quebec Bureau of Statistics, Hotel du Gouvernment, Quebec City, Quebec. It tells in which judicial district of the Superior Court each town in the province is located.

Tracing Your Ancestors in Canada. Public Archives of Canada. Ottawa: Queen's Printer and Controller of Stationery, 1967. This is a good basic guide to research sources in various depositories.

The Ontario Genealogical Society Bulletin, Vol. III, No. 3 (September 1964). Milton Rubincam.

"Canada." Genealogical Research: Methods and Sources. Ed. by Milton Rubincam. Washington, D.C.: The American Society of Genealogist, 1960. pp.261-288.

Post 1815 Settlement in Canada, by Donald Wilson. (Area I, No. 47). Seminar paper from World Conference on Records and Genealogical Seminar. Salt Lake City: The Genealogical Society of The Church of Jesus Christ of Latter-day Saints, 1969.

Canadian Genealogical Periodicals

French Canadian and Acdian Genealogical Review, Case Postale 845, Haut-Ville, Quebec 4, Quebec.

Loyalist Gazette, 23 Prince Arthur Ave., Toronto 180, Ontario.

The Ontario Genealogical Society Bulletin, Box 66, Station Q, Toronto 7, Ontario.

Societe Genealogique Canadienne Francaise. Memoirs, Case Postale 335, Place d'Armes, Montreal 1, Quebec.

RECORDS OF THE IRISH IN OTHER COUNTRIES

- England
- Europe
- Australia
- Wales, Scotland

IRISH IN EUROPE

The Irish have traveled to foreign shores in Europe as military men, church representatives and as regular emigrants in search of a new home.

Due to persecution and deteriorating conditions at home, the Irish were forced into wars abroad by the thousands. Military service during the 16th, 17th, and 18th century saw thousands of Irish fighting with the armies of France, Spain, Austria, and Russia. The Irish Brigade was formed in the 17th century and approximately 11,000 Irishment sailed to France. Many descendents of these military men remain alive today, and some strange adaptations of the last names of the Irish can be found in these European countries.

English Records

Thousands of Irish immigrated to Britain, concentrating on the main industrial centers such as Liverpool in order to obtain employment. (Scotland and Wales as well.) The population of these countries reflect this fact in the living families with Irish surnames which exist today.

Since so many Irish have settled in nearby England, it is not surprising that many English records pertain directly to Ireland and the Irish people, i.e., army enlistment records, Crown books, etc.

The following are possible sources in London:

1. The General Registrar Office, (St. Catherines House, London, W.C.2) Records include: Army birth, marriages and deaths back to 1761; Births and deaths at sea from 1837; Subjects of Britain in foreign countries from 1948; Non Parochial Registers (1642-1837+); And Registered births, deaths and marriages in Wales and England (1837+).
2. Public Records office – Government records (11th century on).
3. National Central Library.
4. British Museum – London (catalog of Irish manuscripts).
5. Parish Registers – (1750+) Kept on the parish level as in Ireland.

6. 1841 & 1851 Census Records – Gives country of origin for people included in the census (which could be Ireland).
7. Society of Genealogists, 37 Harrington Gardens, Kensington, London. SW7 4JX, England.

English Libraries of Interest

1. The Cambridge University Library – Cambridge, England. (See: A catalog of the Bradshaw Collection of Irish Books...) Cambridge, 1916.
2. Archiepiscopal Library – Lambeth Palace, London. (Carew Manuscripts, 1515-1624).
3. Somerset House – London (Prerogative Wills).
4. The Bodleian Library – Oxford (Carte Manuscripts).

Australian Records

The libraries and archives of Australia contain many different sources of genealogical information.

Possible sources:

1. Tasmanian State Library – Has extensive records relative to administrative and immigration matters.
2. Hobart State Archives
3. Canberra National Library – Shipping Index 1803-1857.
4. Registrar General of Tasmania – Birthe, marriages, deaths (1838+). Churches (1804-1838).
5. Mitchell Library – (Sydney) Census returns, passenger lists.
6. The New South Wales Government Gazette – Indexed (1832-1886). Lands, wills, titles, etc., on hand at the major libraries.

Other Libraries of Interest: Scotland & Wales

1. H.M. Register House, Edinburgh, Scotland.
2. National Library of Scotland, Ediburgh, Scotland.
3. National Library of Wales – Aberystwyth, Wales. (Records of Irish emigrants who settled here mainly from 1100-1700).

The Regiments of *The Wild Geese* fighting for France in the 17th and 18th Century.

The Regiment of Colonel William Stanley, 1586-1604

The Regiment of Colonel Henry O'Neill, 1605-1610

The Regiment of Colonel John O'Neill, 1610-1628

The Regiment of Colonel Hugh O'Donnell, 1632-1638

The Regiment of Colonel Owen (Roe) O'Donnell, 1633-1642.

The Regiment of Colonel John Barry, 1636.

The Regiment of Colonel Patrick Fitzgerald, 1639-1641.

The Regiment of Patrick O'Donnell, 1643-1647.

The Regiment of Colonel Dermot O'Sullivan Mor, 1646-1647.

The Regiment of Colonel John Morphy, I, 1646-1659.

The Regiment of Colonel Dudley Costelloe, 1653.

The Regiment of Colonel Charles (Cary) Dillion, 1653.

The Regiment of Colonel Richard Grace, 1658.

The Regiment of Philip O'Reilly, 1655-1660.

The Regiment of Colonel George Cusack, 1656-1662.

The Regiment of Colonel Louis Farrell, 1658-1660.

The Regiment of Colonel James Dempsey, 1660-1662.

The Regiment of Colonel Theodore O'Meara, 1660-1664.

The Regiment of Colonel John Murphy, II, 1667-1669.

The Regiment of Colonel Denis O'Byrne, 1673-1686.

Irish Colonists in the British West Indies. From the "Journal of the American-Irish Historical Society. Vol XXXI, Richard J. Purcell.

ABBREVIATIONS:

A = Ardagh and Clonmacnoise Antiquarian Society Journal.

B = Breifny Antiquarian Society Journal.

C = Journal of the Cork Historical and Archaelogical Society.

G = Journal of the Galway Archaeological and Historical Society.

K = Journal of the County Kildare Archaeological Society.

L = Journal of the County Louth Archaeological Society.

N = North Munster Antiquarian Society Journal.

O = Transactions of the Ossory Archaeological Society.

R = Journal of the Royal Society of Antiquaries of Ireland.

U = Ulster Journal of Archaeology.

W = Journal of the Waterford and South-East of Ireland Archaeological Society.

ADAMS. A Genealogical History of Adams of Cavan. Rev. W. Adams. London, 1903.

ADARE. Memorials of Adare Manor, with historical notices of Adare by her son, The Earl of Dunraven. Caroline, Countess of Dunraven. Oxford. 1865.

ADARE. Notes on the History of Adare. Hon. V. Wyndham-Quin. 1930.

AGNEW. The Agnews in Co. Antrim. John M. Dickson. (U) N.S. 7, 166-'71. 1901.

ALEN. Alen of St. Wolstan's. Henry J.B. Clements. (K) I, 340-'I. 1892-5.

ALEN. An account of the family of Alen, of St. Wolstan's Co. Kildare. H.L. Lyster Denny. (K) IV, 95-110. 1903-5. V, 344-7. 1906-8.

ALLEN. Ladytown and the Allens. Thomas U. Sadleir. (K) IX, 60-69. 1918-21.

ALEXANDER. Memorials of the Earl of Sterling and the House of Alexander. Rev. Charles Rogers, LL.D. 2 Vols. Edinburgh. 1877.

AMORY. Descendants of Hugh Amory 1605-1805. G.E. Meredith. London. 1901.

ANCKETILL. A short history, with notes and references of the... family of Ancketil or Anketell. Belfast. 1901.

ARCHDALE. Memoirs of the Archdales. H.B. Archdale. Enniskillen. 1925.

ARCHER. An Inquiry into the Origin of the family of Archer in Kilkenny with notices of other families of the name in Ireland. J.H. Lawrence-Archer. (R) IX, 220-32. 1867.

MacARTNEY. See MacAulay.

ASH. The Ash Manuscripts... and other family records. Belfast. 1890.

ASTON. See Chamberlain.

MacAULAY. Gleanings in family history from the Antrim coast. The MacAulays and MacArtneys. George Hill. (U) VIII, 196-210. 1860.

AYLMER. The Aylmer Family. Hans Hendrick Aylmer. (K), I, 295-307. 1892-5.

AYLMER. Donadea and the Aylmer family. Rev. Canon Sherlock. (K), III, 169-78. 1899-1902.

AYLMER. The Aylmers of Lyons, Co. Kildare. Hans Hendrick Aylmer. (K) IV, 179-83. 1903-5.

AYLMER. The Aylmers of Ireland. Sir F.J. Aylmer. London. 1931.

BAGENAL. Vicissitudes of an Anglo-Irish family, 1530-1800. Sir P.H. Bagenal. London. 1925.

BAGGE. Genealogical account of the Bagge family of Co. Waterford. Dublin. 1860.

BAGOT. The Bagots of Nurney. Charles M. Drury. (K) VII, 317-24. 1912-14.

BAILIE. History and genealogy of the family of Bailie of the North of Ireland. George A. Bailie. Augusta. 1902.

BAIRDS. British and American Origins. Pedigrees from Ulster. R.M. Sibbett. Belfast. 1931.

BALL. Records of Anglo-Irish families Ball. Rev. W. B. Wright. Dublin.

BALL. Ball family records. Rev. W.B. Wright. York. 1908.

BALLIQUIN. O'Ruark; or Chronicles of the Balliquin Family. Henry J. Monahan. Dublin. 1852.

BANTRY, Brehaven and the O'Sullivan Sept. T.D. Sullivan. Dublin. 1908.

BARNARD. The Barnards. Londonderry. 1897.

BARRINGTON. The Barringtons: a family history. Amy Barrington. Dublin. 1917.

BARRON. Distinguished Waterford families: Barron.Father Stephen Barron. (W) XVII, 47-65,128-34, 137-52. 1914. XVIII, 69-87, 91-104. 1915.

BARRY. Etude sur l'histoire des Bary-Barry. Par C. de Barry. Vieux-Dieu-Les Anvers. 1927.

BARRY. De I'origine des Barry d'Irlande. Par Alfred de Bary. Guebwiller. 1900.

BARRY. Barrymore. Rev. E. Barry. (C) N.S. V, 1-17, 77-92, 153-68, 209-24. 1899. N.S. VI, I-II, 65-87, 129-46, 193-209, 1900. N.S. VII, 1-16, 65-80, 129-38, 193-204. 1901. N.S. VIII, 1-17, 129-50. 1902.

BARRY. The last earls of Barrymore. G.J. Robinson. London. 1894.

BARRY-PLACE. Memoirs of the Barry-Place family. J. Barry Deane. (C) XXXIII, 19-21. 1928.

BARTON. The family of Barton. Rev. Canon Sherlock. (K) IV, 111-13. 1903-5.

BEAMISH. Pedigrees of the families of Beamish. R.P. Beamish. Cork. 1892.

BECK. A Brief History of the Family of Beck. John W. Beck.

BELLEW. Some Notes on the Family of Bellew of Thomastown, Co. Louth. Hon. Mrs. Gerald Bellew. (L) V, 193-7. 1923.

BERMINGHAM (BIRMINGHAM). Notes on the Bermingham pedigree. Goddard H. Orpen. (G) IX, 195-205. 1915-16.

BERMINGHAM. The Bermingham Family of Athenry. H.T. Knox. (G) X, 139-54. 1917-18.

BERMINGHAM. Carbury and the Birminghams' county. Rev. Matthew Devitt, S.J. (K) II, 85-110. 1896-9.

BERMINGHAM. Manual of origin, descent, etc. of Barony of Athenry. (D) 1820.

BERNARD. A memoir of James Bernard, M.P., his son, the first earl of Bandon, and their descendants. 1875.

BERNARD. The Barnards of Kerry. J.H. Bernard. 1922.

BESSBOROUGH. Bessborough (Henrietta Frances, Countess of): Lady Bessborough and her family circle. Earl of Bessborough & A. Aspinall. 1940.

BESNARD. Notes of the Besnard family. T.E. Evans. (C) N.S. XXXIX, 92-99. 1934.

BEWLEY. The Bewleys of Cumberland and their Irish descendants. E.T. Bewley. Dublin. 1902.

BINGHAM. Memoirs of the Binghams. R.E. McCalmont. London. 1913.

BLACK. The Black Family. Isaac Ward. (U) N.S. 8, 176-88. 1902.

BLACKER. History of the family of Blacker of Carrickblacker in Ireland. L.C.M. Blacker. Dublin. 1901.

BLACKWOOD. Helen's Tower. Hon. Harold Nicholson. London. 1937.

BLAKE. Blake Family Records. Martin J. Blake. London. 1902-1905.

BLAYNEY. The Family of Blayney. Notes relating to the Blayney Family of Montgomeryshire and Ireland... E. Rowley-Morris. London. 1890.

BLENNERHASSETT. The Blennerhassetts of Kerry: Earlier English stock. (K) V, 34-9. 1919.

BOLTON. Bolton families in Ireland... C.K. Bolton. Boston. 1937.

BOURCHIER. The Bourchier tablet in the cathedral church of St. Canice, Kilkenny. Richard Langrishe. (R) XXXIV, 365-79. 1904. XXXV, 21-33. 1905.

BOWEN. Ballyadams in the Queen's County, and the Bowen family. Lord Walter Fitzgerald. (K) VII, 3-32. 1912-14.

BOYLE. Memoirs of the Illustrious family of the Boyles. Eustace Budgell. Dublin. 1755.

BOYLE. Genealogical Memoranda relating to the family of Boyle of Limavady. E.M.F.-G. Boyle. Londonderry. 1903.

BARBAZON. Genealogical History of the Family of Barbazon. H. Sharp. Paris. 1825.

BRADSHAW. The Bradshaws of Bangor and Mile-Cross, in the Co. of Down. Francis J. Bigger. (U) N.S. 8, 4-6, 55-7. 1902.

O'BRENNAN. The O'Brennans and the ancient territory of Hy Duach. Rev. Nicholas Murphy. (O) I, 393-407. 1874-9.

O'BRIEN. Carrigogunnell Castle and the O'Briens of Pubblebrian in the Co. of Limerick. Thomas J. Westropp. (R) XXXVII, 374-92. 1907. XXXVIII, 141-59. 1908.

O'BRIEN. The O'Briens in Munster after Clontarf. Rev. John Ryan. (N) II, 141-52. 1941.

O'BRIEN. The sept of Mac-I-Brien Ara. Rev. W.B. Steele. (C), 2nd Ser. III, 10-21. 1897.

O'BRIEN. Historical memoir of the O'Briens. John O'Donoghue. Dublin. 1860.

O'BRIEN. History of the O'Briens from Brian Boroimhe A.D. 1000 to A.D. 1945. Hon. Donough O'Brien. London. 1949.

O'BRIEN. The O'Briens. W.A. Lindsay. London. 1876.

O'BRIEN. Genealogical notes on the O'Briens of Kilcor, Co. Cork. 1887.

BROWNE. Pedigree of the Brownes of Castle MacGarrett. By Lord Oramore and Browne. (G) V, 48-59. 165-177, 227-38. 1907-8.

BROWNLOW. See Chamberlain.

BUCHANAN. The Buchanan book. A.W.P. Buchanan. Montreal. 1911.

BUCHANAN. Later leaves of the Buchanan Book. A.W.P. Buchanan. Montreal. 1929.

BULLOCK. Bullock or Bullick of northern Ireland. J.W. Beck. London. 1931.

BOURKE. (Burke).

BOURKE. The Bourkes of Clanwilliam. James Grene Barry. (R). XIX, 192-203. 1889.

BOURKE. The de Burgos or Bourkes of Ileagh. M. Callanan. (N) I, 67-77. 1936-9.

BURKE. The family of Gall Burke, of Gallstown, in the Co. of Kilkenny. John O'Donova. (K) NS, III, 97-120. 1860.

BURKE. The Rt. Hon. Edmund Burke (1729-97). A Basis for a Pedigree. Basil O'Connell. K.M. (C) N.S. LX, 69-74. 1955.

BURKE. Some notes on the Burkes. M.R. (G) I, 196-7. 1900-01.

BURKE. The De Burgo Clans of Galway. H.T. Knox. (G) I, 124-31. 1900-1. III, 46-58. 1903-4. IV, 55-62. 1905-6.

BURKE. Portumna and the Burkes. H.T. Knox. (G) VI, 107-9. 1909-10.

BURKE. The Burkes of Marble Hill. Thomas U. Sadleir. (G) VIII, I II. 1913-14.

BURKE. Seanchus na mBurcach and Historia et genealogia familiae De Burgo. Thomas O'Reilly. (G) XIII, 50-60, 101-37. 1926-7. XIV, 30-51, 142-66. 1928-9.

BURKE. The de Burghs of Oldtown. Lt.-Col. Thomas J. de Burgh. (K) IV, 467-72. 1903-5.

BUTLER. Some account of the family of Butler, but more particularly of the late Duke of Ormonde. London. 1716.

BUTLER. Genealogical memoranda of the Butler family. W. Butler. Sibsagor, Assam. 1845.

BUTLER. A Genealogical History of the Noble...House of Butler in England and Ireland. London. 1771.

BUTLER. The Testamentary Records of the Butler Families in Ireland (Genealogical Abstracts). Rev. Wallace Clare. Peterborough. 1932.

BUTLER. The Butlers of Co. Clare. Sir Henry Blackall. (N) VI, 108-29. 1952.

BUTLER. Original documents relating to the Butler lordship of Achill, Burrishoole and Aughrim (1236-1640). Prof. Edmund Curtis. (G) XV, 121-28. 1931-3.

BUTLER. The Butlers of Poulakerry and Kilcash. P.J. Griffith. (W) XV, 24-29. 1912.

BUTLER. The Descendants of James, ninth earl of Ormond. Wm. F. Butler. (R) LIX, 29-44. 1929.

BUTLER. An Irish legend of the origins of the barons of Cahir. W.F. Butler. (R) LV, 6-14. 1925.

BUTLER. The Butlers of Duiske Abbey. Rev. James Hughes. (R) X, 62-75. 1868-9.

BYRNE. The Byrnes of Co. Louth. Patrick Kirwan. (L) II, 45-9. 1908-11.

O'BYRNE. Historical reminiscences of the O'Gyrnes, O'Tooles, and O'Kavanaghs and other Irish chieftains. O'Byrne. London. 1843.

O'BYRNE. The O'Byrnes and their descendants. Dublin. 1879.

O'BYRNE. History of the clan O'Byrne and other Leinster septs. Rev. P.L. O'Toole. Dublin. 1890.

MacCABE. The Formorians and Lochlanns. Pedigrees of MacCabe of Ireland and MacLeod of Scotland. John O'Donovan. (U) IX, 94-105. 1861-2.

CAIRNS. History of the family of Cairnes or Cairns. H.C. Lawlor. London. 1906.

CALDWELL. The Caldwell family of Castle Caldwell, Co. Fermanagh. W.H. Greaves-Bagshawe.

O'CALLAGHAN. The chieftains of Pobul-I-Callaghan, Co. Cork. Hubert Webb Gillman. (C) N.S., III, 201-20. 1897.

CAMAC. Memoirs of the Camacs of Co. Down. Frank O. Fisher. Norwich. 1897.

CAMPBELL. Campbell of Skeldon and New Grange. Co. Meath.

CAMPBELL. The Genealogy of Robert Campbell of Co. Tyrone. Rev. F. Campbell. New York. 1909.

CARDEN. Some Particulars about the family and descendants of the First John Carden of Templemore, Co. Tipperary, and Priscilla, his wife. John Carden. 1912.

CARSON. Carsons of Shanroe, Co. Monaghan. Rev. W.T. Carson. Dublin. 1879.

CARSON. Carsons of Monanton, Ballybay, Co. Monaghan. J. Carson. 1907. Belfast.

CAREW. Co. Cork Families-Carew pedigree. (C) N.S. XXIV,132. 1918.

O'CARROLL. Pedigree of the O'Carroll Family. E. O'Carroll. 1883.

CARROLL. True version of the pedigree of Carroll of Carrollton. Maryland. (R) XVI, 187-94. 1883.

MacCARTHY. The Pedigree and succession of the House of MacCarthy Mor. W.F. Butler. (R) II, 32-48. 1921.

MacCARTHY. The Clann Carthaigh. S.J. McCarthy. (K) I, 160-99, 195-209, 233-51, 320-38, 385-402, 477-66. 1908-12. II, 3-24, 53-74, 105-122, 181-202. 1912-14. III, 55-72, 123-39, 206-26, 271-92, 1914-16. IV, 207=14. 1917.

MacCARTHY. Some McCarthys of Blarney and Ballea. John T. Collins. (C) N.S. LIX, 1-10, 82-88. 1954. LX, 1-5, 75-9. 1955.

MacCARTHY. The MacCarthys of Drishane. S.T. MacCarthy. (C) N.S. XXIII, 114-15. 1917.

MacCarthy. A Historical Pedigree of the MacCarthys. D. MacCarthy. Exeter. 1880.

MacCARTHY. The MacFinnin MacCarthys of Ardtully. R. MacCarthy. (C) N.S. II, 210-14. 1896.

CAULFIELD. A short biographical notice of the Caulfield family. Bernard Connor. Dublin. 1808.

CHAMBERLAIN. The Chamberlains of Nizelrath. T.G.F. Paterson. (L) X, 324-6. 1944.

CHAMBERLAIN. The Chamberlains of Nizelrath. Notes on the allied families of Clinton, Aston, O'Doherty and Brownlow. T.G.F. Paterson. (L) XI, 175-85. 1947.

CHAMPION. Leitrim Castle, Co. Cork. Col. James Grove White. 1917.

CHETWOOD. The Chetwoods of Woodbrook in the Queen's Co. Walter G. Strickland. (K) IX, 205-26. 1918-21.

CHICESTER. The history of the family of Chichester. Sir A.P.B. Chichester. 1871.

CHINNERY. George Chinnery, 1774-1852, with some account of his family and genealogy. W.H. Welply. (C) N.S. XXXVII. 11-21. 1932. XXXVIII, 1-15. 1933.

CLARK. The History and genealogy of the Clark family and its connections. Charles Lamartine Clark. Detroit. 1898.

CLAYTON. Some account of the Clayton family of Thelwall, Co. Chester, afterwards of St. Dominick's Abbey, Doneraile and Mallow, Co. Cork. J.P. Rylands. Liverpool. 1880.

CLAYTON. Clayton family, Co. Cork. J.Buckley. (C) N.S. V, 194-7. 1889.

O'CLERY. The O'Cleirigh family of Tir Conaill. Father Paul Walsh. Dublin. 1938.

O'CLERY. The muintir Cleirigh of Tirawley. A.B. Clery. (R) LXXC, 70-75. 1945.

CLINTON. Clinton records. T.G.F. Paterson. (L) XII, 109-16. 1950.

COCHRANS. See Bairds

CODD. Castletown Carne and its owners. Lieut-Col. W.O. Caveagh. (R) XLI, 246-58. 1911. XLII, 34-45. 1912.

COFFEY. Genealogical and historical records of the Sept Cobhthaigh, now Coffey. H.Cofrey. Dublin. 1863.

COGHILL. See Cramer.

COLE. The Cole family of West Carbery. Rev. R.L. Cole. Belfast. 1943.

COLE. Genealogy of the family of Cole, Co. Devon, with branches in Ireland. J.E. Cole. 1867.

COLLES. Records of the Colles family. R.W. Colles. Dublin. 1892.

COLVILLE. The Colville family in Ulster. John M. Dickson. (U) N.S. V, 139-45. 202-10. 1899.

COLVILLE. The Colville Family. (U) N.S. 6, 12-16. 1900.

COMYN. Notes on the Comyn pedigree. David Comyn. (M) III, 22-37. 1913.

O'CONNELL. O'Connell family tracts, No. 1-2. Basil M. O'Connell. Dublin. 1947-48.

O'Connor. The O'Conors of Connaught. C. O'Conor Don. Dublin. 1891.

O'Connor. Memoirs of Charles O'Conor of Belenagare, with a historical account of the family of O'Conor, Rev. C. O'Conor. Dublin. 1796.

O'CONNOR. Memoir of the O'Connors of Ballintubber, Co. Roscommon. R. O'Conor. Dublin. 1859.

O'CONNOR. Lineal descent of the O'Connors of Co. Roscommon. R. O'Connor. Dublin. 1862.

O'CONNOR. Historical and genealogical memoir of the O'Connors, kings of Commaught. R. O'Connor. Dublin. 1861.

CONOLLY. Speaker Conolly and his connections. 1907.

CONWAY. The Conways of Kerry. S.J.M. (K) V, 71-91. 1920

CONYNGHAM. See Lenox-Conyngham.

COOTE. Historical and genealogical records of the Coote family. Lausanne. 1900.

COPINGER. History of the Copingers or Coppingers of Co. Cork. W.A. Copinger. Manchester. 1882.

CORCA LAIDHE. Genealogy of Corca Laidhe. J.O'Donovan. 1849.

CORRY. History of the Corry family of Castlecoole. Earl of Belmore. London. 1891.

COTTER. Notes on the Cotter family of Rockforest, Co. Cork. J.C. (C) N.S. XIV, 1-12. 1908.

COTTER. The Cotter family of Rockforest, Co. Cork. G de P. Cotter. (C) N.S. XLIII, 21-31. 1938.

COWLEY. Some notice of the family of Cowley in Kilkenny. J.G.A. Prim. (R) II, 102-14. 1852.

COX. Claim of J.H.R. Cox to the Baronetcy of Cox of Dunmanway, Co. Cork. With Ancestry Evidence. John. H.R. Cox. London. 1912-1914.

CRAMER. A genealogical note on the family of Cramer or Coghill. (C) N.S. XVI, 66-81. 1910.

CRAMER. Cramer pedigree. J.F. Fuller. (C) N.S. XVI, 143. 1910.

CRAWFORD. The Crawfords of Donegal and how they came there. R. Crawford. Dublin. 1886.

McCREADY. McCreery (McCready) genealogy. C.T. McCready. Dublin. 1868.

CRICHTON. Genealogy of the Earls of Erne. J.H. Steele. Edinburgh. 1910.

CRISPIN. The Crispins of Kingston-on-Hull. M. Jackson Crispin. 1928.

CROFTON. Crofton memoirs: account of John Crowton of Ballymurray, Co. Roscommon, his ancestors and descendants and others bearing the name. H.T. Crofton. York. 1911.

CROSLEGH. Descent and Alliances of Croslegh of Scaitliffe; and Coddington of Oldbridge; and Evans of Eyton Hall. Charles Croslegh. 1904.

CROSSLE. Descent and alliances of Croslegh, or Crossle or Crossley of Scaitliffe. Rev. C. Croslegh. London. 1904.

O'CROWLEY. A defeated clan. Michael Crowley. (C) N.S. XXVI, 24-8. 1920.

O'CROWLEY. O'Crowley pedigree. Carew Mss. and other sources. F.C. Long. (C) N.S. XXXV, 89. 1930.

O'CROWLEY. The O'Crowleys of Coill t-Sealbhaigh. John T. Collins. (C) N.S. LVI, 91-4. 1951. LVII, 1-6, 105-9. 1952. LVIII, 7-11. 1953.

DALY. Families of Daly of Galway with tabular pedigrees. Martin J. Blake. (G) XIII 140. 1926-7.

O'DALY. The O'Dalys of Muintuavara: a story of a bardic family. Dominick Daly. Dublin. 1821.

O'DALY. History of the O'Dalys. E.E. O'Daly. New York. 1937.

D'ARCY. An historical sketch of the family of D'Arcy from the Norman conquest to the year 1853. 1882.

D'ARCY. Complete pedigree of the English and Irish branches of the D'Arcy Family. London. 1901.

D'ARCY. Tabular pedigrees of the D'Arcy family. (G) X, 58. 1917-18.

DAUNT. Account of the family of Daunt. John Daunt. Newcastle-on-Tyne. 1881.

DAVIES. Journal of the very Rev. Rowland Davies, LL.D., from March 8, 1688-9, to Sept. 29, 1690. Richard Caulfield. 1857.

DAVYS. The Davys family records. S.F. O'Clanain. Longford. 1931.

O'DAVOREN. The O'Davorens of Cahermacnaghten, Burren, Co. Clare. Dr. George U. Macnamara. (N) II, 63-93. 149-64. 194-201. 1912-13.

DAWSON. The Dawsons of Ardee. Rev. L.P. Murray. (L) VIII, 22-23. 1933.

DECOURCY. A genealogica history of the Milesian families of Ireland with the monument to Brian Boroimhe. B.W. DeCourcy. 1880.

DELACY Notes on the Family of De Lacy in Ireland. Nicholas J. Synnott. (R) Il, 113-31. 1919.

O'DEMPSEY. The O'Dempseys of Clanmaliere. Lord Walter Fitzgerald. (K) IV, 396-431. 1903-5.

DENHAM. Denham of Dublin. C.H. Denham. Dublin. 1936.

DENNY. Deccys of Cork. Rev. H.L. L. Denny. (C) N.S. XXVIII, 45-6. 1922.

DeRIDELESFORD. The DeRidelesfords. E. St. John Brooks. (R) LXXXII, 45-61. 1952.

DESMONDE. The Olde Countess of Desmonde; Her Identitie; Her Portraiture; Her Descente with and genealogical table. A.B. Rowan. Dublin. 1860.

O'DONNELL. John O'Donnell of Baltimore; his forbears and descendants. E.T. Cook. London. 1934.

DOBBS. Arthur Dobbs, Esquire, 1689-1765. Desmond Clarke. London. 1957.

DODD. The Dodd Family Abroad. Charles Lever.

DOWNEY. A History of the Protestant Downeys of the counties of Sligo, Leitrim, Fermanagh and Donegal and their Descendants. Cairncross C. Downey. New York. 1931.

DOWSE. History of the Dowse Family. 1926.

DRAKE. The Drake family. Fredrick W. Knight. (C) N.S., XXXVIII, 20-30. 1933.

DRAYCOT. The De Verdons and the Draycots. Charles Mac Neill. (L) V, 166-72. 1923.

DRAYCOTT. Some early documents relating to English Uriel, and the towns of Drogheda and Dundalk. Charles McNeil. (L) V, 270-75. 1924.

O'Driscoll. The O'Driscolls and other septs of Corca Laidhe. J.M. Burke. (C) N.S. XVI, 24-31. 1910.

DUNLEVY. A genealogical history of the Dunlevy family. G.D. Kelley. Columbus, Ohio. 1901.

O'DWYER. The O'Dwyers of Kilnamanagh Sir. M. O'Dwyer. London. 1933.

EAGAR. The Eagar family of Co. Kerry. F.J. Eagar. Dublin. 1860.

EAGAR. Genealogical history of the Eagar family. F.J. Eagar. Dublin. 1861.

ECHLIN. Genealogical memoirs of the Echlin family. Rev. J.R. Echlin. Edinburgh. N.D.

EDGEWORTH. The Black Book of Edgeworthstown and other Edgeworth memories, 1585-1817. H.J. Butler and H.E. Butler. London. 1917.

MacEGAN. Two Irish Brehon scripts with notes on the MacEgan family. Martin F. Blake. (G) VI, 1-9. 1909-10.

ELLIS. Notices of the Ellises of England, Scotland, and Ireland. W.S. Ellis. London. 1857-1881.

EMISON. The Emison families with partial genealogies of collateral families. James Wade Emison, Jr. Indiana. 1947.

EMMET. The Emmet family with a bibliographical sketch of Prof. John P. Emmet and other members. Thomas A. Emmet. New York. 1898.

ERNE. Genealogy of the Earls of Erne. John J. Steele. 1910.

EUSTANCE. Kilcullen new abbey and the FitzEustaces. James Fenton. (K) XII, 217-21. 1935-45.

EVANS. The last six generations of the Evans family. W.S. Evans. 1864.

EYRE. A short account of the Eyre family of Eyre Court, and Eyre of Eyreville in Co. Galway. Rev. A.S. Hartigan.

FALKINER. The Falkiners of Abbotstown, Co. Dublin. George H. Federick Nuttall. (K) VIII, 331-63. 1915-17.

FALKINER. A pedigree with personal sketches of the Falkiners of Mount Falcon. F.B. Falkiner. Dublin. 1894.

FARNHAM. Seize Quartiers, connected with Royal Descents of Henry Maxwell, K.P., Seventh Lord Farnham. Cavan. 1850.

FARNHAM. Farnham Descents. Henry Maxwell, Lord Farnham. Cavan. 1860.

FEATHERSTONE. The Featherstones and Halls. Margaret Irwin. 1890.

FERGUSON. Records of the Clan and Names of Fergusson or Ferguson and Fergus. James Ferguson and Robert Menzies Fergusson. Edinburgh. 1895.

FITZEUSTANCE. Fitz-Eustace of Baltiglas. (W)V, 190-5. 1899.

FITZGERALD. Gerladines, Earls of Desmond. Rev. C.P. Meehan. Dublin. 1852.

FITZGERALD. The story of the Slught Edmund from 1485 to 1819. S.M. (K) III, 186-205. 1915.

FITZGERALD. The Fitzgeralds of Lackagh. Lord Walter Fitzgerald. (K) I, 245-64. 1892-5.

FITZGERALD. The Fitzgeralds and the MacKenzies. W. Fitz G. (K), II, 269. 1896-9.

FITZGERALD. The Fitzgeralds of Ballyshannon (Co. Kildare), and their successors threat. Lord Walter Fitzgerald. (K), 888, 425-52. 1899-1902.

FITZGERALD. The history of Morett Castle, and the Fitzgeralds. Lork Walter Fitzgerald. (K), IV, 285-96. 1803-5.

FITZGERALD. The Geraldines of Desmond. Canon Hayman. (R), XV. 215-35. 411-40. 1880-81. XVII, 66-92. 1885.

FITZGERALD. The Fitzgeralds of Rostellane in the Co. Cork. R.G. Fitzgerald-Uniacke. (R) XXV, 163-70. 1895.

FITZGERALD. The Geraldines of the Co. Kilkenny. George Dames Burtchaell. (R) XXII, 358-76. 1892. XXIII, 179-86, 408-20. 1893. XXXII, 128-31. 1902.

FITZGERALD. The Fitzgeralds of Glenane, Co. Cork. R.G. Fitzgerald-Uniacke. (R) XLII, 164-9. 1912.

FITZGERALD. The Fitzgeralds, barons of Offaly. Goddard H. Orpen. (R) XLIV, 99-113. 1914.

FITZGERALD. The Desmonds castle at Newcastle Oconyll, Co. Limerick. Thomas J. Westropp. (R) XXXIX, 42-58, 350-68. 1909.

FITZGERALD. The descendants of the last Earls of Desmond. John O'Donovan. (U), VI, 91-7. 1858.

FITZGERALD. The Fitzgeralds of Farnane, Co. Waterford. G. O'C. Redmond. (W), XIV, 27-39, 72-81. 1911. XV, 168-76. 1912.

FITZGERALD. Unpublished Geraldine documents. Rev. Samuel Hayman. (R) X, 356-416. 1869. XI, 591-616. 1871. XIV, 14-52, 157-66, 246-64, 300-35. 1876-77.

FITZGERALD. The Fitzgerald family. Rev. S. Hayman. Dublin. 1870.

FITZGERALD. Descents of the Earls of Kildare and their wives. Marquis of Kildare. Dublin. 1869.

FITZGERALD. Sketch of the history and descent of the Geraldines of Queen's Co. Mountmellick. 1913.

FITZGERALD. The Earls of Kildare and their ancestors from 1057-1773. Marquis of Kildare. Dublin. 1858-62.

FITZGERALD. Memoirs of an Irish family, Fitzgerald of Decies. Mrs. M. MacKenzie. Dublin. 1905.

FITZGERALD. Initium, incrementum et exitus familiae Geraldinorum Desmoniae. Dominic O'Daly. 1655.

FITZMAURICE. The Fitzmaurices, Lords of Kerry. M.J. Bourke. (C) N.S., XXVI, 10-18. 1920.

FITZRERY. The Fitz Rerys, Welsh lords of Cloghran, Co. Dublin. E. Curtis. (L), V, 13-17. 1921.

O'FLAHERTY. The flight of the O'Flahertys, lords of Moy Soela, to Iar Connaught. Rev. J. Fahy. (R) XXVII, 19-27. 1897.

FLATESBURY. The family of Flatesbury of Ballynasculloge and Johnstown, Co. Kildare. Sir Arthur Vicars. (K) IV, 87-94. 1903-5.

FLEETWOOD. The Fleetwoods of the Co. Cork. Sir Edmund T. Bewley. (R) XXXVIII, 103-25. 1908.

FLEETWOOD. An Irish branch of the Fleetwood family. Sir E.T. Bewley. Exeter. 1908.

FLEMING. Historical and genealogical memoir of the family of Fleming of Slane. Sir W. Betham. 1829.

O'FLYNN. The O'Flynns of Ardagh. J.M. Burke. (C) N.S., XI, 99-101. 1905.

FOLLIN. Follin family. G. Edmonston. Washington. 1911.

FOLLIOTT. The Folliotts of Londonderry and Chester. Sir E.T. Bewley. 1902.

FORBES. Memoirs of the earls of Granard. Hon. John Forbes. London. 1868.

FOX. Some notes on the Fox family of Kilcoursey in King's Co. M.E. Stone. Chicago. 1890.

FRAZER. Notes and papers connected with Persifor Frazer in Glasslough Ireland. P. Frazer. 1906.

FREKE. Mrs. Elizabeth Freke, Her Diary, 1671-1714. Mary Carbery. Cork. 1913.

FRENCH. The families of French of Belturbet and Nixon of Fermanagh and their descendants. Rev. Henry Biddall Swanzy. Dublin. 1908.

FRENCH. The families of French of Dures, Cloghballymore and Drumharsna with tabular pedigree. Martin J. Blake. (G), X, 125-38. 1917-18.

FRENCH. The origin of the families of French of Connaught with tabular pedigree of John French of Grand-Terre in 1763. Martin J. Blake. (G), XI, 142-9. 1920-1.

FRENCH. Some account of the family of French of Belturbet. Rev. H.B. Swanzy. (U) N.S., VIII, 155-60. 1902.

FRENCH. The families of French and their descendants. Rev. H.B. Swanzy. Dublin. 1908.

FRENCH. Memoir of the French family (De la Freyne, De Freyne, Frenshe, ffrench). John D'Alton. Dublin. 1847.

FULLER. Some descents of the Kerry branch of the Fuller family. J.F. Fuller. Dublin. 1880.

FULLER. Pedigree of the family of Fuller of Cork, Kerry and Halstead. J.F. Fuller. 1909.

FULTON. Memoirs of the Fultons of Lisburn. Sir T. Hope. 1903.

GAEDHAL. Irish Family History. Richard F. Cronnelly. Vol. I, 1865.

GALWEY (Galway). The Galweys of Lota. C.J. Bennett. Dublin. 1909.

GALWEY. The genealogy of Galwey of Lota. (C) N.S., XXX, 59-72. 1925.

GARDE. The Garde family. R. Bickersteth. (C) N.S., V, 200-02. 1899.

GAYER. Memoirs of the Gayer family in Ireland. A.E. Gayer. Westminster. 1870.

GERALDINES. Dromona: The memoirs of an Irish family. Theresa Muir Mackenzie. Dublin. 1906.

GERALDINES. The rise, increase, and exit of the Geraldines, earls of Desmond. C.P. Meehan. Dublin. 1878.

GERRARD. Gerrards and Geraldines. Capt. Henry Ge rard. (C) N.S. XXXIV, 30-35, 71-75. 1929.

GIBBON. Recollections from 1796 to 1829. Skeffington Gibbon.

MacGILLYCUDDY. The Macgillycuddy family. (K), III, 176-85. 1915.

GILLMAN. Searches into the history of the Gillman or Gilman family in Ireland. A.W. Gillman. London 1895.

GORGES. The story of a family through eleven centuries. Raymond Gorges. Boston. 1944.

GOUGH. The Story of an Irish Property. Robert S. Rait. Oxford. 1908.

McGOVERN. An Irish sept. Rev. J.B. and J.H. McGovern. Manchester. 1886.

McGovern. Genealogy and historical notes of the MacGauran or McGovern Clan. J.H. McGovern. Liverpool. 1890.

O'GOWAN. A memoir of the name of O'Gowan or Smith. O'Gowan. Tyrone. 1837.

GRACE. A survey of Tullaroan, etc. being a genealogical history of Grace. Dublin. 1819.

GRACE. The origin of the Grace family of Courtstown, Co. of Kilkenny and of their title to the Tullaroan estate. Richard Langrishe. (R) XXX, 319-24. 1900. XXXII, 64-67. 1902.

GRACE. Memoirs of the family of Grace. S. Grace. London. 1823.

GREATRAKES. Notes on the family of Greatrakes. Rev. Samuel Hayman. 1863.

GREEN. Green family of Youghal. Co. Cork. H.B. Swanzy and T. Green. Dublin. 1902.

GREENE. Pedigree of the family of Greene. Lt.-Col. J. Greene. Dublin. 1899.

GREGORY. The house of Gregory. V.R.T. Gregory. Dublin. 1943.

HAMILTON. Monea Castle, Co. Fermanagh and the Hamiltons. Rt. Hon. the Early of Belmore. (U) N.S., I, 195-208, 256-77. 1895.

HAMILTON. Pedigree of the Hamilton family of Fermanagh, Co. Tyrone. J.F. Fuller. London. 1889.

HAMILTON. Hamilton mss. T.K. Lowry. Belfast. 1848.

HAMILTON. Hamilton memoirs. E. Hamilton. Dundalk. 1920.

O'HANLON. Redmond Court O'Hanlon's descendants. (L), II, 61. 1908-11.

O'HART. The last princes of Tara or a brief sketch of the O'Hart ancient royal family. J. O'Hart. Dublin, 1873.

HART. Family history of Hart of Donegal. H.T. Hart. 1907.

HARTPOLE. Notes on the district of Ivory, Coolbanagher Castle, and the Hartpoles. Lord Walter Fitzgerald. (K) IV, 297-311. 1903-05.

HARVEY. The Harvey families of Inishowen, Co. Donegal. G.H. Harvey. Folkestone. 1927.

HASSARD. Some account of the Hassard family. Rev. H.B. Swanzy. Dublin. 1903.

HEACOCK. Richard Heacock. Richard Heacock pedigree. (C) N.S., XI, 47. 1905.

HAUGHTON. Memoirs of the family of Haughton in Ireland. T.W. Haughton. Cullybackey. 1929.

HEALY. The Healys of Donoughmore. John T. Collins. (C), N.S. XLVIII, 124-32. 1943.

HEFFERAN. The Heffernans and their times. Patrick Heffernan. London. 1940.

HENCHY. The O'Connor Henchys of Stonebrook. V. Hussey-Walsh. (K) II, 407-12. 1896-9.

HENRY. The Henry family in Kildare. Rev. Canon Sherlock. (K), III, 386-8. 1899-1902.

HEWETSON. The Hewetsons of the Co. of Kildare. John Hewetson. (R) XXXIX, 146-63. 1909.

HEWETSON. Of the Co. Kilkenny. John Hewetson. (R) XXXIX. 369-92. 1909.

HEWETSON. Of Ballyshannon, Donegal. John Hewetson. (R), XL, 238-43. 1910.

HEWETSON. Memoirs of the house of Hewetson or Hewson in Ireland. Rev. H.B. Swanzy. Dublin. 1903.

HEWSON. Hewsons of Finuge, Kerry, of royal descent. John Hewson. 1907.

HILL. The house of Downshire from 1600 to 1868. H. McCall. 1880.

HOARE. Account of the early history and genealogy with pedigrees from 1330 unbroken to the present time of the families of Hore and Hoare with all their branches. Capt. Edward Hoare of Cork. London. 1883.

HORT. The Horts of Hortland. Sir Arthur F. Hort. (K), VII, 207-16. 1912-14.

HOVENDEN. Lineage of the family of Hovenden (Irish branch). London. 1892.

O'HURLEY (O'Hurly). The family of O'Hurley. Rev. P. Hurley. Cork. 1906.

O'Hurley. Some account of the family of O'Hurly. (C) N.S. XI, 105-23, 177-83. 1905. (C) N.S. XII, 26-33, 76-88. 1906.

JACOB. History of the families of Jacob of Bridgewater, Tiverton and Southern Ireland. H.W. Jacob. Taunton. 1929.

JACOB. Historical and genealogical narration of the families of Jacob. A.H. Jacob of Dublin and J.H. Glascott. Dublin. 1875.

JEPHSON. The English settlement in Ireland under the Jephson family. H.F. Berry. (C) N.S., XII, 1-26. 1906.

JONES. The Jones in Ireland. Robert Leach. Yonkers, New York. 1866.

O'KANE. Some account of the sept of the O'Cathains of Ciannachta Glinne-Geinhin. J. Scott Parker. (U) III, 1-8, 265-72. 1855. IV, 139-48. 1856.

KAVANAGH. The fall of the Clan Kavanagh. Rev. James Hughes. (R) XII, 282-305. 1873.

KEATING. Records of the Keating family. Thomas Mathews.

McKEE. A history of the descendants of David McKee, with a general sketch of the early McKees. James McKee. Philadelphia, 1872.

KELLS. The Kells and Philpotts in Mallow, 1749. H.J. Berry. (C) N.S., XV, 95-98. 1909.

O'KELLY. The O'Kellys of Gallagh, courts of the Holy Roman Empire. Richard J. Kelly. (G) III, 180-5. 1903-4.

O'KELLY. Notes on the family of O'Kelly. Richard J. Kelly. (G) IV, 92-6. 1905-6.

O'KELLY. The pedigree of Maria Anna O'Kelly, countess of Marcolini. (G). IV, 108-10. 1905-6.

O'KELLY. Notes on the O'Kelly family. E. Festus Kelly. (G) XVI, 140-43. 1934-5.

KEMMIS. A short account of the family of Kemmis in Ireland. Lewis G.N. Kemmis. (K) XII, 144-69. 1935-45.

KENMARE. The Kenmare Manuscripts. Edward MacLysaght. Dublin. 1942.

KENNEDY. A family of Kennedy of Clogher and Londonderry c. 1600-1938. Major F.M.E. Kennedy. Taunton. 1938.

O'KENNEDY. Records of four Tipperary septs: O'Kennedys, O'Dwyers, O'Mulryans, O'Meaghers. M. Callanan. Galway. 1938.

KENNEY. Pedigree of the Kenney family of Kilclogher, Co. Glaway. J.C.F. Kenney. Dublin. 1868.

KERR. Joseph Kerr of Ballygoney and his descendants. Mary Alice Kerr Arbuckle. New York, 1904.

KILDARE. The Earls of Kildare and their Ancestors, 1057-1773. Charles W. Fitzgerald, 4th Duke of Leinster. 1857. 2nd edit, 3 vols. 1858-66.

KINGSTON. The Kingston Family in West Cork. Delmege Trimble. 1929.

McKINLEY. The McKinleys of Conagher, Co. Antrim, and their descendants. Thomas Camac. (U) N.S., III, 167-70. 1897.

KIRWAN. Pedigree of the Kirwan family, compiled from the originals. Denis Agar Richard Kirwan and John Waters Kirwan.

LACY. The roll of the house of Lacy. E. deLacy-Bellingarri. Baltimore. 1928.

LALLY. A sept of O'Maolale (or Lally) of Hy-Maine. Miss. J. Martyn. (G) IV, 198-209. 1905-6.

LANDAFF. Genealogy of the earls of Landaff of Thomastown, Co. Tipperary, Ireland.

LANGTON. Memorials of the family of Langton of Kilkenny. J.G.A. Prim. Dublin. 1964.

MacLAUGHLIN. The MacLaughlins or Clan Owen. T.P. Brown. Boston 1879.

LA TOUCHE. The La Touche family of Harristown, Co. Kildare. Miss. M.F. Young. (K), VII, 33-40. 1912-14.

LA TOUCHE. Genealogy of the De La Touche family seated in France, prior to and continued after a branch of it had settled in Ireland, 1690-95. Sir A.B. Stransham. London. 1882.

LATTIN. The Lattin and Mansfield families, in the Co. Kildare. Rev. Canon Sherlock. (K) III, 186-90. 1899-1902.

LATTIN. Notices of the family of Lattin. John M. Thunder. (R) XVIII, 183-88. 1887.

LAVALLIN. History of the Lavallins. George Berkeley. (C) N.S., XXX, 10-15, 75-83. 1925. XXXI, 36-43, 53-59. 1926.

LAWE. Lawe of Leixlip. Rev. H.L.L. Denny. (K) VI, 730-39. 1909-11.

LE FANU. Memoir of the Le Fanu family. T.P. LeFanu. Manchester. 1945.

LEFROY. Notes and documents relating to Lefroy of Carrickglass, Co. Longford. Sir J.H. Lefroy. 1868.

LEINSTER. Emily, Duchess of Leinster, 1731-1814. Brian Fitzgerald. 1849.

LENOX-CONYNGHAM. An old Ulster house and the people who lived in it. M. Lenox-Conyngham. Dundalk, 1946.

LE POER TRENCH. Memoir of the Le Poer Trench family written by Richard, 2nd Earl of Clancarthy, about 1805. Dublin. 1874.

LESLIE. The Leslies of Tarbert, Co. Kerry, and their forebears. P.L. Pielou. Dublin. 1935.

LESLIE. Of Glaslough in the kingdom of Oriel, and of noted men that have dwelt there. Seymour Leslie. Glaslough. 1913.

LEVINGE. Historical notes on the Levinge family, baronets of Ireland. J.C. Lyons. Ladestown. 1853.

LEVINGE. Jottings for the early history of the Levinge family. Sir R. Levinge. Dublin. 1873.

LIMRICK. The family of Limrick of Schull, Co. Cork. Rev. H.L.L. Denny. (C) N.S. XIII, 120-27. 1907.

LINDSAY. The Lindsay memoirs. A record of the Lisnacrieve and Belfast branch of the Lindsay family during the last two hundred years. J.C. Lindsay and J.A. Lindsay. Belfast. 1884.

LINDESAY. The Lindesays of Loughry, County Tyrone. Ernest H. Godfrey. London. 1949.

LLOYD. Genealogical notes on Lloyd family in Co. Waterford. A.R. Lloyd.

LOWRY. The history of the two Ulster manors of Finagh in the County of Tyrone and Coole. Earl of Belmore. London. Dublin. 1881.

LOWTHER. Lowthers in Ireland in the 17th century. Sir E.T. Bewley. 1902.

LUDLOW. Memoirs of Edmund Ludlow. 3 vols. 2nd edition. London. 1721.

LUTTREL. The Luttrels of Luttrelstown. M.J. Borke. (C) N.S., XXVII, 65-69. 1921.

LYONS. Historical notice of the Lyons family and their connections. John C. Lyons. Ladestown. 1853.

LYNCH. Genealogical memoranda relating to the family of Lynch. London. 1883.

LYNCH. Lynch record containing biographical sketches of men of the naem Lynch 16th to 20th century. E.C. Lynch. New York. 1925.

LYNCH. Account of the Lynch family and of the memorable events of tow town of Galway. John Lynch. (G) VIII, 76-93. 1913-14.

LYNCH. Pedigree of Lynch of Lavally, county Galway. Martin J. Blake. (G) X, 66-9. 1917-18.

MacLYSAGHT. Short study of a transplanted family in the seventeenth century. E. MacLysaght. Dublin. 1935.

LYSTER. Memorials of an Ancient House. Rev. H. Lyster Denny. 1913.

O'MADDEN. Records of the O'Maddens of Hy Many. T.M. Madden. Dublin. 1894.

O'Madden. The O'Maddens of Silanchia or Siol Anmachadha, and their descendants from the Milesian invasion of Ireland to the presnet time. Thomas More Madden. (G) I, 184-95. 1900-01. II, 21-33. 1902.

MADDEN (Madan). The Madan family and Maddens in Ireland and England. F. Madan. London. 1933.

MAGENNIS. The Magennises of Clanconnell. Rev. E.D. Atkinson. (U) N.S. I, 30-32. 1895.

MAGENNIS. Magennis of Iveagh. Henry S. Guinness. (R) LXII, 96-102. 1932.

MAGENNIS. Notes on the family of Magennis, formerly lords of Iveagh, Newry and Mourne. E.F. Danne. Salt Lake City. 1878.

MAGENNIS. Pedigree of the Magennis (Guinness) family of N. Ireland and of Dublin. Richard Linn. Christchurch. N.Z. 1897.

O'MAHONY. A history of the O'Mahony septs of Kinelmeky and Ivagha. Rev. Canon O'Mahony. (C) N.S., XII, 183-95. XIII, 27-36, 73-80, 105-15, 182-92, XIV, 12-21, 74-81, 127-41, 189-99, XV, 7-18, 63-75, 118-26, 184-96. XVI 9-24, 97-113. 1906-10.

O'MAHONY (Mahony). The Mahonys of Kerry. (K) IV, 171-90, 223-55. 1917-18.

O'MALLY. Genealogy of the O'Mallys of the Owals. Philadelphia. 1913.

O'MALLEY. Note on the O'Malley lordship at the close of the 16th century. Sir Owen O'Malley. (G) XXIV, 27-57. 1950-51.

MANSFIELD. The Lattin and Mansfield families in the Co. Kildare. Rev. Canon Sherlock. (K) III, 186-90. 1899-1902.

MacMANUS. Genealogical memoranda relating to the Sotheron family and the sept MacManus. C. Sotheron. 1871-73.

MARISCO. The family of Marisco. E. St. J. Brooks. (R) LXI, 22-38, 89-112. 1931.

MARSHAL. The Marshal pedigree. Hamilton Hall. (R) XLIII, 1-29. 1913.

MASSY. Genealogical account of the Massy family. Dublin 1890.

MATHEW. Genealogy of the earls of Llandaff of Thomastown, Co. Tipperary. 1904.

MAUNSELL. History of the Maunsell or Mansel family. R.G. Manusell. Cork. 1903.

MAXWELL. Farnham descents. Henry Maxwell. Cavan. 1860.

MEADE. The Meades of Inishannon. J.A. Meade. Victoria, B.C. 1956.

MEADE. The Meades of Meaghstown Castle and Tissaxon. J.A. Meade.

O'MEAGHER. Historical notices of the O'Meaghers of Ikerrin. J.C. O'Meagher. London. 1887.

MERCER. The Mercer chronicle: an epitome of family history. E.S. Mercer. 1866.

MERRY. The Waterford Merrys.(W) XVI, 30-35. 1913.

MOLYNEUX. An account of the family and descendants of Thomas Molyneux. Capel Moylneux. Evesham. 1820.

MOLYNEUX. Pedigree of Molyneux of Castle Dillon, Co. Armagh. Sir T. Phillips. Evesham. 1819.

MONROE. Foulis Castle and the Monroes of Lower Iveagh. Horace G. Monroe. 1929.

MONTGOMERY. The Montgomery manuscripts (1603-1706). W. Montgomery. Belfast. 1869.

MONTGOMERY. A genealogical history of the family of Montgomery of Mount Alexander. Mrs. E. O'Reilly. 1842.

MONTGOMERY. A family history of Montgomery of Ballyleck, Co. Monaghan. G.S.M. Belfast. 1887.

MOORE. The family of Moore. Countess of Drogheda. Dublin. 1906.

MOORE. The genealogy of John W. Moore. Dublin. 1900.

MOORE. The Moores of Moore Hall. Joseph Hone. London. 1939.

MOORE. Sir Thomas More: his descendants in the male line: the Moores of Moorehall, Co. Mayo, Martin J. Blake. (R), XXXVI, 224-30. 1906.

MORAN. The Morans and the Mulveys of South Leitrim. V. Rev. Joseph McGivney. (A) I, 14-19. 1932.

O'MORE. Notes on an old pedigree of the O'More family of Leix. Sir Edmund T. Bewley. (R), XXXV, 53-9. 1905.

O'MORE. Historical notes on the O'Mores and their territory of Leix to the end of the sixteenth century. Lord Walter Fitzgerald. (K), VI, 1-88. 1909-11.

O'MORE. The O'More family of Balyna in the Co. Kildare by James More of Balyna, ca 1774. (K), IX, 277-91, 318-30. 1918-21.

MORRIS. Morris of Ballybeggan and Castle Morris, Co. Kerry. By the Marquis of Ruvigny and Raineval. 1904.

MORRIS. Memoirs of my family: with some researches into the early history of the Morris families of Tipperary, Galway and Mayo. E.M. Chapman. Frome. 1928.

O'MULCONRY. The O'Maolconaire family. Ed. Edmund Curtis. (G), XIX, 118-46. 1940-41.

O'MULCONRY. The O'Maolconaire family. A Note. E. de Lacy Staunton. (G) XX, 82-8. 1942-3.

O'MULLALLY. History of O'Mullally and Lally Clans. D.P. O'Mullally. 1941.

O'MULLANE. The O'Mullanes and Whitechurch. Sir Henry Blackall. (C) N.S. LVIII, 20-21. 1953.

O'MULLANE. The O'Mullanes. John T. Collins. (C) N.S. LVIII, 97. 1953.

MULOCK. The family of Mulock. Sir E. Bewley. Dublin. 1905.

MUNRO. Story of St. Patrick's Coleraine: The Munro Family of Coleraine. Sam Henry. 42-46.

MacNAGHTEN. Gleanings in family history from the Antrim Coast. The MacNaghtens and MacNeills. George Hill. (U), VIII, 127-44. 1860.

MACNAMARA. The story of an Irish sept. N. MacNamara. London. 1896.

MACNAMARA. Histoire d'un sept irlandais: Les Macnamara. Par Eugene Forques. Paris. 1901.

MACNAMARA. The pedigrees of MacConmara of Co. Clare. R.W. Twigge. 1908.

NANGLE. Ballysax and the Nangle family. Omurethi. (K), VI, 96-100. 1909-11.

NASH. The genealogy of the Nash family of Farrihy. 1910.

O'Neill. The O'Neills of Ulster: their history and genealogy. Thomas Mathews. Dublin. 1907.

NESBITT. History of the family of Nisbet or Nesbitt in Scotland and Ireland. A. Newbitt. Torquay. 1898.

NIXON. The family of Nixon of Nixon Hall, Co. Fermanagh. Henry Biddall Swanzy. Dublin. 1899.

NUGENT. Historical sketch of the Nugent family. J.C. Lyons. Ladestown. 1853.

NUTTALL. The Nuttalls of Co. Kildare. R.W. Smith, Jr. (K) VIII, 180-84. 1915-17.

OLIVER. The Olivers of Cloghanodfoy and their descendants. Major-Gen. J.R. Oliver. London. 1904.

ONSELEY. The name and family of Onseley. Richard J. Kelly. (R) XL, 123-46. 1910.

ORMSBY. Pedigree of the Ormsby family, formerly of Lincolnshire now Ireland. J.F. Fuller. 1886.

ORPEN. The Orpen family. G. Orpen. Frome. 1930.

PALMER. Genealogical and historical account of the Palmer family of Kenmare, Co. Kerry. Rev. A.H. Palmer. 1872.

PALMER. Account of the Palmer family of Rahan, Co. Kildare. T. Prince. New York. 1903.

PARNELL. A Historical sketch of parnell and parnells. R. Johnston. Dublin. 1888.

PARSONS. Notes on families and individuals of the name of Parsons. London. 1903.

PATTERSON. Some family notes. W.H. Patterson. Belfast. 1911.

PENN. Admiral Penn, William Penn and their descendants in the Co. Cork. J.C. (C) N.S. XIV, 105-14, 177-89. 1908.

PENTHENY. Memoir of the ancient family of Pentheny or De Pentheny of Co. Meath. Dublin. 1821.

PHAIRE. Colonel Robert Phaire, "Regicide" his ancestry, history, and descendants. W.H. Welply. (C) N.S. XXIX, 76-80. 1924. XXX, 20-26. 1925. XXXI, 31-36. 1926. XXXII, 24-32. 1927.

PILKINGTON. Harland's history of the Pilkingtons from the Saxon times to the present time. 2nd ed. Dublin. 1886.

PLUNKET. The family of Plunket. W. Lynch. 1830.

POE. Origin and early history of the family of Poe with full pedigrees of the Irish branch of the family. Sir E.T. Bewley. Dublin. 1906.

POLLOCK. The family of Pollock. Rev. A.S. Hartigan. Folkestone.

PONSONBY. Bishopscourt and its owners. Capt. Gerald Ponsonby. (K) VIII, 3-29. 1915-17.

POOL. The Pools of Mayfield and other Irish families. Rosemary ffolliott. Dublin. 1958.

POWER. The Powers of Clashmore, Co. Waterford. Matthew Butler. (C) N.S. XLVII, 121-22. 1942.

POWER. An historical account of the Pohers, Poers and Powers. G. O'C. Redmond. Dublin. 1897.

POWER. Notes and pedigrees relating to the family of Poher, Poer or Power. Edmund. 17th Lord Power. Clonmel.

PRATT. The family of Pratt of Gawsworth, Carrigrohane, Co. Cork. John Pratt. 1925.

PRATT. Pratt family records: an account of the Pratts of Youghal and Castlemartyr, Co. Cork. Millom. 1931.

PUNCH. Punch family of city and county of Cork. (C) N.S. XXXIII, 106. 1928.

PURCELL. Family papers belonging to the Purcells of Loughmoe, Co. Tipperary. Rev. St. John D. Seymour. (N) III, 124-9. 191-203. 1914.

MacQUILLIN. The Clan of the Mac-Quillina of Antrim. M. Webb. (U) VIII, 251-68. 1860.

MacQUILLIN. The MacQuillins of the Route. George Hill. (U) IX, 57-70. 1861-62.

RAM. The Ram Family. Willett Ram and Francis Robert Ram. Halesworth, Suffolk. 1940.

REA. Memoirs of the Rea family, 1798-1857. A.H. Thornton.

REA. The Rea Genealogy. J. Harris Rea. Banbridge. 1927.

RENTOUL. A record of the family and lineage of Alexander Rentoul, LL.D., M.P. E. Rentoul. Belfast. 1890.

REDMOND. Military and political memoirs of the Redmond family. J. Raymond. (C) N.S. XXVII, 22-35, 73-78. 1921. XXVIII, 81-89. 1922. XXIX, 19-28, 87-93. 1924. XXX, 34-40, 96-99. 1925.

O'REILLY. The O'Reillys of Temple-mills, Celbridge with a note on the history of the clann Ui Raghallaigh in general. E. O'H. Dundrum. Co. Dublin. 1941.

O'REILLY. The descendants of Col. Myles O'Reilly in Co. Leitrim (1650-1830) from tradition. Thomas O'Reilly. (B) II, 15-19. 1923.

REYNOLDS. Notes on the MacRannais of Leitrim and their country: being introductiory to a diary of James Reynolds, Lough Scur, Co. Leitrim, for the years 1658-1660. Rev. Joseph Meehan. C.C. (R) XXXV, 139-51. 1905.

RICHARDSON. Six generations of friends in Ireland. J.M.R. London. 1890.

ROBERTS. A roberts family quondam Quakers of Queen's Co. E.J. Adeir Impey. London. 1939.

ROBERTS. The Roberts family of Waterford. William T. Bayly. (W) II, 98-103. 1896.

ROBERTS. Some account of the Roberts family of Kilmoney. Bessie Garvey. (C) N.S. XXXIV, 107-110. 1929.

ROCHE. The Roches, lords of Fermoy. Eithne Donnelly. (C) N.S. XXXVIII, 86-91. 1933. XXXIX, 38-40, 57-68. 1934. XL 37-42, 63-73. 1935. XLI, 20-28. 78-84. 1936. XLII, 40-52. 1937.

ROCHFORD. A Cork branch of the Rochford family. James Buckley. (C) N.S. XXI, 112-20. 1915.

RONAYNE. Some Desmond incidents and notes on the Ronayne family. E.C.R. (C) N.S. XXIII, 104-7. 1917.

RONAYNE. Notes on the family of Ronayne or Ronan of Counties Cork and Waterford. F.W. Knight. (C) N.S. XXII, 56-63, 109-14, 178-85. 1916. XXIII, 93-104, 142-52. 1917.

MacRORY. The Past-MacRorys of Duneane, Castle-Dawson, Limavady and Belfast. R.A. MacRory. Blefast.

ROSBOROUGH. Later history of the family of Rosborough of Mullinagoan, Co. Fermanagh. H.B. Swanzy. 1897.

ROTHE. The family of Rothe of Kilkenny. George Dames Burtchael. (R) XVII, 501-37, 620-54. 1886.

RUDKIN. The Rudkins of the Co. Carlow. Sir E.T. Bewley. Exeter, 1905.

RUMLEY. The Rumley family of Cork. "Hueguenot." (C) N.S. VII, 127. 1901.

RYLAND. Pedigree of Ryland of Dungarvan and Waterford. (R) XV, 562-5. 1881.

ST. LAWRENCE. Notes on the St. Lawrences, lords of Howth, from the end of the twelfth to the middle of the sixteenth century. Lord Walter Fitzgerald. (R) XXXVII, 349-59. 1907.

SANDYS. Some notes for a history of the Sandys family of Great Britain and Ireland. C. Vivian and Col. T.M. Sandys. 1907.

SANKEY. Pedigree of the Sankeys of Engalnd and Ireland. 1881.

SARSFIELD. Dr. Caulfield's records of the Sarsfield family of the County Cork. J.C. (C) N.S. XXI, 82-91, 131-6. 1915.

SARSFIELD. The Sarsfields of Co. Clare. R.W. Twigge. (N) III, 92-107. 170-90, 32-43. 1914-15.

SARSFIELD. Patrick Sarsfield, Earl of Lucan with an account of his family and their connection with Lucan and Tully. Lord Walter Fitzgerald. (K) VI, 114-47. 1903-5.

SAUNDERS. The family of Saunders of Saunder's Grove, Co. Wicklow. T.U. Sadlier. (K) IX, 125-33. 1918-21.

SAUNDERSON. Saunderson of Castel Saunderson. H. Saunderson. Frome. 1936.

SAVAGE. Ancient and noble family of Savages of Ards. G.F. Armstrong. London. 1880.

SAVAGE. A genealogical history of the Savage family in Ulster. G.F.S.-A. London. 1906.

SEAVER. History of the Seaver family. George Seaver. Dundalk. 1950.

SEGRAVE. The Segrave family, 1066 to 1935. C.W. Segrave. London. 1936.

O'SHAUGHNESSY. O'Shaughnessy of Gort (1543-1783):tabular pedigree. M.J. Blake. (G) VII, 53, 1911-12.

SHAW. Some notes on the Shaw family of Monkstown Castle. James B. Fox. (C) N.S. XXXVII, 93-5. 1932.

SHAW. Concluding notes on the Shaw family of Monkstown castle. J.B. Fox. (C) N.S., LX, 53-4. 1935.

SHERIDAN. The lives of the Sheridans. 2 vols. Percy Fitzgerald. 1886.

SHERICAN. The Sheridan family, 1687-1867. Harold Nicolson. London. 1937.

SHERLOCK. Distinguished Waterford families. I. Sherlock. (W) IX, 120-28. 171-5. 1906. X, 42-44, 171-83. 1907.

SHERLOCK. Notes on the family of Sherlock from state papers and official documents. Rev. J.F.M. ffrench. (K) II, 33-47. 1896-9.

SHERLOCK. The family of Sherlock, No. II. Rev. Canon ffrench. (K) VI, 155-9. 1909-11.

SHERLOCK. Extract from the pedigree of Sherlock of Mitchelstown, Co. Cork. W. Devereux. (C) N.S. XII, 51. 1906.

SHIRLEY. Stemmata Shirleiana or annals of the Shirley family. E.P. Shirley. London. 1873.

SINCLAIR. The Sinclair genealogy. C.T. McCready. 1868.

SINCLAIR. Genealogy of the Sinclairs of Ulster. Sir John Sinclair. 1810.

SINNETT, SINNOTT, SYNNOTT. Sinnett genealogy. Rev. C.N. Sinnett. Concord, N.H. 1910.

SIRR. A genealogical history of the family of Sirr of Dublin. London. 1903.

SITLINGTON. The sitlington family of Dunagorr, Co. Antrim. Edmund Getty. (U), N.S. XV, 161-72. 1909.

SKERRETT. Some records of the Skerrett family. Philip Crossle. (G) XV, 33-72. 1931-3.

SLACKE. Records of the Slacke family in Ireland. Helen A. Crofton. 1900-02.

SMITH. The chronicles of a Puritan family in Ireland. G.N. Nuttall-Smith. London. 1923.

SMYTH. Genealogie de l'anienne et noble famille de Smyth de Ballyntray, Comte de Waterford en Irlande.

SOMERVILLE. The Somervilles and their connexions in Cork. P.S. O'Hegarty. (C). N.S. XLVII, 30-33. 1942.

SOMERVILLE. Records of the Somerville family of Castlehaven and Drishane from 1174 to 1904. E. Somerville and Boyle Townshend Somerville. Cork. 1940.

SPEDDING. The Spedding family, with short accounts of a few other families allied by marriage. J.C.D. Spedding. Dublin. 1909.

SPENSER. Pedigree of the poet Spenser's family. (C) N.S., XI, 196. 1905.

SPENSER. Spenser's pedigree. W. Devereux. (C) N.S. XV, 101-2. 1909.

SPENSER. Memorials of Edmund Spenser, the poet, and his descendants in the county of Cork. J.C. (C) N.S. XIV, 39-43. 1908.

SPENSER. The family and descendants of Edmund Spenser. W.H. Welply. (C) N.S. XXVIII, 22-34, 49-61. 1922.

STEWART. The Stewarts of Ballintoy. Rev. George Hill. (U) N.S. VI 17-23, 78-89, 143-61, 218-23. 1900. VII, 9-17. 1901.

STONEY. Some old annals of the Stoney family. Maj. Stoney. London. 1879.

STOUT. The old Youghal family of Stout. Henry F. Berry. (C) N.S. XXIII, 19-29. 1917.

STUART. Genealogical and historical sketch of the Stuarts of Castle Stuart in Ireland. Rev. Andrew G. Stuart. Edinburgh. 1954.

SULLIVAN. Materials for a history of the family of Sullivan of Ardee, Ireland. T.C. Amory. Cambridge, Mass. 1893.

SULLIVAN. A family chronicle derived from the notes and letters selected by Lady Grey. London 1908.

O'SULLIVAN. Bantry, Berehaven and the O'Sullivan sept. T.D. Sullivan. Dublin. 1908.

SWEETMAN. Notes on the Sweetman family. Rev. Canon Sherlock. (K) III, 389-90. 1899-1902.

SYNGE. The family of Synge or Sing. Katherine C. Synge. Southampton. 1940.

TAAFFE. Memoirs of the ramily of Taafe. Count E.F.J. Taaffe. Vienna. 1856.

TALBOT. Genealogical memoir of the family of Talbot of Malahide, Co. Dublin. 1829.

TERRY. Terry pedigree. J.F. Fuller. (C), N.S. IX, 274-76. 1903.

TIERNAN. The Tiernan and other families. Charles B. Tiernan. Baltimore. 1901.

TIERNEY. The Tierneys and the Egmont estates. M.J. Bourke. (C) N.S. XXVII, 10-14. 1921.

TOBIN. The genealogy of Walter Tobin and his family. Presented by Mr. Thomas Shelly. (O), II, 92-5. 1880-83.

TONE. The family of Tone. T.U. Sadleir. (K), XII, 326-29. 1935-45.

O'TOOLE. The O'Tooles, anciently lords of Powerscourt. John O'Toole. Dublin.

O'TOOLE. Les O'Toole. La Reole. 1864.

O'TOOLE. History of the Clan O'Toole and other Leinster septs. Rev. P.L. O'Toole. Dublin. 1890.

TOWNSHEND. An officer of the Long Parliament and his descendants, being an account of the life and times of Colonel Richard Townshend of Castletown and a chronicle of his family. R.&D. Townshend. London. 1892.

TRACY. Tracy Peerage Case. Folio. 1853.

TRANT. Trant family. J.F. Fuller. (K) V, 18-26. 1919.

TRANT. The Trant family. S.M. (K) II, 237-62. 1914. III, 20-38, 1914.

TRAVERS. Hollywood, Co. Wicklow. Lord Walter Fitzgerald. (K), VIII, 185-96. 1915-17.

TRENCH. Memoir of the Trench family. T.R.F. Cooke-Trench. 1897.

TUTHILL. Pedigree of Tuthill of Kilmore and Faha, Co. Limerick. Lt.-Col. P.B. Tuthill.

TWEEDY. The Dublin Tweedys. Owen Tweedy. London. 1956.

TYRCONNEL. Illustrated handbook of the scenery and antiquities of S.W. Donegal. 1872.

TYNTE. Some notes on the Tynte family. H.T. Fleming. (C) N.S., IX, 156-7. 1903.

TYRRELL. Genealogical history of the Tyrrells of Castleknock in Co. Dublin, Fertullagh in Co. Westmeath and now of Grange Castle, Co. Meath. J.H. Tyrrell. London(?) 1904.

TYRRELL. The Tyrels of Castleknock. E. St. John Brooks. (R) LXXVI, 151-54. 1946.

UNIACKE. The Uniackes of Younghal. R.G. Fitzgerald-Uniacke. (C), III, 113-16, 146-52, 183-91, 210-21, 232-41, 245-55. 1894.

USSHER. The Ussher memoirs or genealogical memoirs of the Ussher families in Ireland. Rev. W.B. Wright. London. 1899.

VANCE. An account historical and genealogical of the family of Vance in Ireland. W. Balbirnie. Cork. 1860.

VILLIERS. Pedigree of the family of Villiers of Kilpeacon, Co. Limerick. Lt.-Col. P.B. Tuthill. London. 1907.

WALSH. Notes on the Norman-Welsh family of Walsh in Ireland, France and Austria. (R), LXXV, 32-44. 1945.

WALSH. Nota et synopsis genealogiae comitum de Walsh aut Wallis. (O), II, 95-8. 1880-3.

WANDESFORDE. The story of the family of Wandesforde of Kirklington and Castlecomer. H.B. M'Call. London. 1904.

WARBURTON. Memoir of the Warburton family of Garryhinch, King's Co. Dublin, 1848.

WARREN. History of the Warren family. Rev. Thomas Warren. 1902.

WARREN. Some notes on the family of Warren of Warrenstown, Co. Louth. Mrs. Richard Bellew. (L) IV, 24-34. 1916.

WATERS. The Waters or Walter family of Cork. E.W. Waters. (C) 1939.

WATERS. The Waters family of Cork. Eaton W. Waters. (C) N.S. XXXI, 71-8. 1926. XXXII, 17-23, 104-113. 1927. XXXIII, 35-41. 1928. XXXIV, 36-42, 97-105. 1929. XXXV, 36-43, 102-113. 1930. XXXVI, 26-38, 76-86. 1931. XXXVII, 35-41. 1932.

WAUCHOPE. The Ulster branch of the family of Wauchope. G.M. Wauchope. London. 1929.

WEST. The Wests of Ballydugan, Co. Down; the Rock, Co. Wicklow and Ashwood, Co. Wexford. Edward Parkinson and Captain E. E. West. (U), N.S. XII, 135-41, 159-65. 1906.

WHITE. The Whites of Dufferin and their connections. Major R.G. Berry. (U) N.S. XII, 117-25, 169-74. 1906. XIII, 89-95, 125-32. 1907.

WHITE. The history of the family of White of Limerick, Knockcentry. J.D. White. Cashel. 1887.

WILDE. The Wildes of Merrion Square. Patrick Byrne. London. 1954.

WILKINSON. Fragments of family history. S.P. Flory. London. 1896.

WILLIAMS. The Groves and Lappan, Monaghan county, Ireland. J.F. Williams. Saint Paul. 1889.

WILSON. A brief journal of the life of Thomas Wilson. John Stoddart. Dublin. 1728.

WINGFIELD. Muniments of the family of Wingfield. Viscount Powerscourt. London. 1894.

WINTHORP. Some account of the early generations of the Winthorp family in Ireland. Cambridge. Mass. 1883.

WOGAN. Memoire historique et genealogique sur la famille de Wogan. Par le comte Alph. O Kelly de Galway. Paris. 1896.

WOLFE. The Wolfe family of Co. Kildare. George Wolfe. (K) III, 361-7. 1899-1902.

WOLFE. Wolfes of Forenaghts, Blackhall, Baronrath, Co. Kildare and Tipperary. Lt.-Col. R.T. Wolfe. Guildford. 1893.

WRAY. The Wrays of Donegal, Londonderry and Antrim. C.V. Trench. Oxford. 1945.

WYSE. Ancient and illustrious Waterford families. P. Higgins. (W) V, 199-206. 1899.

YARNER. A collection concerning the family of Yarner of Wicklow. J.C.H. 1870.

YOUNG. Three hundred years in Inishowen being more particularly an account of the family of Young of Culdaff. A.J. Young. Belfast. 1929.

YOUNG. The extinct family of Young of Newtown-O'More, Co. Kildare. W. FitzG. (K), III, 338. 1899-1902.

CO. ANTRIM

Old Ballymena: A history of Ballymena during the 1798 Rebellion. 1938.

The Book of Antrim. George H. Bassett. 1888.

A History of the Town of Belfast. 2 vols. George Benn. London 1877-80.

Thirty Centuries in South East Antrim. Rev. H.J. Clarke. Antrim. 1938.

The Macdonnells of Antrim. George Hill. Belfast. 1877.

Historical Collections relative to the Town of Belfast. Henry Joy. Belfast. 1817.

The History and Antiquities of the Town of Carrickfergus, 1318-1839. Samuel McSkimin. Belfast. 1909.

Sidelights on Belfast History. S. Shannon Millin. 1932.

History of Belfast. 2 Vols. J.D. Owen Belfast. 1921.

Cullybackey, the Story of an Ulster Village. William Shaw. 1913.

On the Shining Ban; Records of an Ulster Manor. R.M. Sibbett. Belfast. 1928.

Historical Notices of Old Belfast, and its Vicinity. Robert M. Young. 1896.

The Town Book of the Corporation of Belfast, 1613-1816. Robert M. Young. 1892.

A History of the Church of Ireland in Ramoan Parish. H.A. Boyd. 1930.

Three Centuries in South East Antrim; the Parish of Coole or Carnmoney. Rev. H.J. St.J. Clarke. Belfast 1938.

St. Colmanell, Ahoghill: A History of its Parish. Rev. W.H.A. Lee. 1865.

The Parish of Lambeg. Rev. H.C. Marshall. 1933.

ARMAGH

Historical Memoirs of the City of Armagh. James Stuart. Dublin 1900.

A Historical and Statistical Account of the Barony of Upper Fews (Amagh). John Donaldson

The History of Charlemont Fort and the Borough in the County Armagh and of Mountjoy Fort in County Tyrone. J.J. Marshall. 1921.

Historical Memoires of the City of Armagh. James Stewart. Dublin. 1900.

The History of St. Patrick's Cathedral, Armagh. John Gallogly. 1880.

Keady Parish; A Short History of its Church and People. Rev. M.B. Hogg. 1928.

The History of Tyan Parish, County Armagh. Thomas Hughes. 1910.

Armagh Clergy and Parishes. Rev. James B. Leslie. 1911.

History of the Parish of Tynan, Co. Armagh. J.J. Marshall. 1932.

The Register of John Swayne, Archbishop of Armagh and Primate of Ireland, 1418-1439. John Swayne. 1935.

CARLOW

History and Antiquities of the County of Carlow. John Ryan. Dublin. 1833.

Carlow Past and Present, with a short account Dalcassion families. Michael Brophy. 1888.

The Antiquities of Leighlin (Co. Carlow). James Coyle.

The Social State of the Southern and Eastern Counties of Ireland in the Sixteenth Century. H.J. Hore. 1870.

CAVAN

The Civic History of the Town of Cavan. 3rd Edition. T.S. Smith. Dublin. 1938.

The Highlands of Cavan. Anomymous. Belfast. 1856.

History of the Diocese of Ardagh. James J. Macnamee. Dublin. 1954.

The Diocese of Kilmore; its History and Antiquities. Philip O'Connell. Dublin. 1937.

Records Relating to the Diocese of Ardagh and Clonmacnoise. Rev. J. Monahan. 1886.

CLARE

An Clar, Official Guide. Dublin. 1954.

A History of the Diocese of Killaloe. D.F. Gleeson. Dublin. 1962.

Ballads of Co. Clare (1850-1976). S.P. OCillin. Galway. 1976.

Northwest Clare, Today, Tomorrow. W. Nolan. Galway. 1974.

Journal 1973, 1977. Dal Geais.

Kilfarboy, A history of a West Clare Parish. S. MacMathuna. Ennis. 1974.

History and Topography of the County of Clare. James Frost. Dublin. 1893.

History of Clare and the Dalcassian Clans of Tipperary, Limerick and Galway. Rev. P. White. Dublin. 1893.

The History and Antiquities of the Diocese of Kilmacduagh. J. Fahey. Dublin. 1893.

The Diocese of Killaloe, from the Reformation to the Close of the Eighteenth Century. Philip Dwyer. Dublin. 1878.

CORK

Cork, A Civic Survey. Cork Town Planning Association. Liverpool. Univ. Press. 1926.

A History of the Diocese of Cork. E. Bolster. Shannon. 1972.

Cork, Past and Present. Cork. 1917.

The Land and the People of Nineteenth Century Cork. J.S. Donnelley. London, 1975.

Rebel Cork's Fighting Story 1916-1921: Told by the men who made it. The Kerryman. 1947.

The New Cork Directory for the Year 1795. Cork. 1795.

City and County Cork Almanac and Directory, 1889-1922. Francis Guy. Cork. 1922.

County and City of Cork Directory, 1875-76. Francis Guy. Cork. 1875.

Cork Almanac and County and City Directory, 1923-1935. Francis Guy. Cork. 1935.

Directory and Pictures of Cork and its Environs. W. West. Cork. 1810.

Guide to Cork. Irish Tourist Assoc. Cork. 1927.

Official Guide to City of Cork. Dublin. 1952.

Official Guide to Cork City and County. Dublin. 1953.

Cork City, its History and Antiquities. Edited by P.J. Hartnett. Cork. 1943.

Port of Cork Handbook. 1953.

Industrial Survey and Business Directory for the City and County of Cork. Dublin. 1960.

Cork Historical and Archaelogical Society Journal. Vol. 1. Cork. 1892.

A List of the Ancient and National Monuments in the County of Cork. Cork. 1913.

History of Bandon. George Bennett. Cork. 1869.

A History of the City and County of Cork. Mary Francis Cusack. Dublin. 1875.

History of West Cork and Diocese of Ross. Rev. W. Holland. Skibbereen. 1949.

Ancient and Present State of the County and City Cork. Charles Smith. Cork. 1893-94.

The Diocese of Cork. C.A. Webster. Cork. 1920.

The History of Bandon and the Principal Towns in the West Riding of County Cork. 2nd Ed. George Bennett. Cork. 1869.

The Council Book of the Corporation of Cork, from 1609-1643; 1690-1800. Richard Caulfield. 1876.

The Council Book of the Corporation of Kinsale. Richard Caulfield. 1879.

The Council Book of the Corporation of Youghal, from 1610-1659; 1666-1687; 1690-1800. Richard Caulfield. 1878.

History of Queenstown, Cork. The Venerable Archdeacon Dennehy. Cork. 1923.

The History of the County and City of Cork. 2 Vols. Rev. C.B. Gibson. London. 1861.

Guide to Youghal, Ardmore and the Black Water. Rev. Samuel Hayman. 1860.

The Social State of the Southern and Eastern Counties of Ireland in the Sixteenth Century. H.J. Hore. 1870.

The History of Kinsale. Florence O'Sullivan. Dublin. 1916.

Place Names and Antiquities of Barrymore (Barony), County Cork. Patrick Power. 1923.

The County and City of Cork Remembrancer. Francis H. Tucky.

Historical and Topographical Notes, etc, on Buttevant, Castletownroche, Doneraile, Mallow, and places in their vicinity. 4 Vols. Col. James Grove White. Cork. 1905-16.

History of Kilbyrne, Donaraile, Cork. Col. James Grove White. Cork. 1915.

Clerical and Parochial Records of Cork, Cloyne and Ross. W. Maziere Brady. London. 1864.

The Parish Registers of Holy Trinity, Cork, 1643-68. Richard Caulfield. 1877.

Annals of St. Fin Barres Cathedral, Cork. Richard Caulfield. 1871.

Church and Parish Records of the United Diocese of Cork, Cloyne and Ross. Rev. J.H. Cole. Cork. 1903.

History of West Cork and the Diocese of Ross. Rev. W. Holland. Skibbereen. 1949.

The Diocese of Cork. Charles A. Webster. Cork. 1920.

The Diocese of Ross. Charles A. Webster. 1924.

DONEGAL

Ballyshannon: its History and Antiquities. Hugh Allingham. Londonderry. 1879.

Inis-Owen and Tirconnell. W. J. Doherty. Dublin. 1895.

Scenery and Antiquities of North West Donegal. William Harkin. Donegal. 1893.

Facts from Gweedore. George Hill. Dublin. 1854.

The Book of Inishowen. H.P. Swan. Buncrana. 1938.

Three Hundred Years in Inishowen. Amy Young. Belfast. 1929.

The History of the Diocese of Raphoe. 2 Vols. The Very Rev. Canon Maguire. Dublin. 1920.

Raphoe Clergy and Parishes. Rev. James B. Leslie. Enniskillen. 1940.

DOWN

The Ancient and Present State of the County Down. Walter Harris. Dublin. 1744.

History of the County of Down. Alexander Knox. Dublin. 1875.

Historical Account of the Dioceses of Down and Connor. James O'Laverty. Dublin. 1878-89.

The City of Down from its earliest days. Edward Parkinson. Belfast. 1927.

Two Centuries of Life in Down: 1600-1800. J. Stevenson. Belfast. 1921.

Local Jottings of Newry Collected and Transcribed. Vols 1-4. Frances C. Crossle. Newry. 1890-1910.

Montgomery Manuscripts, 1603-1706. Rev. George Hill. Belfast. 1869.

A History of Banbridge. Capt. Richard Linn. Belfast. 1935.

The Hamilton Manuscripts. T.K. Lowery. Belfast. 1867.

The Ancient and Present State of the County Down. W. Williamson. 1757.

An Ulster Parish: Being a History of Donaghcloney. Edward D. Atkinson. 1898.

Dromore, an Ulster Diocese. E.D. Atkinson. Dundalk. 1925.

An Ancient Parish, Past and Present, being the Parish of Donaghmore, County Down. J. Davison Cowan. London. 1914.

A Parish Miscellany, Donaghcloney. Josiah Haddock.

Biographical Lists of the Clergy of the Diocese of Down. Rev. James B. Leslie and the Very Rev. H.B. Swanzy. 1936.

An Historical Account of the Diocese of Down & Connor. Rev. James O'Laverty. Dublin. 1878-1889.

The History of the Parish of Holywood from the earliest times. O.J. O'Laverty. No date.

Down and its Parishes. L.A. Pooler. 1907.

Ecclesiastical Antiquities of Down, Connor and Dromore. William Reeves. 1847.

St. Mary's Church, Newry; its History. S.W. Reside. 1933.

Parish of Tullylish; Historical Notes. Rev. David Stewart. No date.

DUBLIN

Dublin Street Guide. Dublin. 1942.

Dublin Delineated. Dublin. 1831.

Dublin and its Environs. Dublin. 1846.

Photographs of Dublin, with Descriptive Letterpress. H.F. Mares. Dublin. 1867.

Parish Guide to the Archdioces of Dublin. Dublin Archdiocese. Dublin. 1958.

Dublin. D. Clarke. London. 1977.

Dublin: Official Guide. Dublin. 1955.

Dublin 1660-1860. M. Craig. Dublin. 1969.

The History of the County of Dublin. J.D. Dalton. No date.

An Essay Towards a Natural History of the County of Dublin. J. Rutty. Dublin. 1772.

History of Dublin. Warburton, Whitelaw & Walsh. Dublin. 1818.

The Neighbourhood of Dublin. W. St. John Joyce. Dublin. 1921.

History of the County of Dublin. Francis Elrington Ball. Dublin. 1902-20.

Dublin, 1660-1860. Maurice Craig. Dúblin & London. 1952.

History of the City of Dublin. John T. Gilbert. Dublin. 1861.

The History and Antiquaries of the City of Dublin from the earliest accounts. Walter Harris. Dublin. 1766.

History of the City of Dublin. John Warburton, James Whitelaw & Robert Walsh. Dublin & London. 1818.

History of Terenure. Brian MacGilolla Phadraig. Dublin. 1954.

History and Description of Santry Clogran Parishes, Co. Dublin and its neighborhood. Francis Elrington Ball, and Everard Hamilton. Dublin. 1895.

Brief Sketches of the Parishes of Booterstown and Donnybrook, in the County of Dublin. Rev. Beaver H. Blacker. 1860-1874.

Traditions of Drimagh, County Dublin and its Neighborhood. Leam Ua Broin. No date.

The Diocese of Meath, Ancient and Modern. Rev. A. Cogan. Dublin. 1862.

The Fasti of St. Patrick's, Dublin. Hugh J. Lawler. 1930.

The Story of Our Parish; St. Peter's Dublin. Catharine M. MacSorley. Dublin. 1917.

The History and Antiquities of the Collegiate Cathedral Church of St. Patrick, near Dublin, from its foundation in 1190, to the Year 1819. William Monk Mabon. Dublin. 1820.

FERMANAGH

History of Enniskillen with some manors of Fermanagh. W.C. Trimble. Enniskillen. 1919-21.

Parliamentary Memoirs of Fermanagh, 1613-1885. Earl of Belmore. Dublin. 1887.

Enniskillen, Parish and Town. W.H. Dundas. Dundalk. 1913.

Derriana consisting to a History of the Siege of Derry and the Defense of Enniskillen in 1688 and 1689, and Biographical notes. Rev. John Graham. 1823.

Enniskillen Long Ago; an Historic Sketch of the Parish of "Iniskeen in Lacu Ernensi". W.H. Bradshaw. 1878.

The Parish of Devenish, County Fermanagh. Rev. W.B. Steele. Enniskillen. 1937.

GALWAY

History of the Town and County of the Town of Galway. James Hardiman. Dublin. 1820.

Old Galway. M.D. O'Sullivan. Cambridge. 1942.

History of Galway. Connacht Tribune. 1926.

History of Clare and the Dalcassian Clans of Tipperary, Limerick and Galway. Dublin. 1893.

The Story of St. Nicholas Collegiate Church, Galway. J. Fleetwood Berry. Galway. 1912.

KERRY

County Kerry Past and Present. Jeremiah King. Dublin. 1931.

Ancient and Present State of the County of Kerry. Charles Smith. Dublin. 1756.

The McGellycuddy Papers. W. Maziere Brady. London. 1867.

History of the Kingdom of Kerry. M.F. Cusack. London. 1871.

A Popular History of East Kerry. T.M. Donovan. 1931.

Selections from Old Kerry Records, Historical and Genealogical. 2 Vols. Mary A. Hickson. London. 1872-74.

The Diocese of Kerry (formerly Ardfert). Rev. Donal A. Reedy. Killarney. No date.

KILDARE

Collections Relating to the Dioceses of Kildare and Leighlin. 3 Vols. Rev. M. Comerford. Dublin. 1883.

The History and Antiquities of the Diocese of Ossory. 4 Vols. Dublin. 1905.

Ossory Clergy and Parishes. Rev. James B. Leslie. 1933.

TIPPERARY

Roscrea and District. George Cunningham. Roscrea. 1976.

A History of the Diocese of Killaloe, Vol. 1. D.F. Gleeson. Dublin. 1962.

Tipperary's Families, being the Hearth money records for 1665-66-67. T. Caffan. Dublin. 1911.

Carrick-On-Suir. P. Power. Dublin. 1976.

South Tipperary. Co. Tipperary. Dublin. 1963.

Tipperary's Annual. Dublin. 1910.

Tipperary's Annual, 1954. Modern Version. Clonmel. 1954.

Tipperary Remembers. Published by Tipperary Remembers Society. Kilkenny. 1976.

History of Clonmel. William P. Burke. Waterford. 1907.

Tipperary. James Cotter. New York. 1929.

The Book of the Galtees and the Golden Vein. Paul J. Flynn. Dublin. 1926.

The Last Lords of Ormond. D.F. Gleeson. London. 1938.

Cashel of the Kings. J. Gleeson. Dublin. 1927.

Clonmel and the Surrounding Country. W. Despard Hemphill. 1860.

Gleanings from Garrymore. M. McIlroy. No date.

Nenagh (Co. Tipperary) and its Neighborhood. E.H. Sheehan. No date.

My Clonmel Scrap Book. James White. No date.

History of Clare and the Dalcassian Clans of Tipperary, Limerick and Galway. Rev. P. White. 1893.

KILKENNY

The History, Architecture and Antiquities of the Cathedral Church of St. Canice, Kilkenny. Rev. James Graves and T. Prim. Dublin. 1857.

Official Guide. Dublin. 1954.

Charter of the City of Kilkenny, Trans. from the original Latin. Kilkenny. 1830.

Journal. Kilkenny and South East of Ireland Archaeological Society. No date.

Liber Primus Kilkenniensis. Kilkenny City Records Edited by Charles McNeill. Dublin. 1931.

A History of County Kilkenny. O. O'Kelly. Donegal. 1969.

OFFALY (KING'S COUNTY)

The Early History of the Town of Birr, or Parsonstown. Thomas L. Cooke. Dublin. 1875.

The Midland Septs and the Pale. F.R.M. Hitchcock. Dublin. 1908.

LIMERICK

The Diocese of Limerick. John Begley. Dublin. 1906-38.

History, Topography and Antiquities of the County and City of Limerick. P. Fitzgerlad & J.J. McGregor. No date.

Limerick: Its History and Antiquities. Maurice Linihan. Dublin. 1866.

Limerick and its Sieges. Rev. James Dowd. Limerick. 1896.

A History of the City of Limerick. John Ferrar. Limerick. 1767

The History of Limerick Ecclesiastical Civil and Military, from the Earliest Records to the Year 1787. John Ferrar. Limerick. 1787.

The German Colony in County Limerick. Richard Hayes. Limerick. 1937.

The Black Book of Limerick. James MacCaffrey. 1907.

History of Clare and the Dalcassian Calns of Tipperary, Limerick, and Galway. Rev. P. White. Dublin. 1893.

St. Mary's Cathedral, Limerick. James Dowd. 1936.

A Descriptive and Historic Guide through St. Mary's Cathedral, Limerick. Francis Meredyth. Limerick. 1887.

LONDONDERRY

The Whole Proceedings of the Seige of Drogheda. Nicholas Bernard. Dublin. 1736.

Some items of Historic Interest about Waterside. Rev. Samuel Ferguson. Londonderry. 1902.

A History of the Seige of Londonderry and the Defense of Enniskillen in 1688 and 1689. Rev. John Graham. 1829.

The County of Londonderry in three Centuries. J.W. Kernohan. Belfast. 1921.

Londonderry: A Particular of the "Howses and Famyleys" in Londonderry, May 15, 1628. Very Rev. R.G. King. Londonderry. 1936.

Historical Gleanings from County Derry. Samuel Martin. Dublin. 1955.

The Londonderry Plantation, 1609-1641. T.W. Moody. Belfast. 1939.

Londonderry and the London Companies, 1609-1629. Sir Thomas Phillips. Belfast. 1928.

Derry and Enniskillen, in the Year 1689. Thomas Witherow. 1873, 1885.

A True Relation of the Twenty Weeks Siege of Londonderry by the Scotch, Irish, and the disaffected English. Thomas Witherow. London. 1649.

Fighters of Derry, their Deeds and Descendants. William R. Young. 1932.

Natural History of Magilligan Parish in 1725. R. Innis. No date.

History of the Parish of Creggan in the Seventeenth and Eighteenth Centuries. Rev. Lawrence P. Murray. Dundalk. 1940.

LONGFORD

History of the County Longford. James P. Farrell. Dublin. 1891.

The Black Book of Edgeworthstown and other Edgeworth memories, 1585-1817. H.T. Butler. 1927.

LOUTH

The History of Drogheda with its Environs. John Dalton. Dublin 1863.

The History of Dundalk and its Environs. John Dalton & J.R. O'Flanagan. Dundalk. 1864.

The Whole Proceedings of the Siege of Drogheda. Nicholas Bernard. Dublin. 1736.

The Boyne and the Aghrim. Thomas Witherow. 1879.

The Siege of Drogheda: or Reminiscences of the Families of Ireland. Anonymous. No date.

History of Kilsaran Union of Parishes, County Lough. Rev. James B. Leslie. Dundalk. 1908.

Tempest's Annual. Tempest. 1936-42.

MAYO

The History of the Archdiocese of Tuam. 2 Vols. Rt. Rev. Monsignor Dalton. Dublin. 1928.

Notes on the Early History of the Diocese of Tuam, Killala and Achonry. J.T. Knox. Dublin. 1904.

History of the County of Mayo to the close of the 16th century. H.T. Knox. Dublin. 1908.

A Narrative of what passed at Killala in the County of Mayo, in the Summer of 1798. Joseph Stock. London. 1800.

St. Patrick and the Parish of Kilkeeran. Rev. Timothy Hurley. No date.

Notes on the Early History of the Dioceses of Tuam, Killala, and Achonry. H.T. Knox. Dublin. 1904.

MEATH

History of the Diocese of Meath. John Healy. Dublin. 1908.

Antiquities of the County of Meath. John Dalton. Dublin. 1833.

History of the Diocese of Meath. John Henry. 2 Vols. No date.

MONAGHAN

History of Monaghan 1660-1860. D.C. Rushe. Dundalk. 1921.

History of the County of Monaghan. Evelyn Phillip Shirley. London. 1879.

Some Account of the Territory and Dominion of Farney, in the Province and Earldom of Ulster. Evelyn Philip Shirley. London. No date.

Lough Fea. 2 Vols. Rev. Evelyn Philip Shirley. London. 1859.

Clogher Clergy and Parishes. Rev. James B. Leslie. 1908.

A Statistical Account or Parochial Survey of Ireland drawn from Communications of the Clergy. 3 Vols. William Shaw Mason. Dublin. 1814.

LEIX

History of the Queen's County. John O'Hanlon. Dublin. 1907-14.

The History of Queen's County. Daniel O'Byrne. Dublin. 1856.

A Statistical Account of the Parish of Aghaboe, in Queen's County. Edward Ledwich. 1796.

Ardfert and Aghadoe; Clergy and Parishes. Rev. James B. Leslie. Dublin. 1940.

ROSCOMMON

Facts and Fictions of Local History. Rev. M. Becket. 1929.

Loch Ce' and it Annals: North Roscommon and the Diocese of Elphin. Francis Burke. Dublin. 1895.

SLIGO

The History of Sligo: Town and County. T. O'Rorke. Dublin. 1889.

History of Sligo, County and Town. W.G. Wood-Martin. Dublin. 1882-92.

Sligo and the Enniskilleners, from 1688-1691. W.G. Wood-Martin. Dublin. 1882.

History, Antiquities and Present State of the Parishes of Ballysadare and Kilvarnet, in County Sligo. T. O'Rorke. No date.

TYRONE

Tyrone Precinct. W.R. Hutchinson. Belfast. 1951.

The History of Charlemont Fort and the Borough in the County Armagh and of Mountjoy Fort in County Tyrone. J.J. Marshall. 1921.

Vesty Records of the Church of St. John, Parish of Aghalow (Caledon, Co. Tyrone). John J. Marshall. No date.

WATERFORD

The Story of Waterford. Edward Downey. Waterford. 1914.

History of County Waterford. Rev. Patrick Power. Waterford. 1933.

Waterford and Lismorc. Rev. Patrick Power. 1937.

The History, Topography and Antiquities of the County and City of Waterford. R.H. Ryland. London. 1824.

The Ancient and Present State of the County and City of Waterford. Charles Smith. Dublin. 1746.

The Barony of Gaultier. M. Butler. No date.

History and Directory of County and City of Waterford. P.M. Egan. No date.

Waterford during the Civil War, 1641-1653. Thomas Fitzpatrick. 1912.

The Holy City of Ardmore, Co. Waterford. F. Ochille. Youghal. No date.

Fasti Ecclesiae Hibernicae: Diocese of Waterford; Diocese of Cashel and Emly. Cotton Henry. Dublin. 1845.

Succession List of Bishops and Clergy of the Diocese of Waterford and Lismore. William H. Rennison. Waterford. 1922.

WESTMEATH

The Annals of Westmeath, Ancient and Modern. J. Woods. Dublin. 1907.

WEXFORD

History of the Town and County of Wexford. Phillip Hore. Dublin. 1900-11.

Ballygullion, County Wexford. Lynn Doyle. 1945.

Notes and Gleanings Relating to the County of Wexford. Martin Doyle. Dublin. 1868.

History of Enniscorthy, County Wexford. W.H. Grattan Flood. No date.

History of the Insurrection of County Wexford in 1798. Edward Hay. Dublin. 1803.

The Social State of the Southern and Eastern Counties of Ireland in the Seventeenth Century. H.J. Hore. 1870.

Ferns Clergy and Parishes. Rev. James B. Leslie. 1936.

WICKLOW

Bray: A Hundred Years of Bray and its Neighborhood from 1770 to 1870. Anomymous. 1907.

MISCELLANEOUS COUNTIES

Derry Clergy and Parishes. Rev. James B. Leslie. Enniskillen. 1937.

Gleanings from Garrymore. Mary McIlroy. No date.

Records relating to the Diocese of Ardagh and Clonmacnoise. Rev. J. Monahan. 1886.

Ferns Clergy and Parishes. Rev. James B. Leslie. 1936.

The Diocese of Kilmore; it History and Antiquities. Philip O'Donnell. Dublin. 1937.

Lisburn Cathedral and its Past Rectors. The Very Rev. W.P. Carmody. 1926.

The Succession of Clergy in the Parishes of S. Bride, S. Michael le Pole and S. Stephen. W.G. Carroll. Dublin. 1884.

The History of the Archdiocese of Tuam. 2 Vols. Rt. Rev. Monsignor Dalton. Dublin. 1928.

St. Multose Church, Kinsale. Rt. Rev. Monsignor Darling. Cork. 1895.

The Diocese of Killaloe, from the Reformation to the Close of the Eighteenth Century. Philip Dwyer. Dublin. 1878.

The Story of St. Patrick's Church, Coleraine. Samuel Henry. No date.

Diocese of Dromore: Brief Historical Sketch of the Parish of Clonduff. Padraic Keenan. Newry. 1941.

The History of Magherafelt. W.H. Maitland. Cookstown. 1916.

The Parish of Fairview including the present parishes of Corpus Christi, Glasnevin, Larkhill, Marino, and Donnycarney. Rev. John Kingston. Dundalk. 1953.

Notes on the Early History of the Dioceses of Tuam, Killala, and Achonry. H.T. Knox. Dublin. 1904.

History of the Diocese of Ardagh. James J. Macnamee. Dublin. 1954.

Raphoe Clergy and Parishes. Rev. James B. Leslie. Enniskillen. 1940.

A Statistical Account or Parochial Survey of Ireland, Drawn from Communications of the Clergy. 3 Vols. William Shaw Mason. Dublin. 1814.

Clogher Clergy and Parishes. Rev. James B. Leslie. 1908.

The History and the Antiquities of the Parish of Dunnamaggan. Richard Lahert. Tralee. 1956.

A History of the Church of Ireland in St. Mary Magdalene Parish. W.S. Leathem. Belfast. 1939.

Some of the Military Records of America before 1900. E. Kay Kirkham. Washington? 1963.

A Survey of American Census Schedules. E. Kay Kirkham. Salt Lake City. 1959.

Directory of Genealogical Periodicals. J.A. Konrad. Ohio. 1975.

A Bibliography of Ship Passenger Lists, 1538-1825. Harold Lancour. New York. 1963.

How to Trace Your Family Tree. American Genealogical Research Institute. Virginia. 1973.

Genealogical Research. American Society of Genealogists. Washington. 1960.

Practical Research in Genealogical. Arizona Temple District Genealogical Library. Arizona. 1955.

Basic Course in Genealogy. Thomas Nelson Community College. Virginia. 1972.

Advanced Genealogical Research. Archibald F. Bennett. Salt Lake City. 1959.

A Guide for Genealogical Research. Archibald F. Bennett. Salt Lake City. 1951.

Searching with Success. Archibald F. Bennett. Salt Lake City. 1962.

Guide to Genealogical Records in The National Archives. Meredith B. Washington. 1964.

Seven Lesson Course in Irish Research and Sources. Betty L. McCay. 1972.

Irish and Scotch-Irish Ancestral Research. Margaret D. Falley. Illinois. 1962.

Wills and Where to Find Them. Jeremy S.W. Gibson. Baltimore. 1974.

In Search of Scottish Ancestry. Gerald K.S. Hamilton-Edwards. Baltimore. 1972.

Check List of Historical Records Survey Publications. Sargent B. Child & Dorothy P. Holmes. Washington. 1943.

State Censuses: An Annotated Bibliography of Censuses of Population Taken After the Year 1790 by State and Territories of the United States. Henry J. Dubester. Washington. 1948.

Search and Research. Noel C. Stevenson. Salt Lake City. 1973.

Directory of State and Provincial Archivists. Society of American Archivist, State and Local Records Committee. Chicago. 1975.

Directory: Historical Societies and Agencies in the United States and Canada, 1975-76. American Association for State and Local History. Nashville. 1976.

The American Archivist. Society of American Archivists.

Check List of Historical Records Survey Publications.

The Morton Allan Directory of European Passenger Steamship Arrivals. New York. 1931.

Ulster, Emigration to Colonial America, 1718-1775. Routledge & K. Paul. London. 1966.

Emigrants from Ireland, 1847-1852. Elish Ellis.

A Dictionary of Scottish Emigrants to the USA Baltimore. Magna Carta Book Co. 1972.

Passengers to America: a Consolidation of Ship Passenger Lists from the New England Historical and Genealogical Register. Genealogical Pub. Co. Baltimore. 1977.

San Francisco Ship Passenger Lists. Louis J. Rasmussen. Genealogical Publishing Co. Baltimore. 1978.

American-Irish Historical Society Journal. New York.

Passenger Lists of Ships Coming to North America, 1607-1825; A Bibliography. A. Harold Lancour. New York.

New England Historical and Genealogical Register.

The Recorder. The American-Irish Historical Society. Boston.

Harp and Sword, 1776. Charles Lucy.

Index of Revolutionary War Pension Applications. National Genealogical Society. 1966.

Report from the Secretary of War... in Relation to the Pension Establishment of the United States. 3 Vols. 1835.

List of Pensioners on the Roll January 1, 1883. 5 Vols. 1883.

Genealogies in the Library of Congress, a Bibliography. Magna Carta Book Company.

U.S. Local Histories in the Library of Congress, a Bibliography. Magna Carta Book Company.

Irish Family Names. Patrick Kelly. 1958.

Some Ulster Surnames. Padraig MacGiolla Domhnaigh. Ed. by Edward McLysaght.

Some Anglicised Surnames in Ireland. Padraig MacGiolla Domhnaigh. 1923.

A Guide to Irish Surnames. Edward MacLysaght. Dublin. 1965.

Irish Families; their names, arms, and origins. Edward MacLysaght. New York. 1972.

More Irish Families. O'Gorman. Galway, Ireland. 1960.

Supplement to Irish Families. Genealogical Book Co. Baltimore. 1964.

The Surnames of Ireland. Edward MacLysaght. Dublin. 1973.

Sloinnte Gaedheal is Gall: Irish Names and Surnames. Patrick Woulfe. Dublin. 1923.

A Survey of American Church Records. 2 Vols. E. Kay Kirkham. Salt Lake City. 1959-60.

Irish Families in Ancient Quebec Records. John O'Farrell. 1872.

Records of Genealogical Interest in the Public Archives of Canada. James Atherton. Salt Lake City. 1969

Tracing Ancestors Through the Province of Quebec and Acadia to France. Roland J. Auger. Salt Lake City. 1969.

Billinger's Postal and Shippers Guide for the United States and Canada. Westwood. New Jersey. Annual.

Gazetteer of Canada. Canadian Permanent Committee on Geographical Names. Ottawa.

Directory-History Societies and Agencies in the United States and Canada. American Assoc. of State and Local History. Tenn. Bi-annual.

Pre-Revolutionary Settlements in Nova Scotia. Salt Lake City. D. Bruce Fergusson. 1969.

Sources for Ge ealogical Research in Ontario. Sandra Guillaume. Salt Lake City. 1969.

The Exodus of British Loyalists (Royalists) from the U.S. to Canada, England, the Caribbean, and Spanish Territories. Robert F. Kirk and Audrey Kirk. Salt Lake City. 1969.

Major Genealogical Sources for Canada, Quebec and Acadia. Salt Lake City. 1969.

Martindale-Hubbell Law Directory. Col. V. Annual.

McGraw-Hill Directory and Almanac of Canada. Toronto.

Church Records of Canada. Millman, Beaudin, Schultz, & Meikleham. Salt Lake City. 1969.

Municipal Guide for the Province of Quebec City. Quebec Bureau of Statistics. 1966.

Tracing Your Ancestors in Canada. Public Archives of Canada. Ottawa. 1967.

The Ontario Genealogical Society Bulletin. Milton Rubincam.

__________, et al. "Canada." Genealogical Research: Methods and Sources. Ed. by Milton Rubincam. Washington. 1960.

Post 1815 Settlement in Canada. Donald Wilson. Salt Lake City. 1969.

Irish Colonists in the British West Indies. Richard J. Purcell.

How to Read the Handwritting and Records of Early America. E. Kay Kirkham.

The O'Loughlin Book. Michael C. O'Laughlin. Kansas City, MO. 1980.

The O'Donoghue Book. Michael C. O'Laughlin. Kansas City, MO. 1980.

History and Bibliography of American Newspapers, 1690-1820. Clarence S. Brigham. Worcester, Mass. 1947

American Newspapers, 1821-1936. Winifred Godfrey. New York. 1937.

Directory: Historical Societies and Agencies in the U.S. and Canada, 1975-76. American Association for State and Local History. Nashville. 1976.

A Survey of American Church Records. Salt Lake City. 1959-60.

The Library of the National Society. Daughters of the American Revolution. 1776 D. St. N.W., Washington, D.C. 20006.

Irish Families. Edward MacLysaght.

Genealogical Research Methods and Sources. The American Society of Genealogists.

The Researcher's Guide to American Genealogy. Val. D. Greenwood.

Genealogy as Pastime and Profession. Donald Lines Jacobus.

Know Your Ancestors. Ethel W. Williams.

Tracing Your Ancestry. 2 Vols. F. Wilbur Helmbold.

American & British Genealogy & Herladry. P. William Filby.

Genealogical Books in Print. Netti Schreiner-Yantis.

The Genealogical Helper. Everton Publishers, Inc. Bi-monthly magazine. Logan. Utah.

National Genealogical Society Quarterly. National Genealogical Society. Washington, D.C.

A Topographical Index of the Parishes and Townlands of Ireland in Sir William Petty's MSS. Barony Map (1655-1659). Y. M. Goblet, Ed. Dublin. 1932.

The Parliamentary Gazetteer of Ireland. 1841, 1844, 1846.

Philips Handy Atlas of the Counties of Ireland. P.W. Joyce. 1881.

Topographical Dictionary of Ireland. 2 Vols. Lewis. London. 1837.

Registry of Deeds, Dublin, Abstracts of Wills, 1708-1745; 1746-1785. Ed. P. Beryl Eustance. Dublin.

Catalogue of the Manuscripts in the Library of Trinity College. T.K. Abbott and E.J. Gwynn. Dublin. 1900.

Catalogue of the Irish Manuscripts in the Royal Irish Academy. E. Fitzpatrick & K. Mulchrome. Dublin. 1948.

Freeman's Journal Index: The Freeman Journal. A Dublin newspaper 1763-1780; 1783-1786.

New England Historical and Genealogical Register. "Two Early Passenger Lists, 1635-1637." "List of Emigrants from England 1773-1776." "List of Emigrants to America from Liverpool 1697-1707.

Emigration from Ulster to North Carolina, etc. from Papers of the late W.C. Houston. Philadelphia. 1736-37.

The Drumgooland Vestry Book, 1789-1828. 1892.

Passenger Lists sailing from Newry, Co. Down and Warrenspoint, Co. Down. 1791-1792.

Lists of Persons Naturalized in New York. 1802-14.

Ordance Survey Documents. Contains emigrants 1833-35. The National Archives Library.

The General Index to the Accounts Papers, Reports of Commissions. etc. 1801-52.

The Devon Commission. 1847.

Fasti of the Irish Presbyterian Church. McConnell. Belfast. 1935.

History of the Irish Presbyterians. W.T. Lattimer. Belfast. 1902.

Guide to Irish Quaker Records. Olive Goodbody.

Quakers in Ireland 1654-1900. Isabel Grubb. London. 1927.

Immigration of the Irish Quakers into Pennsylvania, 1682-1750. Albert Cook Meyers. 1902.

Archivium Hibernicum. Catholic Society of Ireland. Dublin. 1912.

Catholic Directory and Almanac. 1837

Protestant Exiles from France in the reign of Louis XIV. D.C. Agnew. London. 1871-74.

Ulster Journal of Archaelogy. Vols. 1-4. 1853-56.

Irish Pedigrees.. 2 Vols. John O'Hart. Dublin. 1892.

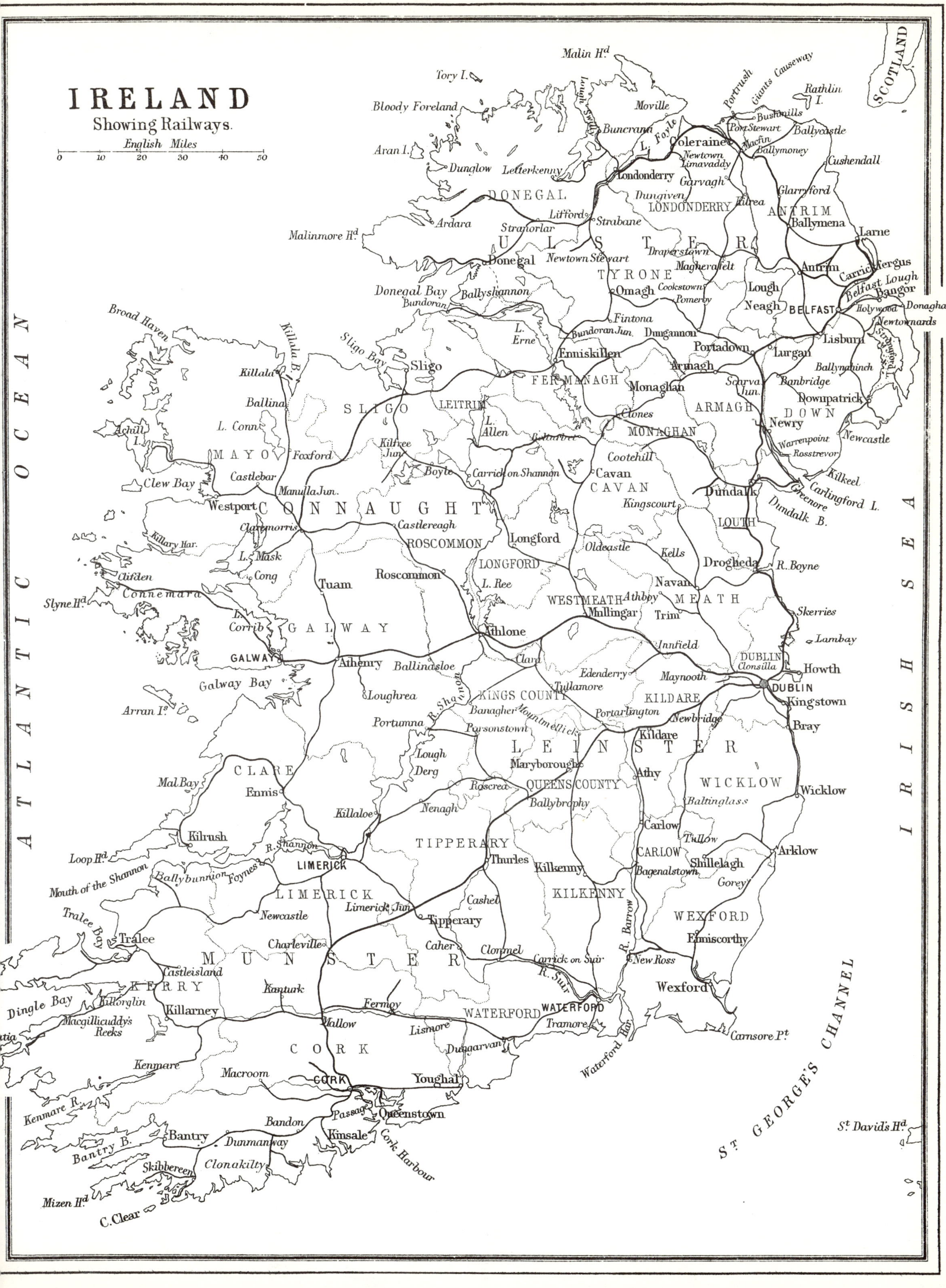

IRELAND
Showing Railways.
English Miles
0 10 20 30 40 50
ATLANTIC OCEAN
IRISH SEA
ST GEORGE'S CHANNEL
SCOTLAND
ULSTER
CONNAUGHT
LEINSTER
MUNSTER
DONEGAL
LONDONDERRY
ANTRIM
TYRONE
FERMANAGH
ARMAGH
DOWN
MONAGHAN
CAVAN
LOUTH
SLIGO
LEITRIM
MAYO
ROSCOMMON
LONGFORD
WESTMEATH
MEATH
DUBLIN
GALWAY
KINGS COUNTY
QUEENS COUNTY
KILDARE
WICKLOW
CARLOW
KILKENNY
WEXFORD
CLARE
LIMERICK
TIPPERARY
WATERFORD
KERRY
CORK
Malin Hd.
Tory I.
Bloody Foreland
Aran I.
Rathlin I.
Portrush
Giants Causeway
Bushmills
Port Stewart
Ballycastle
Macfin
Ballymoney
Cushendall
Moville
Lough Swilly
Buncrana
L. Foyle
Coleraine
Newtown Limavaddy
Garvagh
Londonderry
Dunglow
Letterkenny
Dungiven
Kilrea
Glarryford
Ballymena
Larne
Lifford
Strabane
Ardara
Stranorlar
Malinmore Hd.
Draperstown
Magherafelt
Antrim
Carrickfergus
Belfast Lough
Bangor
Donaghadee
Holywood
Newtownards
Donegal
Newtown Stewart
Omagh
Cookstown
Pomeroy
Lough Neagh
BELFAST
Donegal Bay
Bundoran
Ballyshannon
Fintona
L. Erne
Bundoran Jun.
Dungannon
Portadown
Lurgan
Lisburn
Strangford
Ballynahinch
Broad Haven
Killala B.
Sligo Bay
Sligo
Killala
Enniskillen
Armagh
Monaghan
Scarva Jun.
Banbridge
Downpatrick
Ballina
L. Conn
Achill I.
L. Allen
Kilfree Jun.
Belturbet
Clones
Newry
Warrenpoint
Rosstrevor
Newcastle
Foxford
Boyle
Carrick on Shannon
Cootehill
Cavan
Kilkeel
Carlingford L.
Greenore
Clew Bay
Castlebar
Manulla Jun.
Westport
Dundalk
Dundalk B.
Kingscourt
Claremorris
Castlereagh
Longford
Killary Har.
L. Mask
Cong
Oldcastle
Kells
Drogheda
R. Boyne
Clifden
Connemara
Tuam
Roscommon
L. Ree
Navan
Athboy
Trim
Mullingar
Slyne Hd.
L. Corrib
Athlone
Skerries
Lambay
GALWAY
Athenry
Ballinasloe
Clara
Innfield
Howth
Clonsilla
Maynooth
Edenderry
DUBLIN
Kingstown
Galway Bay
Loughrea
R. Shannon
Tullamore
Banagher
Mountmellick
Portarlington
Newbridge
Arran Is.
Portumna
Parsonstown
Kildare
Bray
Lough Derg
Maryborough
Athy
Mal Bay
Ennis
Roscrea
Ballybrophy
Baltinglass
Wicklow
Nenagh
Killaloe
Carlow
Kilrush
Tullow
Arklow
Loop Hd.
R. Shannon
Thurles
Kilkenny
Shillelagh
LIMERICK
Bagenalstown
Gorey
Mouth of the Shannon
Ballybunnion
Foynes
Cashel
Limerick Jun.
Newcastle
Tipperary
R. Barrow
Tralee Bay
Tralee
Charleville
Caher
Clonmel
Enniscorthy
Carrick on Suir
New Ross
Castleisland
R. Suir
Wexford
Dingle Bay
Killorglin
Kanturk
Killarney
Fermoy
WATERFORD
Macgillicuddy's Reeks
Mallow
Lismore
Tramore
Carnsore Pt.
Waterford Har.
Dungarvan
Kenmare
Macroom
CORK
Youghal
Kenmare R.
Passage
Queenstown
Bandon
Bantry
Dunmanway
Kinsale
Cork Harbour
St. David's Hd.
Bantry B.
Skibbereen
Clonakilty
Mizen Hd.
C. Clear

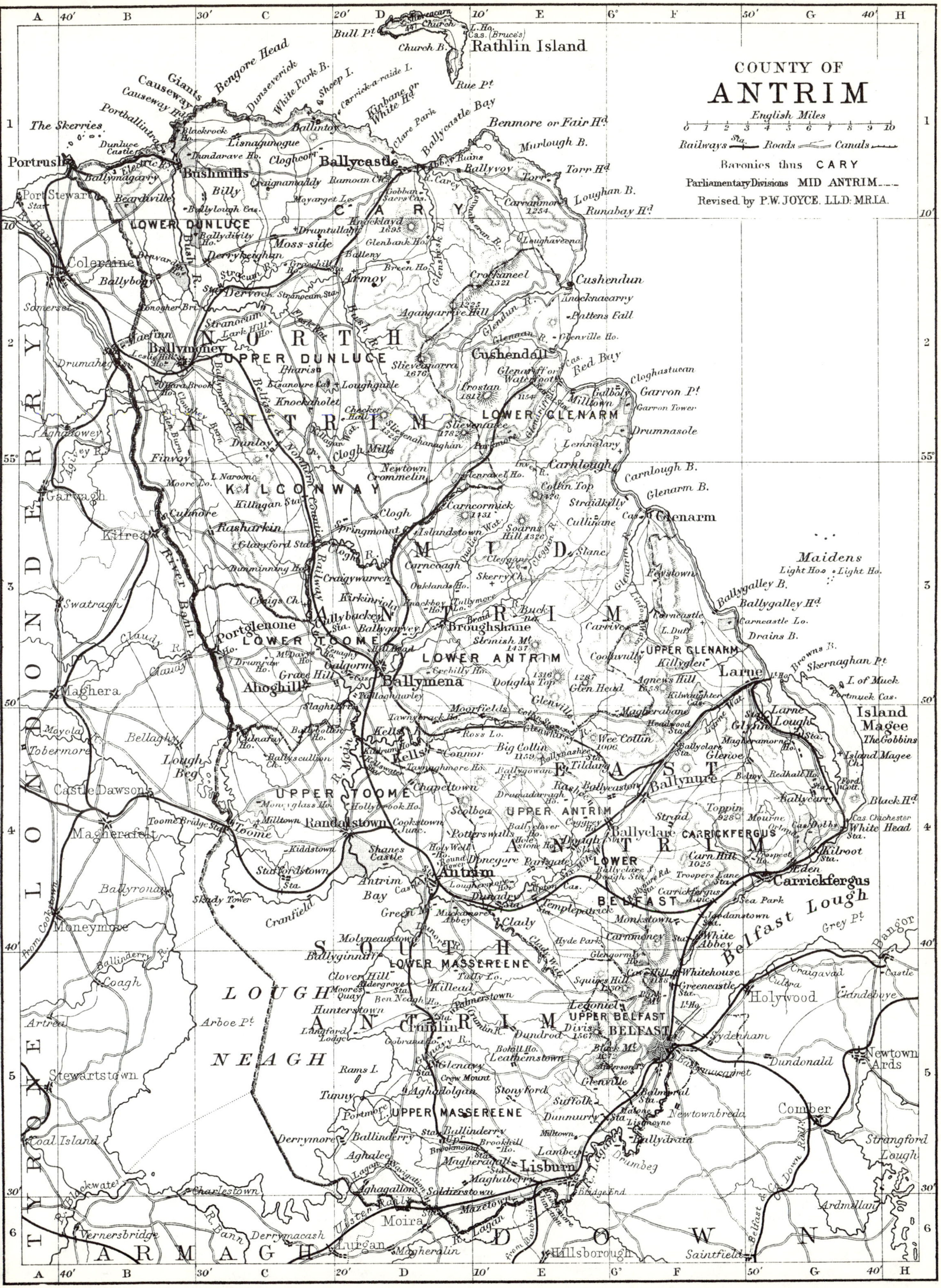
COUNTY OF
ANTRIM
English Miles
0 1 2 3 4 5 6 7 8 9 10
Railways Sta. Roads Canals
Baronies thus CARY
Parliamentary Divisions MID ANTRIM
Revised by P.W. JOYCE. LL.D. M.R.I.A.
Rathlin Island
Bull Pt.
Church B.
Rue Pt.
The Skerries
Portrush
Port Stewart
Giants Causeway
Bengore Head
Bushmills
Ballycastle
Ballycastle Bay
Benmore or Fair Hd.
Murlough B.
Torr Hd.
Loughan B.
Runabay Hd.
Cushendun
Cushendall
Red Bay
Garron Pt.
Carnlough B.
Glenarm B.
Glenarm
Maidens
Ballygalley Hd.
Larne
Larne Lough
Island Magee
The Gobbins
Black Hd.
White Head
Carrickfergus
Belfast Lough
Bangor
Holywood
Belfast
Lisburn
Coleraine
Ballymoney
Ballymena
Antrim
Randalstown
Toome
Portglenone
Ahoghill
Crumlin
Whitehouse
Newtown Ards
Comber
Strangford Lough
Moira
Lurgan
Hillsborough
Saintfield
Magherafelt
Moneymore
Maghera
Garvagh
Kilrea
Castle Dawson
Stewartstown
Coal Island
LOUGH NEAGH
NORTH ANTRIM
MID ANTRIM
EAST ANTRIM
SOUTH ANTRIM
CARY
LOWER DUNLUCE
UPPER DUNLUCE
KILCONWAY
LOWER GLENARM
UPPER GLENARM
LOWER TOOME
UPPER TOOME
LOWER ANTRIM
UPPER ANTRIM
LOWER BELFAST
UPPER BELFAST
CARRICKFERGUS
LOWER MASSEREENE
UPPER MASSEREENE
LONDONDERRY
TYRONE
ARMAGH
DOWN

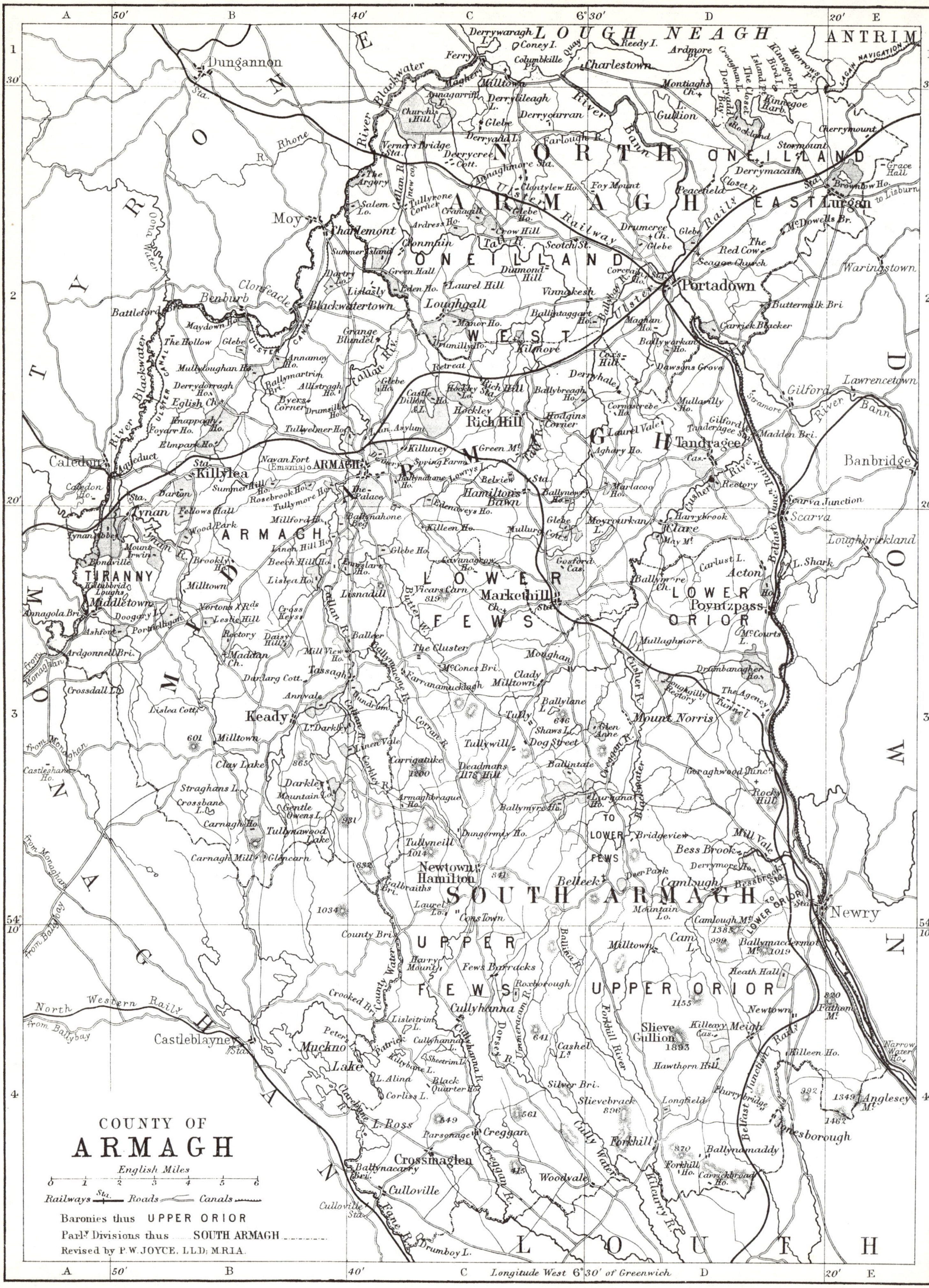
COUNTY OF
ARMAGH
English Miles
0 1 2 3 4 5 6
Railways Sta. Roads Canals
Baronies thus UPPER ORIOR
Parl.y Divisions thus SOUTH ARMAGH
Revised by P. W. JOYCE, LL.D; M.R.I.A.
Longitude West 6° 30' of Greenwich
LOUGH NEAGH
ANTRIM
TYRONE
MONAGHAN
DOWN
LOUTH
NORTH ARMAGH
MID ARMAGH
EAST ARMAGH
SOUTH ARMAGH
ONEILLAND EAST
ONEILLAND WEST
ARMAGH
TIRANNY
LOWER FEWS
UPPER FEWS
LOWER ORIOR
UPPER ORIOR
Dungannon
Moy
Charlemont
Benburb
Blackwatertown
Loughgall
Portadown
Lurgan
Tandragee
Rich Hill
ARMAGH
Killylea
Caledon
Tynan
Middletown
Keady
Markethill
Poyntzpass
Scarva
Banbridge
Newry
Bess Brook
Camlough
Newtown Hamilton
Cullyhanna
Crossmaglen
Creggan
Forkhill
Jonesborough
Castleblayney
Culloville
Muckno Lake
Slieve Gullion
Mount Norris
Gilford
Lawrencetown
Waringstown
Loughbrickland
Charlestown
Milltown
Lagan Navigation
Ulster Railway
Ulster Canal
North Western Railway
River Blackwater
River Bann
Callan R.
Cusher River
Belfast Junction Railway

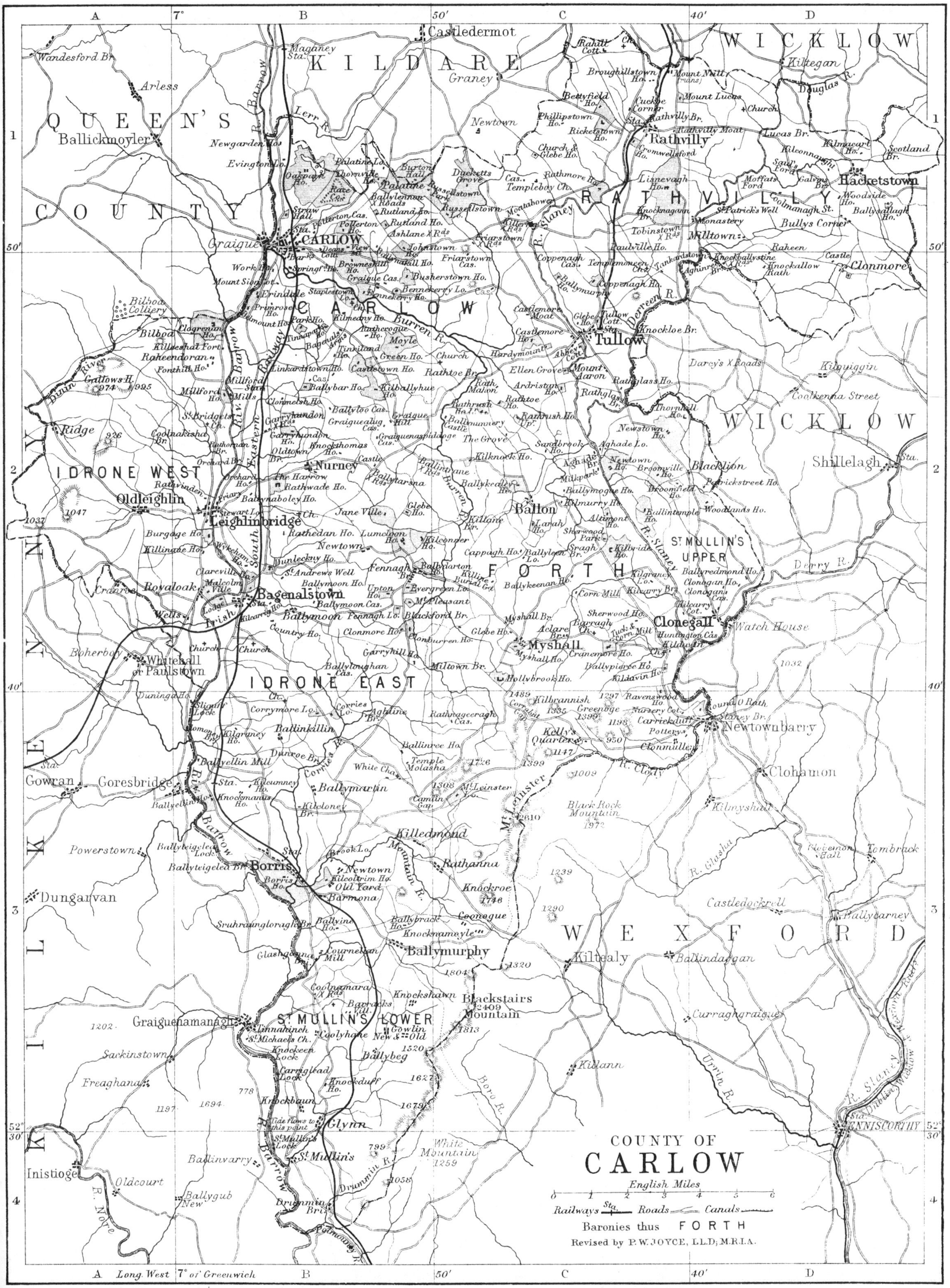
COUNTY OF
CARLOW
English Miles
0 1 2 3 4 5 6
Railways Sta. Roads Canals
Baronies thus FORTH
Revised by P. W. JOYCE, LL.D; M.R.I.A.
A Long. West 7° of Greenwich B 50' C 40' D
KILDARE
QUEEN'S COUNTY
WICKLOW
WEXFORD
KILKENNY
CARLOW
RATHVILLY
IDRONE WEST
IDRONE EAST
FORTH
ST. MULLIN'S UPPER
ST. MULLIN'S LOWER
Castledermot
Carlow
Tullow
Rathvilly
Hacketstown
Clonmore
Leighlinbridge
Bagenalstown
Oldleighlin
Nurney
Ballon
Myshall
Clonegall
Newtownbarry
Borris
Goresbridge
Gowran
Graiguenamanagh
Ballymurphy
Blackstairs Mountain
Mt. Leinster
Black Rock Mountain
White Mountain
Shillelagh
Enniscorthy
Inistioge
Kiltealy
Killedmond
Royaloak
Whitehall or Paulstown
Ballickmoyler
Dunganvan
St. Mullin's
Glynn
R. Barrow
R. Slaney
R. Nore
Burren R.

COUNTY OF
CAVAN
English Miles
0 1 2 3 4 5 6 7 8
Railways Sta. Roads Canals
Baronies thus CLANKEE
Parliamentary Divisions...EAST CAVAN
Revised by P.W. JOYCE, LL.D, M.R.I.A.
FERMANAGH
MONAGHAN
LEITRIM
LONGFORD
ROSCOMMON
MEATH
WEST MEATH
TULLYHAW
TULLYHUNCO
LOWER LOUGHTEE
UPPER LOUGHTEE
TULLYGARVEY
CLANKEE
CLANMAHON
CASTLERAHAN
WEST CAVAN
EAST CAVAN
CAVAN
Longitude West 7° of Greenwich

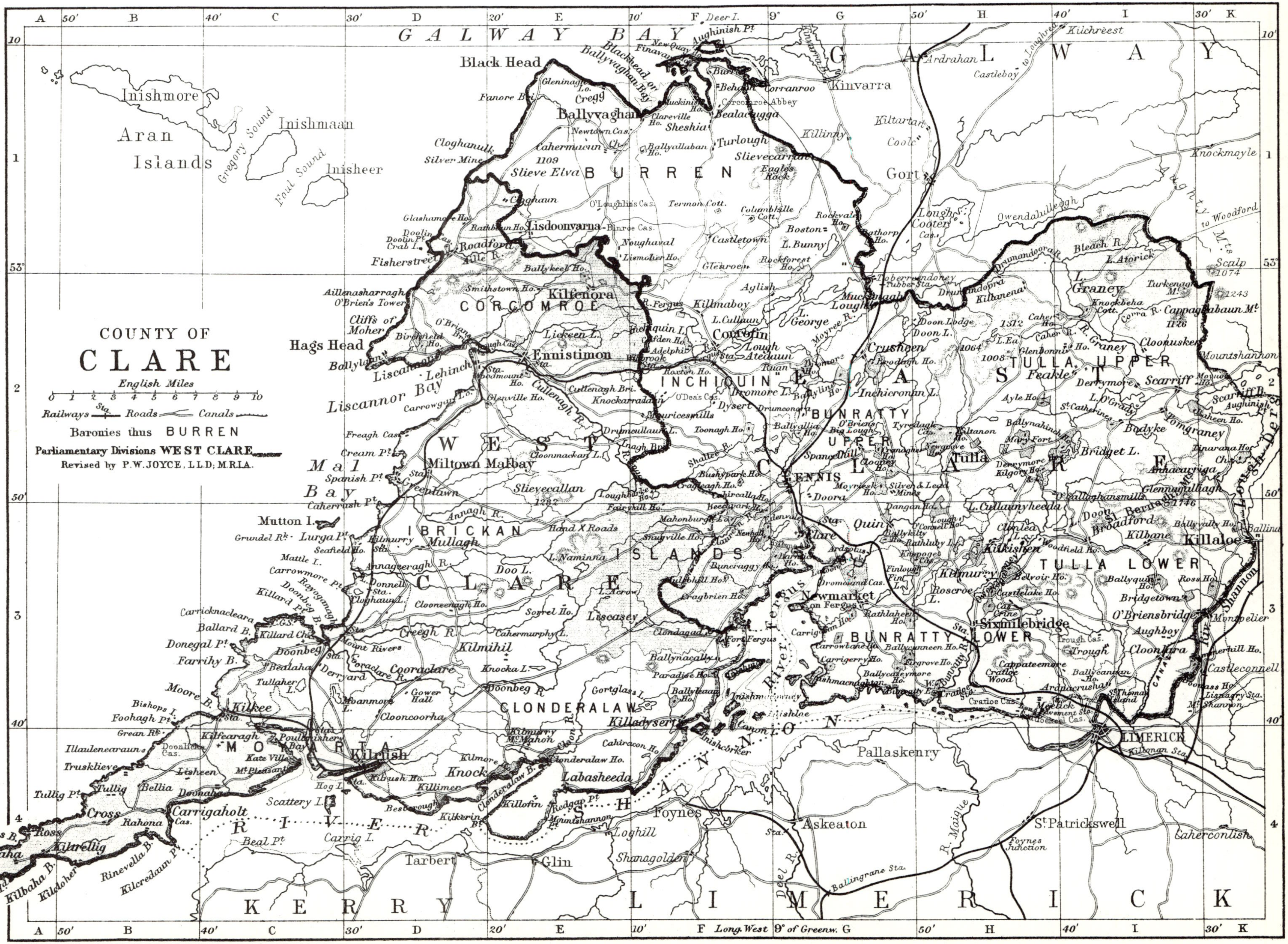
COUNTY OF
CLARE
English Miles
0 1 2 3 4 5 6 7 8 9 10
Railways Sta. Roads Canals
Baronies thus BURREN
Parliamentary Divisions WEST CLARE
Revised by P.W. JOYCE, LL.D; M.R.I.A.
GALWAY BAY
GALWAY
LIMERICK
KERRY
Aran Islands
Inishmore
Inishmaan
Inisheer
BURREN
CORCOMROE
INCHIQUIN
IBRICKAN
ISLANDS
CLONDERALAW
MOYARTA
BUNRATTY UPPER
BUNRATTY LOWER
TULLA UPPER
TULLA LOWER
ENNIS
Kilrush
Kilkee
Ennistimon
Lisdoonvarna
Killaloe
LIMERICK
Loop Head
Hags Head
Black Head
Long. West 9° of Greenw.

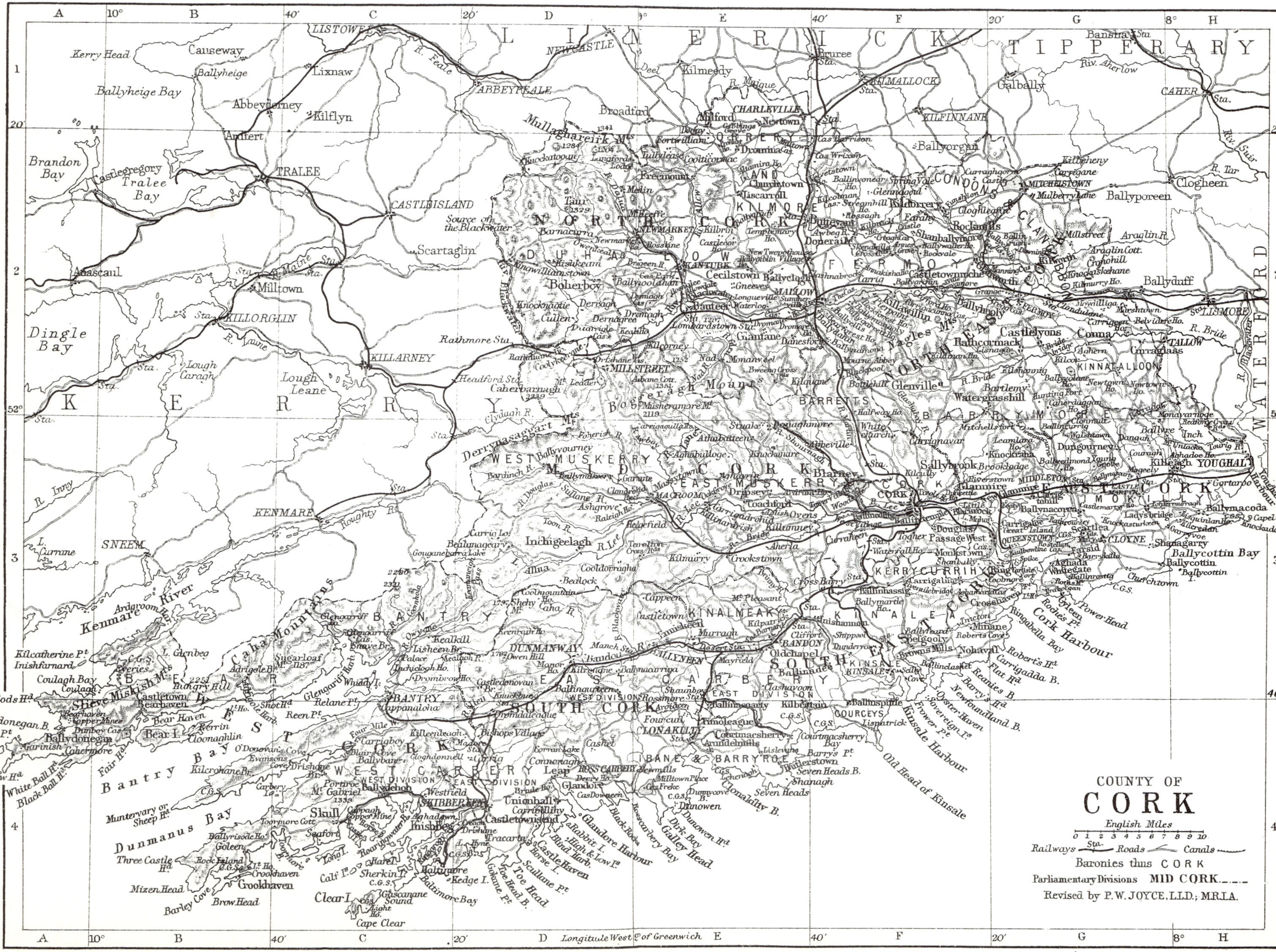
COUNTY OF
CORK
English Miles
Railways Sta. Roads Canals
Baronies thus CORK
Parliamentary Divisions MID CORK
Revised by P. W. JOYCE, LL.D.; M.R.I.A.
LIMERICK
TIPPERARY
WATERFORD
KERRY
NORTH CORK
MID CORK
SOUTH CORK
EAST CORK
WEST CORK
CORK
Longitude West of Greenwich

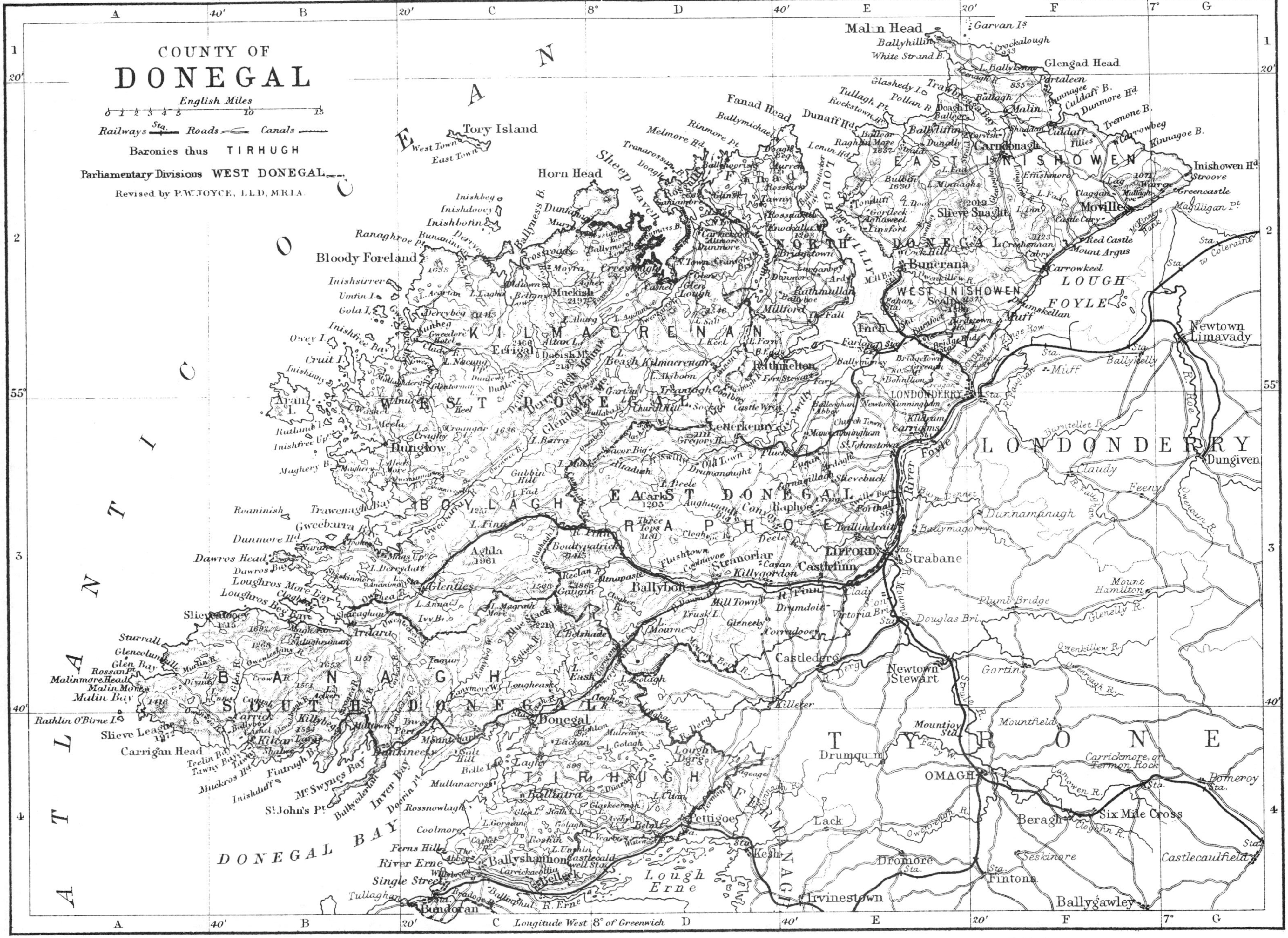
COUNTY OF
DONEGAL
English Miles
0 1 2 3 4 5 10 15
Railways Sta. Roads Canals
Baronies thus TIRHUGH
Parliamentary Divisions WEST DONEGAL
Revised by P.W. JOYCE, LL.D, M.R.I.A.
ATLANTIC OCEAN
DONEGAL BAY
Tory Island
West Town
East Town
Horn Head
Sheep Haven
Bloody Foreland
Ranaghroe Pt
Inishbofin
Inishdooey
Inishbeg
Inishsirrer
Gola I.
Owey I.
Cruit I.
Aran I.
Rutland I.
Inishfree Upr.
Maghery B.
Roaninish
Trawenagh Bay
Gweebarra B.
Dunmore Hd.
Dawros Head
Dawros Bay
Loughros More Bay
Loughros Beg Bay
Slieve Tooey
Sturrall
Glencolumbkille
Glen Bay
Rossan Pt.
Malinmore Head
Malin More
Malin Bay
Rathlin O'Birne I.
Slieve League
Carrigan Head
Teelin Bay
Tawny Bay
Muckros Hd.
Inishduff
Fintragh B.
Mc Swynes Bay
St. John's Pt.
Inver Bay
Doorin Pt.
Rossnowlagh
Coolmore
Ferns Hill
River Erne
Single Street
Tullaghan
Bundoran
Ballyshannon
Belleek
Lough Erne
Malin Head
Garvan Is.
Inishtrahull
Glengad Head
Fanad Head
Melmore Hd.
Rinmore Pt.
Dunaff Hd.
Tullagh Pt.
Inishowen Hd.
Stroove
Greencastle
Moville
Magilligan Pt.
Red Castle
Mount Argus
LOUGH FOYLE
LOUGH SWILLY
Carndonagh
Malin
Culdaff
Buncrana
Slieve Snaght
EAST INISHOWEN
WEST INISHOWEN
NORTH DONEGAL
Fanad
KILMACRENAN
WEST DONEGAL
BOYLAGH
EAST DONEGAL
RAPHOE
BANAGH
SOUTH DONEGAL
TIRHUGH
Dunfanaghy
Creeslough
Muckish
Errigal
Dunglow
Gweedore Hotel
Rathmullan
Milford
Ramelton
Letterkenny
Kilmacrenan
Glenties
Ardara
Killybegs
Kilcar
Carrick
Donegal
Ballyshannon
Ballintra
Pettigoe
Lough Derg
Stranorlar
Ballybofey
Killygordon
Castlefinn
Lifford
Raphoe
Convoy
Manorcunningham
St. Johnstown
Newtown Cunningham
Inch
Burnfoot
Muff
Aghla
Blue Stack Mts.
Derryveagh Mts.
Glendowan Mts.
Newtown Limavady
Dungiven
LONDONDERRY
Londonderry
Claudy
Feeny
Dunnamanagh
Strabane
Plumb Bridge
Mount Hamilton
Douglas Bri.
Newtown Stewart
Castlederg
Killeter
Gortin
Mountjoy Sta.
Mountfield
TYRONE
Drumquin
OMAGH
Carrickmore, or Termon Rock
Pomeroy Sta.
Six Mile Cross
Beragh
Seskinore
Castlecaulfield
Fintona
Dromore
Ballygawley
Lack
Kesh
Irvinestown
FERMANAGH
Longitude West 8° of Greenwich

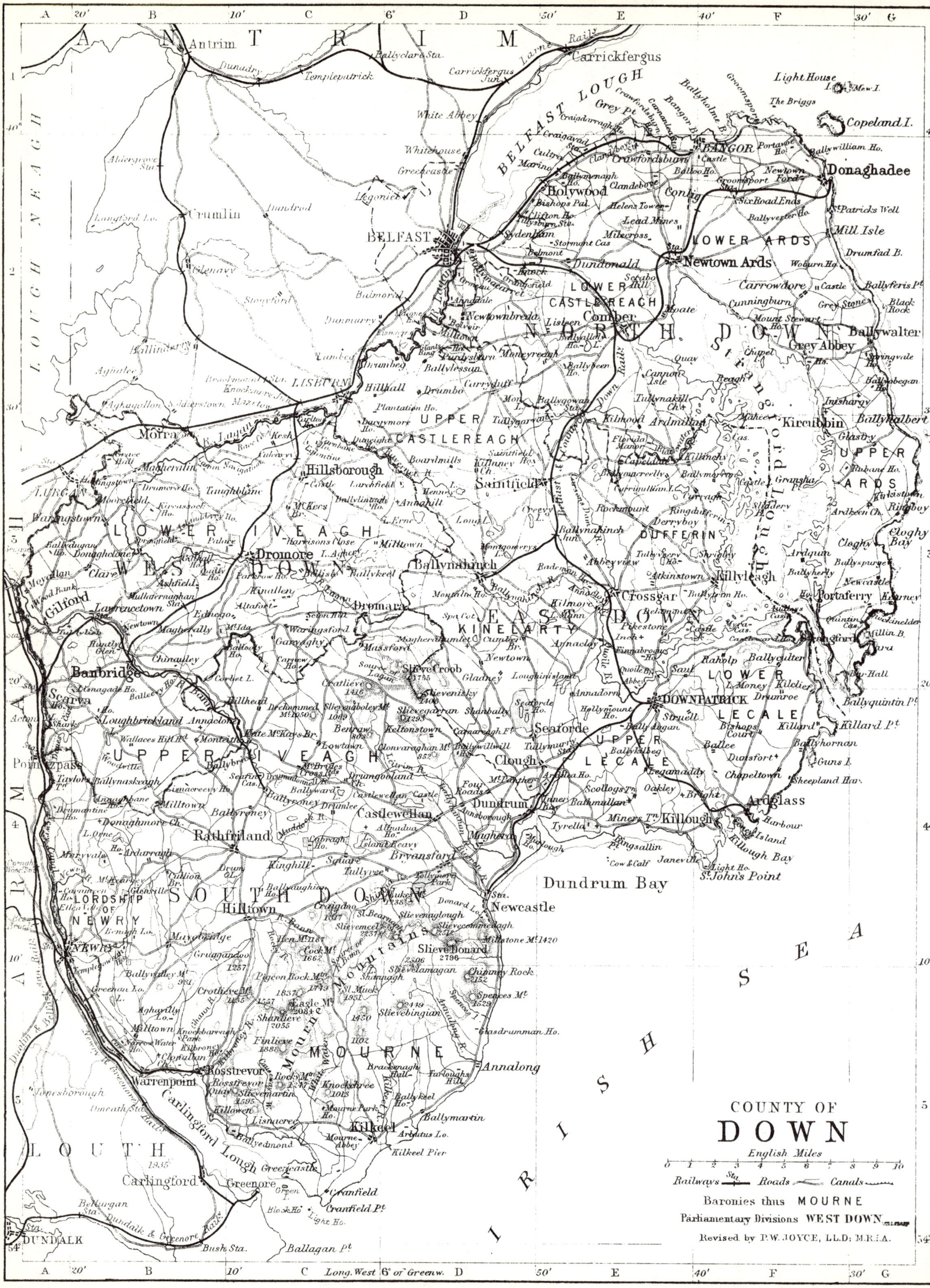

COUNTY OF
DOWN
English Miles
0 1 2 3 4 5 6 7 8 9 10
Railways Sta. Roads Canals
Baronies thus MOURNE
Parliamentary Divisions WEST DOWN
Revised by P.W. JOYCE, LL.D; M.R.I.A.
ANTRIM
LOUGH NEAGH
ARMAGH
LOUTH
BELFAST LOUGH
IRISH SEA
Dundrum Bay
Carlingford Lough
Killough Bay
Strangford Lough
NORTH DOWN
EAST DOWN
WEST DOWN
SOUTH DOWN
LOWER ARDS
UPPER ARDS
LOWER CASTLEREAGH
UPPER CASTLEREAGH
LOWER IVEAGH
UPPER IVEAGH
DUFFERIN
KINELARTY
LOWER LECALE
UPPER LECALE
LORDSHIP OF NEWRY
MOURNE
Mourne Mountains
Antrim
Carrickfergus
Templepatrick
Crumlin
BELFAST
Holywood
BANGOR
Donaghadee
Copeland I.
Newtown Ards
Comber
Dundonald
Lisburn
Moira
Lurgan
Hillsborough
Saintfield
Ballynahinch
Dromore
Killyleagh
Crossgar
Portaferry
Kircubbin
Ballywalter
Grey Abbey
Ballyhalbert
DOWNPATRICK
Ardglass
Killough
Dundrum
Clough
Seaforde
Castlewellan
Newcastle
Slieve Donard 2796
Rathfriland
Banbridge
Gilford
Scarva
Loughbrickland
Poyntzpass
Newry
Hilltown
Warrenpoint
Rosstrevor
Kilkeel
Annalong
Greenore
Carlingford
Dundalk
St. John's Point
Killard Pt.
Cranfield Pt.
Long. West 6° of Greenw.

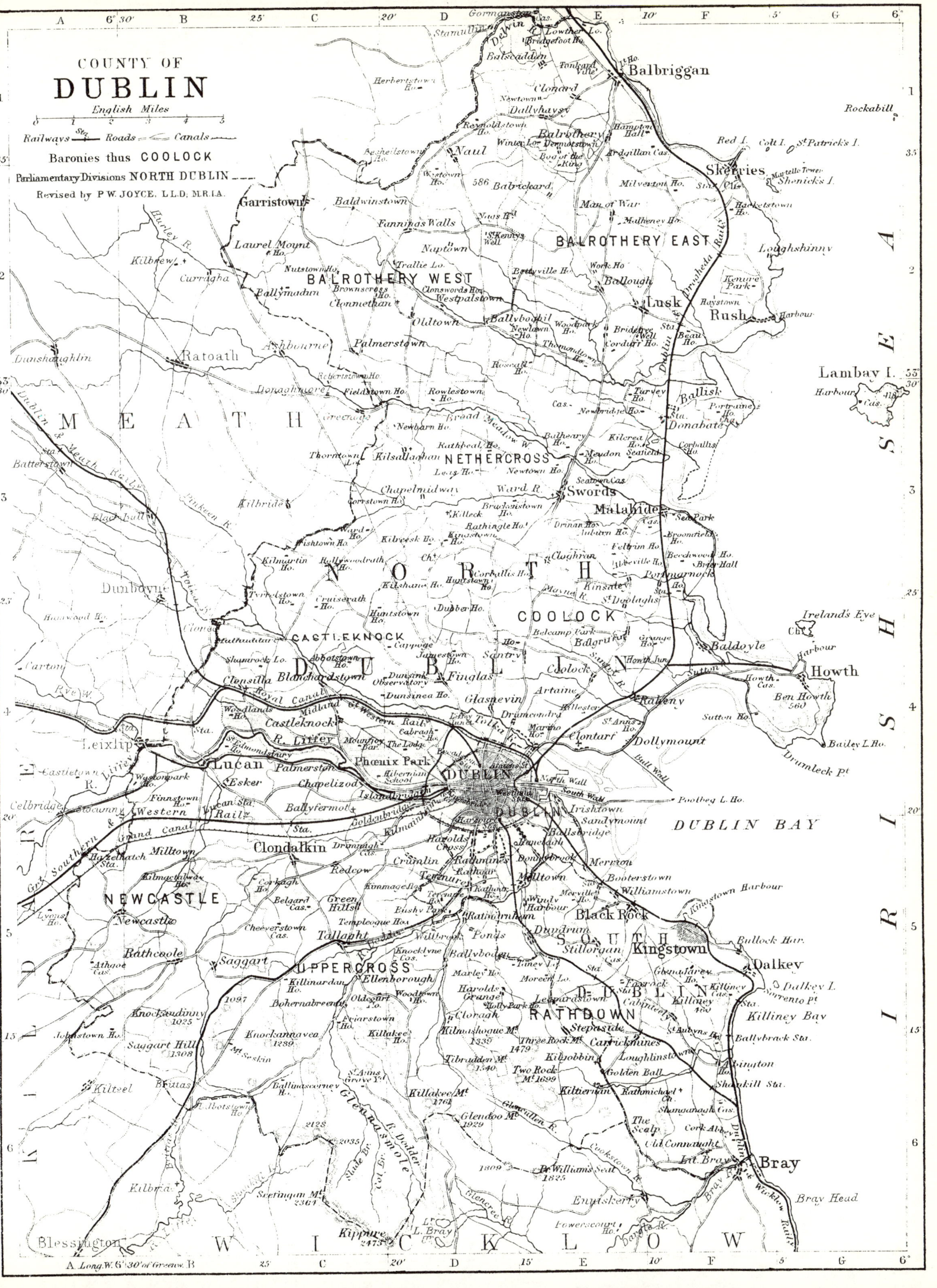
COUNTY OF
DUBLIN
English Miles
0 1 2 3 4 5
Railways Sta. Roads Canals
Baronies thus COOLOCK
Parliamentary Divisions NORTH DUBLIN
Revised by P.W. JOYCE. LL.D. M.R.I.A.
BALROTHERY WEST
BALROTHERY EAST
NETHERCROSS
COOLOCK
CASTLEKNOCK
NORTH DUBLIN
NEWCASTLE
UPPERCROSS
RATHDOWN
SOUTH DUBLIN
MEATH
WICKLOW
KILDARE
IRISH SEA
DUBLIN BAY
Balbriggan
Skerries
Rush
Lusk
Garristown
Naul
Balrothery
Ratoath
Dunshaughlin
Ashbourne
Swords
Malahide
Donabate
Portmarnock
Baldoyle
Howth
Ben Howth
Ireland's Eye
Lambay I.
Rockabill
Shenick's I.
Finglas
Glasnevin
Santry
Raheny
Clontarf
Dollymount
Drumcondra
Phœnix Park
Castleknock
Blanchardstown
Clonsilla
Dunboyne
Leixlip
Lucan
Chapelizod
Celbridge
Clondalkin
DUBLIN
Kilmainham
Rathmines
Donnybrook
Ballsbridge
Sandymount
Irishtown
Merrion
Booterstown
Black Rock
Kingstown
Dalkey
Dalkey I.
Killiney
Killiney Bay
Stillorgan
Dundrum
Rathfarnham
Tallaght
Saggart
Rathcoole
Newcastle
Stepaside
Carrickmines
Bray
Bray Head
Enniskerry
Kippure
Blessington
Glenasmole
Royal Canal
Grand Canal
R. Liffey
Dublin & Drogheda Rail.
Midland Gt Western Rail.
Gt Southern & Western Rail.
Dublin & Meath Rail.
Dublin & Wicklow Rail.
Poolbeg L. Ho.
Bailey L. Ho.
A. Long. W. 6° 30' of Greenw. B

COUNTY OF
FERMANAGH
English Miles
0 1 2 3 4 5 6 7 8
Railways Sta. Roads Canals
Baronies thus CLANAWLEY
Parliamentary Divisions NORTH FERMANAGH
Revised by P.W. JOYCE, LL.D; M.R.I.A.
Longitude West 8° of Greenwich
DONEGAL BAY
DONEGAL
TYRONE
LEITRIM
CAVAN
MONAGHAN
NORTH FERMANAGH
SOUTH FERMANAGH
LURG
MAGHERABOY
CLANAWLEY
TIRKENNEDY
MAGHERASTEPHANA
CLANKELLY
KNOCKNINNY
COOLE
LOUGH ERNE
UPPER LOUGH ERNE
Lough Melvin
Lough Macnean Upper
ENNISKILLEN
Ballyshannon
Belleek
Pettigoe
Kesh
Ederny
Lack
Irvinestown or Lowtherstown
Ballinamallard
Derrygonnelly
Garrison
Kiltyclogher
Manor Hamilton
Belcoo
Swanlinbar
Lisbellaw
Tempo
Brookeborough
Maguires Bridge
Lisnaskea
Newtown Butler
Clones
Rosslea
Fivemiletown
Clogher
Augher
Fintona
Dromore
Trillick
Omagh
Beragh
Ballintra
Boa Island
Belmore Mtn 1312
Cuilcagh 2188
Slieve Beagh
Enniskillen Railway
Ulster Railway

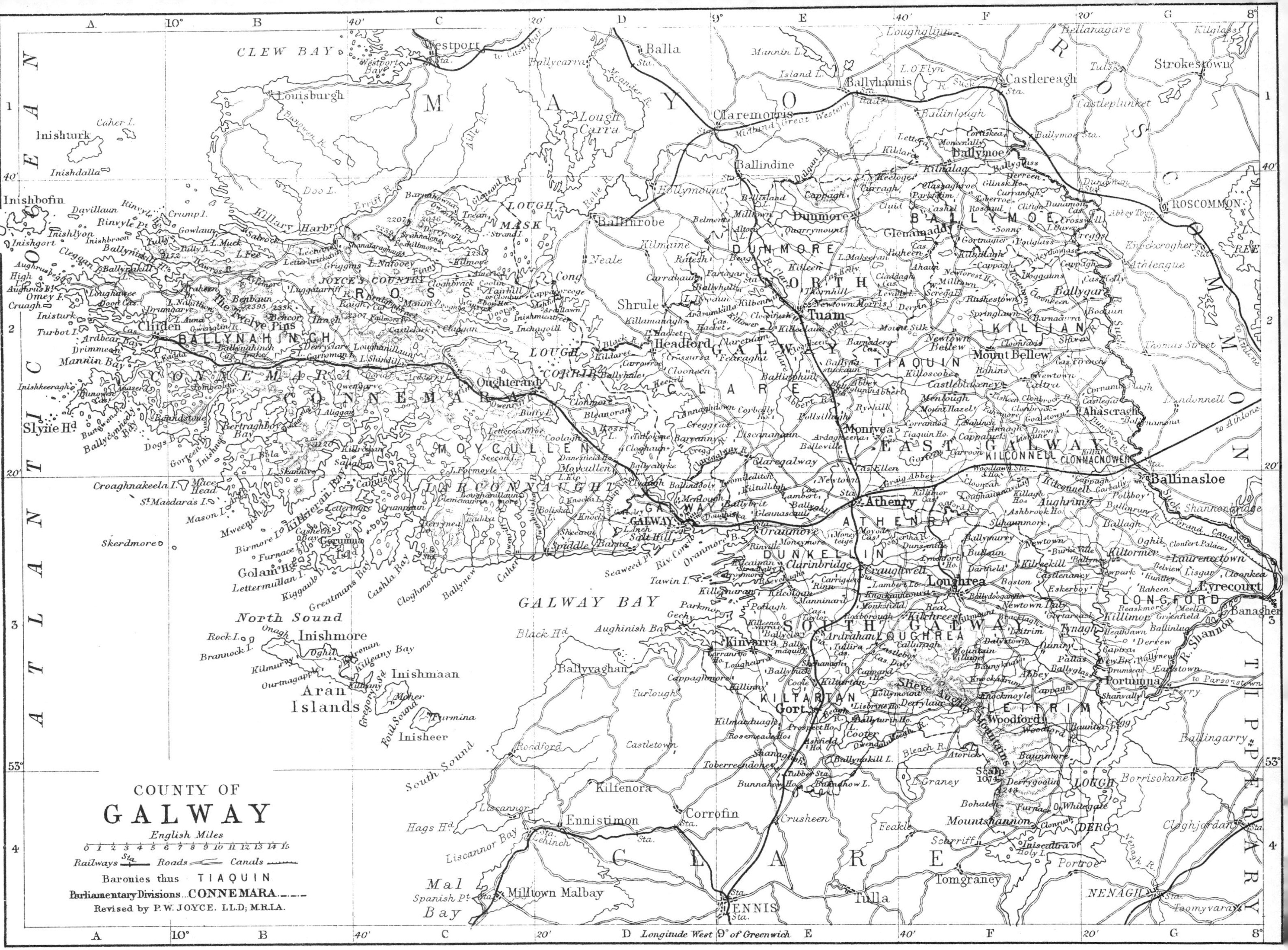

COUNTY OF
GALWAY
English Miles
Railways Sta. Roads Canals
Baronies thus TIAQUIN
Parliamentary Divisions...CONNEMARA
Revised by P. W. JOYCE. LL.D; M.R.I.A.
Longitude West 9° of Greenwich

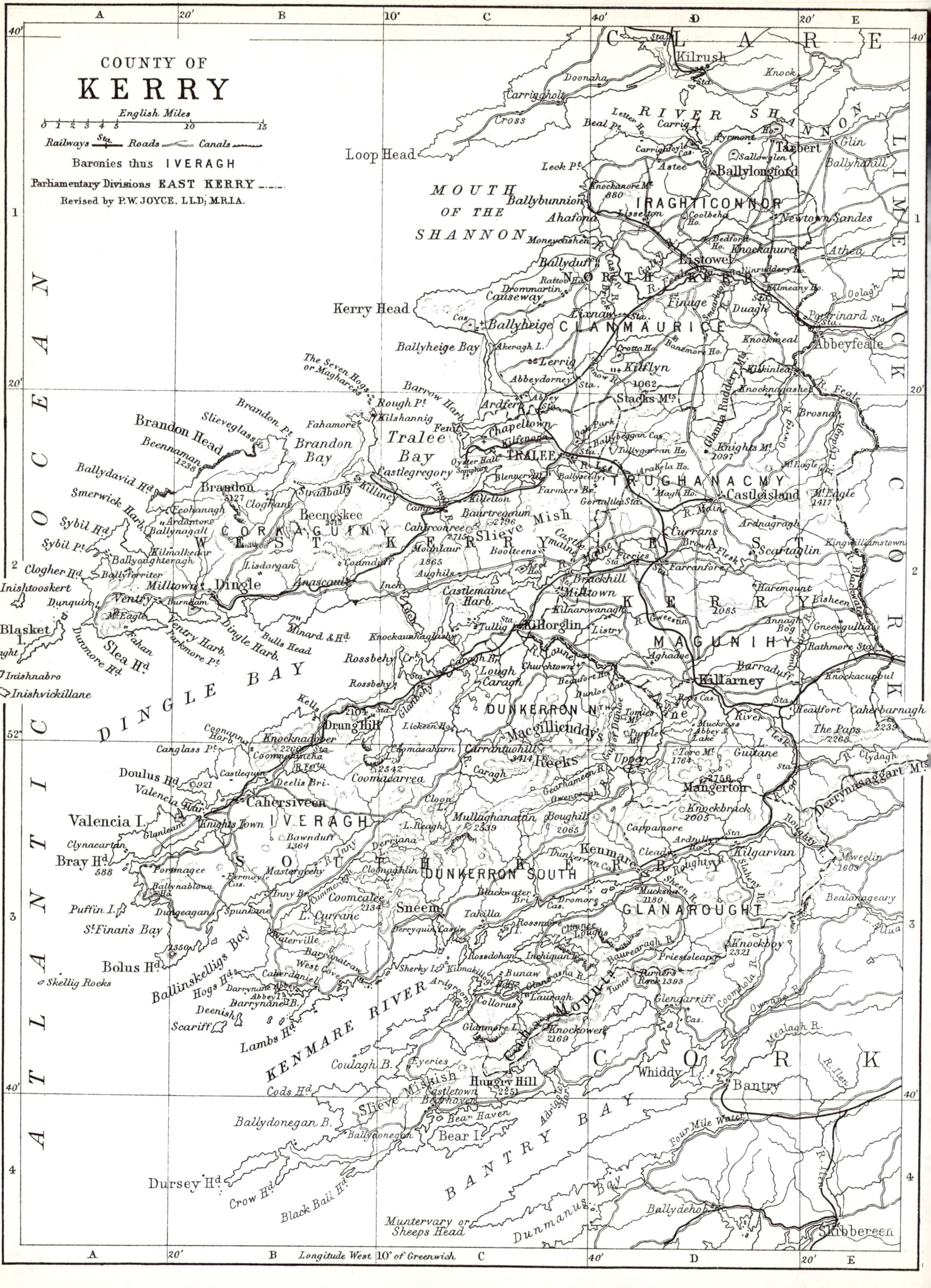
COUNTY OF
KERRY
English Miles
0 1 2 3 4 5 10 15
Railways Sta. Roads Canals
Baronies thus IVERAGH
Parliamentary Divisions EAST KERRY
Revised by P.W. JOYCE. LLD; M.R.I.A.
CLARE
LIMERICK
CORK
ATLANTIC OCEAN
RIVER SHANNON
MOUTH OF THE SHANNON
Kilrush
Loop Head
Tarbert
Ballylongford
IRAGHTICONNOR
Ballybunnion
Newtown Sandes
Listowel
NORTH KERRY
Kerry Head
Ballyheige
CLANMAURICE
Abbeyfeale
Tralee Bay
TRALEE
Brandon Head
Brandon Bay
Castlegregory
TRUGHANACMY
Castleisland
CORKAGUINY
WEST KERRY
EAST KERRY
Slieve Mish
Dingle
Ventry
Gt. Blasket I.
Tearaght
Inishtooskert
Slea Hd.
DINGLE BAY
Killorglin
MAGUNIHY
Killarney
Castlemaine Harb.
DUNKERRON NTH
Macgillicuddy's Reeks
Carrantuohill 3414
Mangerton
Valencia I.
Cahersiveen
IVERAGH
SOUTH KERRY
DUNKERRON SOUTH
Kenmare
GLANAROUGHT
Kilgarvan
Sneem
Bolus Hd.
Skellig Rocks
Ballinskelligs Bay
KENMARE RIVER
Glengarriff
Bantry
BANTRY BAY
Bear I.
Castletown Berehaven
Hungry Hill 2251
Dursey Hd.
Crow Hd.
Black Ball Hd.
Muntervary or Sheeps Head
Dunmanus Bay
Skibbereen
Longitude West 10° of Greenwich

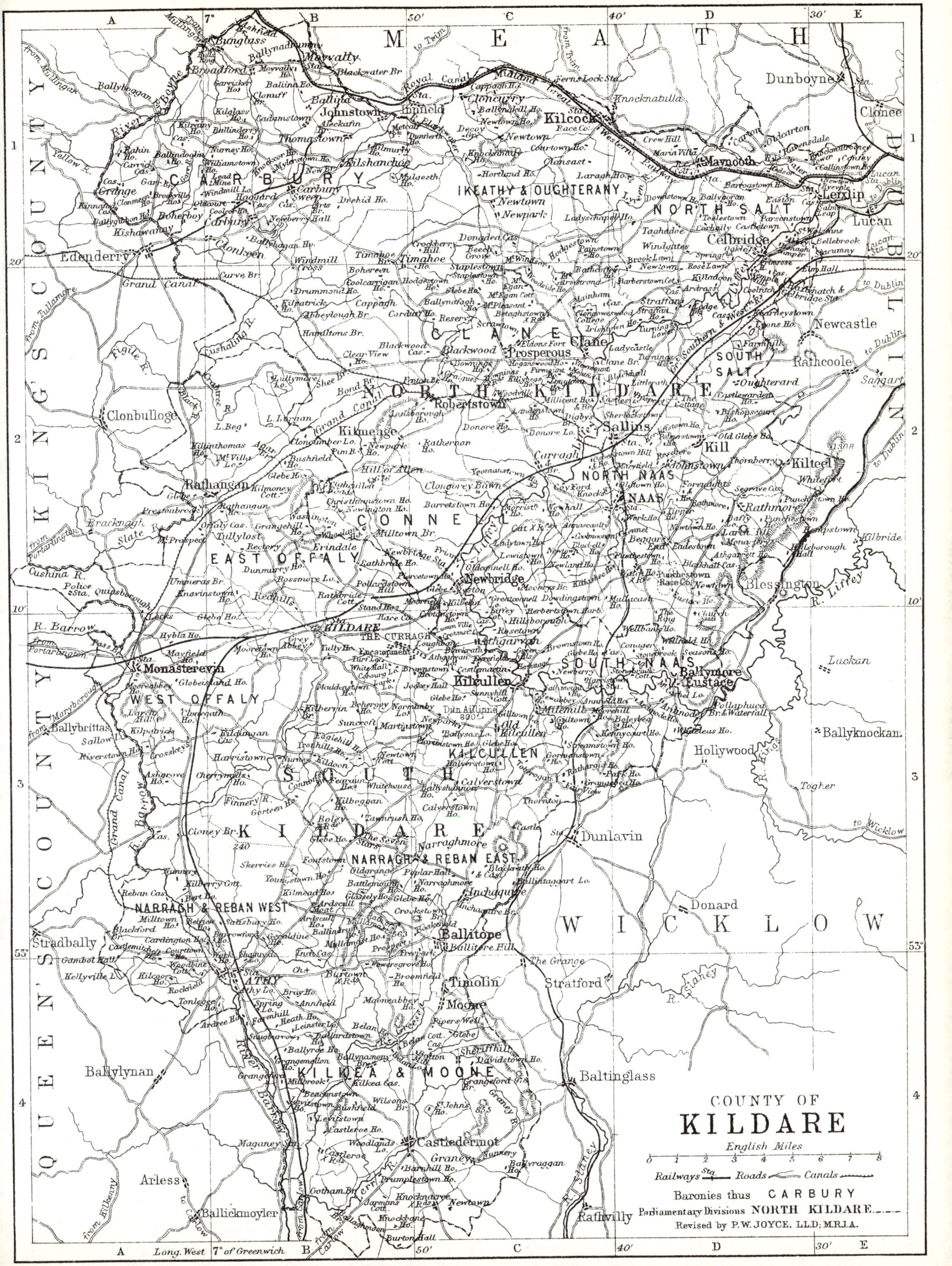
COUNTY OF
KILDARE
English Miles
0 1 2 3 4 5 6 7 8
Railways Sta. Roads Canals
Baronies thus CARBURY
Parliamentary Divisions NORTH KILDARE
Revised by P. W. JOYCE, LL.D; M.R.I.A.
Long. West 7° of Greenwich
MEATH
DUBLIN
WICKLOW
KING'S COUNTY
QUEEN'S COUNTY
CARBURY
IKEATHY & OUGHTERANY
NORTH SALT
SOUTH SALT
CLANE
NORTH KILDARE
CONNELL
NORTH NAAS
SOUTH NAAS
EAST OFFALY
WEST OFFALY
KILCULLEN
SOUTH KILDARE
NARRAGH & REBAN EAST
NARRAGH & REBAN WEST
KILKEA & MOONE
Maynooth
Kilcock
Leixlip
Celbridge
Clane
Naas
Newbridge
Kildare
Monasterevin
Rathangan
Robertstown
Kilcullen
Athy
Ballitore
Castledermot
Edenderry
Dunlavin
Baltinglass
Blessington
Grand Canal
Royal Canal
R. Liffey
R. Barrow
R. Slaney

COUNTY OF
KILKENNY
English Miles
0 1 2 3 4 5 6 7 8
Railways Sta. Roads Canals
Baronies thus GOWRAN
Parliamentary Divisions SOUTH KILKENNY
Revised by P. W. JOYCE, LL.D; M.R.I.A.
QUEENS CO.
TIPPERARY
WATERFORD
CARLOW
WEXFORD
NORTH KILKENNY
SOUTH KILKENNY
GALMOY
FASSADININ
CRANNAGH
KILKENNY
SHILLELOGHER
GOWRAN
KELLS
KNOCKTOPHER
IDA
IVERK
Kilkenny
Castlecomer
Ballyragget
Durrow
Freshford
Johnstown
Urlingford
Callan
Thomastown
Graiguenamanagh
Goresbridge
Bennettsbridge
Inistioge
Knocktopher
Mullinavat
Carrick on Suir
Piltown
Waterford
New Ross
Carlow
Leighlinbridge
Bagenalstown
Borris
Long. West 7° of Greenw.

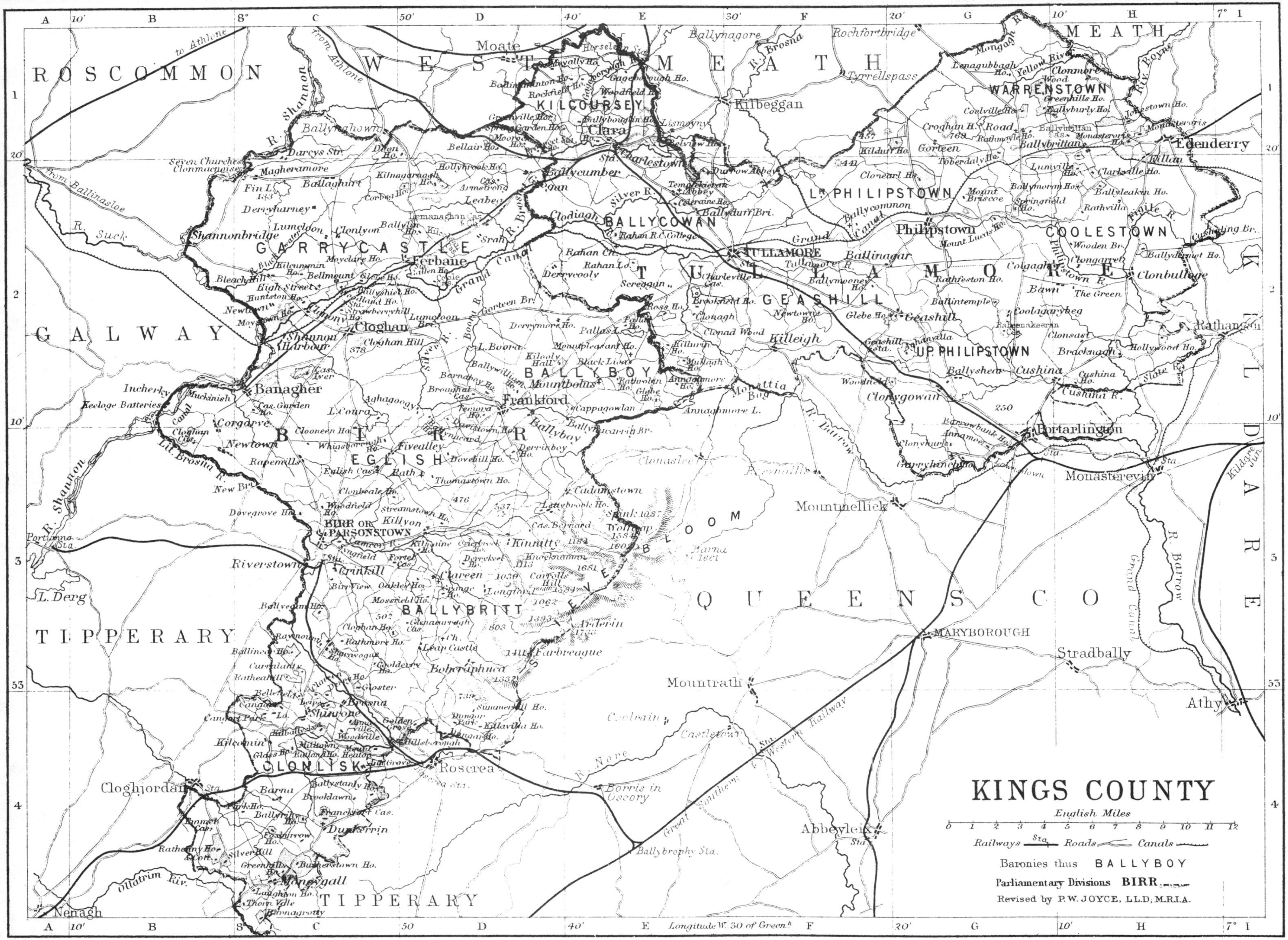

KINGS COUNTY
English Miles
0 1 2 3 4 5 6 7 8 9 10 11 12
Railways Sta. Roads Canals
Baronies thus BALLYBOY
Parliamentary Divisions BIRR
Revised by P.W. JOYCE, LL.D, M.R.I.A.
Longitude W. 30 of Green.h
ROSCOMMON
WESTMEATH
MEATH
KILDARE
GALWAY
TIPPERARY
QUEENS CO
WARRENSTOWN
KILCOURSEY
L.R PHILIPSTOWN
COOLESTOWN
BALLYCOWAN
GARRYCASTLE
TULLAMORE
GEASHILL
UP. PHILIPSTOWN
BALLYBOY
EGLISH
BALLYBRITT
CLONLYSK
BIRR
SLIEVE BLOOM
TULLAMORE
BIRR OR PARSONSTOWN
Philipstown
Edenderry
Clara
Kilbeggan
Moate
Banagher
Frankford
Ferbane
Cloghan
Shannonbridge
Portarlington
Monasterevin
Mountmellick
Maryborough
Stradbally
Mountrath
Athy
Abbeyleix
Roscrea
Cloghjordan
Nenagh
Borris in Ossory
Riverstown
Kinnitty
Shinrone
Moneygall
Killeigh
Daingean
Rathangan
Tyrrellspass
Rochfortbridge
Ballynagore
Grand Canal
R. Shannon
R. Brosna
R. Barrow
R. Suck
R. Nore
L. Derg
Great Southern & Western Railway

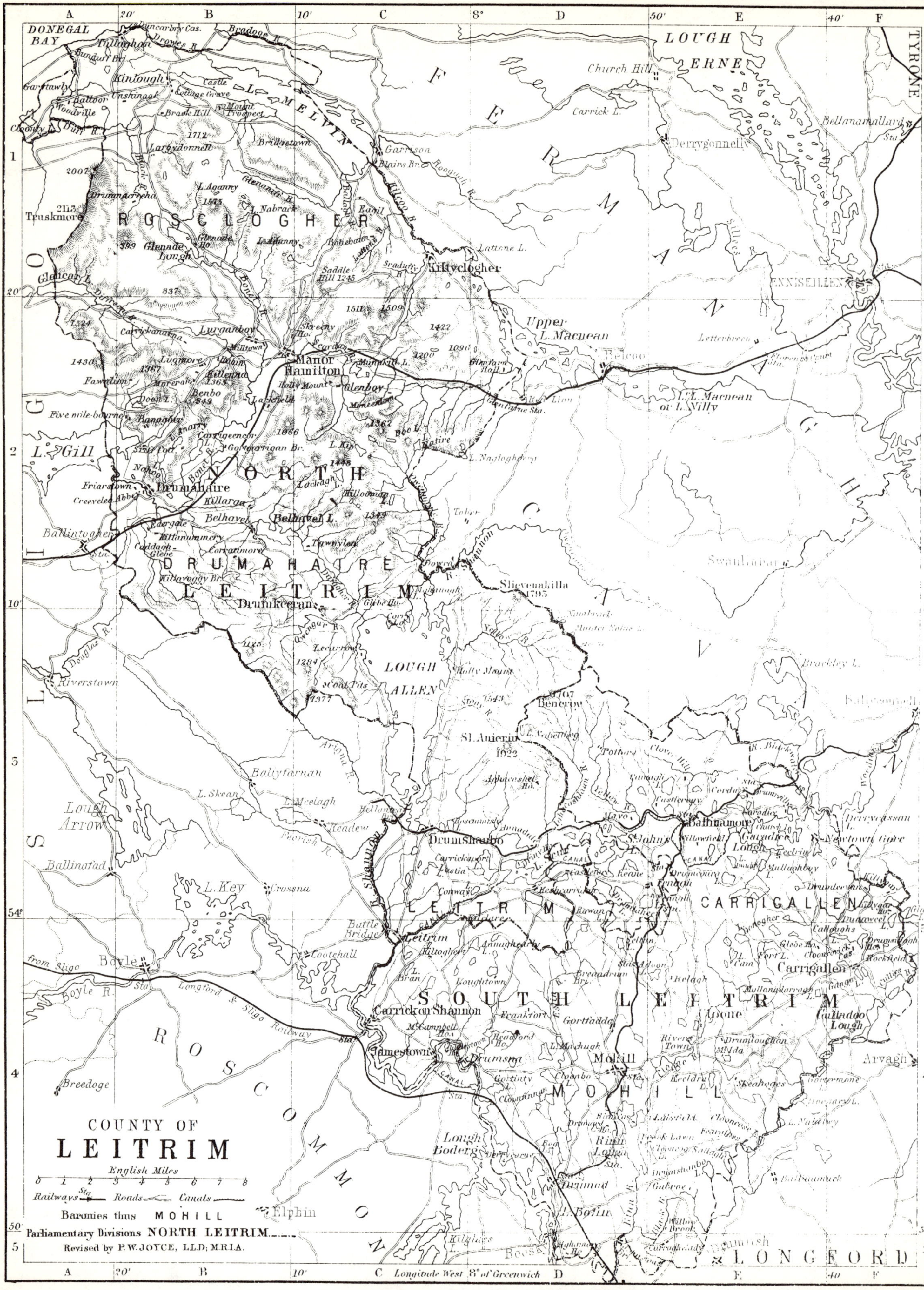
COUNTY OF
LEITRIM
English Miles
0 1 2 3 4 5 6 7 8
Railways Sta Roads Canals
Baronies thus MOHILL
Parliamentary Divisions NORTH LEITRIM
Revised by P.W. JOYCE, LL.D; M.R.I.A.
Longitude West 8° of Greenwich
DONEGAL BAY
LOUGH ERNE
TYRONE
FERMANAGH
CAVAN
LONGFORD
ROSCOMMON
SLIGO
ROSCLOGHER
NORTH
DRUMAHAIRE
LEITRIM
SOUTH LEITRIM
CARRIGALLEN
MOHILL
L. MELVIN
LOUGH ALLEN
Tullaghan
Kinlough
Manor Hamilton
Kiltyclogher
Drumshanbo
Drumkeeran
Carrick on Shannon
Mohill
Ballinamore
Carrigallen
Jamestown
Drumsna
Leitrim
Boyle
Belcoo
Enniskillen
Derrygonnelly
Lough Gill
Lough Arrow
L. Key
Lough Boderg
Glencar L.
Dromod
Drumahaire
Ballintogher
Riverstown
Ballyfarnan
Arvagh
Breedoge
Elphin
Roosky
Truskmore
Slievenakilla 1793
St. Aniern 1922
Longford & Sligo Railway

COUNTY OF
LIMERICK
English Miles
Railways Sta. Roads Canals
Baronies thus OWNEYBEG
Parliamentary Divisions WEST LIMERICK
Revised by P.W. JOYCE, LL.D; M.R.I.A.
Long. West 9° of Greenw.
LIMERICK
Newmarket on Fergus
Sixmilebridge
O'Briensbridge
Castleconnell
Newport
Foynes
Askeaton
Glin
Tarbert
Shanagolden
Pallaskenry
Adare
Patrickswell
Rathkeale
Croom
Ardagh
Newcastle
Abbeyfeale
Ballingarry
Bruff
Hospital
Kilmallock
Kilfinnane
Charleville
Dromcolliher
Cappamore
Pallas Grean
Galbally
Ballylanders
Mitchelstown
Tipperary
Buttevant
SHANID
KENRY
PUBBLEBRIEN
CLANWILLIAM
OWNEYBEG
COONAGH
CONNELLO LOWER
CONNELLO UPPER
GLENQUIN
COSHMA
COSHLEA
SMALL COUNTY
WEST LIMERICK
EAST LIMERICK
RIVER SHANNON
Ballyhoura Hills
Mullaghareirk Mts
Slievefelim Mts
Galty Mts
CLARE
TIPPERARY
CORK
KERRY

COUNTY OF
LONDONDERRY
English Miles
0 1 2 3 4 5 6 7 8 9 10
Railways Sta. Roads Canals
Baronies thus COLERAINE
Parliamentary Divisions NORTH DERRY
D O N E G A L
LOUGH FOYLE
NORTH DERRY
SOUTH DERRY
KEENAGHT
TIRKEERAN
COLERAINE
LOUGHINSHOLIN
N.E. LIBERTIES OF COLERAINE
N.W. LIBS OF L'DERRY
LONDONDERRY
COLERAINE
Portrush
Port Stewart
Bushmills
Ballymoney
Magilligan Pt.
Inishowen Hd.
Moville
Greencastle
Carndonagh
Malin
Culdaff
Muff
Newtown Limavady
Dungiven
Garvagh
Kilrea
Swatragh
Maghera
Tobermore
Draperstown
Magherafelt
Moneymore
Bellaghy
Castle Dawson
Claudy
Feeny
Sperrin Mounts
Sawel Mt. 2240
Benbradagh 1536
Binevenagh 1260
Slieve Gallion
Lough Beg
Portglenone
Toome Sta.
Cookstown
Newtown Stewart
Omagh
Stewartstown
T Y R O N E
A N T R I M
LOUGH NEAGH
River Bann
R. Roe
R. Foyle
Long. West 7° of Greenw.
55°
A B C D E F G
1 2 3 4 5

COUNTY OF
LONGFORD
English Miles
0 1 2 3 4 5 6 7
Railways Sta. Roads Canals
Baronies thus GRANARD
Parliamentary Divisions NORTH LONGFORD
Revised by P.W. JOYCE, LL.D; M.R.I.A.
Longitude West 7° 40' of Greenwich
LEITRIM
CAVAN
WESTMEATH
ROSCOMMON
NORTH LONGFORD
SOUTH LONGFORD
GRANARD
LONGFORD
ARDAGH
MOYDOW
RATHCLINE
SHRULE
LONGFORD
Granard
Edgeworthstown
Drumlish
Ballymahon
Newtown-Forbes
Lanesborough
Killashee
Ballinalee
Abbeylara
Arvagh
Mohill
Drumod
Roosky
Jamestown
Drumsna
Ardagh
Keenagh
Ballinamuck
Cloondara
Legan
Abbeyshrule
Ballynacarrigy
Rathowen
Ballymore
Moyvore
Forgney
Tashinny
Carrickboy
Bellananagh
Crossdoney
Inchcleraun
River Shannon
Inny River
Royal Canal
Camlin R.
Lough Gowna
Lough Ree
Lough Iron
Lough Owel
Derravaragh L.
Glen Lough
Gulladoo Lough
Lough Bodera
Lough Bofin
Rinn Lough
Rinn Riv.
Black Riv.
River Erne
Great Northern & Western Railway
Longford & Sligo Railway
Mullingar & Longford Railway
Cavan Junction Railway
to Mullingar
from Athlone

COUNTY OF
LOUTH
English Miles
0 1 2 3 4 5 6
Railways Sta. Roads Canals
Baronies thus FERRARD
Parliamentary Divisions SOUTH LOUTH
Revised by P.W. JOYCE, LL.D, M.R.I.A.
40' A 6° 30' B 20' C 10' D
Longitude West 6° 30' of Greenwich
54°
50'
40'
1
2
3
D O W N
A R M A G H
M O N A G H A N
M E A T H
I R I S H S E A
CARLINGFORD LOUGH
D U N D A L K
B A Y
LR. DUNDALK
UPR. DUNDALK
NORTH LOUTH
LOUTH
ARDEE
SOUTH LOUTH
FERRARD
DUNDALK
DROGHEDA
Dundalk Harb.
Slieve Gullion
Jonesborough
Forkill
Crossmaglen
Creggan
Cullaville
Warrenpoint
Rosstrevor
Omeath
Carlingford
Carlingford Mt. 1935
Greenore Point
Greencastle
Ballagan Pt.
Whites Town
Cooley Pt.
Knockbridge
Louth
Castlebellingham
Annagassan
Dunany Point
Ardee
Collon
Dunleer
Clogher Head
Termonfeckin
Baltray
Mouth of the R. Boyne
Mornington
Drogheda Bay
Slane
Navan
River Boyne
Windy Harbour
Drumcondra
Laytown Sta.
Dulcek Sta.
to Dublin

COUNTY OF
MAYO
English Miles
Railways Sta. Roads Canals
Baronies thus GALLEN
Parliamentary Divisions EAST MAYO.
Revised by P. W. JOYCE, LL.D, M.R.I.A.
Longitude West 10° from Greenwich

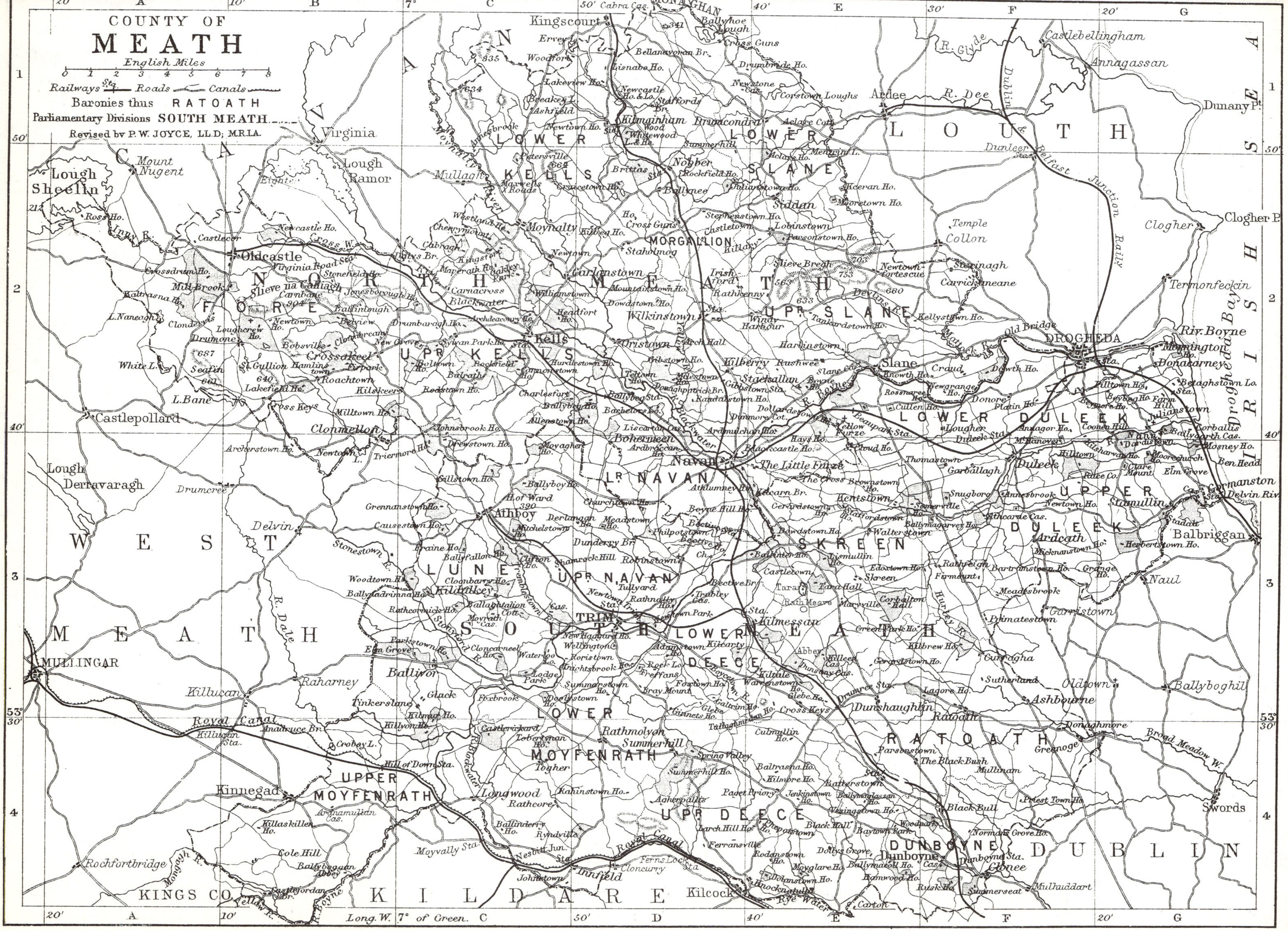
COUNTY OF
MEATH
English Miles
Railways Sta. Roads Canals
Baronies thus RATOATH
Parliamentary Divisions SOUTH MEATH
Revised by P. W. JOYCE, LL.D., M.R.I.A.
NORTH MEATH
SOUTH MEATH
WEST MEATH
LOUTH
DUBLIN
KILDARE
KINGS CO.
CAVAN
IRISH SEA
Drogheda Bay
Long. W. 7° of Green.
Kells
Navan
Trim
Drogheda
Oldcastle
Athboy
Slane
Dunboyne
Ratoath
Mullingar
Balbriggan
Swords
Kilcock
Lough Sheelin
Lough Ramor
Lough Derravaragh

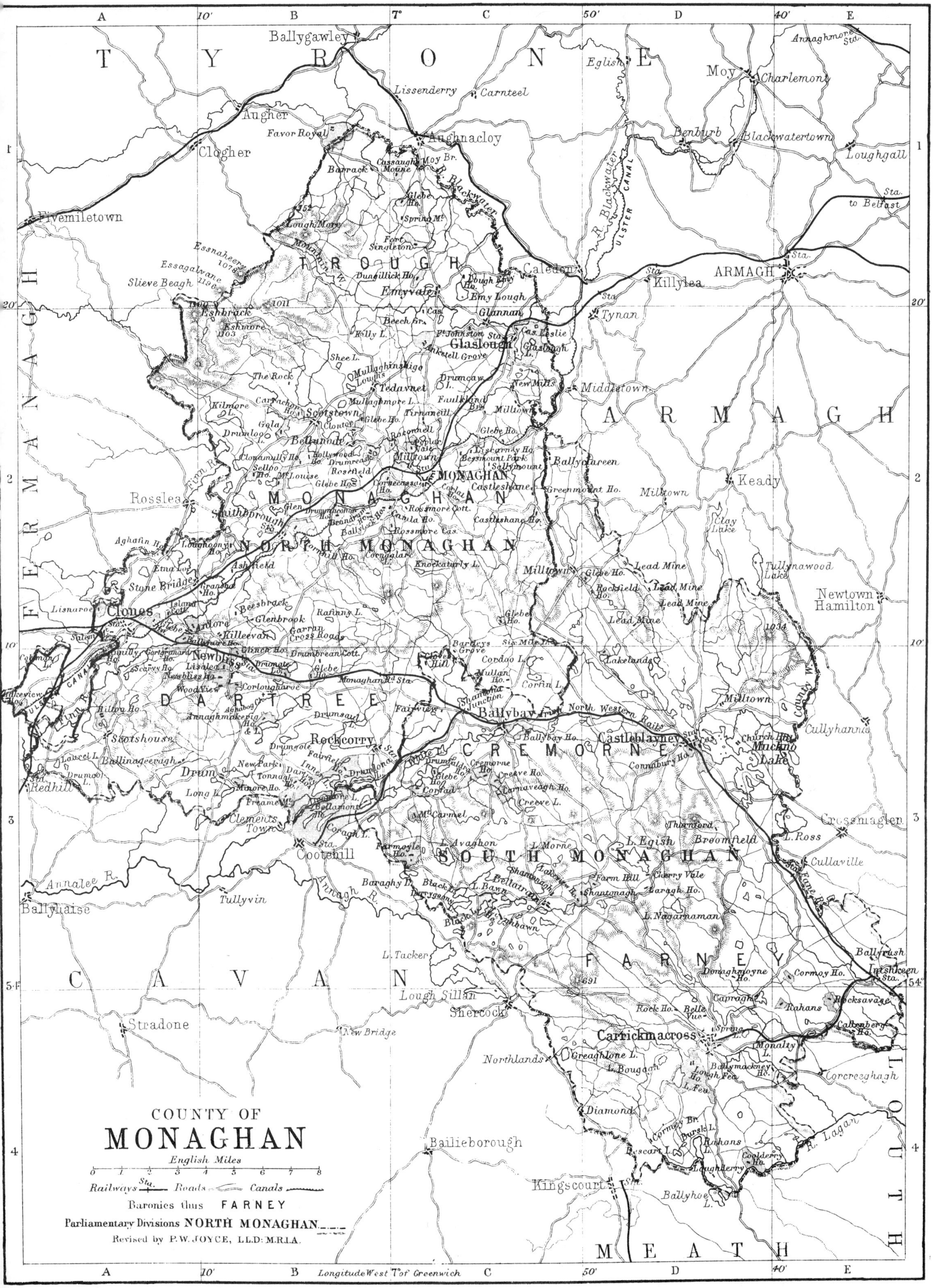
COUNTY OF
MONAGHAN
English Miles
0 1 2 3 4 5 6 7 8
Railways Sta. Roads Canals
Baronies thus FARNEY
Parliamentary Divisions NORTH MONAGHAN
Revised by P.W. JOYCE, LL.D: M.R.I.A.
Longitude West 7° of Greenwich
TYRONE
FERMANAGH
ARMAGH
CAVAN
MEATH
LOUTH
TROUGH
MONAGHAN
NORTH MONAGHAN
DARTREE
CREMORNE
SOUTH MONAGHAN
FARNEY
Ballygawley
Augher
Clogher
Fivemiletown
Aughnacloy
Caledon
Moy
Charlemont
Benburb
Blackwatertown
Loughgall
ARMAGH
Killylea
Tynan
Middletown
Keady
Newtown Hamilton
Emyvale
Glaslough
Scotstown
MONAGHAN
Clones
Newbliss
Smithborough
Rosslea
Ballybay
Castleblayney
Rockcorry
Cootehill
Shercock
Carrickmacross
Crossmaglen
Cullaville
Inishkeen
Bailieborough
Kingscourt
Stradone
Ballyhaise
Tullyvin
Redhill
Slieve Beagh
Muckno Lake
ULSTER CANAL
R. Blackwater
Annalee R.
R. Lagan

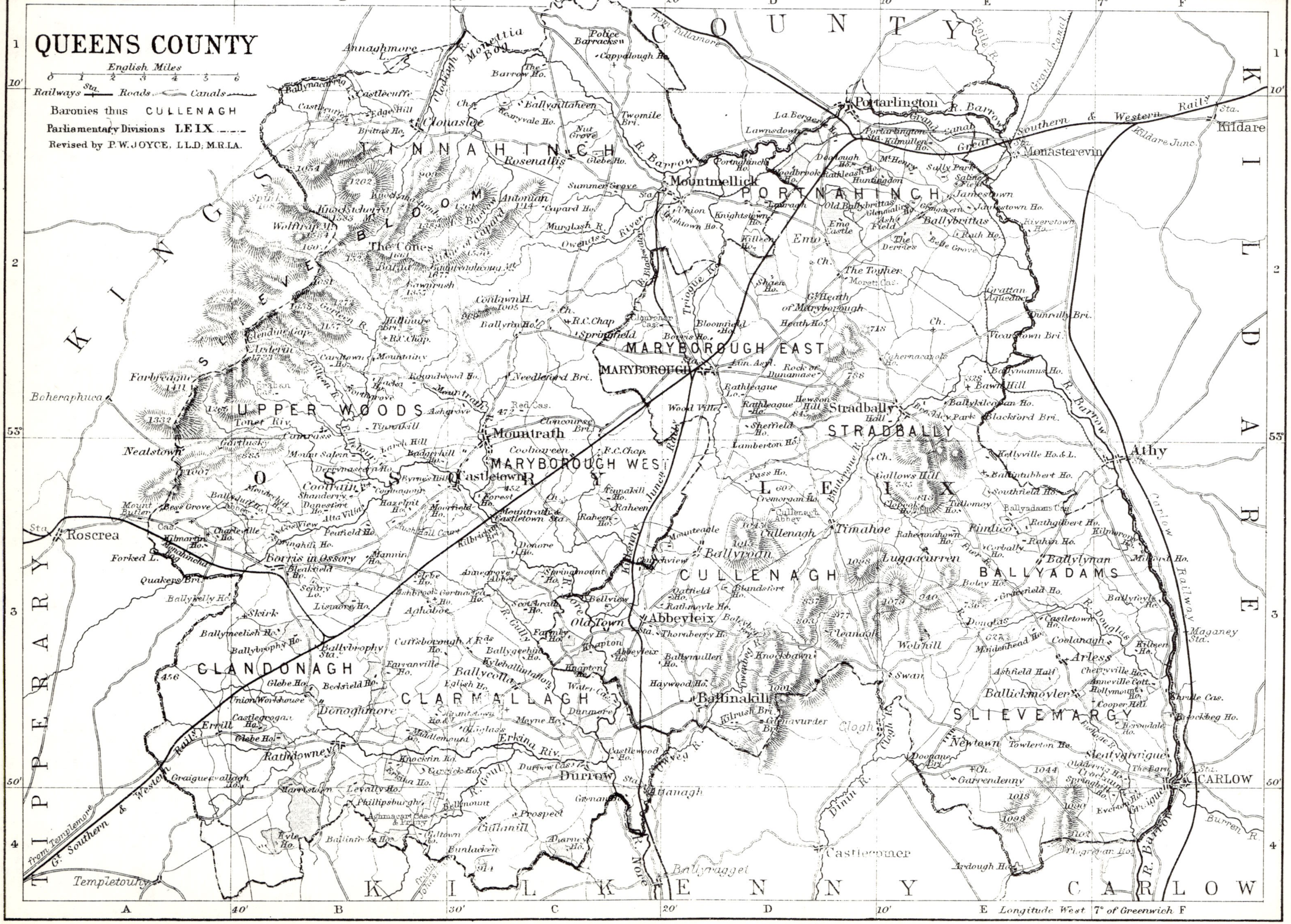
QUEENS COUNTY
English Miles
0 1 2 3 4 5 6
Railways Sta. Roads Canals
Baronies thus CULLENAGH
Parliamentary Divisions LEIX
Revised by P.W. JOYCE, LL.D, M.R.I.A.
KINGS COUNTY
TIPPERARY
KILKENNY
CARLOW
KILDARE
SLIEVE BLOOM
TINNAHINCH
PORTNAHINCH
UPPER WOODS
OSSORY
MARYBOROUGH EAST
MARYBOROUGH WEST
STRADBALLY
LEIX
CULLENAGH
BALLYADAMS
SLIEVEMARGY
CLANDONAGH
CLARMALLAGH
Maryborough
Mountmellick
Portarlington
Monasterevin
Kildare
Athy
Carlow
Stradbally
Mountrath
Castletown
Abbeyleix
Ballinakill
Durrow
Rathdowney
Borris in Ossory
Roscrea
Clonaslee
Rosenallis
Timahoe
Luggacurren
Ballylynan
Arless
Ballickmoyler
Newtown
Donaghmore
Ballybrophy
Emo
Ballybrittas
Templetouhy
Castlecomer
Great Southern & Western Railway
Grand Canal
R. Barrow
R. Nore
Longitude West 7° of Greenwich

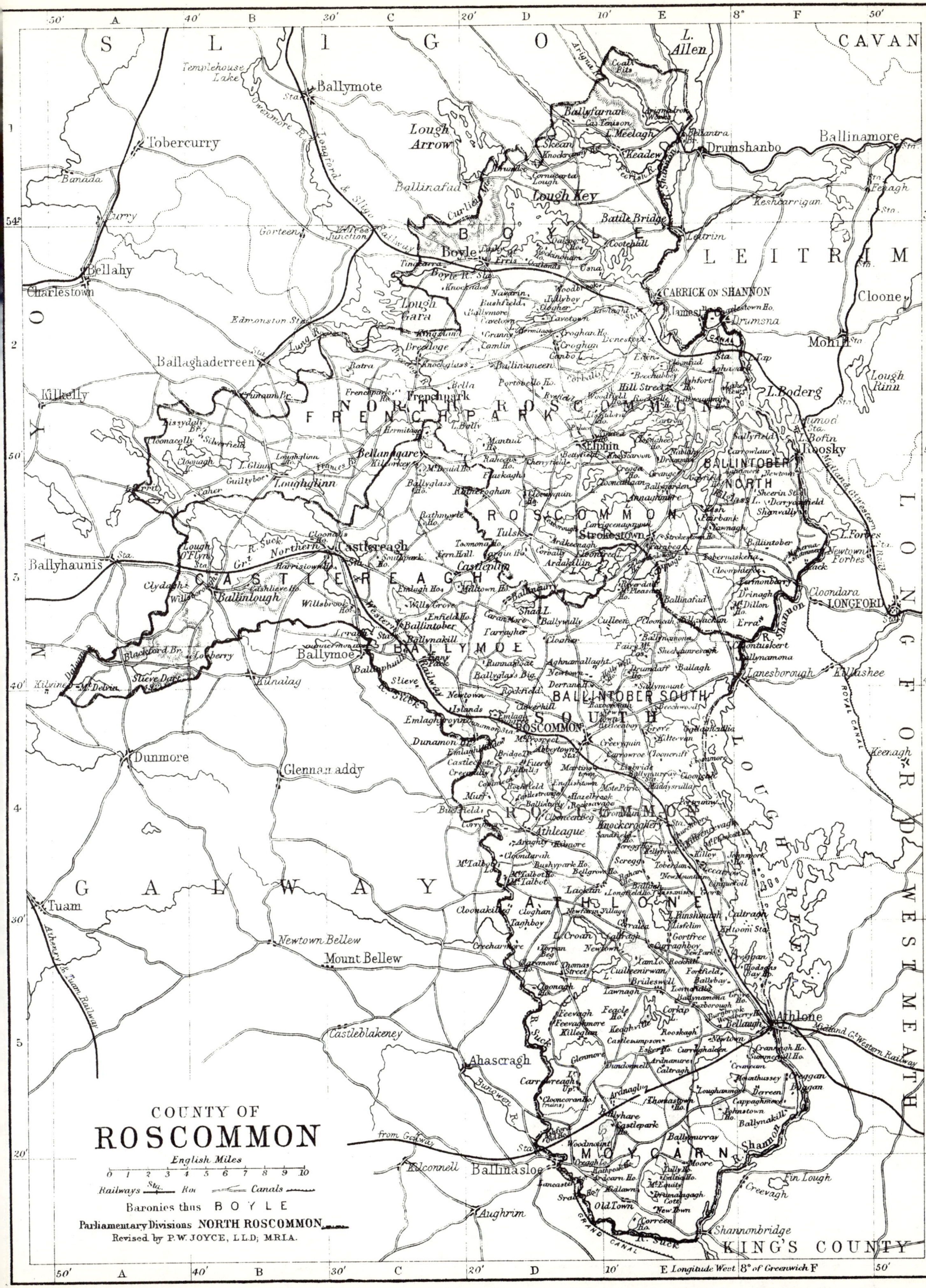

COUNTY OF
ROSCOMMON
English Miles
0 1 2 3 4 5 6 7 8 9 10
Railways Sta. Roads Canals
Baronies thus BOYLE
Parliamentary Divisions NORTH ROSCOMMON
Revised by P. W. JOYCE, LL.D; M.R.I.A.
SLIGO
MAYO
GALWAY
LEITRIM
LONGFORD
WESTMEATH
KING'S COUNTY
CAVAN
BOYLE
FRENCHPARK
CASTLEREAGH
BALLYMOE
ROSCOMMON
BALLINTOBER NORTH
BALLINTOBER SOUTH
ATHLONE
MOYCARN
NORTH ROSCOMMON
SOUTH ROSCOMMON
Lough Key
Lough Gara
L. Allen
L. Boderg
Lough Ree
Boyle
Elphin
Strokestown
Castlereagh
Roscommon
Athlone
Ballinasloe
Carrick on Shannon
Longitude West 8° of Greenwich

COUNTY OF
SLIGO
English Miles
0 1 2 3 4 5 6 7 8 9 10
Railways Roads Canals
Baronies thus LEYNY
Parliamentary Divisions NORTH SLIGO
Revised by P. W. JOYCE, LL.D; M.R.I.A.
DONEGAL BAY
DONEGAL
FERMANAGH
LEITRIM
MAYO
ROSCOMMON
SLIGO BAY
KILLALA BAY
CARBURY
TIRERAGH
LEYNY
CORRAN
TIRERRILL
COOLAVIN
NORTH SLIGO
SOUTH SLIGO
Sligo
Ballysadare
Collooney
Coolaney
Ballymote
Tobercurry
Easky
Dromore
Inishcrone
Killala
Ballina
Foxford
Swineford
Charlestown
Bellahy
Curry
Aclare
Boyle
Drumshanbo
Leitrim
Carrick on Shannon
Manor Hamilton
Drumahaire
Drumkeeran
Bundoran
Grange
Cliffony
Riverstown
Ballinafad
Ballyfarnan
Keadew
Inishmurray
Lough Gill
Lough Arrow
Lough Gara
Lough Allen
Lough Melvin
Lough Conn
Lough Cullin
Lough Key
Ox Mountains
Slieve Gamph
Curlieu Hills
Bricklieve Mts
Benbulbin
Truskmore Mt
Kings Mt
River Moy
R. Shannon
Longford & Sligo Railway
Foxford & Ballina Railway

COUNTY OF
TIPPERARY
English Miles
0 1 2 3 4 5 6 7 8 9 10 11 12
Railways Sta Roads Canals
Baronies thus ELIOGARTY
Parliamentary Divisions MID TIPPERARY
Revised by P. W. JOYCE. LL.D, M.R.I.A.
GALWAY
KINGS COUNTY
QUEENS COUNTY
CLARE
LIMERICK
KILKENNY
CORK
WATERFORD
LOWER ORMOND
NORTH TIPPERARY
UPPER ORMOND
OWNEY & ARRA
IKERRIN
ELIOGARTY
MID TIPPERARY
KILNAMANAGH UPPER
KILNAMANAGH LOWER
SLIEVEARDAGH
MIDDLETHIRD
EAST TIPPERARY
CLANWILLIAM
IFFA & OFFA EAST
SOUTH TIPPERARY
IFFA & OFFA WEST
Galty Mountains
Knockmealdown Mts
Portumna
Birr or Parsonstown
Roscrea
Nenagh
Borrisokane
Cloghjordan
Templemore
Thurles
Killaloe
Newport
Tipperary
Cashel
Cahir
Clonmel
Fethard
Carrick on Suir
Mitchelstown
Ballyporeen
Clogheen
Mountrath
Abbeyleix
Durrow
Callan
Johnstown
Longitude West 3° of Greenwich

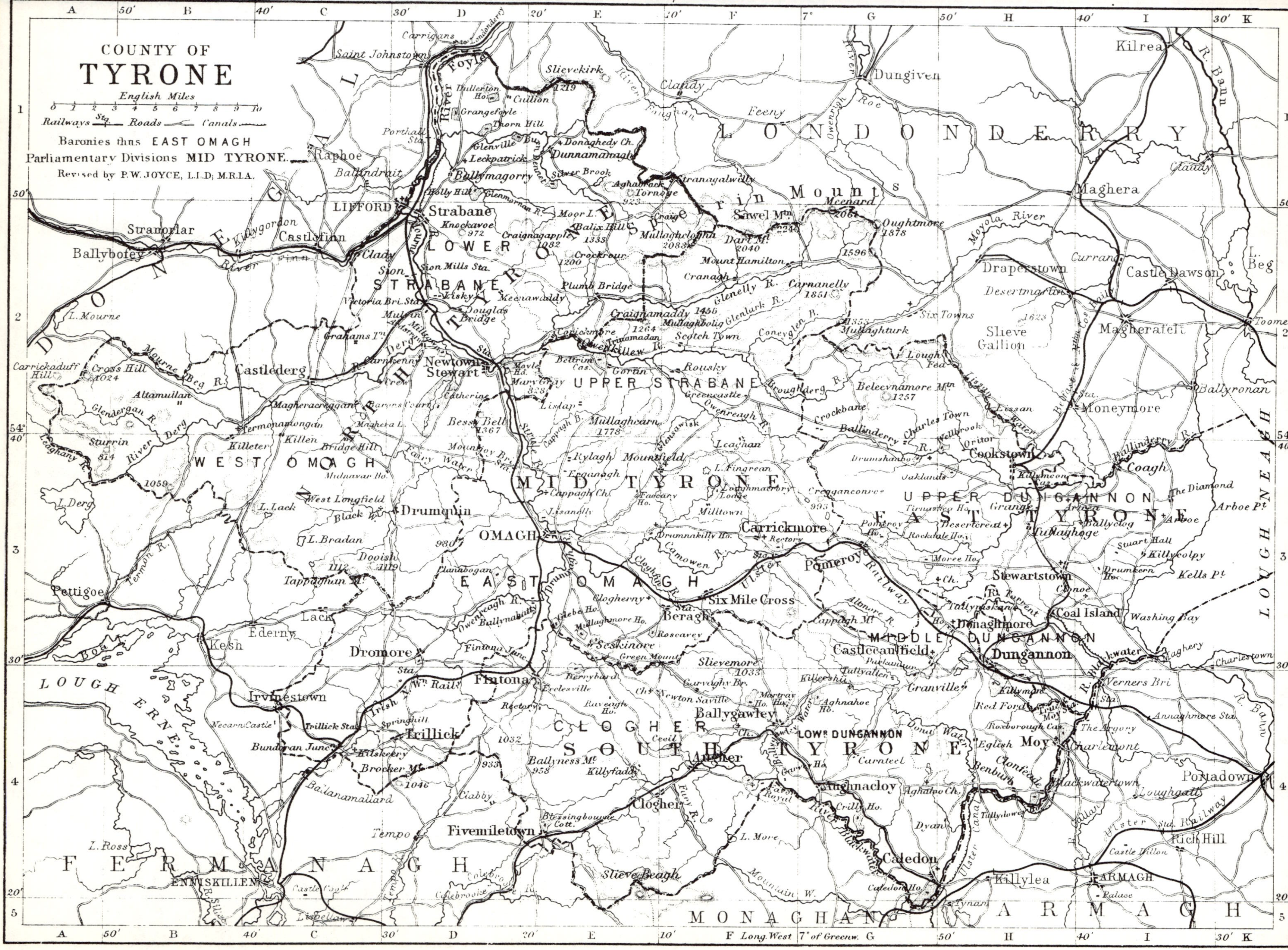
COUNTY OF
TYRONE
English Miles
Railways Sta. Roads Canals
Baronies thus EAST OMAGH
Parliamentary Divisions MID TYRONE
Revised by P.W. JOYCE, LL.D; M.R.I.A.
LONDONDERRY
DONEGAL
FERMANAGH
MONAGHAN
ARMAGH
LOUGH NEAGH
LOUGH ERNE
LOWER STRABANE
UPPER STRABANE
NORTH TYRONE
WEST OMAGH
EAST OMAGH
MID TYRONE
UPPER DUNGANNON
EAST TYRONE
MIDDLE DUNGANNON
CLOGHER
SOUTH TYRONE
LOWr DUNGANNON
Strabane
Omagh
Dungannon
Cookstown
Newtown Stewart
Castlederg
Drumquin
Dromore
Fintona
Trillick
Fivemiletown
Clogher
Augher
Ballygawley
Aughnacloy
Caledon
Moy
Coal Island
Stewartstown
Pomeroy
Carrickmore
Six Mile Cross
Beragh
Donaghmore
Castlecaulfield
Benburb
Sperrin Mounts
Long. West 7° of Greenw.

COUNTY OF
WATERFORD
English Miles
0 1 2 3 4 5 6 7 8 9 10
Railways Sta. Roads Canals
Baronies thus GAULTIERE
Parliamentary Divisions EAST WATERFORD
Revised by P.W. JOYCE, LL.D; M.R.I.A.
TIPPERARY
KILKENNY
WEXFORD
CORK
ATLANTIC OCEAN
UPPER THIRD
MIDDLE THIRD
GAULTIERE
GLENAHIRY
DECIES WITHOUT DRUM
DECIES WITHIN DRUM
COSHMORE & COSHBRIDE
EAST WATERFORD
WEST WATERFORD
Waterford
Dungarvan
Lismore
Cappoquin
Tramore
Youghal
Clonmel
Carrick on Suir
Tallow
Dungarvan Harbour
Waterford Harbour
Tramore Bay
Youghal Bay
Knockmealdown Mts
Comeragh Mts
Drum Hills
River Suir
R. Blackwater
Lon. West 30' of Greenw.

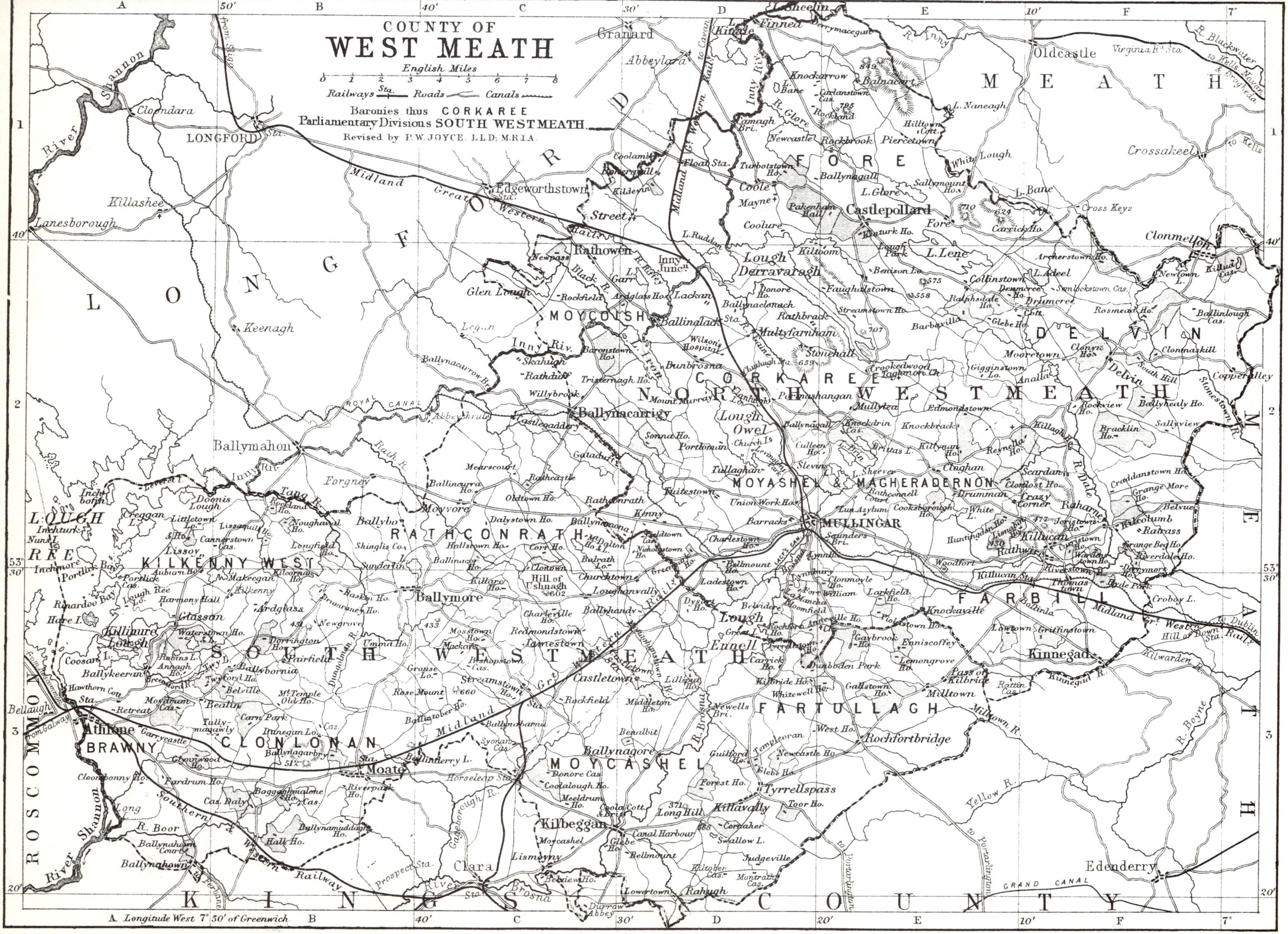
COUNTY OF
WEST MEATH
English Miles
Railways Roads Canals
Baronies thus CORKAREE
Parliamentary Divisions SOUTH WESTMEATH
Revised by P.W. JOYCE. LL.D; M.R.I.A.
LONGFORD
MEATH
ROSCOMMON
KINGS COUNTY
NORTH WESTMEATH
SOUTH WESTMEATH
CORKAREE
MOYCASHEL
FARTULLAGH
FARBILL
DELVIN
FORE
RATHCONRATH
KILKENNY WEST
CLONLONAN
BRAWNY
MOYCASHEL
MOYASHEL & MAGHERADERNON
MULLINGAR
Athlone
Moate
Kilbeggan
Castlepollard
Edenderry
A. Longitude West 7° 50' of Greenwich

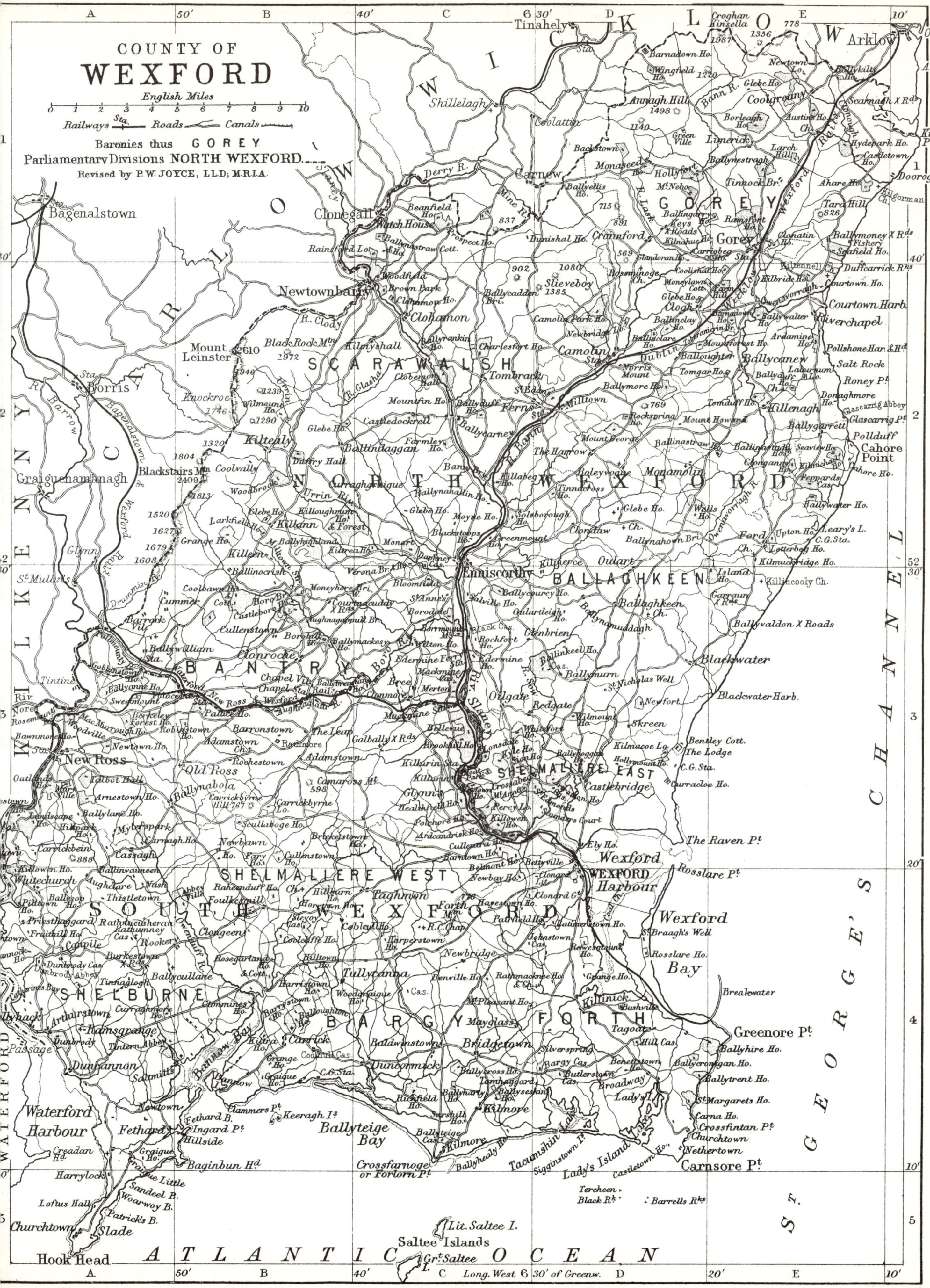
COUNTY OF
WEXFORD
English Miles
0 1 2 3 4 5 6 7 8 9 10
Railways Sta. Roads Canals
Baronies thus GOREY
Parliamentary Divisions NORTH WEXFORD
Revised by P. W. JOYCE, LLD; M.R.I.A.
WICKLOW
CARLOW
KILKENNY
WATERFORD
GOREY
SCARAWALSH
NORTH WEXFORD
BALLAGHKEEN
BANTRY
SHELMALIERE EAST
SHELMALIERE WEST
SOUTH WEXFORD
SHELBURNE
BARGY
FORTH
ST. GEORGE'S CHANNEL
ATLANTIC OCEAN
Arklow
Gorey
Enniscorthy
Wexford
WEXFORD Harbour
Wexford Bay
New Ross
Newtownbarry
Ferns
Tinahely
Shillelagh
Bagenalstown
Borris
Graiguenamanagh
Mount Leinster 2610
Blackstairs Mtn 2409
Courtown Harb.
Cahore Point
Blackwater
The Raven Pt.
Rosslare Pt.
Greenore Pt.
Carnsore Pt.
Ballyteige Bay
Bannow Bay
Waterford Harbour
Hook Head
Saltee Islands
Lit. Saltee I.
Grt. Saltee I.
Tuskar
Long. West 6 30' of Greenw.

COUNTY OF
WICKLOW
English Miles
0 1 2 3 4 5 6
Railways Sta. Roads Canals
Baronies thus ARKLOW.
Revised by P.W. JOYCE, LL.D; M.R.I.A.
DUBLIN
KILDARE
CARLOW
WEXFORD
LOWER TALBOTSTOWN
UPPER TALBOTSTOWN
RATHDOWN
NEWCASTLE
BALLINACOR NORTH
BALLINACOR SOUTH
ARKLOW
SHILLELAGH
WICKLOW
BRAY
Bray Head
Greystones
Delgany
Enniskerry
Blessington
DUNLAVIN
BALTINGLASS
Stratford
Rathvilly
HACKETSTOWN
TULLOW
TINAHELY
Shillelagh
CARNEW
CLONEGALL
NEWTOWNBARRY
GOREY
Coolgreany
ARKLOW
Arklow Head
Rathdrum
Aughrim
Redcross
Brittas Bay
Mizen Head
Wicklow Head
Glendalough
Roundwood
Kilcoole
NEWTOWN MT. KENNEDY
Rathnew
Ashford
Glen of Imaale
Lugnaquillia
Wicklow Gap
Kilteel
KILCULLEN
BALLYMORE EUSTACE
Longitude West 6°30' of Greenwich

INDEX.

NOTE.—The *letters* and *numbers* after the names correspond with those in the borders of the map, and indicate the square in which the name will be found.

Abbert & R., Galway E 2
Abbey, Tipperary D 4
Abbey, The, Donegal C 4
Abbey Cott., Carlow C 2
Abbey I., Kerry B 3
Abbeydorney, Kerry C 1
Abbeyfeale, Limerick B 3
Abbeylara, Longford E 2
Abbeyleix, Sta. & Ho., Queen's Co. C 3
Abbeylough Br., Kildare B 2
Abbeyshrule, Longford D 3
Abbeyside, Waterford D 3
Abbeytown, Mayo D 1
Abbeytown Sta., Roscommon D 4
Abbeyview, Down E 3
Abbeyview Cott., Wicklow D 3
Abbey Ville, Limerick E 2
Abbeyville, Sligo F 3
Abbey Ville, Wexford B 4
Abbeville, Cork F 3
Abbeville Ho., Dublin E 3
Abbeville He., Tipperary B 1
Abbotstown Ho., Dublin C 4
Abington, Limerick G 2
Abington Ho., Dublin F 6
Acanon L., Cavan G 3
Acartan L., Donegal C 2
Acaun Br., Carlow D 1
Achill Island & Hd. Mayo A 2
Achill Sound, Mayo B 2
Achillbeg I., Mayo A 2
Achonry & Ho., Sligo E 3
Aclare, Sligo C 3
Aclare Br., Carlow C 2
Aclare Cott., Meath E 1
Aclare Ho., Meath E 2
Acleery L., Donegal B 3
Acrow L., Clare E 3
Acton, Armagh D 3
Acurry L., Cavan G 3
Adamstown & Ch., Wexford B 3
Adamstown Ho., Meath D 3
Adanny L., Leitrim B 1
Adare Sta. & Manor Ho., Limerick E 2
Adeel L., West Meath F 2
Adelphi, Clare F 2
Adoon L., Leitrim E 4
Adrigole Br., Cork B 3
Adrigole Har., Cork B 3
Adrumkilla, Galway E 2
Affane Ho., Waterford C 3
Agangarrive Hill, Antrim D 2
Aganive L., Donegal D 2
Aganny L., Leitrim B 1
Agar Br., Kildare B 2
Agency, The, Armagh D 3
Aghaboe, Queen's Co. B 3
Aghabog Ch., Monaghan B 3
Aghabrack, Tyrone E 1
Aghabulloge, Cork E 3
Aghacashel Ho., Leitrim D 3
Aghacashlaun R., Leitrim D 3
Aghada, Cork G 3
Aghade Br. & Lodge, Carlow C 2
Aghadoe, Kerry D 2
Aghadoe Ho., Cork H 3
Aghadolgan, Antrim D 5
Aghadowey, Londonderry F 2
Aghadowey R., Londonderry E 2
Aghadown, Cork C 4
Aghafin Ho., Monaghan A 2
Aghagallon, Antrim D 5
Aghagoogy, King's Co. C 2
Aghagower, Mayo C 2
Aghagreagh, Up. & Lo., Longford D 2
Aghalee, Antrim D 5
Aghaloo Ch., Tyrone G 4
Aghamarta Cas., Cork F 3
Aghamore, Fermanagh F 3
Aghamore, Mayo E 2
Aghamore, Roscommon E 3
Aghamore Ho., Leitrim D 5
Aghanloo, Londonderry D 2
Aghanvilla, King's Co. G 2
Agharra, Longford D 3
Aghatruhan Br., Wicklow E 3
Aghavannagh Barks., Wicklow C 3
Aghavea Ch., Fermanagh F 3
Aghavilly Lo., Down B 5
Aghavrin, Cork E 3
Aghaward, Roscommon E 2
Aghaweel, Donegal E 2
Agher L., Donegal C 2
Aghern, Cork G 2
Agherpallis, Meath D 4
Aghery L., Down C 3
Aghinree Bri., Carlow D 2
Aghla, Donegal C 3
Aghlem Bri., Donegal C 4
Aghline Br., Carlow B 3
Aghmacart Cas. & Pry. Queen's Co. B 4
Aghmore, Longford E 2
Aghnagarron, Lo. & Up., Longford D 2
Aghnahoe Ho., Tyrone G 4
Aghnamallaght, Roscommon D 3
Aghnameadle Cas., Tipperary C 2
Aghnaskea Bri., Longford B 2
Aghory Ho., Armagh D 2
Aghowle Ch., Wicklow B 4
Agivey & R., Londonderry F 2
Aglish, Clare F 2
Aglish, Cork E 3
Aglish, Kilkenny C 5
Aglish, Waterford B 3
Agnews Hill, Antrim F 3
Ahabeg Ho., Limerick F 2
Ahafona, Kerry C 1
Ahaphuca, Limerick G 3
Ahare Ho., Wexford E 1
Aharney Ho., Queen's Co. C 4
Ahascragh, Galway G 2
Ahaun, Galway F 2
Ahaunboy, Cork C 4
Aherla, Cork E 3
Aherlow R., Tipperary B 4
Ahnagurra Ho., Limerick G 3
Ahoghill, Antrim C 3
Aille R., Clare D 1
Aille R., Mayo C 2
Aillenasharragh, Clare D 2
Air Hill, Wicklow D 3
Akeragh L., Kerry C 1
Akiboon L., Donegal D 2
Aleckafin Bri., Kildare B 1
Aleck More L., Donegal B 3
Aliggan L., Galway B 2
Alina L., Armagh C 4
Alistragh Ho., Armagh B 2
Alla, Londonderry B 3
Allaghaun R., Limerick B 3
Allen Dale, Wicklow A 3
Allen, Hill of, Kildare B 2
Allen Lough, Leitrim C 3
Allenstown Ho., Meath C 2
Allick L., Mayo D 1
Allow River, Cork E 2
Allua Lake, Cork D 3
Almondstown, Louth C 3
Altaconey R., Mayo C 1
Altadush, Donegal D 3
Altafort, Down C 3
Altahullion, Londonderry C 3
Altamira Ho., Cork E 2
Altamullan, Tyrone B 2
Altan L., Donegal C 2
Alta Villa, Limerick D 2
Alta Villa, Queen's Co. B 3
Altbeagh Cott., Cavan F 3
Altidore Ho., Wicklow E 2
Altimont Ho., Carlow C 2
Altmore, Donegal D 2
Altmore R., Tyrone G 3
Altmover, Londonderry C 3
Altnadua Ho., Down D 4
Altnapaste, Donegal D 3
Altore L., Galway E 2
Aluirg L., Donegal C 2
America, Galway C 2
Amiens Sta., Dublin D 4
Anagloy Cross, Louth A 3
Analla L., West Meath F 2
Ananima L., Donegal B 3
Anascaul, Kerry B 2
Anaserd, Galway A 2
Anaverna, Louth C 1
Anderson's Town, Antrim F 5
Anglesborough, Limerick H 3
Anglesey Mt., Louth C 1
Anketell Grove, Monaghan C 2
Anlore, Monaghan B 2
Ann Grove, King's Co. C 4
Anna L., Donegal C 3
Anna Carter Br., Wicklow D 2
Annacarriga, Clare I 2
Annacarty, Tipperary B 3
Annaclone, Down B 4

B

C

Carrick, Londonderry D 2
Carrick, Wexford B 4
Carrick Cas., Kildare A 1
Carrick Ho., Queen's Co. B 3
Carrick Ho., West Meath D 3
Carrick Ho., West Meath E 1
Carrick L., Fermanagh C 2
Carrickacottia, Donegal C 4
Carrickanarna, Leitrim B 2
Carrickaneane, Meath F 2
Carrickanna, Waterford E 3
Carrickaport L., Leitrim C 3
Carrick-a-raide I., Antrim D 1
Carrickart, Donegal D 2
Carrickbeg, Waterford E 1
Carrickbein, Wexford A 3
Carrick Blacker, Armagh D 2
Carrickborrahane Ho., Waterford E 3
Carrickboy, Longford C 3
Carrickbroad Ho., Armagh D 4
Carrickbyrne Hill, Wexford B 3
Carrickbyrne Lo., Wexford B 3
Carrickdale Pt., Sligo C 1
Carrickduff, Carlow C 3
Carrickedmond Ho., Louth B 1
Carrickfergus Bar. & Tn., Antrim G 4
Carrickfergus Junction, Antrim F 4
Carrickhugh Sta., Londonderry C 2
Carrickmacross, Monaghan D 4
Carrickmines, Dublin E 6
Carrickmore, Tyrone F 3
Carricknacleara, Clare C 3
Carrick-on-Shannon, Leitrim C 4
Carrick-on-Suir, Tipperary E 4
Carrickshock, Kilkenny C 4
Carrick Water, Galway C 2
Cary Barony, Antrim D 1
Carrig, Cork D 4
Carrig, Cork F 2
Carrig, Tipperary C 1
Carrig Hill, Cavan D 2
Carrig I., Kerry D 1
Carrig Lo., Cork D 3
Carrigacunna Cas., Cork F 2
Carrigadda Bay, Cork G 3
Carrigadoon Hill, Tipperary E 4
Carrigafoyle Cas., Kerry D 1
Carrigagulla Ho., Cork E 3
Carrigaholt, Clare B 4
Carrigaline, Cork F 3
Carrigallen, Leitrim F 4
Carrigaloe, Cork G 3
Carrigan Hd., Donegal A 4
Carrigane, Cork G 2
Carrigans & Sta., Donegal E 3
Carrigbeg Ho., Wexford D 1
Carrigboy, Cork C 4
Carrigeen, Galway E 3
Carrigeen Ho., Cork G 2
Carrigeenagappul, Roscommon E 3
Carrigeencor L., Leitrim B 2
Carrigeenina, Tipperary B 4
Carrigeennaveagh, Waterford G 2
Carrigerry Ho., Clare G 3
Carrighahorig, Tipperary B 1
Carrighallen Barony, Leitrim E 3
Carrigillihy, Cork D 4
Carriglead Lock, Carlow B 3
Carrignavar, Cork F 3
Carrigogunnel Cas., Limerick E 2
Carrigoran Ho., Clare G 3
Carrigtohill, Cork G 3
Carrigtuke, Armagh C 3
Carrigullian L., Down E 3
Carrive, Antrim E 3
Carrolls Hill, King's Co. D 3
Carron Mtn., Limerick F 4
Carroon, Galway F 2
Carrow, Longford B 3
Carrowbeg, Donegal F 2
Carrowdore & Cas., Down F 2
Carrowgar Lo., Clare D 2
Carrowilkin, Sligo D 3
Carrowkee Hill, Sligo F 3
Carrowkeel, Donegal F 2
Carrowkeribly L., Mayo D 1
Carrowlaur, Roscommon F 2
Carrowmenagh, Londonderry E 3
Carrowmore, Galway E 3
Carrowmore, Mayo D 3
Carrowmore Ho., Mayo D 1
Carrowmore L., Mayo B 1
Carrowmore L., Mayo D 2
Carrowmore Pt., Clare C 3
Carrowmorris, Sligo D 2
Carrownabanny L., Sligo D 3
Carrownisky R., Mayo B 2
Carrowreagh, Sligo D 2
Carrowreagh, Upper & Lower, Roscommon D 5
Carrowroe, Galway D 2
Carrowroe, Roscommon E 4
Carrowwilkin, Sligo D 3
Carrs Bri., Fermanagh E 3
Carryduff, Down D 2
Carsons Dam R., Down E 3
Castlereagh Barony, Roscommon D 3
Carstown, Louth C 3
Cartanstown L., Louth B 3
Carton, Kildare D 1
Cartown Ho., Limerick D 2
Cartron, Roscommon E 2
Cartron, Sligo C 3
Cartron Ho., Longford C 3
Casheen Bay, Galway B 3
Cashel, Cork D 4
Cashel, Donegal B 4
Cashel, Donegal D 2
Cashel, Galway F 2
Cashel & Sta., Tipperary C 3
Cashel Lo., Longford B 3
Cashel Loughs, Armagh C 4
Cashel Upper, Donegal C 4
Cashen R., Kerry D 1
Cashla Bay, Galway C 3
Cashlieve Ho., Roscommon B 3
Cassagh, Wexford A 3
Cassaugh Moune, Monaghan C 1
Castle Archdall, Fermanagh D 2
Castle Blunden, Kilkenny C 3
Castle Caldwell, Fermanagh C 2
Castle Cambie, Tipperary A 2
Castle Cary, Donegal F 2
Castle Cauldfield, Tyrone G 3
Castle Chichester, Antrim G 4
Castle Comfort, Limerick G 2
Castle Cosby, Cavan E 3
Castle Daly, West Meath B 3
Castle Dargan Ho., Sligo F 2
Castle Dawson, Londonderry F 4
Castle Farm, Limerick G 3
Castle Fogarty, Tipperary C 3
Castle Forbes, Longford B 2
Castle Freke, Cork E 4
Castle Garde, Limerick H 2
Castle Garden Ho., King's Co C 2
Castle Gray, Limerick D 2
Castle Haven, Cork D 4
Castle Howard, Wicklow D 3
Castle Hume, Fermanagh D 2
Castle I., Cork C 4
Castle I., Down F 3
Castle Jevers, Limerick F 3
Castle Leslie, Monaghan C 2
Castle Lloyd, Limerick H 2
Castle Lodge, Limerick F 2
Castle L., Cavan H 3
Castle Nogent, Longford D 2
Castle Oliver, Limerick G 3
Castle Otway, Tipperary B 2
Castle Park, Cork E 2
Castle R., Londonderry D 2
Castle Rock Sta., Londonderry E 1
Castle Saunderson, Cavan E 2
Castlebar & L., Mayo C 2
Castlebellingham & Sta., Louth B 2
Castleblakeney, Galway F 2
Castleblayney & Sta., Monaghan D 3
Castleboro Ho. & Cas., Wexford B 3
Castleboy, Galway E 3
Castlebridge, Wexford D 3
Castlecaldwell Sta., Fermanagh C 2
Castlecaulfield, Tyrone G 3
Castlecomer & Ho., Kilkenny C 2
Castleconnell & Sta., Limerick G 1
Castleconor, Sligo B 3
Castlecoo Hill, Louth C 3
Castlecoote, Roscommon C 4
Castlecor, Meath A 2
Castlecor Ho., Cork E 2
Castlecore Ho., Longford C 3
Castlecuffe Cas. & Hamlet, Queen's Co. B 2
Castlederg, Tyrone C 2
Castledermot, Kildare C 4
Castledockrell, Wexford C 2
Castledonovan Br., Cork D 3
Castlefield Ho., Kilkenny D 3
Castlefinn, Donegal E 3
Castlefore, Leitrim D 3
Castlegaddery, West Meath C 2
Castlegannon, Kilkenny C 4
Castlegar, Galway G 2
Castlegregory, Kerry C 2
Castlegrogan Ho., Queen's Co. B 3
Castlehill Ho., Mayo C 1
Castleisland, Kerry D 2
Castlejordan Bri., Meath B 4
Castlekevin, Wicklow D 2
Castlekirk, Galway C 2
Castleknock & Barony, Dublin C 4
Castlelackan, Mayo D 1
Castlelake, Tipperary C 3
Castlelake Ho., Clare H 3
Castlelough, Tipperary A 2
Castlelyons, Cork G 2
Castlemagarret Ho., Mayo E 2
Castlemaine & Harb., Kerry C 2
Castlemartin, Kildare C 3
Castlemartyr, Cork H 3
Castlemartyr Ho., Cork G 3
Castlemitchell Ho., Kildare A 3
Castlemore, Mayo F 2
Castlemore Ho. & Moat, Carlow C 2
Castlemorris, Kilkenny C 4
Castlenancy, Galway F 3
Castlepark Ho., Roscommon E 5
Castlepark Ho., Tipperary B 3
Castleplunket, Roscommon D 3
Castlepollard, West Meath E 1
Castlequin, Kerry B 3
Castlerahan Barony, Cavan G 3
Castlerea, Longford C 3
Castlereagh, Mayo D 1
Castlereagh, Town, Bar., & Sta., Roscommon C 3
Castlereagh, Lower Barony, Down E 2
Castlereagh, Upper Barony, Down D 3
Castlerickard, Meath C 4
Castleroberts, Limerick E 2
Castleroe Ho. & Cross Rds., Kildare B 4
Castleroe Ho., Londonderry E 2
Castlerogy, Leitrim E 3
Castleruddery Ho., Wicklow B 3
Castlesampson, Roscommon E 5
Castleshane & Ho., Monaghan C 2
Castlesize, Kildare D 2
Castlestrange, Roscommon D 4
Castle Tenison, Roscommon D 1
Castletimon Ford, Wicklow E 3
Castleton Ho., Limerick D 2
Castletown, Clare F 1
Castletown, Cork E 3
Castletown, Kildare D 1
Castletown, Queen's Co. C 3
Castletown, Limerick E 3
Castletown, Longford B 2
Castletown, Meath D 2
Castletown, Meath E 3
Castletown, Sligo F 2
Castletown & Sta., West Meath C 3
Castletown Ho., Carlow B 2
Castletown Ho., Queen's Co. E 3
Castletown Ho., Kilkenny B 4
Castletown Ho., Sligo B 2
Castletown Ho., Sligo B 2
Castletown Ho., Wexford D 4
Castletown Ho., Wexford E 1
Castletown R., Louth B 1
Castletownarra Ch., Tipperary A 2
Castletown Bearhaven, Cork B 4
Castletown Conyers, Limerick E 3
Castletownoche, Cork F 2
Castletownsend, Cork D 4
Castle View, Queen's Co. B 3
Castleview Ho., Tipperary B 2
Castle Waller, Tipperary A 3
Castleward Ho., Down F 3
Castlewarden Ho., Kildare D 2
Castle Warren, Kilkenny D 2

Castlewarren, Kilkenny D 2
Castlewellan, Down C 4
Castlewellan, Cas., & L., Down D 4
Castle Willington, Tipperary B 2
Castlewood Ho., Queen's Co. C 3
Castle Wray, Donegal D 3
Catherine L., Tyrone D 2
Catherines Bay, Wexford A 4
Cat Cross Rds., Kildare C 2
Catstown, Kilkenny C 4
Causetown Ho., Meath C 3
Causeway, Kerry C 1
Causeway Hd., Antrim B 1
Causeway W., Down C 5
Cavan, Donegal D 3
Cavan, Sta., & College, Cavan E 3
Cavan Junct., West Meath D 3
Cavanagrow Ho., Armagh C 2
Cave Hill, Antrim F 5
Cave of Dunmore, Kilkenny C 2
Cavetown & L., Roscommon D 2
Cecil Ho., Tyrone F 4
Cecilstown, Cork E 2
Celbridge, Kildare D 1
Chaffpool Ho., Sligo E 3
Chanter Hill, Fermanagh E 2
Chapel Is., Down F 2
Chapel Vil. & Sta., Wexford B 3
Chapelizod, Dublin C 4
Chapelizod Ho., Kilkenny C 3
Chapelmidway, Dublin D 3
Chapeltown, Antrim D 4
Chapeltown, Down F 4
Chapeltown, Kerry C 2
Charlemont, Armagh B 2
Charlesfort, Meath C 2
Charlesfort, Sligo C 2
Charlesfort Ho., Wexford C 2
Charles Town, Tyrone G 2
Charlestown, Armagh D 1
Charlestown, King's Co. E 2
Charlestown, Louth A 2
Charlestown, Mayo E 2
Charlestown Ho., Leitrim C 4
Charlestown Ho., West Meath D 2
Charleville, Cork E 1
Charleville, Louth B 2
Charleville Cas., King's Co. E 2
Charleville Ho., Mayo D 2
Charleville Ho., Queen's Co. A 3
Charleville Ho., West Meath C 3
Charleville Ho., Wicklow D 1
Charleville Junc., Limerick F 3
Checker Hall, Antrim D 2
Cheekpoint, Waterford G 2
Cheeverstown Cas., Dublin C 5
Cherry Green, Limerick E 3
Cherryfield, Roscommon D 3
Cherrymills Ho., Kildare B 3
Cherrymount, Armagh E 2
Cherrymount, Meath C 2
Cherrymount Ho., Wicklow D 3
Cherry Vale, Monaghan D 3
Cherryville Ho., Queen's Co. F 3
Chimneyparks, Sligo D 3
Chimney Rock, Down D 5
Chinauley, Down B 3
Christhianstown Ho., Kildare B 2
Christianstown Ho., Louth B 2
Church Bay, Antrim D 1
Churchboro, Roscommon E 4
Church Hill, Armagh C 2
Church Hill, Donegal D 3
Church Hill, Fermanagh C 2
Church Hill, Monaghan D 3
Church Is., Sligo F 2
Church Is. (L. Owel), West Meath D 2
Church L., Leitrim E 3
Church Mt., or Slieve Gadoe, Wicklow B 2
Church Village, Mayo D 1
Church Town, Donegal E 3
Churchtown, Cork E 2
Churchtown, Cork G 3
Churchtown, Kerry C 2
Churchtown, Limerick C 3
Churchtown, West Meath C 3
Churchtown, Wexford A 5
Churchtown Ho., Meath D 3
Churchview Ho., Queen's Co. C 3
Cinquefoil, Roscommon E 4
Clabby, Fermanagh F 2
Cladagh R. & Bri., Fermanagh D 3
Cladagh or Swanlinbar R., Fermanagh D 3
Claddagh Cas., Galway E 2
Clady, Tyrone C 2
Clady & Water, Antrim E 4
Clady R., Donegal C 2
Claggan Donegal F 2
Claggan, Galway C 2
Clammers Pt., Wexford B 4
Clanabogan, Tyrone D 3
Clanawley Barony, Fermanagh D 3
Clanboy Bri., Longford D 2
Clandeboye Sta., Down E 2
Clandonagh Barony, Queen's Co. B 3
Clane Barony & Village, Kildare C 2
Clane Br., Kildare C 2
Clangibbon & Condons Barony, Cork G 2
Clanhugh Lo. & Sta., West Meath D 2
Clankee Barony, Cavan G 3
Clankelly Barony, Fermanagh G 3
Clanmahon Barony, Cavan E 3
Clanmaurice Barony, Kerry D 1
Clanmorris Barony, Mayo D 2
Clansast, Kildare C 1
Clanwilliam Barony, Limerick F 2
Clanwilliam Barony, Tipperary B 4
Clara, King's Co. E 1
Clara Bri., Wicklow D 3
Clara Cas., Kilkenny D 2
Clare, Armagh D 3
Clare, Clare G 3
Clare, Down B 3
Clare or Claremorris, Mayo E 2
Clare Barony, Galway E 2
Clare Is., Mayo A 2
Clare Mount, Meath G 3
Clare R., Galway E 2
Clare R., Tipperary A 3
Clareen, King's Co. C 3
Clareen, King's Co. D 3
Claregalway, Galway E 2
Claregalway R., Galway D 2
Claremount Ho., Mayo E 2
Claremount Ho., Roscommon D 5
Clare Park, Antrim D 1
Claret Rock Ho., Louth B 1
Claretuam, Galway E 2
Clare View, Limerick A 2
Clareville Ho., Carlow B 2
Clareville Ho., Clare F 1
Clarina, Limerick E 2
Clarinbridge, Galway E 3
Clarkville Ho., King's Co. H 2
Clarmallagh Barony, Queen's Co. C 3
Clashavoon, Cork E 3
Clashawley R., Tipperary D 4
Clashmore, Waterford C 3
Clashnabrock, Cork F 2
Clashymore Harb., Sligo D 1
Classaghroe, Galway F 2
Classylaun Harb., Sligo F 1
Claudy, Londonderry C 3
Claudy & R., Londonderry F 3
Claureen R., Clare F 3
Clawinch, Longford A 3
Clay Lake, Armagh B 3
Cleady, Kerry D 3
Cleanagh, Queen's Co. D 3
Clear, Cape, Cork C 4
Clear I., Cork C 4
Clear View Ho., Kildare B 2
Cleggan B., Galway A 2
Cleggan Lo. & R., Antrim E 3
Clements Town, Cavan G 2
Clermont, Louth B 2
Clermont, Wicklow E 2
Clermont Carn, Louth C 1
Clew Bay, Mayo B 2
Clifden, Kilkenny D 3
Clifden Cas., Galway A 2
Clifden Ho., Clare F 2
Clifton, Galway F 2
Clifton Ho., Down E 2
Clifton Ho., Meath C 3
Clifton Lo., Fermanagh F 3
Cliff Lo., Waterford G 3
Cliffony, Sligo F 1
Clifford Ho., Cork F 2
Cliffort, Cork E 3
Clinoe Cott., Limerick F 2
Clobemon Hall, Wexford C 2
Clodiagh R., King's Co. E 2
Clodiagh R., Queen's Co. B 1
Clodiagh R., Tipperary B 3
Clodiagh R., Waterford E 2
Clody R., Wexford B 2
Cloganodfoy Cas., Limerick G 4
Clogga, Kilkenny C 5
Clogh, Kilkenny C 1
Clogh, Wexford D 2
Clogh & R., Antrim D 3
Clogh Mills, Antrim D 2
Clogh R., Kilkenny D 1
Cloghage Brook, Wicklow D 2
Cloghagh R., Kilkenny C 2
Cloghan, Roscommon D 4
Cloghan, West Meath E 2
Cloghan & Hill, King's Co. C 2
Cloghan Cas., King's Co. B 3
Cloghan Ho., King's Co. C 3
Cloghane, Kerry B 2
Cloghanodfoy Cas., Limerick F 4
Cloghans, Kerry B 2
Cloghany, Fermanagh D 3
Cloghanulk, Clare D 1
Clogharinka Cas., Kilkenny C 2
Cloghastucan, Antrim F 2
Cloghaun, Clare E 1
Cloghaun, Galway D 2
Cloghaun L., Clare D 3
Cloghboy, Donegal B 3
Cloghbrack, Galway C 2
Cloghchurnel Lowr., Longford E 2
Cloghchurnel Upr., Longford D 2
Cloghcorr, Antrim C 1
Cloghdonnell, Cork C 4
Clogheen, Tipperary C 4
Clogher, Longford B 2
Clogher, Longford B 3
Clogher, Louth C 3
Clogher, Roscommon D 2
Clogher, Roscommon D 3
Clogher, Sligo F 4
Clogher & Barony, Tyrone E 4
Clogher Hd., Kerry A 2
Clogher Hd., Louth C 3
Clogher Ho., Mayo D 2
Clogher R., Donegal C 3
Clogher R., Donegal D 3
Cloghernagh Br., Waterford G 2
Clogherny, Tyrone E 3
Cloghfin R., Tyrone E 3
Cloghjordan, Tipperary B 2
Cloghleafin, Cork F 2
Cloghmore & Sta., Galway C 3
Cloghran, Dublin E 3
Cloghroe R., Donegal D 3
Cloghy & Bay, Down G 3
Clogrenan Ho., Carlow B 2
Clohamon & Ho., Wexford C 2
Clomoney Bri., Carlow B 3
Clonabream, Meath B 2
Clonacody Ho., Tipperary D 4
Clonad Wood, King's Co. F 2
Clonagh, King's Co. E 2
Clonakilty & Bay, Cork E 4
Clonallan Ch., Down B 5
Clonamully Ho., Monaghan B 2
Clonard, Dublin E 1
Clonard, Grt. & Lit., Wexford D 4
Clonaslee, Queen's Co. B 2
Clonatin Ho., Wexford E 1
Clonbeale Ho., King's Co. C 3
Clonbrock & R., Galway F 2
Clonbulloge, King's Co. H 2
Clonburren Ho., Carlow B 2
Cloncarneel Ho., Meath C 3
Cloncloney Ho., Kilkenny C 5
Cloncoskoran Ho., Waterford D 3
Cloncourse Bri., Queen's Co. C 2
Cloncumber Lo., Kildare B 2
Cloncurry, Kildare C 1
Clondagad, Clare F 3
Clondalkin, Dublin C 5
Clondaw, Wexford D 2
Clonderalaw Barony, Clare E 3

Clonderalaw Ho. & Bay, Clare E 4
Clondervis, Meath A 2
Clondrohid Rect., Cork D 3
Clone Ho., Kilkenny B 2
Clonea, Waterford E 2
Clonea Cas., Waterford D 3
Clonea Cas., Waterford E 2
Clonearl Ho., King's Co. F 2
Clonee, Meath F 4
Cloneen Ho., Tipperary D 4
Clonegall, Carlow C 2
Clonegath Ho., Kildare A 3
Clonelly Ho., Fermanagh D 1
Clonervy, Cavan F 2
Clones & Sta., Monaghan A 2
Cloney Bri., Kildare A 3
Clonfeade, Tyrone H 4
Clonfert Palace, Galway G 3
Clonganny Ho., Wexford E 2
Clongarret, King's Co. H 2
Clongeen, Wexford B 4
Clongorey Bawn, Kildare C 2
Clongoweswood College, Kildare C 2
Clonkeen, Kildare B 1
Clonkerdin Ho., Waterford C 3
Clonlea L., Clare H 3
Clonlisk Barony, King's Co. C 4
Clonlonan Barony, West Meath B 3
Clonlost Ho., West Meath E 2
Clonlyon, King's Co. C 2
Clonmacken Ho., Limerick E 2
Clonmacnoise, King's Co. B 2
Clonmacnowen Barony, Galway G 2
Clonmain, Armagh C 2
Clonmannan Ho., Wicklow E 2
Clonmaskill, West Meath F 2
Clonmeen Ho., Kildare A 1
Clonmel, Tipperary D 4
Clonmellon, West Meath F 1
Clonmelsh Ho., Carlow B 2
Clonmethan, Dublin C 2
Clonmines Ho., Wexford B 4
Clonmore, Galway D 2
Clonmore, King's Co. H 1
Clonmore, Wexford C 3
Clonmore, Wicklow B 4
Clonmore & Cas., Carlow D 2
Clonmore Ho., Carlow B 2
Clonmoyle Ho., West Meath E 3
Clonmullen, Carlow C 3
Clonmass B., Donegal D 2
Clonmult, Cork G 3
Clonoe, Tyrone H 3
Clonogan Ho. & Cas., Carlow D 2
Clonough R., Wexford E 1
Clonony, King's Co. C 2
Clonoulty, Tipperary C 3
Clonown, West Meath C 2
Clonreher Cas., Queen's Co. C 2
Clonroche, Wexford B 3
Clonrush, Galway F 4
Clonsast, King's Co. H 2
Clonshavoy, Limerick G 2
Clonshire Riv. & Ho., Limerick D 2
Clonsilla, Dublin B 4
Clonswords Ho., Dublin D 2
Clontarf, Dublin E 4
Clontoe, Monaghan B 2
Clonty L., Cavan D 2
Clontylew Ho., Armagh C 2
Clonuff Bri., Kildare B 1
Clonvaraghan Mt., Down D 4
Clonygowan, King's Co. G 2
Clonyharp Cas., Tipperary C 3
Clonyhurk, King's Co. G 3
Clonyn Ho., West Meath F 2
Cloon L., Kerry C 3
Cloon L., Mayo C 2
Cloon R., Clare E 4
Cloonacleigha L., Sligo E 3
Cloonacolly L., Roscommon A 2
Cloonacool, Sligo D 3
Cloonagh Ho., Roscommon D 5
Cloonagh L., Roscommon A 3
Cloonaghlin, Cork B 4
Cloonaghlin L., Kerry C 3
Cloonaghmore R., Mayo D 1
Cloonahee Ho., Roscommon E 2
Cloonakilleg, Roscommon C 4
Cloonakillina L., Mayo F 1
Cloonalis Ho., Roscommon B 3
Cloonart Bri., Longford B 2
Cloonbalt Ho., Longford C 2
Cloonbarry Ho., Meath C 3
Cloonbarry Ho., Sligo C 3
Cloonbo L., Leitrim D 4
Cloonbony Ho., Longford B 2
Cloonbonny Ho., West Meath A 3
Clooncah, Galway F 3
Clooncah, Roscommon E 3
Clooncah, Roscommon E 4
Clooncallow Ho., Longford C 3
Clooncoe L., Leitrim E 4
Clooncogaile, Waterford C 2
Clooncoorha, Clare D 3
Clooncoose, Longford C 2
Clooncoran Ho., Roscommon D 5
Clooncorick Cas., Leitrim F 4
Clooncose L., Longford C 1
Clooncraff, Roscommon E 4
Clooncullaan L., Roscommon E 3
Cloondara, Longford B 2
Cloondarah, Roscommon D 4
Cloone & R., Leitrim E 4
Cloonee, Longford C 2
Cloonee Cott., Limerick E 3
Cloonee Loughs, Kerry C 3
Clooneen, Galway D 2
Clooneen Beg, Roscommon D 4
Clooneen Ho., King's Co. C 3
Clooneen R., Sligo E 3
Clooneenagh Ho., Clare D 3
Clooney Ho., Clare G 2
Clooney L., Donegal B 3
Cloonfad Ho., Roscommon E 2
Cloonfaris, Galway F 2
Cloonfin L. & Ho., Longford D 2
Cloonfinlough Ho., Roscommon E 3
Cloonfree L., Roscommon D 3
Cloonfush, Galway E 2
Cloongowla, Mayo D 3
Clooningan, Sligo C 3
Cloonkea, Galway G 3
Cloonkeen, Galway E 2
Cloonkeen, Galway F 2
Cloonker, Longford C 3
Cloonlara, Clare I 3
Cloonmachan L., Clare E 2
Cloonmore, Roscommon E 4
Cloonmore Ho., Mayo E 2
Cloonphierce, Roscommon E 3
Cloonshannagh Ho., Longford D 2
Cloontuskert, Roscommon F 3
Cloonty, Leitrim A 1
Cloonty L., Sligo F 1
Cloonusker, Clare I 2
Cloonyquin Ho., Roscommon D 3
Clopook Ho., Queen's Co. E 3
Cloragh, Dublin D 5
Clorane Ho., Limerick F 3
Closet, The, & Riv., Armagh D 2
Clough, Down D 4
Cloughey Burn, Antrim B 2
Cloughjordan, King's Co. B 4
Clover Hill, Antrim D 5
Clover Hill, Leitrim E 3
Clover Hill, Monaghan C 3
Cloverhill, Cavan E 2
Cloverhill, Roscommon D 4
Cloverhill Ho., Sligo E 2
Cloyne, Cork G 3
Cluid, Galway E 2
Cluster, The, Armagh C 3
Clydagh, Galway D 3
Clydagh, Roscommon A 3
Clydagh R., Kerry E 2
Clydagh R., Kerry E 3
Clydagh R., Mayo D 2
Clynacartan, Kerry A 3
Coachford, Cork E 3
Coagh, Tyrone I 3
Coagh L., Sligo E 3
Coal Ch., Wexford D 4
Coal Island, Tyrone H 3
Coalbrook Ho., Tipperary D 3
Coalville Ho., King's Co. G 1
Cobourg Lo., Kildare B 3
Cock Brook, Wicklow B 2
Cock Hill, Donegal E 2
Cock Mt., Down C 4
Cods Hd., Cork A 4
Coggrey Ho., Antrim E 4
Cogush, Donegal B 3
Cole Hill, Meath B 4
Colebreene, Londonderry F 2
Colebrooke & Riv., Fermanagh F 2
Coleman L., Monaghan A 3
Coleraine & Barony, Londonderry E 2
Coleraine Ho., King's Co. E 2
Coleraine Ho., Tipperary C 3
Coleraine, N. E. Liberties of, Londonderry F 2
Colgagh, King's Co. G 2
Colgagh Ho. & L., Sligo F 2
Colligan R. & Br., Waterford C 3
Collin Top, Antrim E 3
Collinstown, West Meath E 2
Collinstown Ho., Kildare E 1
Collon, Louth B 3
Collooney & Sta., Sligo E 2
Collorus, Kerry C 3
Colt I., Dublin F 1
Columbkille Cott., Clare F 1
Columbkille Pt., Armagh C 1
Comber, Down E 2
Comeragh Mts., Ho., & L., Waterford D 2
Conager, Kildare D 3
Condons & Clangibbon Bar., Cork G 2
Cones, The, Queen's Co. B 2
Coney Island, Armagh C 1
Coney Island, Down F 4
Coney Island, Sligo E 2
Coneyburrow Bri., Louth B 2
Coneyglen B., Tyrone F 2
Confey, Kildare E 1
Cong, Galway D 2
Conlawn H., Queen's Co. C 2
Conlig, Down E 2
Conn Lough, Mayo D 1
Conna, Cork G 2
Connabury Ho., Monaghan D 3
Connamara, Galway B 2
Connello, Lower Bar., Limerick D 2
Connello, Upper Bar., Limerick D 3
Connonagh, Cork D 4
Connons Bri., Kildare B 3
Connor, Antrim D 4
Conogher Bri., Antrim B 2
Conor's Is., Sligo E 1
Cons Town, Armagh C 3
Convamore, Cork F 2
Convent Ho., Waterford C 3
Convoy, Donegal D 3
Conway L., Leitrim C 3
Cooanmore Bay, Sligo C 2
Cooksborough Ho., West Meath E 2
Cookstown, Sligo B 2
Cookstown, Tyrone H 3
Cookstown Ho., Louth A 2
Cookstown Junc., Antrim D 4
Cookstown R., Wicklow D 1
Coola Cott. & Bri., West Meath C 3
Cooladangan Ho., Wicklow D 4
Coolagarybeg, King's Co. G 2
Coolagh, Galway D 2
Coolaghflags, Kilkenny B 3
Coolalough Ho., West Meath C 3
Coolalug & Bri., Wicklow C 4
Coolamber, West Meath D 1
Coolamoney, Louth A 2
Coolaney, Sligo E 2
Coolattin, Wicklow B 4
Coolattin Park, Wicklow C 4
Coolavin & Barony, Sligo F 4
Coolavoher, Londonderry C 3
Coolavully, Antrim F 3
Coolballintaggart Lo., Wicklow C 3
Coolbeha Ho., Kerry D 1
Coolbawn Ho., Wicklow C 4
Coolbawn Ho. & Cott., Wexford B 3
Coolboy, Donegal D 3
Coolboy & Ho., Wicklow C 4
Coolcarrigan Ho., Kildare B 2
Coolcashin Ho., Kilkenny B 2
Coolcliffe Ho., Wexford B 4
Coolcor Ho., Kildare B 1
Coolcull Ho., Wexford B 4
Coolcullen R., Kilkenny D 2
Coolderry Ho., King's Co. C 3

Coolderry Ho., Monaghan D 4
Cooldorragha, Cork D 3
Coole, Galway E 3
Coole, West Meath D 1
Coole Barony, Fermanagh F 3
Coole Cas., King's Co. D 2
Coole Cas. & L., Fermanagh E 2
Coole Ho., Tipperary C 4
Cooleen, Sligo C 3
Cooleen Ho., Limerick E 3
Coolestown Barony, King's Co. H 2
Cooley Pt., Louth D 2
Coolfin Ho., Waterford F 2
Coolfitch, Kildare D 2
Coolgreany, Wexford E 1
Coolhull Cas., Wexford B 4
Coolin, Galway C 2
Coolishal Ho., Wexford D 2
Coolkenna Street, Wicklow B 4
Coolkeeragh, Londonderry B 2
Coolkirk, Louth C 3
Coolmanagh St., Carlow D 1
Coolmeen, Roscommon D 4
Coolmoonan, Kildare C 2
Coolmore, Cork G 3
Coolmore, Donegal C 4
Coolmore Ho., Kilkenny D 4
Coolmountain Ho., Cork D 3
Coolnagour, Queen's Co. B 3
Coolnagour Ho., Waterford C 3
Coolnahau, Kilkenny D 4
Coolnakisha Br., Carlow A 2
Coolnamara Cross Rds., Carlow B 3
Coolnamuck, Waterford E 1
Coolnamuck Ho., Kilkenny D 4
Coolamunna Ho., Tipperary B 2
Coolnareen, Queen's Co. C 3
Coolnasillagh, Londonderry E 3
Coolnavoe, Donegal D 3
Coolock & Barony, Dublin E 4
Coologe L., Cavan D 2
Coolpark, Sligo C 2
Coolrain, Queen's Co. B 3
Coolroe Ho., Kilkenny E 3
Coolrus Ho., Limerick E 3
Coolticormac, Cork E 2
Coolum Lo., Waterford G 3
Coolure, West Meath D 1
Coolvally, Wexford B 2
Coolyermer L., Fermanagh D 3
Coolyhane, Carlow B 3
Coolykeerane, Cork D 2
Coomacarrea, Kerry C 3
Coomasaharn, Kerry C 3
Coomcalee, Kerry B 3
Coomhola River, Cork C 3
Coomnahincha & Harb., Kerry B 3
Coonagh, Limerick E 2
Coonagh Barony, Limerick H 2
Coonana, Kerry A 3
Cooneen & C. Water, Fermanagh G 3
Coonen Hill, Meath G 2
Coonlanagh, Queen's Co. E 3
Coonogue, Carlow C 3
Cooper Hill, Queen's Co. F 3
Cooperhill Ho., Limerick E 2
Cooperhill Ho., Sligo F 3
Cooralacare & Riv., Clare D 3
Coosan Lough, West Meath A 3
Cootehall, Roscommon E 2
Cootehill & Sta., Cavan G 2
Cooter L., Galway E 3
Copeland Island, Down G 1
Coppanagh Gap, Kilkenny D 3
Coppenagh Cas., Carlow C 2
Copperalley, West Meath G 2
Coppony L., Cavan F 2
Copse Ho., Wicklow D 3
Coragh L., Cavan G 2
Coragh L., Monaghan B 3
Corballis, Meath G 2
Corballis Ho., Dublin D 3
Corballis Ho., Dublin F 3
Corbally, Kildare D 1
Corbally, Roscommon D 3
Corbally Ho., Galway E 2
Corbally Ho., Queen's Co. E 3
Corbally L., Roscommon D 2
Corbally Sth., Sligo B 3
Corbalton Hall, Meath E 3
Corbeg Ho., King's Co. C 2
Corbet L., Down B 3
Corboley, Galway D 3
Corbollis Ho., Louth B 2
Corboy Upr., Longford C 2
Corcomroe Abbey, Clare F 1
Corcomroe Barony, Clare E 2
Corcrain Ho., Armagh D 2
Corcreeghagh, Louth A 2
Corderry Ho., Louth A 2
Cordoo L., Monaghan C 3
Corduff, Leitrim E 3
Corduff Ho., Dublin E 2
Corduff Ho., Kildare C 2
Corfad, Monaghan C 3
Corfin L., Monaghan C 3
Corglass L., Cavan E 3
Corglass L., Longford C 1
Corgrave, King's Co. C 2
Corick Mt., Londonderry E 3
Corickmore, Tyrone E 2
Cork & Barony, Cork F 3
Cork Abbey, Dublin F 6
Cork Harbour, Cork G 3
Corkagh Ho., Dublin C 5
Corkaguiny Barony, Kerry B 2
Corkaree Barony, West Meath D 2
Corkeen Is., Tipperary A 2
Corker R., Donegal B 3
Corkhill Ho., Silgo D 2
Corkip L., Roscommon E 5
Corkley R., Armagh C 3
Corlat Ho., Monaghan C 2
Corlea, Longford B 3
Corliss L., Armagh C 4
Corlougharoe, Monaghan B 3
Cormaglava Ho., Longford B 3
Cormeen Cott., Cavan G 4
Cormey Bri., Monaghan D 4
Cormoy Ho., Monaghan E 3
Cornabrass L., Fermanagh F 4
Cornacarta Lough, Roscommon D 1
Cornadrung Cott., Longford D 1
Cornagillagh, Donegal D 3
Cornaglare L., Monaghan B 2
Cornaglea Ho., Cavan G 3
Cornagrow L., Cavan F 3
Cornaher, West Meath D 3
Cornakill Ho., Cavan H 4
Cornamucklagh, Galway G 2
Cornamucklagh, Londonderry F 3
Cornapark, Longford D 3
Cornasaus, Cavan H 3
Cornascreeb Ho., Armagh D 2
Cornashesk, Cavan G 4
Cornecassa Ho., Monaghan B 2
Cornfield Ho., Mayo D 2
Coronation Plantation, Wicklow C 2
Corr Ho., West Meath C 2
Corra R., Clare I 2
Corrabella Ho., Tipperary C 4
Corrabut Gap, Carlow C 3
Corrachro Ho., Fermanagh E 3
Corradoo L., Sligo F 3
Corradooey, Donegal E 3
Corradoon Ho., Waterford C 2
Corradoran L., Louth A 2
Corraghbridge Ho., Limerick D 2
Corralea, Roscommon E 5
Corralongford L., Fermanagh G 2
Corramore, Roscommon D 4
Corran Barony & L., Sligo E 3
Corran Lake, Cork D 4
Corran R., Armagh C 3
Corrandoo, Galway F 2
Corraneary L., Cavan G 3
Corraneary Lo., Cavan D 3
Corranroo, Clare G 1
Corranroo Ho., Galway E 3
Corratimore, Leitrim B 2
Corratinner L., Cavan G 3
Correen Ho., Roscommon E 6
Corrib, Lough, Galway D 2
Corrib R., Galway D 3
Corries Lo. & R., Carlow B 3
Corrigadrohid, Cork E 3
Corrinshigo Ho., Cavan I 3
Corrofin, Clare F 2
Corrstown Ho., Dublin C 3
Corry L., Fermanagh G 3
Corry Lo., Leitrim C 3
Corrymore Lo., Carlow B 3
Corsleive, Mayo B 1
Corstown Loughs, Meath E 1
Cortial L., Louth A 1
Cortiskea, Galway F 1
Corville, Cavan D 2
Corville Ho., Tipperary C 2
Corvish, Donegal F 2
Cosby Castle, Cavan E 3
Coshlea Barony, Limerick G 3
Coshma Barony, Limerick F 3
Coshmore & Coshbride Barony, Waterford B 3
Costello Barony, Mayo E 2
Cot Br., Dublin C 6
Cottage, The, Kildare D 2
Cottage Grove, Leitrim B 1
Coulagh & Bay, Cork A 3
Coumbeg, Tipperary A 2
Coumduala L., Waterford D 2
Coumduff, Kerry B 2
Coumshingaun L., Waterford D 2
Country Ho., Carlow B 2
County Bri., Louth C 1
County Bri. & Water, Armagh C 4
County Water, Monaghan E 3
Coura L., King's Co. C 2
Couragh, Cork G 3
Courceys Barony, Cork F 4
Cournellan Mill, Carlow B 3
Court, The, Kilkenny D 3
Courtaur Cas., Kilkenny C 3
Courtbane L., Louth A 1
Courtmacsherry & Bay, Cork E 4
Courtnacuddy Cross Rds., Wexford B 3
Courtown Ho., Kildare C 1
Courtown Ho. & Harb., Wexford E 2
Courttown Ho., Kildare A 3
Cow & Calf, Down E 4
Cox's Hill, Armagh D 2
Coy Ford, Kildare C 2
Crab Island, Clare D 1
Crab Lane, Wicklow B 4
Crabtree R., Kildare B 2
Craddanstan Ho., West Meath F 2
Cradockheel Cas., Clare H 3
Craigbrien Ho., Clare F 3
Cragg Ho., Tipperary A 3
Cragny L., Donegal C 3
Cragleagh Ho., Clare F 2
Craig, Tyrone F 2
Craig Abbey, Galway F 3
Craigagh, Londonderry D 3
Craigavad Sta., Down E 2
Craigavole, Londonderry E 3
Craigdarroch Ho., Down E 1
Craigdoo, Down C 4
Craiggore, Londonderry D 2
Craigmore, Londonderry E 3
Craignagapple, Tyrone E 2
Craignamaddy, Antrim C 1
Craignamaddy, Tyrone E 2
Craigs, Donegal E 3
Craigs Ch., Antrim C 3
Craigywarren, Antrim D 3
Crana R., Donegal F 2
Cranagh, The, Londonderry F 2
Cranagh, Tyrone F 2
Cranagh Ho., Tipperary C 2
Cranagher Ho., Clare G 2
Cranagill, Armagh C 2
Cranalagh, Longford D 2
Crancam, Roscommon F 5
Cranemore Ho., Carlow C 2
Cranfield, Antrim C 4
Cranfield & C. Pt., Down C 5
Cranford Bri., Donegal D 2
Cranna Ho., Tipperary A 2
Crannagh Barony, Kilkenny B 2
Crannagh Ho., Roscommon F 5
Crannford, Wexford D 1
Cranroe, Kilkenny D 2
Cratlieve, Down C 3
Cratloe Cas., Sta., & Wood, Clare H 3
Craud, Meath F 2
Craughwell & Sta., Galway E 3
Crawfords Lo., Tipperary D 2
Crawfordsburn, Down E 2

D

E

F

G

H

I

J

K

L

M

N

O

P

Q

R

S

T

U

V

W

Y

Classics . . . In Irish Family Heritage

As Internationally Advertised in 'Ireland of the Welcomes'

2nd Edition 100 NEW PAGES

THE COMPLETE BOOK FOR TRACING YOUR IRISH ANCESTORS

'THE FIRST MAJOR WORK OF CONSEQUENCE IN OVER 20 YEARS!'

Contains all the standard 'handbook' information plus so much more. Twenty illustrated steps for the beginner. Geographical guide including terms & understanding. Survey & census illustrations in Ireland and America dating back to the 1600s. Thousands of surnames listed in the Birth Index and elsewhere.

Of course it includes the records and repositories in Ireland, the U.S.A., and Canada. Where to write — whom to see. Parish registers listed along with hundreds of books for further reference, passenger lists, etc.

Absolutely unique. No other book contains all that this one does. PERMANENT HARD BINDING IS GOLD STAMPED.

ORDER #300 **PRICE: HARDBOUND $29.95**

- **HARDBOUND**
- **FULL SIZE 8½"x11"**
- **EASY TO READ & UNDERSTAND**
- **OVER 100 NEW PAGES** (OVER 250 PAGES IN ALL)
- **GOLD STAMPED**
- **MAPS & ILLUSTRATIONS**

(Includes N. Ireland)

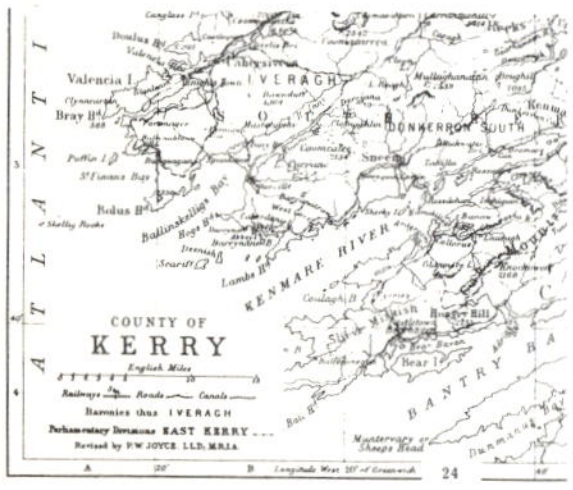

Over 40 maps — Ancient & modern. Full size county maps, just added.

ADMINISTRATIVE DIVISIONS

The Province

Ancient Kingdoms of Ireland. The four provinces were: (1) Ulster in the north; (2) Leinster in the east; (3) Connaught in the west, and (4) Munster in the south. The old province of Meath became incorporated into Leinster. The kingdoms of Oriel and Aileach merged with Ulster in the 17th century.

The County

The largest local administrative division of more modern times. The first 12 counties came into existence in the year 1210, and the last county (Wicklow) was formed in 1605.

Explanation of terms & understanding

Proprietor (1641)	Denominacion of Lands	Acres

Also of interest in this cc rolls in the Public Record

Hearth Money Rolls - Lists assessed house h Armagh 1664; Cavan 1664 Louty 1664; Monaghan 16(

1740 Householders List

Illustrated census' & surveys beginning in the 1600s

The Birth Index of Ireland (1800s)

NAME	BIRTHS	PREDOMINANT COUNTIES	NAME	BIRTHS	PREDOMINANT COUN
*Abbott (10)	11		Barry	217	Cork, Limerick, Water(
Abernethy	6		*Bartley (8)	10	
*Abraham (8)	9	Armagh	Barton	20	Fermanagh, Dublin

Pinpointing the Counties of Location for over 1,000 surnames

BY POPULAR DEMAND!

FROM THE 'IRISH ARCHIVES' THEMSELVES!

OVER 400 OF THE

"GREAT FAMILIES OF IRELAND"

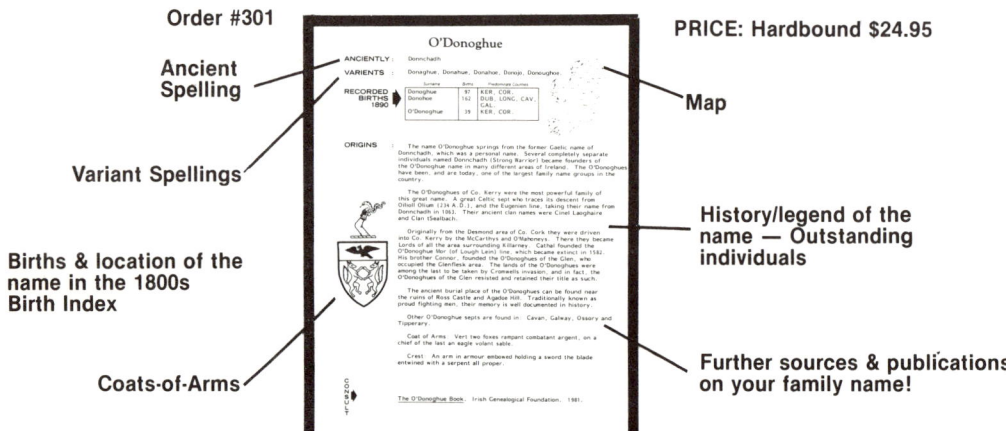

Pinpoint the exact location of your family in ancient Ireland — and that of your Irish friends as well. Easy to read summary of the history of the 'Clan'. Original and ancient spellings. Published works on your family name. Indexed. Hardbound — Gold Stamped. Information as found in the archives.

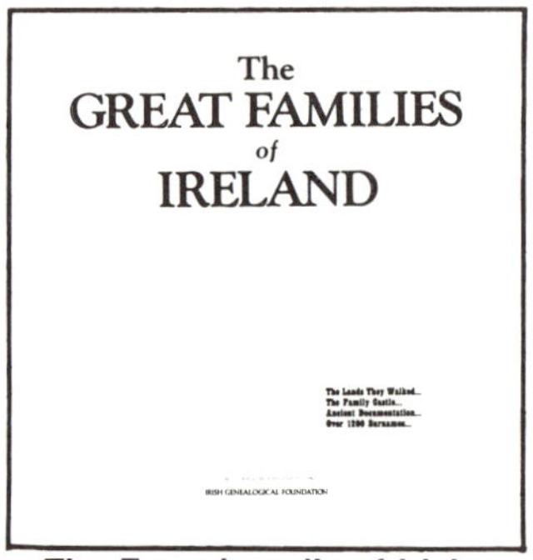

- The Encyclopedia of Irish surnames!
- Hardbound, full size 8½x11
- **INDEXED**
- The most often asked for book from the Archives
- A must for any Irish family researcher or proud family member
- All books will ship before Christmas 1981

Order #301 **PRICE: Hardbound $24.95**

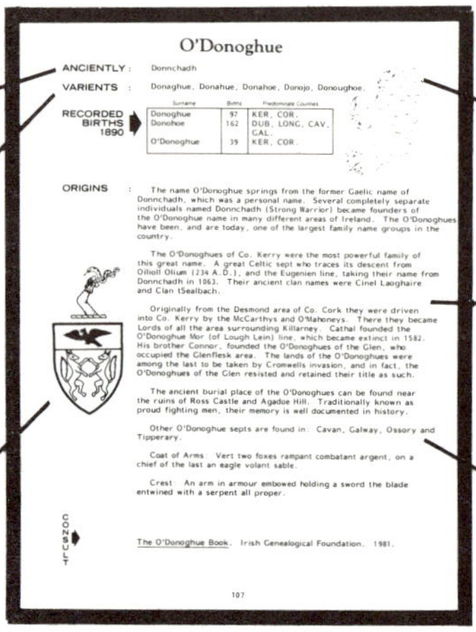

O'Donoghue

ANCIENTLY : Donnchadh

VARIENTS : Donaghue, Donahue, Donahoe, Donojo, Donoughoe.

RECORDED BIRTHS 1890

Surname	Births	Predominant Counties
Donoghue	97	KER, COR.
Donohoe	162	DUB, LONG, CAV, GAL.
O'Donoghue	39	KER, COR.

ORIGINS : The name O'Donoghue springs from the former Gaelic name of Donnchadh, which was a personal name. Several completely separate individuals named Donnchadh (Strong Warrior) became founders of the O'Donoghue name in many different areas of Ireland. The O'Donoghues have been, and are today, one of the largest family name groups in the country.

The O'Donoghues of Co. Kerry were the most powerful family of this great name. A great Celtic sept who traces its descent from Oilioll Olium (234 A.D.), and the Eugenien line, taking their name from Donnchadh in 1063. Their ancient clan names were Cinel Laoghaire and Clan tSealbach.

Originally from the Desmond area of Co. Cork they were driven into Co. Kerry by the McCarthys and O'Mahoneys. There they became Lords of all the area surrounding Killarney. Cathal founded the O'Donoghue Mor (of Lough Lein) line, which became extinct in 1582. His brother Connor, founded the O'Donoghues of the Glen, who occupied the Glenflesk area. The lands of the O'Donoghues were among the last to be taken by Cromwells invasion, and in fact, the O'Donoghues of the Glen resisted and retained their title as such.

The ancient burial place of the O'Donoghues can be found near the ruins of Ross Castle and Agadoe Hill. Traditionally known as proud fighting men, their memory is well documented in history.

Other O'Donoghue septs are found in: Cavan, Galway, Ossory and Tipperary.

Coat of Arms: Vert two foxes rampant combatant argent, on a chief of the last an eagle volant sable.

Crest: An arm in armour embowed holding a sword the blade entwined with a serpent all proper.

CONSULT The O'Donoghue Book. Irish Genealogical Foundation. 1981.

107

A LIBRARY IN ITSELF! Order both volumes offered on this page and **SAVE $10.00.** A 54.90 Value for only $44.90. Must be ordered before Christmas 1982 (when Irish eyes will be smiling!).

An Exciting and Stimulating Link With Your Family's Past!

Ready for Immediate Shipment!

"THE BOOK" ON YOUR IRISH FAMILY!

The most comprehensive series on Irish family histories ever published

• Origins • History • Location • Maps of Occupied Territory
• Hundreds of Descendants • Contributions from readers

A BOOK WRITTEN FOR YOU & YOUR SURNAME ALONE.

The Murphy Book

Pinpoints the **exact location** and origins of your name. The first man to bear your Irish family name. The legend and tradition of the clan. Ancient pedigree along with hundreds of descendants. Coat of Arms, variant spellings. Includes several maps of territory occupied. Records of the name in more ancient times. A 'must' for any researcher or proud family member. A great heirloom.

Also includes: Pedigree/marriage and will records taken from the Irish Archives along with sources on your particular surname. Notable people of the name throughout the world. The family castle.

ORDER # THE BOOK APPROX. 50 PAGES BOUND ON EACH BOOK PRICE $9.95 PER BOOK
PLEASE SPECIFY SURNAME.

The O'Sullivan Book

SEE FOR YOURSELF, SOME ACTUAL EXCERPTS FOLLOW:

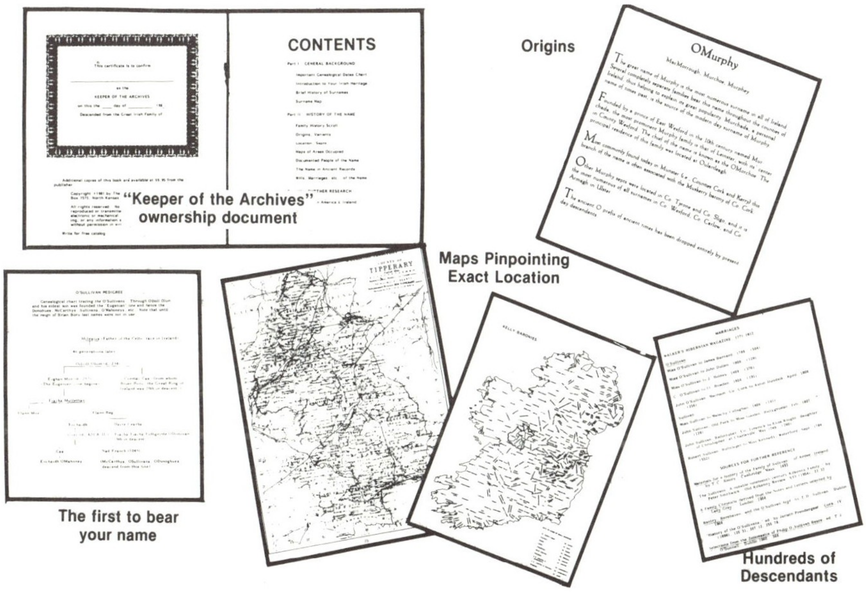

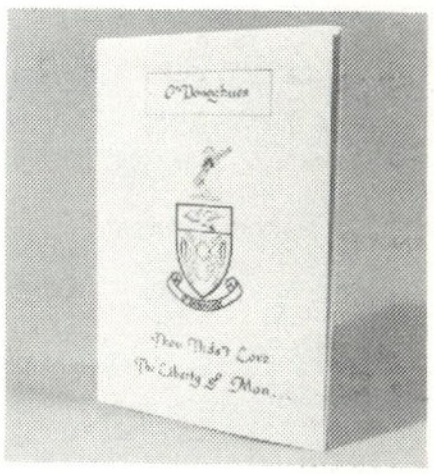

The O'Donaghue Book

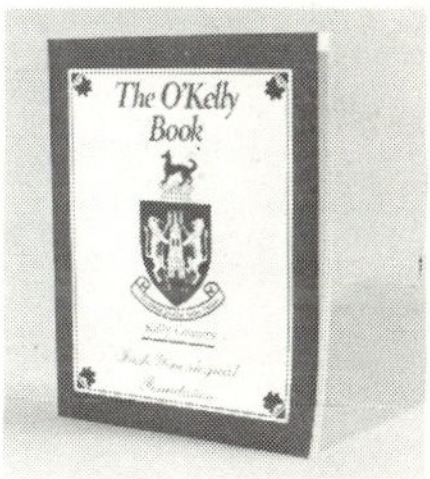

The Kelly Book

AVAILABLE IMMEDIATELY FOR THE:

Murphy
(O)Sullivan
(O)Donaghue
Kelly
O'Reilly
and O'Loughlin families!

The O'Reilly Book

LIMITED EDITION! Only 250 books printed on each available surname. Decision to continue production will be based solely on demand. Each book is deinitely 'one of a kind' — So get yours today!

FREE LISTING OF YOUR FAMILY TREE (or Ancestors) in these books when you order promptly. Make contact with your long lost cousins. Find the missing link in your pedigree. An unbelievable **FREE OFFER** from the Foundation — Our way of saying 'Thanks.' Just send us what you have — We'll do the rest.

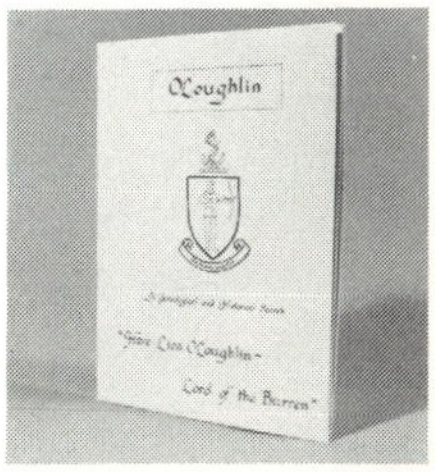

The O'Loughlin Book